MIDNIGHT PEARL

ACACIA ROSE

INDIA • SINGAPORE • MALAYSIA

Notion Press

Old No. 38, New No. 6
McNichols Road, Chetpet
Chennai - 600 031

First Published by Notion Press 2018
Copyright © Acacia Rose 2018
All Rights Reserved.

ISBN 978-1-64429-879-4

This book has been published with all efforts taken to make the material error-free after the consent of the author. However, the author and the publisher do not assume and hereby disclaim any liability to any party for any loss, damage, or disruption caused by errors or omissions, whether such errors or omissions result from negligence, accident, or any other cause.

No part of this book may be used, reproduced in any manner whatsoever without written permission from the author, except in the case of brief quotations embodied in critical articles and reviews.

Dedicated To

The millions of souls - who are India and Pakistan.

Chapter One

Amritsar, India, 1919

RAVINDER PRESSED HIS tiny hand into his grandfather's warm, secure palm as he trotted after him into the large compound.

'Come along child. You will meet your cousins and aunty today.'

'Yes Papaji.' Ravi looked up into the laughing brown eyes that he knew so well. His heart swelled with excitement. There was a definite thrill in the atmosphere. Hundreds, thousands of people were already gathered in small family clusters around the edges of the compound and bigger groups of people were sitting cross legged in the middle of the field; some talking, some it seemed staring into the distance as if waiting for the arrival of a bigger destiny than they dared think about.

'Papaji?'

'Yes child.'

'Why is everyone here today?'

'Everyone?'

'There are so many people and not just….'

'Not just our Sikh brothers and sisters from the Gurudwara?'

'Yes. There are so many others.'

'Child,' the old man patted the little boys hand with his free hand, 'today is a very important day. We must stand up to the British. They are deporting our leaders from Amritsar and they have forbidden us to gather today like this.'

'Why can't we gather Papaji?'

'That is a very good question young man. Now, there are your cousins. Let us go and join them. I see your Aunty has brought some treats for us to celebrate Bishakhi Day.'

Ravi laughed. 'That is good then Papaji. We will have meethi pooris to eat.'

'Indeed you will you little imp.'

Ravi skipped alongside his grandfather, tugging at his hand in his excitement and anticipation of the sweet food his aunty would soon push into his mouth.

It was 5.10 pm in the afternoon on 13 April 1919. The crowd clapped in support of the second resolution, to condemn the British firing on a peaceful demonstration of Sikhs.

'Papaji?' 'Yes child.'

'Why did the British people kill us?'

'They don't want us to be free like they are. They don't like us gathering together to talk about our freedom, to live peacefully as we used to live under the great Sikh.'

'Why not Papaji?' Ravi suddenly felt very cold and sad as if all the sweetness had left his mouth from Aunty's pooris. He wanted to cry and he gripped his grandfather's hand tightly.

'There are some things that even I do not know Ravi and there are some people that I too don't understand.'

'Papaji you are crying.'

The old man made no attempt to remove the tears flowing down his cheeks. For a moment he had glanced towards the entrance of the compound. The crowd was thick towards the centre of the uneven ground where the speakers had raised the resolutions to stop British oppression and violence against them. The throng of people, Sikhs, Muslims, Hindus and a tiny smattering of Christians were enthralled by the prospect of defying the British as they had on two occasions in as many weeks. The surge of freedom was palpable, a communal heart beating throughout the gathering. The old man cast his eyes around him, witnessing his neighbours, cousins from nearby villages, businessmen, religious leaders and mothers closely guarding their children, thinking and seeing as one. As his eyes crossed their heads he caught a measure of movement at the opening of the compound.

'Ravi, you sit here in my lap.' He quickly unbuttoned his long tunic.

Ravi buried his head into his grandfather's chest and thrust his arm inside the open tunic. For a second he could feel the hilt of the tiny sacred sword tucked into the belt of the kacchera. He breathed a sigh of relief as his grandfather wrapped his strong arms around his tiny body.

Ravinder felt the jerk in his grandfather's body at the same time as he heard the noise of the gunfire. A gush of blood spurted onto his head and into his mouth. He tried to spit it out and move his head to look upwards into his grandfather's face but he couldn't move. He hung on with all his strength feeling his grandfather stiffen as he fought to stay upright. Suddenly, there were screams all around him. More shots of gunfire. Bullets flew in all directions. Children running… mothers shrieking. His aunty….he heard her call his cousins and start running away from the noise that was everywhere. The sound was deafening and the smell of blood made him want to vomit. He clamped his mouth shut to stop the blood that was pouring from his grandfather's chest from going inside his mouth. But he couldn't block his nose. He needed to breathe; frantic breaths mixed with panic, confusion and an overwhelming sense to stay exactly where he was and not to move. He could still hear the gunfire. It must have been only a minute, less than that.

Ravi's entire world changed in that moment. All he could hear was silence. There was no warmth, no beating heart of his grandfather's heart, no soft words to calm and quieten him, no encouraging smile. His grandfather's arms were still locked around him as they crashed to the ground together, falling sideways, his head still buried in his grandfather's chest as he felt the life suddenly drain from his body. Ravi was all alone, hugging the lifeless body that was once the person he loved most in the world, the silence of death pounding in his ears.

Ravinder heard his own cries of grief. 'Papaji, Papji.' There was no response. The tears mixed with the blood on his cheeks and in his mouth. He spat out the rest of the blood and lay still. For a moment all he could hear was the pounding of blood in his ears, getting louder and louder as if his head would burst as his heart raced with fear. Then his ears opened to the world around him and he heard the screams and shrieks again, the thudding of feet on the ground and bodies falling. Carefully, he pushed his head away from his grandfather's chest; cold and unwelcoming. He turned his head to look sideways along the ground at the chappalled feet running in blind panic. A group of women, some with blood stains on their saris and some with hair streaked with a mix of dust and blood suddenly surged towards the open well. Ravi drew in his breath in sheer horror as they leaped one after another into the well, one woman dragging her child with her.

'No!' Ravi whispered unable to shout as he wanted to. He looked around him for his Aunty. His eyes met little eyes like his own. His baby cousin, five years old this month, her hand stretching towards him, the other arm limp, the hand blown off, blood soaking the dust next to her body. He reached out to her, grasping a finger, two fingers, clasping her whole hand, pulling her towards him. She smiled, her dainty mouth curving upwards in its cheeky way. Then she looked at her arm torn by the violence around them, unable to comprehend. A soft cry, her tears, then the hand in his went limp.

It was midnight. Ravinder woke to a soft groan near his grandfather's cold and stiff body. He pushed himself into a sitting position. The blood had dried on his shirt but his trouser pants were wet and warm. He realised that he had wet himself in his sleep. The thirst gripped his throat and he desperately wanted to find water. He searched around with his hands on the ground for his aunty's tiffin for the yoghurt milk that she always carried with her when she came visiting. His baby cousin was still, her hand stretched out; her eyes wide open; unblinking. The groaning turned into a cry and Ravinder knew that it was a man who had fallen half across his grandfather's legs. He looked at him, the jagged wound in his thigh glistening in the almost full moon risen high above the compound. Ravi looked into the desperate eyes. He wanted to reach out to the man has he did his baby cousin, but he couldn't bring himself to do it. The tears started and Ravi found himself without thinking, crawling forwards to the man's head near his grandfather's feet. He began to frantically unwind the man's turban from his head. His tears turned into loud cries as he pulled the last of the cotton material into his hands pushed it into the seeping wound on the man's leg. Sobbing, Ravi pushed with all his strength. He felt the man's hand close over the top of his hand, then carefully push away his hand and replace it with his own.

'Dhanavada.' He whispered. 'Tuhada dhanavada.'

Exhausted by emotion and the effort, Ravi sat up then fell forwards over his grandfather, slipping back into a dreamless sleep.

The harsh screech of vultures woke Ravi early in the morning as the dawn light caught the tops of the buildings around the edges of the compound. He pushed himself up and sat blinking in the early morning light. There was no movement in the compound. Littered around him were dozens of dead people; women, children, men, his grandfather …

Ravinder wanted to scream but no sound came from his parched throat. His mouth felt stale and he needed to vomit again but nothing would come up from his stomach still tight with fear. He stood up and looked around him. The well was only twenty or thirty steps away at the most. He looked again. There was no one to stop him, no one to tell him that he couldn't go for water. There was no sign of men with guns and there were no longer any bullets flying around him, killing, killing.

Chapter Two

Delhi, India March 1940

EDWARD STEPPED ONTO the dusty plain of India with a sigh of relief.

'Well, I suppose that's that.'

'Edward?' The voice was quiet, lilting and somehow familiar. 'You must be David.'

Edward shook his hand.

'How do you do. Or I should say *"namaste."* That's what we all say over here.'

'Namaste? I suppose that means *"lovely day?"*'

'Well actually Edward, it means *"I bow to the light within you"* and if you want to be pedantic about it, you can fold your hands and give a little bow.' David gave a comical demonstration.

Edward laughed. 'Nice introduction David. Does a sword to the back of the neck follow?'

'You're fast Edward. Yes there is great deal of tension here. There have been more deaths.' David paused.' The situation looks as if it will get worse before it gets any better but we can talk about that later. First things first. Let's go and find you a drink. Do you need the john?' David asked discreetly.

'Thanks, I'd appreciate that.' Edward was aware of how grimy he was. Edward squinted into the dusty light. The edges of the airfield were indistinct apart from a neat rampart of military tents on one side of the field. Some of the tents were closed to wandering animals, some half open with men busily tooing and froing between the tents and the metal building that served as the base.

'We're hoping to open airlanding training field later this year.' David said soberly.'

'Airlanding?'

'For the combined forces of course. Landing fields in this part of the world are generally pretty rough. Besides, our Ghurka friends over there,' David pointed to a small unit of men in brightly coloured headdress marching towards the Dakota, 'are some of the best fighters you would find anywhere. Imagine strapping them into parachutes and dropping them near the Burmese border.'

'Burma?'

'You must know course that we are expecting an invasion at some time. Japan.'

'Japan is not a part of the war David!'

'The Australian signals intelligence tells us something is afoot in the Pacific.

Besides, the Japanese will want to cut off the route through Burma to China.'

'I see.' Edward was thoughtful.

'How was the flight?' David's eyes twinkled.

'Rough. Very little padding in the fuselage, but thankfully we were securely strapped in by the harness. Mind you, that didn't stop one hell of a headache. The noise!' Edward grimaced at the memory.

'That's the RAF for you. No frills.'

'The Qantas Empire Class Flying boat service would have been fun I suppose.' Edward grinned.

'Luxury class! If you have the time and money definitely the best way to travel. Can't imagine anything better, London To Sydney via the Middle East and India courtesy of the Empire.' David gave him a friendly slap on the back.

'I wish,' Edward said ruefully. 'Apparently the Short Sunderland flight is a holiday in itself!'

David laughed out aloud. 'Champagne, caviar, somewhere comfortable to sleep, wander around the cabin and a very clear view of the sky.'

'I suppose *"The Reporter"* has a schedule.' Edward said ruefully. 'Mind you, there was a Sunderland on Lake Habbaniya when we arrived. I would have given anything to swap planes at that point.'

'You refuelled at RAF Dhibban?'

'Yes. Quite a spot I must say. All the services and comforts. Those boys know how to live it up, even in wartime. But I'm afraid my travelling companion Petes had some business in Baghdad so we drove straight there for a little shopping. Then we were back on the Dakota at first light, so very little time to enjoy the hospitality of the RAF as it were.'

'Still, you are here safely and it is not exactly easy to travel overland.' David mused.

'Well I am definitely no Marco Polo but having said that, there is no way anyone could travel overland these days.'

'Hmm, not with Jerry on the march through Europe.'

'Pretty grim I must stay from all accounts. I should be at home reporting in London, but my Chris insisted that I have a break from the war. The point is which war! By the way, this is for you.' Edward handed him a small parcel.

'Thanks. Empire Airmail via "safe hand."' David grinned. 'Good old Chris. He doesn't miss much. How is *"The Reporter"* coming along by the way?'

'Busy - but we have good sources, which saves us a bit of time rummaging around for information. The war is definitely hotting up in Europe though. Anything interesting in your package?'

'Lots.' David tucked the parcel into his shirt. 'A bit of light reading you might say.'

'Knowing Chris, it's anything but light reading.'

'I have to be a bit low key here. British Raj you know. Could be pulled up for treason or thrown in gaol for 'sedition' if I step out of line.'

'He did mention your position was sensitive. But then England has to look after her own territories.' Edward smiled. 'Even if they aren't really hers.'

'What *is* it like in London at the moment Edward.' David asked quietly.

Edward sensed the soft sadness in his new friend's tone. 'Nothing you would want to go home for at this moment David. Meat rationing is in and of course, we spend so many nights under a blackout. No lights, that sort of thing.'

'Sounds a bit grim.'

'You would be surprised. People are pretty cheerful at home. Churchill keeps their spirits up with his enthusiasm and confidence. Britain will win the war. That sort of stuff.'

David laughed.

'Mind you, not much fun on the London bus system at the moment. The windows are covered with a sort of sticky brown mesh to stop the glass shattering if a bomb goes off nearby. A bit dull for travellers.'

'Good planning.' David said thoughtfully.

'The hardest part though are the air raid warnings. The sirens are pretty piercing and of course, everyone has that "chilled moment" before going into the shelters. They can go off at any time you know.' Edward paused as if he were reliving the moment. 'Even during the middle of the night you have to get out of bed and go outside and huddle in your Anderson Shelter.'

'Very unnerving Edward.' David felt his mind watching as if expecting a bomb any moment.

'It can be.' Edward laughed lightly. 'Mostly of course, the "All Clear" siren comes soon enough then we all pop out of our tunnels and underground shelters like a warren of rabbits.' He grinned.

David slapped him on the back. 'Welcome to India Edward. This will be a real holiday for you.'

The two men approached the Austin 8. 'Hop in.' David said cheerfully. 'Strictly on loan from the one of the boys at the base.' He grinned. 'They prefer military vehicles only out here.'

'You have your own car?'

'Car and driver. Morris. But I drove to the airfield myself this time Edward, to collect you. You will feel more comfortable with your own for first impressions of India.'

'Thank you.' Edward was genuinely grateful.

'This is car is a bit of fun for us chaps don't you think?' David turned over the engine. The sound was strangely comforting after the roar of the

Dakotas twin engines. Edward felt as though he could still be somewhere in the Middle East, except that there were distinct differences in the clothing and the men looked decidedly less fierce. The airfield buzzed with activity. There seemed to be a limitless number of natives busily running errands and parcels from tent to tent. Uniformed men strolled across the polo ground with the speed of a Sunday picnic. Red-turbaned coolies ran frantically to and fro, shouting and yelling at one another as they jostled to carry bigger and bigger loads. Edward found himself transfixed to the sight of an old man with an impossible pile of cases perched on his head. His frail legs wobbled as each new case was stacked on top the others. But, he held his head high, his back erect as mastered the load.

A corporal called out merrily 'Hello grandpa! Can you carry my kitbag?'

The old man grinned toothlessly, wavering for a moment with suppressed laughter before he straightened himself again by precariously moving one leg in front of the other. The cases shifted, threatening to spill into the dust.

'It's like that over here. You'd better get used to it. Nothing that you would see anywhere else in the world mind you; limbless beggars, child prostitutes, poverty that makes your heart weep and yet some of them here are richer than the King of England.' David noticed Edward's visible shock at the abuse of the old man. 'Don't get sentimental about it Edward. There's nothing any of us can do. Try and help one of them and a whole lot comes running at you out of nowhere like a goddamned horde of flies. They stick around you with that pathetic look in their eyes and grab at your clothes, your shoes, anything. If you give them a single morsel, then in less time than you can draw breath, you'll have another ten hanging off you. Besides, it upsets the natural order. Everything and everyone has a place in India. Like it or not, their caste system works.'

'You must be joking of course.' Edward was appalled.

'No I'm not. Take away that old man's work and he has nothing. Give the beggars food and they would start to riot and fight each other. They have their systems and pecking order just like everyone else. Let people know that you accept their station in life and they're happy. Try and change it and the whole damned lot will come tumbling down on top of you. Don't take it to heart Edward, they're far better off than you think. The whole structure is like some Parsi tower of death. It exists for a good reason. If you can imagine five million destinies intricately connected by a thread called "caste," you begin to get the picture. Pull that thread out and there would only be chaos. Between you and me Edward,' David continued, 'I can't wait to see the whole damned lot of them out of here. They're completely out of context with mother England and some of them take the British Raj thing much too far if you ask me.'

Edward laughed coarsely. 'I see you're a reluctant supporter of the cause.'

'I didn't say that. However, from a common-sense point of view, our time in India is over and that's the truth of it. Gandhi isn't going to let the matter rest as long as he lives so it's time to pack up shop and go home.'

'Well if that's the way you see it David, I guess there's merit in it. Besides, I'm supposed to be here on a sort of a working holiday so the last thing that I want to do is to start a social crusade.'

'Leave it to the Mahatma. He has the story.' 'You know Gandhi?'

'Yes of course. Didn't Chris tell you, we go to his meetings from time to time, just to keep up to date with what going through the old man's mind. Looks as though he isn't about to give up the fight easily. There's going to be more blood before it's over though, mark my words. Some of these Raj types are a bit reluctant to let go of their make-believe kingdoms. Too used to having it all their way I suppose. And especially since they overlord the Indians, it's a bit of a humiliation for them to let it all go.'

'So you're not on the side of the British David.'

'I didn't say that I was, but then I didn't say that I wasn't. Have to do the diplomatic thing you know. There's the john. I'll wait here for you.'

'Thanks. Haf a mo.' Edward disappeared then reappeared feeling and looking relived and refreshed. The Dakota's engine gave a warning rumble and Edward spun around to see the plane taxiing towards the fuel dump.

'Won't be there for long Ed. Refuel, load up, change pilots and take off.'

'Christ, they don't hang about!'

'Important mail to deliver.' David laughed.

'Alone in the far reaches of The Empire.' Edward said grimly. 'Don't worry, you'll be safe with me.'

'Guess that's it. I'm stranded for now.'

'Let's go and have that chai and we'll be out of here.'

'Chai?'

'Best tea on earth, the way the Indians do it. Spice it up and add loads of buffalo milk, bring the whole lot to the boil, throw in a handful of tea and there you have chai.'

'Can't hurt to try. Looks as though I have a bit of adjusting to do.'

'Bye the way, try not to eat anything from the street stalls while you are in India. Don't know what you're getting. We've got a good cook at the base and and have my personal cook also so you can be sure that the food is clean.'

'Chris warned me.'

'Same goes for drinks. Boil everything first.'

'Thanks for the tip. What's that lot doing over there?'

'You mean the chai-wallahs?'

'Is that who they are.' Edward's voice was tinged with intrigue.

'Street vendors. They come out to the base to sell their sweets and so on. You see them everywhere, especially on the railway platforms. Fruit, tea, pooris, knick- knacks, you name it. Once the trains come into Karachi, Lahore, Amritsar and Delhi, the place goes berserk. The chai's boiled and safe to drink. He'll hang around until you give him back the cup but take your time.'

Edward accepted a chipped cup of milky tea and waited until David handed the chai-wallah a couple of coins.

'Here's to your health and a successful trip.'

'Cheers.' The tea was sweet and as David warned, spicy. The milk was welcome nourishment and Edward found himself wanting a second cup. David motioned the awkward and gnarled vendor to pour them another round from his battered and handleless kettle. The little man gave them a toothless grin; his lips and gums stained a beetroot red.

'Beetle nut. They chew it over here. Keeps them awake. It's a narcotic. Wouldn't touch it though Edward, it's quite addictive.'

'I won't! Not if that's how I'll look afterwards.' Edward chuckled.

The man turned his head while keeping his eyes planted on the Englishmen, hawked and spat into the dust. He hawked again and coughed from his chest, spitting reddened phlegm and sputum.

'Charming.' Edward remarked.

The man settled back onto his haunches, his beady eyes fixed on Edward, but somehow far away. They were sharp and cunning, nevertheless glazed by a languishing intoxication. His grubby hand reached towards David. David handed him a coin, drained his cup and held it out to the vendor. Edward watched the hand take the cup, rinse it with a little tea and place it on a hook protruding from his belt.

'Finished?' David took the cup from Edward and handed it to the man. 'Let's get out of here. There's more of them heading this way, probably to sell us sweets and what nots.'

'Lucky you have a car.'

'It's not as easy when you don't. They hang off you like leeches and you can't get rid of them. Just yell "*cello*" at them if they get too much. That means, "*go away.*"

'Rightio. Can't say I blame them though, they have to make a living like everyone else.'

'Don't fall for it Edward. They'll make a living, don't you worry. Speaking of which. I have an errand to run on the way to the compound I'm afraid. The journey will be a little longer than our usual direct route. Hang on for the ride.' David's Morris Ten sputtered into life. He gave the horn a long blast and turned the wheel towards the group of vendors.

The car accelerated dangerously towards the huddle. In a split second, carts men and produce hurtled by as they veered to safety.

'That was close.' Edward gripped both sides of the seat.

'Do it all the time.' David grinned. 'They do it to me, I do it to them. Give them a bit of their own curry.'

The car gathered speed, billowing dust and contempt into the atmosphere of heckling and determined business. Through the side mirror, blurred by heat, Edward briefly glimpsed the Dakota spiralling upwards through an imaginary doorway in the dust. For a second, the sound of the engine drowned out the petrol- whine of the car before being silenced as it banked steeply to the east. Edward felt his head spin with a thousand images; Ruth, the woman in his dreams, the war, Gandhi and David upon whom he now depended. He felt momentarily sick and afraid, as if he had no control over the events into which he been involuntarily cast.

David jerked the wheel to the right and leant his horn for a good five to six seconds.

'Damned cows, can't go anywhere here without one of them wandering across the road.'

'She didn't look too concerned.' Edward snapped back to the present.

'Never are. They own India. Who cares about the Jinnahs and the Gandhis? At the end of the day, it's four hooves and a pile of dung that keeps this country on its feet.' David hooted the horn again and waved his arm at a cyclist heading towards them on the wrong side of the road. 'Run him off if he's not careful.' David pointed the car directly at the rider. The cyclist slowed to an almost heart- stopping halt then pulled the wheel onto the side of the road. He wobbled crazily, the urns balanced by a pole on either side spilling precious drops of milk, before righting himself and assuming his place on the strip of dirt that served as the lifeline to market. He looked in the rear vision mirror and gave him the thumbs up sign.' Crazy nut. Can't teach them to ride on the right side of the road. Want to take up the whole damned space for themselves. They'll never learn you know. Life and death, it doesn't matter. What matters is if you win a little bit over the next person.'

The milk vendor was unable to return David's insult, his hands fiercely gripping the handlebars to maintain his balance and dignity and his course set determinedly to the middle of the road.

'See what I mean.' David nodded into the mirror. 'Stubborn as a mule.'

Edward was more than mildly alarmed, his English repose once again shattered, this time by a rude and 'dog eat dog' introduction to India. His armpits were sweaty and the grit of the airfield and road stuck to his teeth. The sky was still brown and indistinct, moulding shapes into indefinite realities and Edward's sense of place and order could not find even a tiny footing in the shifting, treacherous manners of the road. The cyclist was a vivid close-up view of the apparent margins between life and death and the insistence of an ancient land on being her own keeper. Mother India, *"Bharat"* determined her own minor and major justices, gathering, embracing and positioning her flock within her tolerant and accommodating arms. There was no room for protest at the bosom of the Mother. Ultimately, there was no room for any who dared despise her infinite wisdom and calling. She was as ancient and timeless as the gods. No matter the fecundity and possessiveness of corporeal mothers; they were insignificant against the omnipotent demands of the Mother Bharat.

Edward felt his powerlessness acutely. The vastness of the land was steeped into the barren soil peppered with little piles of dung. The omnipresence of humanity was continually recorded in the creaking rickshaws that lurched across the road at unexpected and dangerous intervals and the hordes of huddling beggars relentless in their pursuit of an anna or a rupee. Here, there were increasing throngs of people on foot jammed into village market places, and the sharp, penetrating eyes of the chai wallah.

The car hurtled through the unkempt and transient settlements, its route disdainful of chickens, donkeys or stray dogs that dared to linger in its path. Occasional souls, accustomed to idling in conversation, were thrown into temporary and startled disorder as David pushed through narrow streets, regardless.

'Can't afford to stop. Once you stop, they're at the window trying to sell you this or that. Keep going. That's the best thing to do.'

The shanty settlements clinging to the edge of the town crowded Edward's mind like a thousand lives clamouring for space, climbing for recognition and pushing one another aside with grim disregard. The sea of faces become an ocean of living waves, pounding the sedate shore of his English upbringing into a storm-wrecked landscape of broken images, coarse feelings and human debris. There was no letting up, no escape from the tide of humanity that breached the once fortified wall of his sensibilities and rushed across the plains of his experience and exposure, scattering a myriad of forms, faces, colours, creeds and castes into his consciousness.

Edward gazed giddily at the blur of human beings, pressing to catch his own face through the visage of English superiority, as his side window whisked into and out of their view. At times, the car slowed to an agonising crawl and the hands and faces found a foot-hold in his psyche; the curious grasping, the unhidden contempt and despising of land-lost peoples, somehow blaming, somehow desperate.

David drove on in good-humoured repose, quietly whistling a tune to, from time to time, breaking his self-confident air with a 'damn' or to hammer the horn until the cluttered and unwieldy path cleared before him. Then the sun broke through the haze as if to heighten Edward's powerlessness, forcing its unstoppable heat onto the car.

'Pull the shades down if you like Ed. There's one for your side window and one in the back.'

David noticed Edward's discomfort. The sudden sun could easily tip the balance between 'just managing' and 'hysteria.'

'If you want, have a nap.' David honked the horn and swerved to avoid a group of rag-clad women squatting in a circle around tousling cockerels.' There's a cushion behind you. We'll be there in about an hour.' David was content to leave it at that. He had his hands full and he needed time to assess Edward silently, unobtrusively.

'Thanks. I might do that.' Edward tugged at the blind cord until it mercifully covered his side window. He was reluctant to obstruct David's view in this maelstrom of human survival by shading the back, side window. Nevertheless, David insisted.

'Don't worry about me Ed. They will see me before I see them. Law of life, 'move out of the way if you want to keep it.'

Edward relented and settled into a grateful but troubled doze. He didn't know how he would manage being here in India. Whilst he had David to guide him and forge the way through the unlimited throngs of carts, bicycles, street stalls, the maddening stationary cows and huddles of "doing nothing" human beings, he would undoubtedly manage. Alone, he would feel as vulnerable as a blindfolded party-trick, thrown from hand to hand until unmasked and told to pin the tail on the donkey. This time, there was no pictures with which he could identify and in any case, the images and impressions were constantly moving like a coloured maelstrom. There was no pinning the tail in India, no chance of orienting himself and taking a chance at where he stood in relation to the bigger picture. He was dizzy, blind-man and had no idea where to find the donkey.

Sleep was the familiar escape, but the images of the world outside his shaded window penetrated his mind and disturbed Edward's dreams. He saw handless maidens squatting in the dung, young boys racing wildly from train carriage to train carriage selling spindles and pencils, old men sitting in seeping puddles of spent body fluids, equally old, toothless women clutching rags to their breasts, furtively extending grasping hands at passers by.

Amidst the chaos, perfectly wound turbans sat upon proud heads with unseeing eyes. The bejewelled turbans converged in a kaleidoscope of glittering menace, bobbing amongst the flowing white robes of pretender-priests and unmasking the still stranger soldier garbs, that martialled order and obedience. Among the moving sea of souls, women veiled and hidden from desire by black and coarse cloth, wafted in small clusters, in and out of Edward's vision.

Then from behind the curtain, the same eyes emerged. The scintillating and magnetic gaze of the pearl-like eyes accelerated out of the crowd and caught his own staring eyes for a tortuous moment, then retracted in an instant behind the veil once more.

Faces and people began to race before him until they moved in an endless blur of colour into long strands, twisting and intertwining into a shimmering gossamer- like rope, dancing and rippling across the depth and breadth of India. With each thought and breath of semi-sleep, the waves bounced from end to end as if held by a distant hand. As the waves redoubled and met, they heightened into a single form, Hindu, Buddhist, Muslim, Parsi woven into a solitary bond. Then on one side, Christ appeared, a lonely shadow, tall, silent and on the other, Gandhi. The two Saints caught the strands, one by one, untwisting and separating one from the other. Then with gentle fingers, they held them to the light, caressing each thread until the colours resonated with 'I am, I am, Amen, Amen, I am, I am, Aum, Aum.'

The final 'Aum' droned into a long chant, rhythmically emanating from each cord in a symphony of love, a resplendent canopy of light and sound across the dying plains of India.

Edward heaved to the side, his head jerking from the left shoulder to his right and then agonisingly forwards onto his chest. He struggled to lift his head, fighting against sleep for consciousness to lighten the weight of his head. His head lolled forwards again, sending sharp thrusts of pain into his forehead. The sleep suddenly snapped and with his awakening, the illusion of security also broke. He groaned at the strain of lifting his head to the vertical. He closed his eyes to cut out the throbbing, moving his head to the right shoulder to make the movement easier. The noise and smell of petrol was sickening and the dust crawled through tiny cracks between metal and glass, settling at the edges of his mouth and nose.

'Here, have a swig of this.' David passed Edward a small silver flask. 'It will wake you up and take the edge off the dust. 'God awful isn't it. Can't go anywhere without being covered by the stuff. Better than the monsoon though. The place starts to crawl with vermin. Snakes too. Have to watch out for them, but you won't be here that long I expect. Did you have a good nap? Can't say you missed much. Just a load of camels carrying all manner of things, pots, bolts of cloth, sticks, you name it. By the way Edward, if you need to relieve yourself, we can stop here for a few minutes. Pit stop if you know what I mean.'

Edward nodded. He would do anything to stop for a few moments, to collect his thoughts and have a break from the reeking invasion of petrol fumes. David pulled up unceremoniously at a roadside stall and killed the engine. He stepped out of the car with amazing alacrity slamming the door shut and locking it behind him.

'Can't trust them around here. More thieves than Ali Baba's cave.'

David walked into the low-roofed lean-to without hesitation. He relieved himself, walked back whistling into the sunlight and indicated for Edward to follow suit.

'Turn a blind eye to it Ed. Just do what you have to do and leave. That's it.'

There was no toilet. It was simply an overflowing pit of human excreta. Muck covered every available space on the floor and the stench rose up like an exploding bomb of inhumanity and poverty.

Edward's instinct was to vomit - violently against the country that defied his dignity and decency. The urge to run from the incongruous pit that claimed to be a "toilet" almost overpowered his urge to void. David's words jammed his mind with reason, forcing him to stay and relieve himself rather than flee from the insulting stench. He closed his eyes as an urgent arc of urine formed and fell into the steaming pool, triggering further waves of fecundate gases. The moment of urination was an initiation far worse than months of systematic brutalisation in any English boarding school or military establishment. The utter humiliation of being forced into the waste of numberless, faceless, defecating Indians tore from Edward, the last of his resistance. He vomited heaving from the depths of his stomach and at the same time, felt as though he were losing all contact with his own culture, his sense of respectability and control.

Then it was over. He could hear David calling, anxious to continue before the car attracted beggars. Edward drew his strength to face the cesspit for the last time and retreated into the blinding and scornful sun.

'You all right? You look a bit pale around the gills.' David couldn't suppress his mirth. 'Weren't sick in there were you Ed?'

Edward nodded, too weary to speak.

'Happens to most of us first time. Bit overpowering but then you get over it and treat it like any other john. Don't think about it too much. This is India. Bye the way, there's a bit of scotch left in the flask. Take a swig and rinse your mouth out. It will take the edge off the nausea and the bitter taste in your mouth. There's a good chap. You'll be on top of all this in no time.'

David swung open the car door and before seating himself properly, kicked the engine into life.

'Let's get a move on. Soon there'll be a horde of them heading this way. "*Mango Sahib, grraape, coconut. Sahib, please you want incense sahib.*" Say nothing, look at no one, and keep moving.'

David turned towards Edward, 'Once they catch your eye, that's it, they have got you. It is as if a worm goes straight inside, reads you like a book then takes you for everything you have. Leaves salesmen in the west for dead. Don't know how they do it. Greatest psychologists on earth these chaps. Take one merchant-wallah from here and pit him against ten of best salesmen in England and the Indian will win outright every time. You have to have a policy of "no buy" whenever you go out or you're done for. If you want anything Ed, souvenirs for your wife or whatever let me know and I will send one of the servants out to shop for it. Don't trust any of them. They'll increase the price ten times without batting an eye. But not to their own kind. Same goes for getting taxis, you name it. Fix the price or they'll fleece you outright. It's the way it is. David became philosophical, 'Can't say I blame them, with our lot parading officialdom and wealth under their poor noses. I'd do the same I suppose.'

The shanties merged into a long string of rubble. David increased the throttle, happy that the obstacles were less now that the road was more distinct from the huddles of human inhabitants. 'We're out of the woods now. This is the edge of the main centre Edward. We just have to drop off some mail then we are on the way home. Can't say the next hour will be much fun. Fascinating though. Hang onto your hat, we're going in.'

Edward felt much relieved after abandoning abhorrence and revulsion in the communal latrine. The scotch, as David promised, took the edge off his nausea. He was content to sit and absorb the sights and sounds of the encroaching city.

'Things are very quiet today Ed. It hasn't always been the case, as you would know. Once the Indians got the vote, they also got a taste of their own power. That's the problem. Don't know how to use it and most of the time, took it out on each other. Wouldn't do much to us, but they can be pretty hard against their own kind. The war's taken the gas out their balloon for now though.'

'Are the Indians involved in the war?'

'Of course. Just like the other wars Mother's fought this century, she's relying heavily on Indian military support, and money; don't ask about the money from the Maharajas Edward.' David drew in his breath. 'The idea is to then form a sort of government with the Maharajas, but under British control, a sort of dominion set up. Gandhi doesn't like it a bit.'

'I don't wonder. Puppet government and the wealth goes to Britain rather than these millions of poor excuses for human beings.' Edward waved an expansive hand towards the shanties flitting out of view.

'That's it. Britain's doing it all over again and all in the name of war. Independence doesn't get a look in. Not that the Indians had much choice. The Viceroy made the decision without consulting any of the ministries so that was that. So far, they have done a bit of a deal. Congress wants complete Independence in return for co-operation during the war. Mind you, I don't think that Gandhi agreed to it. He's had his fingers burnt by the British. The situation is a bit delicate at the moment. No one is really sure what Gandhi will do next. "Look out!" 'David shouted into the ether. 'Damned fool. Could see me from a mile away and what does he do? Waits until the last moment and dashes out into the middle of the road. That's Indians for you Edward.'

David paused, and grinned despite himself.' Amazing thing is that they make such good fighters, surprising ability, especially those turbaned fellows. Sikhs. Can't beat them in any hand to hand combat and they're darned good horsemen as well.'

'Strange that you should mention it. I was dreaming about them before we stopped. It was weird, like a cacophony of coloured turbans swirling in front of my eyes. Not that there was any noise, but the colours! All shades of the rainbow and everything in between. It just looked like a pile of heads bobbing beneath this moving mirage of material.'

'Quite a vivid dream. Do you always have them like that?'

'Seem to lately.'

'What else?'

'They were all there, all varieties. Those Hindu priest-types, Buddhists and of course huddles, of women covered with veils. Only the eyes appeared again.'

'Eyes?'

'Yes, the same eyes I dreamt about on the plane to Baghdad. Hauntingly beautiful David She was wearing a purdah. I've never seen anything like them.'

'My word. Hope you don't have any mix-ups with the Muslims old chap. Could lose your head the way they're acting at the moment. Mind you, the Hindus aren't much better.'

'I hope not too. Chris wants me to cover the Amritsar story. I hope it's not a premonition. You must know that Sir Michael O'Dwyer was murdered the other day David?'

'Yes, we heard all about it on the BBC. Bit of a problem over here of course. Bound to stir up a lot of old feeling. We have to keep our heads down for a while otherwise there will be more riots to deal with.'

'That bad? What about going to Amritsar?'

David looked alarmed 'Are you sure that's a good idea?'

'Well, what do you think?'

'I think that we'd better check out the mood before you go launching into the wilds of Sikh sentiments. Don't want you to become the next sacrificial lamb. When the Indians run hot Edward, they simply over boil. There's no stopping them once they get started and you don't want to be the next action. Gandhi's the only one who can settle them down. They all treat him like a Saint, as if he's their own venerated grandfather. Especially the Harijans. He is the only one they've got.'

'Harijans?'

'The untouchables. The people that empty the can and collect the cow dung.'

'Didn't empty the one we just visited.' Edward smiled.

'Wouldn't want to either.' David shot him a wry look.

Chapter Three

THE TWO MEN settled into a companionable silence as David negotiated his way through the thickening streets. His speed sobered considerably as his thoughts mulled over Amritsar and the dis-ease of Gandhi. The situation in India was not only hot; it was volatile, especially in the big cities where news travelled fast. There was no point in provoking anyone into stoning their car, or turning it over and burning it, because of his usual reckless and contemptuous driving. This was Delhi and not some backward village peopled more by cows than recalcitrant new nationals.

The car engine cut out with a soft splutter as it pulled into the compound.

'Just in time eh! This old girl has nearly done her time.' David stepped agilely out of the car.

Edward followed suit, his bones weary and reluctant to stir. Perhaps it was just the burden of life. The recent ordeals with Ruth and now the disturbing re- arrangement of the cultural landscape seemed to have aged him in days.

'Here we are Edward.' David offered. 'First, a hot drink and a wash, then you must sleep properly for a few hours before we talk. I think that you've been through enough for one day don't you?'

Edward nodded with tired and grateful resignation as David collected his luggage from the boot and led him towards the cottage.

'This place is like a village - could be anywhere you like in England. You can block out the entire outside world if you want to. This is where I live. You are welcome to stay as long, as you want Edward. The company will do me good I expect and I'd love to hear a bit of news about mother country at the same time.'

'Thanks. I'd be happy to catch you up on some of it.'

'That's settled then. Welcome to my humble abode in this vast and wondrous kingdom!'

The two men laughed as David opened the door with a good humoured flourish. Inside, the 'cottage' was stark with whitewashed walls and very little furniture.

A collection of hand-woven rugs, carefully arranged, softened polished marble floors.

'Tasteful.'

'I like the local produce - these people really know crafts. This is your room Edward.' David flung David's bags onto a chair at the end of the bed. 'There's a bathroom attached. Nothing fancy. Just a place to wash and shave. You'll be OK in here for a while. No disturbances. Everything here is cotton, *"Khadi"* - the mattress, quilts and so on. It's actually very comfortable. Much better than blankets.'

'Thanks.' Edward was lost for words. 'What time will I come looking for you?'

'I'm around and about today. A local woman comes to cook for me at 6 o'clock so I'll expect to see you at about half past six if that's all right with you. I'm a vegetarian. Hope you don't mind.'

'No.'

'Good. Enjoy your rest. If you need anything, just yell. The water is quite hot so don't burn yourself under the tap.'

'Thanks David, I mean it.'

'Don't mention it.' David smiled broadly and closed the door behind him leaving Edward to contemplate a much needed and welcome wash.

Edward pulled out his travelling kit and headed into the bathroom. The bathroom was scrubbed clean, but nothing fancy. The toilet bowl was as equally ancient as the washbasin. A metal bucket with a cup-like scoop seemed to be the only apparatus for a full wash. The water was steaming hot as David had promised and warned. Edward filled the ceramic basin to wash his face and shave. 'Well, if this is how they do it here, guess I had better get used to it.' He half-filled the bucket with hot water and added the cold until it was a bearable temperature. Then he stripped off his filthy and now pungent trousers and shirt and flung them into a pile in the corner of the bathroom. God, it was good to get the smell off his body.

The water was refreshing and miraculously therapeutic for his tiredness. Edward almost felt civilised as he poured cupfuls of the water over his head and watched it flow harmlessly towards the drain. The soap scorched his eyes and threatened to clog the drain, but he continued to lather his skin as if the memories and insults of the journey would disappear along with the Indian dirt and grime.

David had thoughtfully left a few towels lying over the back of a chair - Khadi. Edward swept one towel over his head and the other around his waist then planted himself on the crude surface of the chair. This was heaven. Nothing and no-one to worry about for the moment. Ruth could wait! She was far enough away for Edward to treasure the privacy of his bath and the company of another man.

He dried himself carefully and completely before heading into quiet comfort of the quilt aware of how he wanted the protection of the loose fitting cottons of the Indians.

Chapter Four

Europe Two Weeks Earlier
THE THUNDERCLOUDS OF war gathered in the European skies. Not even the 'Holy City' of Europe, The Vatican, was completely immune. By 1939 the Pope had engaged in intensive, pre-war diplomacy in an effort to avert the coming war that would sweep across multiple nations bringing with, it the slaughter of millions of innocents. Nevertheless, Thomas felt safe in Italy. Despite the tensions present in the early months of the war, there was still concourse between the great spiritual institutions, the Church of England and the Roman Catholic Church. There were also regular transmissions between The Vatican and England through its ecclesiastical diplomat, the Papal Apostolic nuncio in London, William Godfrey. The Vatican was after all, *"Christ's seat of power"* in the world and Rome by geographical and historical association, the home for the papal throne. The Church of England, although not Roman Catholic, was a key and important member of the Christian Church, and Rome would make sure that relations would remain strong and communications always open.

Pope Pius XII was deeply opposed to the war. By April 1939 he announced peace plans in at attempt to mediate negotiations between Italy, France, Poland, Germany and England. In the early months of 1940, the Pontiff talked to both the British and German generals who wanted to overthrow Hitler. At the same time, he ordered the Vatican Radio to broadcast reports on the persecution of the Catholic Church in Poland. His efforts were to no avail, but the Vatican City was safe; the Holy City free for now of occupation by Nazi Germany. Thomas felt driven to visit his beloved city Rome. At the University of Oxford he was absorbed in studying religious architecture, its significance during times of war and peace, the role and influence of great buildings on the human mind and civil order. More than that, more than his thesis for his doctoral studies, Thomas loved the intricate design and compelling curves of St Peter's Basilica, the grand and commanding St Peter's Square, the frescoes, furnishings and artworks that so articulately, illustrated and described the heart and soul of Christian belief.

It was inevitable that his studies would draw him back into the bosom of The Vatican City; it was fortunate that he could indulge his senses in the splendour of St Peter's, when war threatened to destroy the great buildings and their works that were otherwise eternal representations of holy belief and order. He was overjoyed when the Head of the Faculty organised the through the Papal Apostolic nuncio in London, safe passage directly to The Vatican where he could spend as long as he needed to write his doctoral thesis.

Thomas's presence in Rome, was a good sign that diplomacy still worked during the time of war, even when the neutrality of the Pontiff was required by treaty with Mussolini. Any exchange that kept alive communications and dialogue, that furthered the human spirit of enquiry, was welcome.

He felt a deep inner gratitude to his Dean and faculty. The war had hardly registered in his mind, fascinated and absorbed as he was in the study of great religious architecture and its relationship to any and every theory on God, the origin of life and the intangible human soul. Just as he studied the drawings of great buildings in minute detail, he plumbed the depths of the laws of karma and the human condition! He cared not whether threads of meaning emanated from bricks and mortar across or religious texts; the writings of Mohammed, Abraham, Christ, or The Bhudda, the Mithrain or existential strands of thought. All were significant and created a single lineage in human thought and development. He felt equally inspired by Donato Bramante and Michaelangelo, as by Christopher Wren and the great English artists, Van Dyck, Constable and Turner. Art, architecture and the scriptures were for Thomas a singular chord in the grand design. He could as lose himself as easily poetry as in prose, in art or by wandering through the catacombs and great cathedrals of the world. The mystic, literal and practical were one and the same to Thomas. When not lost in the timeless majesty of great works of the human mind, Thomas was anyway absorbed in his own reflection upon universal harmony, order and the cosmos. As he stared skywards at the Spire, Thomas felt the thrill of the sublime. Time stood still as he gazed at the beauty of the St Peter's Dome.

'Signor, you had better come inside.' The guard was clearly worried, his tone both hushed and urgent. The guard recognised that his unexpected visitor was English. Like a startled crab, he scurried over to hustle him out of view. He was not as worried for the English man absorbed in the architectural beauties of old Rome, as he was for himself. He was a self-respecting Italian and this was not the time to be seen 'consorting' with an Englishman, welcome though he was at the Holy See. There were the ever-present eyes of the Curia to consider along with his job and it was never clear whether Rome and The Vatican had formalised the neutrality of the the Church during the escalating war.

'Oh?' Thomas looked towards the ridiculous figure waving his arms and beckoning him into the looming confines of St Peter's Basilica. 'And why my dear fellow?' Thomas replied with his good-natured ease. 'Do you think it might rain on my English head?' Thomas could not resist. He enjoyed making fun of the little man and besides, he had a perfect right to be in Rome. Thomas moved towards the little man, at first extending his hand and instead, stooping into a sweeping bow.

'Signor' replied Thomas 'It is a great honour to be in your wonderful city and the weather is very conducive to the study of religious architecture, but it seems that you think there are better things to see inside.'

'Indeed there are Signor.' The guard was visibly relieved.

As the guard led him inside, Thomas allowed his mind to flow to the transcendental curves and arches of such complete magnificence. His feet simply and dutifully followed the guard's comical, yet determined gait as his mind contemplated the divine.

The guard turned, impatient more than concerned for his charge. 'Signor, Signor. Watch out!'

Thomas, semi-levitated upon the ascendant beauties of religious form and structure heard the guard. His foot stepped into the space; his mind had kept uncluttered for so long, the space without the firm bedrock of substance and steadfastness. As he fell, Thomas saw the wonderful roof spiral and swirl above him, beckoning him to join the angels, tempting him with their corporeal vision cast in plaster and rock. He seemed to fall deeper and deeper before he felt his head connect with a sharp crack. Then the waves of blackness washed into the void of consciousness. There was no longer any feeling of lightness, no longer any absorption in the giddying heights of the ceiling, nor light of illumination entrancing his mind into deeper secrets or journeys; only a searing, painful and endless blackness. The light had gone out.

Thomas was dead.

Chapter Five

RUTH OPENED THE telegram with a sense of surprise. This was unlike Thomas to call whilst he was overseas. Generally, Thomas was completely absorbed in his research, so that the best he could do to remember England and his family was to jot into his diary to bring Ruth home something 'out of the ordinary.' For Edward, Thomas's journeys meant an interesting artefact uncovered and returned to London; or an unexpected and exciting disclosure on the past, that threw new light on the present. Edward and Thomas had spent many hours into the early mornings discussing religion, philosophy and 'truth,' if there were such a thing, each discussion taking them further into the subtle differences of existence, mind, God and eternity. For Edward, their discussions meant new and stimulating territory. For Thomas esoteric existentialism was his love, his passion and his reason for being. Thomas was grateful that Edward was such a willing conversationalist who sufficiently understood the subtleties of his discourse to challenge Thomas's enthusiasm and open naivety. The creased telegram appeared to be, written in haste. Thomas probably had some exciting news; perhaps the extra time he wanted in Rome. As she read the lines, Ruth's natural amusement with her brother dropped into frozen shock and her mind buckled under the steel trap of finality.

> "Dear Mrs. Thompson, I regret to inform you that your brother fell whilst visiting St Peter's Basilica this morning. The doctor confirmed that his death was instant. Your name was cited as 'Next of Kin' in his wallet and so it is my unfortunate duty to request instructions for the disposal of his body."

1 March 1940.

'I'm so sorry Ruth.' Edward spoke quietly.

Ruth nodded, unable to speak - fresh tears and sobs welling to the surface.

Edward walked softly out of the living room into the kitchen and opened the coffee grinder. Ruth would need time to collect her thoughts and at the moment, he needed to collect his own thoughts before consoling here. Ruth's grief belonged with Thomas, and so Edward knew enough to leave her alone until she wanted him there. He measured sufficient grounds for four cups of coffee into the grinder and absorbed himself in the task, deliberating over the quality of the brew. The grinder whirred as Edward turned the handle, the grating sound a welcome break to the emotions searing the kitchen. Then he lit the gas and measured enough water to allow the coffee to brew until it was mature and strong. Ten minutes would do nicely. In that time, the kitchen would fill with the sounds of clinking cups and saucers and the aromas of a warm and intimate breakfast.

Ruth's tiny cough was the cue for Edward. He returned to the living room with the tray full of coffee, cream, sugar and a few of the delicate chocolates dedicated to their dinner party for his work colleagues. She smiled, her mouth and eyes softening to thank Edward for his discretion. Edward returned the smile, an unobtrusive twitch at the corners of his mouth. He sat next to her, and then poured her coffee, stirring in the precious and rationed cream and sugar. He knew Ruth would need encouragement to eat and drink. Right now, she needed immediate warmth, normality. She raised the cup to her lips, trying to control the quiver in her mouth and tremor in her hands. The coffee was hot, comforting and sweet. Edward always ordered the best. The aroma mingled with her tears somehow brought the present into focus.

Edward smiled as Ruth sniffed, wiping her tears with one hand, cup in the other.

'Here, let me take it for a moment Ruth.' Edward caught the cup balancing it in his left hand as Ruth blew her nose, then hid her face in her hands.

'Edward, how could it happen? I don't understand, he was safe.'

Edward quickly put both cups down and held his wife, allowing her to bury her head in his chest as if she were a child. He rocked her until the tears flowed endlessly, soaking into his sweater. It was two hours before she finally fell asleep. Cradled in Edward's arms, she mourned her brother now lost to the world and the war he did not fight. Edward held her until her only movement was the quiet breathing of deep sleep. Then he laid her head on the lounge and went to find her blankets. He walked to the hall table and picked up the phone.

'Chris? It's Ed. I can't come in today. Do you mind?' 'Of course not Ed. Something happen at home?' 'You might say that. Can I call you a bit later?'

'Sure thing. Nothing urgent here at the moment.'

'Thanks Chris. I mean it.' Edward placed the received back on the hook and went back into the kitchen. He wanted more coffee and, breakfast. His stomach ached with emptiness, but more so, his mind from questions, from worrying about Ruth and wondering how they would bring Thomas home. Ruth would never be able to face the ordeal. He would have to arrange for the body to come home himself, for Thomas's funeral and burial. Ruth would only be able to think about the living Thomas, and more than likely, could and would not comprehend or organise the aftermath of death.

Ruth finally stirred. The coarseness of the blanket was rough comfort, incongruous against the outline of her dream. The struggle between the transient comfort of her subconscious and the raw edge of reality continued until the weight of the blanket forced her into waking. Then she woke, refreshed and comforted by the familiar impressions of her home, Edward and her sanctuary against the war and her fears. Then, the sudden loneliness, the surge of helplessness descended like a shroud.

'Edward.' A few seconds lapsed. 'Edward.' Ruth was exhausted with her tiny effort.

Edward heard Ruth's faint call and dismissed it as imagination. He heard her the second time, her voice breaking his long musings on Thomas.

'Strange. Thomas has consumed my mind for hours.' Edward inwardly remarked. He remembered vividly the pipe playing at Thomas's lips, the smoke curling through his hair almost as beautiful as Ruth's, but a shade coarser and duller. He was sure that the sparkle of Thomas's eyes in that moment was as real is if he were present, reciting long stanzas of Kabir or Tagore. Edward smiled. He often listened quietly, admiring Thomas's grasp of literature as much as he mused at his passion for religion. Thomas educated him as no teacher could, his fervour and dramatics breathing life into the ancient tales and lore of India. Edward could almost feel and touch the wonderful battleground where Arjuna fought his cousins and smell the scorching heat as Rama and his army of monkeys set alight to Ceylon. In great detail and colour, Thomas would recant the epics of the Pandavas, drawing complex and extended genealogies for Edward as if the characters of the Mahabharata were part of his own family. Then he would switch to the ventures of Christ and the yogis' stories of Jesus in India before and after his time as Christ the teacher. Edward would listen in fascinated disbelief to his brother-in-law, wanting to discount his fantastic tales, yet somehow trapped by their logical authenticity.

Then there was Rome, Rome! Thomas's great hope. He longed to spend weeks exploring the ancient city and its surrounds, searching for signs, remnants of the Caesars. For Thomas, Rome more than London or New York was the pulse of the modern world. The secrets of his English past were in Rome. It was in Rome, that Thomas could make sense of his own religion. He could suffuse himself in the ancient city; seductive, irresistible, an obsession. The same Rome held in its underground and private passages, trails of spiritual intrigue, death and destruction. Rome was for Thomas, the beginning of his spiritual journey and, now it marked the end.

Oxford was tolerant of Thomas's pursuits, happy that within the scholar, was also an enthusiast, and engineer who could build across time, culture and religion, bridges of learning and understanding. Through Thomas's subtle - even brilliant mind - the most seasoned professors could travel through time, cross the far seas and taste the spiritual essence of both the East and the West. Thomas was deeply engaged in the exercise of linking mythological and historic beams to the bridge of human understanding, culminating not in Constantinople, but in Rome. He was fascinated by the overarching, mythological symbols that clearly connected East to West, ancient India, to Greece, Persia to Rome and inevitably, Catholic Rome to Protestant Anglo-England. It wasn't a new philosophical journey and it was unlikely he would uncover new information. The journey was however the context and framework that could potentially enlighten and nourish the Anglican Church in England; its origins and relationship with the far East.

Thomas's intellectual power and enthusiasm persuaded his professors to support his enquiry into the origins of Christian thought and its relationship to the secular and everyday matters of modern Britain. He possessed an equally powerful sense of religious form, the significance of artefacts and architecture, their symbology and links to ancestral archetypes. The influence of a few pieces of wood and metal on the course of nations was to Thomas as intriguing as the origins of the Bible or literality of the Koran.

> *"Even more extraordinary Edward, is Hitler's retrieval of the talismanic Crucifixion Spear. Or so he thought! Legend has it that the possessor of the Spear would have enough power to rule the world - the corporeal link to the Divine. The Spear has supposedly been the property of a succession of powerful souls including St Maurice, Charles IV,*
>
> *Charlemagne and Napoleon. And now it belongs to the Hapsburgs. Still, it isn't theirs any longer. Hitler has it safe and sound at Nuremberg. As if the Nazis could have a spiritual centre!"*

Edward recalled Thomas's wide-eyed disclosures at Hitler's deep obsession with the occult and involvement with the Thule society, his dabbling in alchemy and strange interest in the symbology and power of eastern religions. Thomas confided,

> *"Most worrying, is Hitler's identification with Parsifal. You know Edward; Wagner has more power over Hitler than even Hitler's*

mother. I hate to think what he is going to do masquerading as Klingsor. No doubt, he sees all of Europe as the treasured Holy Grail. Or perhaps he hopes to crush Christianity. Whatever Edward, I do not like the omens.

Imagine a lunatic like Hitler ruling the world with black magic. God! I don't want anything to do with the war. It's not about territory or ideals; it's about the survival of good in a dark world. If Hitler is Klingsor, I wonder who is the prophesied Parsifal?"

Edward shuddered. Thomas plumbed the depths of meaning too deeply for him and he, Edward preferred to protect his Christian sensibilities. Rome was nevertheless, the seat of Christian power therefore, it was natural that Rome would ultimately draw Thomas into its embrace. In Rome, Thomas could search for the elusive Holy Grail, no matter the glaring paradox of crowded streets, the dirt and crumbling buildings that screeched out *"the fallibility of all great men."* Indeed, it was the transparency and frailty of human life appealed mostly to Thomas. How magnificent were the aspirations and achievements of men, yet how simply were they all shattered at death. Edward sighed, inwardly aching. Perhaps Thomas tempted fate once too often. Suddenly, Edward snapped out of his trance.

'Ruth!' He moved quickly to the sitting room and caught his wife in his arms. He held her, stroking her cheek, soothing her face crumpled by her broken reality. 'It's all right, I'm here now.'

Ruth let go relieved she was not alone. 'I couldn't sleep. I just kept dreaming about Thomas, about our childhood. Edward, he's gone.' Ruth began to weep; unaware Edward mirrored her tears in his own. Finally, she collapsed into a second sleep; her grief spent and mind washed clean of pain and disbelief. Thomas would never come home.

Edward waited until Ruth was completely quiet, then left her to sleep. This time, she would sleep long untroubled hours, without memories of the past or any anguish of the future.

Chapter Six

EDWARD WAS RIGHT. The pearls looked beautiful against Ruth's Scottish skin. Handed down from her mother, they were still stunning in their simplicity and strength. Double stranded and held at the shoulder by a tiny golden clasp, the pearls had a virginal, yet regal quality. Now they were perfectly showcased, against Ruth's off-the-shoulder, midnight blue dress that she wore to Thomas's funeral, and now out to dinner together.

Ruth treasured the pearls as much as she treasured the diamond brooch Edward gave her for their engagement. The jeweller had shaped the brooch into an elm leaf; the tiny diamonds scattered along its stem and the veins. She wore the brooch with the pearls, their contrast and complement perfect.

Chris had found the brooch in India on one of his sojourns to report on the rising Congress movement. Hidden in a jeweller's shop in Calcutta, it was destined for the daughter of a wealthy Srinagar Sikh. Ultimately, the heiress decided on a more subtly crafted bracelet. So the jeweller held the brooch carefully, secreting it away from prying eyes, until the right customer came along. For the privilege of ownership, Chris paid a handsome price, but the brooch was worth every anna. He was attracted to its beauty immediately he saw it in its blood red, silk casket. He had hardly noticed the shop until a collection of children raced in front of him breaking his stride and forcing him to step aside.

The shop was unobtrusive, clean and obviously catered to an elite clientele. Immediately, Chris remarked to himself how well India kept its secrets as he revelled in the unexpected discovery of the jeweller and his shop. On his travels, Chris often looked for small trinkets or items of interest for his family and friends. This time, he knew that the exquisite beauty of the brooch would be right for Ruth. It didn't take much to convince Edward. After all, Chris was a single man without sisters or cousins. Edward agreed. The brooch meant more to him than any other gift he had ever received.

Edward pushed his worry for Ruth to the back of his mind. He couldn't give the attention of his thoughts to her for now. There was a lot of correspondence to catch up on, telegrams to read and phone calls to make. It was an important time for the whole of Europe. No one was safe until the allies defeated Germany and in the interim, the new alliance with Italy would make the pressure on England more intense. He winced. His migraines had been more severe over the last week. It was hardly surprising considering the extra worry he had for Ruth. His neck stiffened automatically to block the pain, but it was too late. The jab of pain seared at the right side of his neck and into the shoulder muscles. Edward closed his eyes and waited for the spasm to pass. The pain was unbelievably intense and shot into his skull as if to burst the delicate membranes around the brain. He wanted to double up and vomit but he knew that after two or three seconds of unbearable hot jolts into his neck, the spasm would pass.

After the pain left him, Edward felt dizzy and disoriented. From time to time, he would also lose his immediate and short-term memory. The neurologist advised Edward to reduce his intake of coffee and red wine - and the chocolate. Nevertheless, his habits chained him as securely as the brass handles on Thomas's coffin. Maybe not all those years of studying and writing in his half-lighted study helped. Coffee had kept him focused and able to read the vast amounts of literature, newspaper clippings and articles that were essential to his university studies and entry into the world of journalism.

Now his office was poorly lighted and dusty. England was running on reduced power. There were economies at every turn to aid the war effort and working at night was especially difficult. There were often blackouts following the wailing of sirens. Then came the hurried movement of Londoners to their designated shelters. Radio communications were at a minimum and cable correspondence was the best that Edward could expect to use to create a picture of the war. His boss and Editor Chris, knew how to extract war photos from the photographic interpretation centre and Edward often relied more upon the photographs rather than cable reports to construct his stories. Chris had free access to the non-classified photographs essential to match and verify cabled reports from Europe. This formed the basis of his war reporting.

Chapter Seven

CHRIS COOKE WAS a stocky character, in both build and personality. His shock of hair was jet black with few signs of grey except at the temples. He possessed a well-proportioned frame, somewhat small in stature. What he lacked in height he projected through the force of his personality and convictions. His hands were rough and broad like stonemasons, in contrast to the meticulous and well-cut design of his clothes. There was not much he wouldn't tackle, and 'look out' to those who tried his patience or were unfortunate enough to be considered by Chris to be 'a fool,' or worse still, 'a blind and degenerate idiot.' He was a man who had little time for small talk and treated the top brass much the same as he did his work colleagues. He had a completely, and deliberately, undeveloped sense of social grace. In Chris Cooke, there was plenty of experience in the art of seduction, sycophancy and political strategy. The truth was that he simply could not be bothered with the pretence that was part of the business of 'winning the ear' of politicians, business houses and other influential individuals.

Chris shook hands with life in the same rough and tough manner that he admired in the working classes: no secret signs or hidden languages to confer favour and opportunity. If he could not do it based on his own effort, then he did not do it. That was his motto for life, "take me as I am and I'll take you as you are. Give anyone a hand up and out and lay off the little folk or on my oath, you'll go down in screaming flames in my newspaper."

The Editor of the tiny and influential London newspaper, was not afraid of the consequences. Nobody would dare to close him down. He knew how to be discreet. He also knew when to cross the line hence, there were a good handful of members of the House of Lords who regarded him with respect. He was a man who would accept no favours and who feared few. Chris Cooke simply didn't care if they rotted in hell or fell into the holes of their own making. For a man in his mid forties, he was a self-made success, modest, but substantial. His independent newspaper in Bouverie Street - close enough to the Fleet Street press to feel the same pulse - was a thriving and insightful weekly that raised as many eyebrows through its probing reports, as it did silence critics.

Through Edward's eyes, Chris was the mentor and figure of easy and rough success that he needed. The competitive and constraining world of mainstream journalism was not for the faint-hearted. Chris was a man who called his own shots and said 'to hell with the rest of them.' And in Edward, Chris found a genuine friend, a keen and accurate mind and a good conversationalist. Their working relationship proved to be easy and on equal terms, Chris deferring to Edward as often as he gave instructions or applied his broad and unashamed editorial hand.

Chapter Eight

A FEW YELLOWED envelopes lay scattered on the desk as Edward walked into the office. The smell of stale smoke, dust and sweat was revolting and he momentarily felt like returning home. Edward hesitated pushing aside the papers and envelopes but picked an envelope marked:

"*Mr. Edward Thompson. In Confidence.*"

'Coffee first' muttered Edward. There would be plenty of time to sift through the papers, cables and sort the photos before applying himself to the story. It was not as if he could ring and check the facts. Phone calls out of England to France and Germany were risky and there was a good chance that his contacts would be exposed if he tried anyway. The newspaper reports were risky enough and he had to be careful to conceal part of the facts in order not to reveal their source. Nevertheless, the photos were OK. Jerry would accept that there were English planes flying over Europe taking photos. The morning looked grim. The editor and junior reporters were already at work, sorting articles and developing the news for the next edition.

'Morning Edward.' Chris greeted him quietly.

'Morning.'

'How's Ruth?'

'She's fine thanks Chris. She's sleeping well and seems to have come to term's with Thomas's death. Uncanny really.'

Chris smiled broadly.' Glad you're feeling up to it today. There's quite a bit of correspondence on your desk. You've probably seen it.'

'Yes I have. I must say Chris I don't feel good about some of these stories. I'd hate to think what would happen if Jerry caught any of them pushing through these reports.'

'I also worry Edward, but as you know all the information goes through the Home Office first and they wouldn't put anyone in the field unnecessarily at risk.'

'You're right, of course.' Edward was relieved that Chris was Editor. He did not relish that role.

'I guess it's one way of keeping up morale. Mind you, some of the stories are pretty bad. You wouldn't want it to be your own father or son, your own brother or husband Chris.'

Edward shuddered. 'No, but at least Jerry knows he's got a real fight on his hands. Coffee hot?'

'Sure is. There are some fresh buns if you feel like breakfast.' 'Thanks Chris. I had something before I came.'

'Digestive biscuits?'

'Yes.' Edward grinned.

'If you want some help with the correspondence, I'm all yours.'

'That's wonderful. I might need it today. I must admit I'm finding it a bit difficult to feel switched on today. Thomas's death …'

'It's much easier when you are doing all the arranging Ed and can forget about your own feelings. Do you want to talk about it?'

'Ah, I'll be OK. You know Chris; Thomas was really involved in that trip to Rome. He was convinced that there was really something behind the artefacts of Christ. He believed they held almost magical powers. I remember him saying something about the artefacts getting into the wrong hands. It's a bit strange don't you think? Here we are trying to make head or tail of the war and Thomas takes himself off to Rome in the middle of it all. Quite brave really. I wonder if he was serious about looking into the Vatican treasures. Maybe there was more to Thomas than any of us knew. In any case, that won't help him now I expect.'

'It was an accident Ed.' Chris half questioned him.

'I haven't any reason to think otherwise Chris. The Coroner's report was consistent with accidental death. Just one of those extraordinarily, unlucky things. It has me thinking though.'

'You're not thinking of going there yourself are you Ed. Thomas was safe but there's a war on and you're a journalist.' Chris sounded the soft warning.

'No of course not, but maybe after things have settled down, I wouldn't mind going into some of Thomas's ideas anyway. It's sort of intriguing me.'

'I see. I'll think about it Ed. It might give you a break from war reporting. Try writing something different to lighten the news for the rest of us.' Chris smiled despite the his foreboding.

Chapter Nine

March 15 1940, London, England,
UDHAM SINGH WALKED to Regent's Park Railway Station. It was a particularly wet afternoon and he was grateful for the train that would take him quickly to his destination a few stations from where he lived. The streets were unusually quiet this afternoon. It must have been the unseasonably cold, windy and wet spring weather. Even the train was quiet with a scattering of men, heads buried in the afternoon paper, not noticing his presence at all. The minutes passed slowly and then the train pulled smoothly into St James's Park Station. Udham alighted onto the platform and walked up the stairs and out into the dreary London weather.

Within minutes he was at his destination walking up the six or so steps to the front door of Number 10 Caxton Street London. He felt a familiar thrill, his heart fluttering quietly against his chest as he remembered the reason why he was here at the meeting of the East India Association and the Royal Central Asian Society.

This was no ordinary gathering. It was a remarkable meeting of senior ex-pats from India; Lord this and General that, military people and civilians both, who had served Britain in India and were now permanently home in London during the Second World War or on short leave from their far flung posts.

A hand reached out for his ticket as Singh entered the hall. He smiled briefly, passing over his ticket to the minor official who guarded the door. He quickly turned his thoughts to the the topic of the lecture, "Afghanistan: The Present Position."

Singh looked briefly for a place to stand in the overfull meeting hall. He had timed his entry exactly, when there were already, over one hundred seated and another dozen more, crammed along the sides where there was only standing room. He carefully moved to the front of the hall standing casually against the wall as the spaces quickly filled behind him. Singh had a clear view of the stage and the men now seated ready to speak. He wanted to hear what they had to say, how they saw the Far East and the spilling over of tensions from India to Afghanistan, the lawless tribal people living on the fragile borderlands between the Punjab, Kashmir and the Sindh. He listened carefully, enthralled by the experiences and reflections of the overlords from Britain who had changed the fate of his homeland, India, and the Punjab where he and his siblings grew up; motherless, fatherless, left to the mercy of the orphanage.

Of all of the speakers, it was Lord Zetland who captured his imagination.

> *"That there is a powerful bond of common interest between India and Afghanistan, must be apparent to anyone who considers the geographical, the political and the economic circumstances of the two countries."*

Economic circumstances? For his whole life he had struggled against adversity, poverty and homelessness. Yet he knew that he had a motherland where his religious devotion was nurtured and his passion for freedom for himself and his homeland was born. Singh felt the bond keenly, not with Afghanistan, but with freedom and with his right to self-determination, his right to become someone, someone of significance, that would put the past right, a past that hid the brutal and savage murder of his own people in their home town of Amritsar.

Suddenly, the speeches and the meeting were over. The military man who had served in the Punjab, O'Dwyer stood up to thank the speaker.

Udham Singh felt his chest momentarily tighten, his breath quicken and for a moment, the world slowed to an agonising standstill, as if his thoughts and the people now standing on their feet and moving across the stage, were actors in slow motion. His mind was suspended in the moment, then cold logic forced him to open the booked lightly clasped in his left hand and lift out the revolver. He fired two shots directly at Sir

O'Dwyer as he stepped forwards to meet Lord Zetland. The man dropped dead to the floor. Before the crowd had a chance to react, he fired again, and again, and again wounding the three men who had wounded the Punjab, India and his sense of freedom, fairness and justice.

Suddenly, he was running up the aisle of the hall, shouting for people to move aside, to let him escape from the throng that would rapidly close around him if he wasted another moment. He looked up and a woman stood before him, blocking his path, catching both of his shoulders to stop him where he was. He could not move or push her away, she was a woman. It was too late, a man forced him to the ground and the revolver flew out of his hand, empty of six shots, the remainder of the ammunition and a small knife still in his pockets ready for his planned exit back into the dreary streets of London.

Chapter Ten

'WE HAVE A new story this morning Ed. I went straight to Caxton Hall when I heard about the murder.'

'Murder?'

'General Dwyer. The chap who was the governor of Punjab when all that sedition stuff and the riots in India started with Gandhi, you know around 1919.'

'Oh.'

'I got there just in time to get the gist of the story. Pretty gruesome affair I'm afraid.'

'Right. We're not exactly used to murder under our feet. Death isn't that easy to report and write about, even when it is from the other side of the Channel.'

'This fellow was a Sikh. The man who did it. He was still at Caxton Hall when I arrived. Interesting looking chap. They have him in custody as we speak.'

'I see.' Edward paused to think. 'Do you want me to follow up with the police, go to the trial, that sort of thing Chris?'

'The police report could be useful for a start Ed if you wouldn't mind.' Chris smiled wanly aware that Ed was walking into another sad story. 'Let me know if it's too fresh. The death thing I mean.' Chris said quickly.

'Thanks Chris. I think that I am OK. Really.' Edward was grateful for the distraction from his thoughts and worrying about Ruth and her fragile mental state. He missed Thomas absolutely, but it grief somehow in someone close to you seemed far worse than death itself. The police report would be matter of fact and it would be a good chance to catch up with friends in the force.

Chapter Eleven

'ED, YOU KNOW, I've been thinking. You can only do this war reporting for so long. Not you in particular, but any of us. It gets you down after a while every day reading the correspondence and not being able to do anything to change the war.'

'That doesn't sound like you Chris.'

'Well, it is true don't you think. I mean, sometimes I come in here and feel depressed. So many people killed, so many villages destroyed. Its all senseless and no-one really knows whether or not London will be bombed today or tomorrow and what can you or I do about it Ed?'

'Well we are. That is why we are here Chris. Our role and duty is to keep up the public morale, and belief that Jerry won't destroy England. I mean, imagine if no one knew what was going on! It wouldn't take much for people to panic.'

'Ed, Chris tried to open the conversation again, 'You need a break. Rest your heart. Go somewhere for a while. Take Ruth for a holiday. You've been working so hard that she rarely gets to see you.'

'Thanks for the thought, but there aren't many places to go at the moment. Canada maybe, Australia and New Zealand are in the throes of war and there is nowhere safe in Europe.'

'What about India?' 'India?'

'Yes. Maybe you could nose around while you're there and see what's happening in the Punjab. Gandhi is bound to be garnering for another 'hartal' of sorts, defying the British as he does.'

'Sounds like more work Chris.' Edward laughed.

'Well, a little maybe. I've been wondering about the murder of General Dwyer. Do you think that you could visit Amritsar, you know, get a bit of background on the location, talk to people, see what the mood is in India?'

'What about Ruth? From your own accounts Chris, it isn't a picnic there at the best of times.'

'The Raj have done all right haven't they?'

'Yes but we're not the Raj Chris. We're just a lowly paid newspaper reporter and his wife.'

'Thanks very much.' It was Chris's turn to grin. 'I do still have good friends in India you know. David is stationed at Delhi and he can organise your trip to Lahore from there. He would welcome a fellow Londoner. Especially now, with sentiments heating up the way they do.'

'Hmm.'

'Even if Ruth doesn't feel up to it, you go and have some time away from this office and England.'

'You're right, the break from one another would do us both the world of good.' 'Edward, you know David has a real sense about something happening at this meeting that Jinnah is cooking up.'

'Jinnah? You mean the Muslim chap?'

'The very one. Apparently he and Gandhi don't see eye to eye on everything and I would put my money on Jinnah wanting to bring on a separate Muslim state.'

'Where does Britain stand?'

'That is of course the very question, since England has from the beginning, supported the Muslim League, it makes it very tricky now with the Muslims wanting a separate home state.'

'Do you think he will get what he wants?'

'Gandhi has I take it, attempted to persuade Jinnah towards a united India.'

'I see. It could be quite interesting, from a reporting point of view I mean.'

'Absolutely, that with Amritsar would make it very worthwhile sending you over.'

'The Viceroy?'

'Ask David when you see him.'

'I see. That's settled then.' Edward grinned.

'Let me know tomorrow Edward. There's a good man. There won't be any problems here so don't worry about the office.' Chris left the room with his customary smile and a slight nod to his head.

Chris had offered him a lifeline. and it was an offer he could hardly refuse. At least over dinner, there would be an opportunity to talk to Ruth about the idea. Edward poured some coffee and sat down in front of the pile of correspondence, telegrams and hastily scribbled memos, passed from behind the lines to the allies. He shuffled the pile for a few minutes, distractedly looking for a theme or a string of letters that would make sense. Sometimes the news was disjointed. Bits and pieces came from here and there, but from time to time, he would get a lead. It was a bit of good luck when the story gelled. Ed's first instinct was to show Chris the report. Classified information was classified information and Chris could not afford to take risks that would put the lives of correspondents and supporters at risk. He would generally ring the Home Office with the news and wait for the OK to print. Sometimes the leads were so significant that the Office would congratulate them on their information. At other times, it was nothing of importance either way. Needless to say, the Home Office had bits of news to chaff out the story. Chris knew that their efforts were good and in its own way, the newspaper was doing its bit.

Edward found it a hard to concentrate. His thoughts were constantly distracted to Ruth, her pale and drawn face, her white hands clutching at her handkerchief, the dark shadows under her eyes.

'Hell!' Edward slammed down the letters.

'Something up?' the junior reporter looked up from his work. 'No, no nothing. Sorry, I forgot that I wasn't alone in here.'

'If there's anything I can do…'

'No, it's OK thanks. Actually, can you pour me another coffee while I make a telephone call?'

'Sure. Anything else you'd like? Did you try those buns?' Adam grinned. 'They taste good. Two or three?'

'Two's fine. No jam though.' Edward patted his stomach. 'Can't let myself go just yet.'

Adam retreated to salvage the buns for Edward and pour him a coffee from the fresh brew. Edward took the receiver off the hook, hesitating for a moment and wondering what to say to her.

'Ruth.'

Ruth was surprised to receive the call so early in the day. 'Ed, is everything OK?'

'Yes Ruth. Just thought I'd ring to see how you're getting along.'

'Oh. Well, I've hardly started Ed. I just can't seem to concentrate for some reason.'

'Why don't you go for a walk Ruth. Don't hang around home if you don't feel like it. Tell you what; let's go out to dinner. Can you ring up, and book a table.'

'Why not. That sounds like a grand idea.' Ruth attempted cheer.

'Good. Then I'll meet you at home and don't forget to dress warmly Ruth. There's a bit of a chill in the air today.'

Ruth had to smile. Edward had a tendency to mother her and she was capable and independent without him. She survived for months on end when he was away without anyone to worry about whether she was warm enough or not.

'I'll put on a coat. How's Chris?'

'Chris is fine. He just offered me a break. But I'd rather talk to you about it tonight Ruth.'

'Sounds fine. Looks like I'll have to wait for the sweet surprise.'

Ruth put down the telephone. She felt a bit more like her spirited self. Often she bantered with Edward when he became overly protective toward her. A baby would be a good solution for him. Not that either of them was in a hurry. Ruth suddenly felt guilt descend like a dark cloud. She hadn't told him yet.

'God Ruth. And now you're pregnant!' She snapped aloud to herself. At first, she thought it was the stress of Edward being constantly overseas. She hadn't been eating well so it didn't overly concern her that she had missed the last couple of months. However, it became all too obvious when Dr. Anderson insisted on taking a sample. The news could not have come at a worse time.

'Are you sure Ruth?' Dr. Anderson probed gently.

'I haven't felt anything like that towards Edward for ages' confessed Ruth. 'Ever since Ed has been going overseas, I've just lost interest. Even in myself.' She added almost as an afterthought.

Dr. Anderson nodded. 'And drinking too much Ruth.'

Dr. Aubrey Anderson was old. Many families had grown up under his care and he was used to seeing women having their ups and downs in marriage, not wanting a baby and then suddenly becoming pregnant. He was happy for Ruth, but a little worried that she was strong enough to carry a child to term.

'Ruth, are you sure?' he repeated.

'Doctor Anderson, of course I am sure. Edward and I…' Ruth's voice trailed away.

'I see. Ruth.' Dr. Anderson paused to measure his words. 'Ruth, I would do anything to make it easier for you.'

'I know that - but I have to tell him myself.' Ruth was adamant. 'It would be better for both of you of course.'

Ruth looked into the eyes of the man whom she had known since she was a child. It was almost as if he knew more about her than her own father. Yet, Dr. Anderson did not judge her. He knew that she somehow, somewhere, lost interest in life and could not find her feet no matter what she tried. Yet, this man seemed eternally patient, never doubting her, never reprimanding her carelessness.

'Don't worry Ruth.' Dr. Anderson continued. 'Edward will want the best for you after all.'

Ruth suddenly quietened with the realisation that he was right. She would have to sort this one out for herself and face Edward knowing that he would be hurt, but also that he would be practical and accepting of her.

'I want you to take these for the next couple of weeks.' Dr. Anderson handed her a bottle. 'They're not much better than alcohol - but they will make you sleep better. Try not to drink - especially if you are taking the tablets.'

Ruth took the tablets, fumbling, as she pushed them into her purse. Her eyes were bright with fresh tears.

'They're not forever Ruth, you know that.'

She nodded and stood up. 'Thank you Dr. Anderson.'

'No need Ruth. Just call me if you want to talk. We'll get you through this one.' Dr. Anderson placed a gentle hand on her arm, his eyes reassuring, yet faintly tinged with disappointment.

She nodded silently and waited for him to open the door.

'Goodbye Ruth. And remember, you don't have to suffer it out alone.' The door closed and Ruth was suddenly facing the clinic nurse.

'Everything all right Ruth? You look a bit shaken?'

'Yes. I'm fine.'

Ruth wanted desperately to run, to run out of the confines of the surgery, which neatly filed and categorised her sad secrets. She wanted to lose herself in the ruthless winter winds. She needed to feel the cold air buffet the torn and sullied sails on the ailing and broken vessel of her life.

At 6.25 p.m., Edward parked the Riley a block away from their home. There were a number of cars around despite effects of the depression years and now the war. Incredible really. The war economy strangely stimulated confidence and even though it robbed England of household goods and necessities, at the same time, industry flourished and new industries were born and moulded on the forge of 'national interest and safety.' The dinner and cinema would cost him, but it would be money well spent. Edward was usually prudent but tonight was to be a celebration.

Ruth also wanted to forget her pain. She wanted to remember the days when she and Edward were deeply in love and be able to wash her feelings away with more than just drink.

Edward dropped his briefcase on the hall table and hung his overcoat on its rack.

'I'm home Ruth.'

Ruth came to meet him at the door, a soft smile pulling at the corners of her eyes.

'Ruth, good to see the colour in your cheeks again.' Edward was surprised and happy at the change in her. 'Let's have a coffee first.' he suggested.

'OK. Can you make it Ed? I need a few minutes to get dressed. Sorry I'm not ready.'

'I'll make it. What are you wearing?'

Ruth dropped her head. 'The pearls I suppose.'

'Good. Don't be too long. We don't want to miss the start of the film.' Edward felt better now that Ruth had picked up. She would enjoy tonight.

Together they would come through the difficult time and although it was new and shaky ground, Edward felt sure that he could navigate them to a safe place of acceptance, if not genuine regard for one another. Ruth relied heavily on him for emotional support almost as if she were helplessly floating downstream without a boat or lifebelt. More than once had Edward dived in to rescue her from her sense of powerlessness and a lack of direction and purpose. Ruth had no real anchors other than Thomas and himself. Moreover, Thomas - the reliable good humoured, rock solid Thomas - entered the raging torrent of death. That left him. Now Chris, bless his soul, had given him an out. Tonight would be it!

'Edward.'

'Mmm.' Edward turned at the lightness in her voice.

'I can't seem to hold my hands steady to tie the clasp.'

'Come here, I'll fix it for you.' Edward leaned forwards and neatly caught the two ends of the clasp together. The pearls dropped in an elegant crescent around her neck. 'You look just beautiful.' Edward beamed as he spoke.

Ruth smiled back, no longer shy and embarrassed. 'Where's that coffee?'

'Coming up Ruth. Looking forwards to dinner?'

Ruth's eyes lit up with excitement. 'Yes. You know Edward, even though it is war time, it still feels as though we can go anywhere, at least anywhere other than Europe.'

'Let's see shall we Ruth. Nothing's impossible.'

'Well it would be a change wouldn't it. Smuggle opium out of India and tea out of China?'

'This isn't the dark ages you know. I'm not sure that I'd like Captain Kidd as an associate anyway.'

'You could do worse Ruth. He was pretty good at his job and probably far more interesting than a dull British journalist.'

Ruth laughed her face transformed into the mesmerising beauty that Edward hadn't seen in her for a long time.

'That's better Ruth. Let's go shall we.' Edward gave her a quick hug and opened the door into the softly moonlit night.

With the city lights eerily dimmed, the moon assumed a subtle and strangely friendly appearance. Ruth peered up through the side window of the car, craning her neck to see whether it was full or half.

'Ed, the moon's just lovely tonight.' 'So are you.'

'Do you think that we were once smugglers Ed?' Ruth preferred adventure.

'Hmm. Maybe. Perhaps you and Tom were. You know, how you spent all those years together rowing up and down the Oxford River.'

Ruth was startled back to Thomas's death. 'Do you think, is it possible, I mean, do you believe in reincarnation Ed?' 'Do you?'

'I'm not sure. I mean if we did, then we'd know, wouldn't we?'

'Not necessarily Ruth. Thomas always used to say it would take the fun out of life if you were carrying the past around with you. You know, like heavy baggage or wet clothes on your back.'

'Oh?'

'Over dinner. Now we'd better drink that coffee and make tracks before the moon makes our passage too visible and dangerous.'

'Edward!'

'Smugglers? Why not.' Edward laughed. 'You're just teasing.'

Ruth couldn't resist a small laugh at his imagery. 'So you think I've still got a dagger in my belt, a scraggy scarf on my head and a pair of pantaloons!'

'You look so lovely tonight Ruth.' Edward tried to be serious.

'You're fairly irresistible yourself. But you didn't answer my question Ed.'

'No, I can't see any daggers in your belt, but then, Thomas couldn't have known that step was waiting for him either. We just don't know Ruth that's all. What's around the corner. We don't even know how we got there in the first place. I mean, we know that we drive from A to B or fly from Y to Z but we aren't always aware of the events that lead up to the now we are in. In fact, if we knew all that, chances are we would take a different direction and miss out on the things that we were meant to see and experience.'

'That's too deep for me Edward and you're trying to tell me that Thomas's death was a good thing!' Ruth reprimanded him softly.

'No Ruth. I'm not saying it was a good thing, but neither you, Thomas nor I could have known what he was going into and none of us could have known what would happen.'

'I understand that Edward.' Ruth remained thoughtful for a while. 'I guess that's true, it isn't Thomas's fault that he's dead, nor is it yours or mine or anyone's for that matter.'

'That's right Ruth. And it probably isn't God's fault either.' Edward gently added. Ruth drew her breath in a held it until it hurt too much. She started to cry, tears wetting her cheeks and dropping onto the shawl that covered her breast.

'Sorry Ruth. I didn't mean to upset you.' Edward braked and pulled the car into a parking space. 'We're here Ruth. Can you manage it?'

'I'm fine.' Ruth rallied her emotions. 'Nothing can spoil tonight, not even Thomas.'

'Not even God you mean Ruth.' Edward countered.

Ruth looked deeply into her husband's eyes. 'Do you think anyone cares Ed?'

Edward looked back into her eyes with a sensitivity and softness that she had only seen a few times in her life. She remembered her father when he told her about her mother's illness and the picture was as clear as the time when Thomas had saved a dying swan, caught in a tangle of rubbish and weeds on the river. Now she felt the same softness in Edward.

'Ruth, I'm sure people do care. I care. But that's not going to bring Thomas back.' He pressed her arm firmly and looked directly at her. 'Let's go inside, it will be warmer in there.'

The flush in Ruth's cheeks faded for a moment but quickly returned as she recovered her composure.

'Ed,' Ruth turned to catch his arm as Edward opened the car door for her.

'Thanks. I mean it. I couldn't have coped with any of this without you.'

Edward smiled. 'Come on. It's too cold out here.'

The scattered lights of the Soho looked as magical as Ruth had hoped, only more brilliantly now that the spirit of London at war was somewhat dimmed.

Chapter Twelve

THE FEELING IN the tiny restaurant was every bit as warm as Edward had promised, only more so with the addition of a bottle of red wine. The food was good, honest and simple, but nevertheless nourishing and filling. Ruth picked for a while at her food, then ate heartily noticing Edward's good appetite and concentration on his food.

Ruth pushed her plate away. 'That was delicious.'

'Dessert Ruth?'

'I don't know whether I've any more room Edward.'

'Nonsense. You can eat three times as much as me when you want to.'

'How about some more wine?'

'Only with dessert.' Ruth relented.

'Good.' Edward called for the waiter. 'Could we see the menu again please.'

'Ruth, I don't know how to put this to you but, I'm having a break from work in London.' Edward waited until the effects of good food and wine softened the edges of Ruth's logic. 'There's not much doing in England at the moment apart from the war, so I'm having a short stint overseas.'

'Ed. I had no idea you were thinking of such a thing.'

'I wasn't. It's Chris's idea.'

'Chris! Why would he suggest such a thing in the middle of the war? Your work is too important Ed and I'm sure he can't really afford to let you go.'

'My work isn't that important Ruth and besides, Chris thought I could do a bit of work anyway while I'm away.'

'A sort of working holiday then.'

'Something of that sort.'

The waiter returned to the table with the menus.

'Let's see Ruth. How about caramel pudding?'

'Sounds delicious.'

'Two puddings and a small bottle of port thank you.'

The waiter discreetly collected the menus white napkin dutifully draped over his arm, then retreated to the kitchen.

'Ruth, I think it's a good idea, good for both of us. You and I need a break from one another. You know, you need time to think about Thomas. What do you think?' Edward felt sure his timing was impeccable.

'It's all come so suddenly Ed. I don't know. I need time to think.' Ruth touched her hand on her husband's arm. 'It would do us both good I suppose. Where are you thinking of going?'

'India.'

'India!' It could have been the moon. 'India?' Ruth repeated.

'Yes - India. It might be a bit hot, but there are a couple of important stories to cover.'

'Well it does sound exotic Edward. But are you sure we can afford it?'

'Don't worry about that. *"The Reporter"* is covering all costs. Besides, Chris has his contacts in India so I will stay with them.'

'Stories?'

'Gandhi is hotting up the Congress movement at the moment, he is still working on India cutting ties with England, you know, Independence. Then there is that Muslim chap Jinnah wants a separate state and then we had the murder of General Dwyer yesterday.'

'Edward you can't seriously think that is a good idea.' Ruth was aghast.

'It will be perfectly safe. I will be with British friends of Chris, not wandering around alone like some sort of a wandering mystic like Thomas lost in a foreign land.'

'Edward! That's not fair. Thomas…'

'Sorry Ruth. That was not fair at all. But what I am trying to say…'

'You are right Edward. Thomas died in a silly accident and you will be as safe as, well, you will probably be safer in India than he was in Italy.'

'Ruth I *am* sorry.'

'It's alright Edward. Go. You are right. The break will do us both good. And besides, there is your work and you can't let Chris down, not now.'

'Chris thought I could cover that story, you know, about General Dwyer and visit Amritsar to see what the place is all about. No doubt England is too busy to take much notice of what is happening in India, but it should provide some light relief from news of the war and the loss of our chaps in Europe.'

'It does sounds lovely Edward. I couldn't go if I wanted to though Edward. I'm pregnant.' Ruth blurted it out.

'Ruth!' It was Edward's turn to be surprised. 'That's wonderful! But how…'

'I don't know.' Ruth started to clutch at her napkin, her face distorted into an anguished frown.

'Ruth, if there's something I don't know…'

'Edward I don't know. I don't know how it happened; I don't know when it happened. I just know that I'm pregnant. Dr. Anderson insisted on doing the tests. I didn't want to but he knew better.'

The waiter returned to their table with their deserts and the port. He expertly placed the bowls of steaming pudding in front of his charges, then poured half glasses of port into small glasses. He glanced at both their faces, aware of the sudden change of mood.

'Would you like the bill sir?'

Edward roused himself from the shock. 'Yes, thank you.'

The waiter gave a small bow and walked stiffly to the counter.

'Ruth.' She remained silent. 'Ruth. I'm not sure what to say or to think. I just don't know where this is coming from and I'm not sure that I want to know.'

Ruth couldn't speak. She crumpled into herself like a forlorn and lost child. The silence was cold and painful. Edward looked as if the life had drained from his cheeks and Ruth remained absorbed in a private, childlike world that no one could access. The waiter returned and placed the bill under Edward's plate.

'Thank you.' The words choked him.

'Edward, I honestly don't know.'

'I suspect you don't Ruth. It's no wonder. I'm away so often and you're left alone in that house. I'm sorry Ruth.' It was Edward's turn to feel guilty.

They drove back to London in silence, Ruth clutching and unclutching her handkerchief, Edward's hands gripping the wheel determinedly. The night seemed colder than it was and Ruth was glad when they finally arrived home. Edward got out and quickly moved to open Ruth's door. She caught his hand as she climbed out and Edward pulled her up to look directly into her eyes. There was a savage, possessive look in his eyes.

'Go to bed Ruth. I'll sleep on the lounge.'

Ruth recoiled in shock at the sudden change in him. She retracted her hand and moved quickly to the front door. Edward opened the door and Ruth ran upstairs closing the bedroom door behind her. She felt an overwhelming temptation to fling herself onto the bed and scream with rage.

'Why, why? Why this?' With Thomas gone, Edward represented the last remaining remnant of reality. Desperate for consolation, she tore off the pearls and the dress, still adorned with the delicate diamond brooch, and flung them onto the floor.

Chapter Thirteen

IT WAS SEVERAL hours before Edward decided to go to his wife. 'Probably one of those slimy charity sharks,' Edward muttered under his breath. 'I knew that crowd was no good for you Ruth. If only you'd have listened. Too late now! You're pregnant Ruth. Well, that's bad luck, I'm going to India with so it looks as if you'll have to carry this one by yourself.'

Edward was not going to help her this time. It was something she would have to face herself. It was her baby and she was the one to make the decisions about whether to keep it or not. 'How can you.' Edward gave himself a sarcastic look as he passed the hall mirror. 'So now you don't believe in god either. Well you deserve it after all your prattling on about reincarnation. I suppose the baby is Thomas.' Edward felt like vomiting. The irony of it all. How fate had sadistic and arrow- sharp twists. No matter what, Ruth would never be his. 'You idiot Edward. It would have been better to let her rot in her own juice in the first place, then at least she might have come to her senses.' Edward walked into the bedroom, feeling half-angry and half-disgusted for being such a fool.

Ruth lay huddled beneath the bedclothes, her soft hair spread across the pillow. He wondered how he had ever loved her. It was like loving a delicate flower who wilted whenever exposed to the sun or the wind. He loved her nevertheless.

'Ruth.' Edward shook her. Ruth stirred and opened her eyes. She was ghost-like with the dark shadows ringing her eyes once again. Her face was paler than the moon; her lips tinged with the traces of lipstick sickly red, stark against her skin. Edward kissed her on the forehead and put his arms around her. 'Good night angel.' he whispered in her ear.

Ruth slept soundly, not moving, not rising to wakefulness until the sun was playing and dancing on the windows.

Chapter Fourteen

EDWARD SLEPT FITFULLY, dreaming that the snow was a shroud of death clouding his consciousness. In between, there were glimpses and flashes of light, scenes from the past. Thomas, Ruth lying prone and bleeding, India, submerged in heat and dust. Then a beautiful young woman as pure as a pearl, gazing into his eyes from beneath her purdah. He awoke feeling thirsty, headachy and disturbed. Nevertheless, he was going to India, he was sure of that. He knew that he needed time out from Ruth as much as she needed time away from him. Now the pregnancy! Edward was angry. He dressed, moody, discontented and with the stale taste of disgust in his mouth. Coffee would clear the bitterness. He headed for the kitchen. Ruth had already made toast and delicately arranged the butter and marmalade between the milk jug and napkins.

'That looks inviting.' Edward cheered.

Ruth smiled briefly and turned quickly to finish making the coffee.

'Anything I can do?' Edward asked seating himself so he could watch her movements.

'Edward, I've been thinking. You should go to India. It will be good for you. I'll have to think about the baby. Either way, I won't be able to go anywhere. It's too risky for me to travel and I know that Dr. Anderson would be against it.' Ruth was not about to waste time with small talk.

Edward spread a tiny portion of butter on his toast. He added a quarter of a teaspoon of marmalade and bit into the crust and chewed for a few minutes.

'Ed?'

'Ruth, sit down. Look, I'm sorry this had to happen. It isn't your fault. I should have known not to leave you alone for so long. What are you going to do?'

'Of course Ruth. He can probably give you more support than I can at the moment. Are you going to keep the baby?'

'I don't know.' Ruth looked a bit tearful.

'Well just don't do anything you don't want to. We can bring the child up together as if it were our own.'

Her tears burst openly in relief.

Edward patted her hand and waited for a few moments, then continued quietly eating his breakfast.

'Ruth, I'll only be away for only three weeks or so. Do you think you'll be all right?' Edward raised his eyebrows at her, not expecting a verbal answer.

She nodded as Edward continued.

'Chris will organise a flight with the RAF. He'll have my whereabouts and I'll make sure he rings you everyday to let you know how everything is going. There's nothing to worry about. It's probably a lot safer in India than it is in England at the moment.'

Ruth stared into her coffee. 'I'll be fine Edward. Don't worry at all. When do you plan to leave?' Ruth found it hard to get the last words out.

Edward looked up, a little concerned and met her eyes. 'Tomorrow.'

'Tomorrow!'

'Yes. It's better don't you think? We both need time to sort things out and I'd rather be there doing something rather than moping around here.'

Ruth gathered the breakfast things together onto a tray and started to stack the plates near the sink.

'I'm going in to the office today Ruth. I'll call you this evening and let you know what time the plane leaves. You won't have to come to see me off, we can say goodbye in the morning.'

Ruth was relieved that Edward went to work, for once feeling that she had no reason to be sad, no reason to pine after him or want him home sooner than he was ready. She had to sort out her problems herself. Dr. Anderson was there, but this was her baby. Ruth ran her hands across her belly. She felt warm, safe and somehow, complete.

'You must be so tiny.' It was hard to suppress just a faint feeling, of contentment and happiness. This was new. She was a mother now, not just Edward's wife or the charity flower without any substance of her own. She could feel the unfamiliar stirrings of a new strength, a solid conviction that she was more than the fragile Ruth that everyone knew.

Chapter Fifteen

CHRIS OPENED THE office door for Edward, sensing rather than hear him walk up the stairs. The office was dark, but had two small windows facing the Bouverie St entrance. There were a cluster of newspaper stands scattered along the street now humming with the news and activity of the war. The war had been good for business, Chris reminded himself. One couldn't be too, sentimental about things. In any case, he was convinced that they played a vital part for England, transferring news along the lines and keeping tabs on Jerry in their own way. The office could well afford to send Edward to India. Chris had however, his suspicions that Edward would find more in India than he had bargained for. Edward wouldn't need much time to arrive at the heart of the situation and make it into good news.

The Congress movement was fighting an enormous battle in India, no less monumental than the Second World War in Europe. England had barely spared a passing thought for India, apart from her usefulness to the Allied cause. There was in the meantime, the unavoidable and misrepresented anniversary of the massacre at Amritsar. The news of General Dwyer's murder flashed across the front pages of the *"The Reporter."* Then the main newspapers created a short-lived furore out of the incident, briefly reviving General Dyer from the ashes of his anonymity whilst simultaneously condemning the Sikh, Udham Singh as did Gandhi.

> *"Gandhi seditious? What rot!"* thought Chris *"Englishmen can be such brutes and justify their heinous acts in the name of defending a woman. Still, Miss Marcella was an innocent, taken to, by the Indians and fair enough that the British Raj were keen to stop any further attacks."*

Chris smiled at Edward as he walked into the office. 'Morning Ed. Everything OK?'

'Hi Chris. Yes I'm OK.'

'Ruth?'

'Ruth? Ruth's pregnant.'

'Congratulations old boy. When's the happy day?'

'The baby isn't mine.' Edward looked directly into Chris's eyes.

'What. You're joking me. Ed!' Chris's vice trailed away into dismay.

'Not joking Chris. She can't remember whom or when damn her.'

'I don't believe it Ed. Not Ruth!'

'I'm at a total loss. I have no idea either.'

'I'm so sorry Ed. It's not exactly what you need right now is it.

'I'd still like to go to India Chris, if it's all right. Ruth can sort herself out for the time being. Dr. Anderson has an eye on her and right now I'm sure he'll do a better job than I can.'

'Ed. You are taking it to heart.'

'Too right. Wouldn't you? All the patience and time I've given that woman Chris. Child more like it. Then she goes and does this. What would you do?'

'I don't know. I swear I don't Ed. But hell, I can imagine I would feel like getting out - for a while I mean - while she cools her heels and comes to her senses.'

'That's exactly what I intend doing. It's about time she grew up and faced a few things by herself Chris. All this stuff about her mother, and her father who was never there. Who does she think I am? A surrogate parent or something?'

'Well, you'd make a damn good parent Ed, that's for sure.'

'Thanks. But it won't change things. India will do us both the world of good. A change from stuffy Europe and being locked into this ridiculous war.'

'Right. How do you feel about dropping in on Amritsar?' Chris was quick to take the cue.

'Amritsar?'

'Didn't you know Ed? Sir Michael O'Dwyer murdered. The papers are hot on the trail of the young Sikh. Just a boy you know when he got caught up in the massacre when O'Dwyer's man Colonel Dyer opened fire in the compound. Hundreds of people shot apparently.'

'Just a boy? God. Why aren't men decent at war? I suppose it's always the men who win and the women and children who lose.'

'I feel the same. However, I thought you might get a better idea of what happened by visiting the compound.'

'Go there? Capture the memories as it were?'

'The well and the wall are where most of the action took place. Would make it a bit more relevant for us here.'

'Nice assignment. Thanks.' Edward felt faintly nauseous.

'Not so fast. There's also Gandhi to catch up with. I'd like you to see what he's up to, what's happening with the Congress movement. He really is a thorn in Churchill's side.' Chris grinned.

'I see. You can't really help yourself Chris. Stir up the old man when he is at his most vulnerable.' Edward laughed.

'Interesting that a tiny Saint could be so intolerable.'

'You think he will have the same effect on me?'

Chris laughed aloud. 'You are too patient, and too polite. On the other hand that Jinnah chap could get under anyone's skin; the Muslim leader. That might make the trip more interesting trip for you.'

'A bit of a whirlwind tour of the politics of the subcontinent by the sound of it!'

'You can have your holiday too Edward. See the sights. Go with our man in Delhi. He'll take you around.'

'That's a relief then. I can't imagine navigating the caste or political divides successfully let alone finding the tourist spots in the heat of the moment.' Edward allowed his dry humour to surface.

Chris looked carefully at his man. He was happy that Edward had more or less taken the bait to take a break and a trip. 'You might as well drop into the Kashmir, before Muslim-Hindu relations degenerate any further that is. I've heard that Srinigar is a beautiful place for a spot of relaxation.'

'Thanks Chris. You're hanging me out to dry a bit you know.'

'Behind the scenes Ed and strictly off the record,' Chris looked soberly into the distance. 'Our lot are keen to see the Muslim people satisfied after the loss of the Khalifat during the First World War. I'm not sure how well Gandhi will manage his people once they get a sense that there could be a division of Muslim and Hindi India.'

'Expecting trouble?'

'Well, put it this way Ed. Gandhi had his work cut out once the Muslim League and Jinnah found their voice and place in India.'

'Jinnah is going it alone?'

'Not entirely. Some of the others are also champing at the bit I hear. At the Viceroy's meeting last October, he made it clear that he wanted dominion status only for India. They were all there at the meeting; Gandhi, Nehru, Bose, Patel and Jinnah along with over 40 other provincial leaders. The Working Committee rejected the Viceroy's offer and stated they would give no support to Great Britain. Gandhi wasted no time in voicing his profound disappointment in Britain's policy of *"Divide and Rule."* By 15 November, the Congress ministries resigned. You can imagine Jinnah's response! He declared 22 December as *"a day of deliverance from tyranny, oppression and injustice during the last two and half years,"* meaning of course, that he was not happy about the power of the Congress ministers. In addition, that was one of the critical points in the breakdown of relationship between Congress and the Muslim League. So the door is now open my friend, for Jinnah and the Muslim League to walk through and create a separatist Muslim state.'

'You mean through conflict?'

'It could not be any other way Edward. You can't imagine the Boses and Jinnahs of India agreeing to terms and sharing power. Not even with Gandhi cajoling them into unity.' Chris added as an afterthought.

'Too many young bulls in one field?'

'Precisely. So I expect that you will act with absolute discretion and tact Edward. Don't want to add fuel to the fire. Gandhi supports Britain at war, however Congress at large, is no longer pro-British, believe me.'

'Speaking of which. I told Ruth I'd be leaving tomorrow.'

'Tomorrow? So fast?'

'Why not. No use moping around here Chris. I'd rather be somewhere where I can forget about her. I don't trust my feelings at the moment. She looked so beautiful last night. I thought she'd finally grown out of herself Chris, you know, become a mature woman. I thought our time together had at last come. Then she had to drop the bombshell that she was pregnant! Can you believe that?'

'No. I understand Ruth less than you do Edward, but I know that it is completely out of character for her to fool around behind your back. You're right. The break will be good for you both.' Chris paused to give Edward time to collect himself. 'I'm just waiting to hear back from the RAF about their flights. You'll have to go via Baghdad Edward. No point hovering over Europe waiting to be shot down by some trigger-happy German.'

'But we'll have to fly over Europe anyway, so what's the difference.'

'You'll do a dogleg to skirt around the war zone and drop towards the Middle East. Can't take risks.'

Edward felt relieved by Chris's practical approach and planning. 'So where do I stay?'

'Delhi of course. David - our contact with the British Raj - will meet you at the airport and take you to the British sector. Nothing too fancy, but you'll be comfortable. I don't want you hanging around the social snobs Edward. You won't get much of a picture that way. Try to keep low profile, but do as much snooping as you need in order to get the drift. David still knows his way around both the Congress and the Viceroy's camp so he'll be able to put you on the right track.'

'Sounds all too easy' Edward murmured.

'Well it won't be. Pretty tense over there at the moment I imagine. Especially after O'Dwyer's murder. Can you fit Lahore into your agenda? Possibly Karachi if you can. I'd like to get a view of the Muslim side of things. See what this communal tension is all about.'

'All in three weeks?'

'Take longer if you need. I'll talk to Ruth if you want.'

'Thanks. I think I'd prefer to Chris. It's about time she learnt to handle herself and get used to my job. I'd like her to come of course, but she never wants to anyway. There's always some or another charity function on. Blasted charities! They're a complete waste of everyone's time and money Chris. And now one of them has gone and got her pregnant.'

'Steady on. It could be worse. At least she isn't running off with someone to Rhodesia.'

Edward had to laugh. 'Half her luck. I suppose it would be more interesting than hanging around with a stuffy English journalist for the rest of her life.'

Chris rose quickly to the banter. 'I hope that's no reflection on the editor Edward?'

'I didn't mean that… '

'Just joking. Did you say you were going to make the coffee today? Get on with it so I can find out about your flight. Don't forget the buns. I'm starving.'

Edward went in search of the immortal nectar of newspaper offices – caffeine along with cups, and plates for the buns. He returned to the office, arms loaded, in time to catch the tail end of Chris's conversation.

'Yes Delhi.' Chris shouted over the telephone. 'And with our luck your plane will land in Persia or the Arabian Sea.'

'Hang on a bit. You could go by boat if you wanted to.' The reply was brusque and the voice cultured with the words clipped to effect.

'I don't want a boat. I'm running a newspaper, not a tea business so your hot air won't help me to get there.'

The RAF clerk laughed at the suggestion. 'I thought all you newspaper buffs drank coffee, not tea.'

'We do, but that's not going to get my man to Delhi any sooner is it?'

'Give me an hour. I'll call you back'

'Good oh. Don't forget to mention that he'll need a bit of spare room for his typewriter as well as his baggage. I want him to arrive safely do you hear?' Chris snarled.

'Give it a break. He can swim for all I care.'

'Call me back within the hour.' Chris put down the phone. It wasn't often that he pulled strings with the RAF but he could when he wanted to. He was well known and respected. The RAF would be happy to oblige him. 'Ed!' Chris hadn't lowered his voice since his conversation with the RAF. 'Where's that coffee?' Tea indeed! Britain was addicted to tea. If it weren't for the tea trade with China, there would be no place for Britain in India. India was taken for a fool in Chris's eyes. Yet he knew that she wasn't that, not at all. The Company got its foot in the door and paved the way for the Raj. A lot of pompous old men sucking the flesh, off a dying cow. That's what the British in India were as far as he was concerned. As for their women? They were no better, strutting around like peacocks looking around for a better nest than they could build for themselves in England.

'It's ready Chris.'

'Thanks. Smoke?'

'No thanks. That chest infection got the better of me.'

'You don't mind if I do?'

'Go ahead. The RAF sounds as though they'll come through with the goods.' Edward noted.

They'll give me a call in about an hour.' Chris sounded confident of his success. 'Don't forget your typewriter. I expect a cable every day with an update on where you've been and what you've uncovered. Keep an eye especially on the mood o the Indians. Can't say I feel confident Edward. O'Dwyer's murder didn't cause much of a shakeup here, but I imagine the sentiment is still running hot in India.'

Edward was quiet. There was no point commenting until he had a first-hand picture of India for himself. He was glad that Chris wasn't going to stick him in with the stuff shirts.

David was good value. Edward met Chris's *"Man in India,"* last time David came to England. He was the quiet, hard-working civil servant type. Didn't get his nose dirty and didn't necessarily support the illicit activities of the British either. He simply worked hard to do the job he was given and that was all. Chris relied on him from time to time for the odd report. Officially, he wasn't a correspondent, but he had a good eye for detail and could report as accurately as any journalist on a situation. He had repeatedly updated Chris on the growth of the Congress movement and had been to visit Gandhi in his ashram several times. However, he couldn't travel around much. Not like Edward would be able to. The Raj expected David to be loyal to Britain and toe the Viceroy's line.

'I'm sure David will fill me in on all the details. Does he know I'm coming?'

'Sent him a cable this morning. He'll be delighted and grateful for fresh news and company from home. He's happily single…'

'Half his luck.'

'Hey, don't take it so seriously. She has the problem, not you.'

'You're right. Christ. I've got to stop brooding about her.'

Chris gave Edward a broad smile. 'India will get the wind up you Edward - you won't have time to think about Ruth. There's something about the place that rather hooks you, then you find yourself increasingly entangled and wonder how she's got under your skin. A sort of a fascination I suppose. Then there's the other side - the sheer revulsion - the filth and poverty, the blatant indifference of the upper classes, the so-called brahmins to the sacrificial impotence of the shudras. It's a sort of social creed and form of ritualised suffering, the caste-system. It's an outrageous crime Edward, so much wealth and so much poverty. Look at the children; from birth, they pay for their existence. Some have their limbs chopped off so that they make better beggars for their parents. Polio deforms whoever is left. You'll love it and you'll hate it.

Take India in Ed. You'll see England differently once you've been in India. You have to. You can't survive the experience otherwise. What you have here is nothing compared to India. What would Britain understand? She's only at war with men and machines. India is at war with her soul. Even the social fabric is as rough and rustic as Gandhi's beloved Khadi. That's the power of India Ed. It's the millions and millions of hands and feet that drive the spinning wheels and till the god-forsaken soil. It isn't the clever minds and megalomaniac motives of the Hitler's that have the real power. It is the sheer devotion of men like Gandhi to their Hindu gods that have the power to move the masses.

Don't look at your own life when you are in India Ed. Just absorb the vastness, the enormity of a population struggling for a foothold. Feel and live their day to day obstacles of life. See what's it means to struggle to find enough food to eat or clean water to drink. Just to find a place on the earth to sleep is a battle for many of them. It stinks Ed. It stinks. I'm ashamed to be British when I see how the Raj have garnered the remnants of India's wealth to line their own pockets and play king in a land that they shouldn't even be in. I should say "we've" I suppose. I tell you, I can't and won't associate myself. Sure, I'm loyal to the king, but then I'm not an imperialist. Never was.

Sorry Ed, I don't want to cloud your vision of the place, but as you can tell I'm not a fan of the British in India, or a fan of Britain anywhere else for that matter! That's another story though for another time. In any case, you'll form your own views but I'm determined that you see the other side before being seduced by the landed gentry - British or Indian. The privileged classes will suck you in with the veneer of opulence and self-importance. Don't let that happen Edward! Good man.'

It could have been Thomas. It could have been Thomas's voice schooling him, warning, advising. Edward sat in stunned silence as if he had heard a re-write of one of Thomas's inspired monologues. India would suck his essence dry! Not even Ruth could have that sort of power. Maybe that's what Thomas had done for him. Thomas had given him a broader vision, a wealth of spiritual strength and new perspectives through which to see his life. Then where did Chris get it? It was almost as if fate had taken Thomas and used Chris instead to catapult him forwards on his journey. There was no going back. The dye was cast and like it or not, he would be soon immersed in the living experience of Thomas's lectures and his enthused outbursts on the Gita, Mahabharata and Ramayana. Perhaps the Hindu gods were more compassionate than the British one. Maybe they just had a bigger field to play on, more actors, more scenes, more by-plots. He would be an insignificant dot on the landscape, a piece of the vast puzzle that formed life on the sub-continent.

And Gandhi? How had he managed to rise out of the dust of the vast epic of life and death and grasp the reigns of self-rule? How had one man taken on the power of a kingdom as mighty as Britain and challenged its very roots in India. Gandhi snubbed the *"Grandest Society of Merchants in the Universe"* through insisting on the economic and political liberation of India from Britain. How could a country as poor as India brace itself three centuries later to shake off the complex economic bondages that bound it to perpetual poverty. The shackles of dependency were as severe and intractable as the worst karmic bondage. Gandhi intended to free India from one of the greatest nations of the industrialised world through the humble spindle and handmade spinning wheel.

Edward felt he was already immured in the monumental spiritual landscape traversed by Thomas and now Chris. The journey from his protected Protestantism to the enormity of the great epics of Hinduism was inconceivable, yet somehow fixed by fate. Thomas tempted his intellect, then his heart and now his soul and frightening thought that soon he would be a part of the mass of humanity, the endless moving sea, of souls journeying from birth to death and into rebirth. There was no recourse from the finality of death. There would be no escape from the spinning cosmic wheel. It would trap and bind him with its karmic spokes; its course and momentum set with terrifying and unchangeable surety.

Edward shuddered. What would he find there? India was presumably a wasteland of human life where death was common currency. Then of what purpose was life? Life was the unavoidable abandonment of compassion, humanity and dignity on the spoked wheel of fate. Would he meet his own fate and return enlightened and emboldened, as Thomas would have? Or would destiny simply string him like a, on the pyre of mortality with the ever-patient vultures wheeling overhead?

Ruth - it was certain - had no hold over the surging river that was carrying him away from her. Like the Ganges in full flood, the future would deposit him as flotsam onto the floodplains upon which millions of others lived and died. There would be no Ruth in India. In India, he would be unable to hide behind England or the robes of her Christian Church.

Thomas had loved the Church nevertheless. He had loved his Oxford Chapel, the Bach cantatas and flickering candles, beckoning and succouring him in death as they had in life. Thomas had found no need to reject his faith, impassioned as he was by the greater order of the three hundred and thirty million household gods and goddesses that graced the homes of millions more. Thomas loved Christ as his own, yet he saw in Gandhi another Christ, a Christ of infinite wisdom, compassion, tolerance and living forgiveness.

Gandhi also loved Christ. It was an overwhelming yet somehow comforting and pleasant reassurance. The unknown was also the known and Edward instantly knew, that in Gandhi he would find a solid core of spiritual truths, an example in the man of practical religion and an essence that embodied human life.

Edward's instinct told him that what he would find in Gandhi, would be both sobering and uplifting.

Yes, he would go, but not in awe of the British Raj, annexed as it now was to the wonderful, limitless empire spanning five continents and several centuries. He would travel to India aware of the five thousand-year history of the oldest surviving religion on earth. This was an ancient culture with its roots deeper than the oak; roots that penetrated the soil of humanity in a way that Christianity never could. These were ancient roots that held firm against the relentless droughts, floods and famines of a continent far more immense in its history, more diverse and and densely populated than the floating isles that formed his own home, Britain.

He would go with the open mind that Thomas had nurtured in him, a willing soul free from expectation or the baggage of his own culture. Edward would complete for Thomas, the part of his own journey that he had not had the time to continue, the evolving of his faith into experience and wisdom. Gandhi would be the bridge for the Thomas that Edward carried in his heart, the living Ashram, the virtual Vatican of Thomas's endless curiosity.

Chris munched his way through two buns, drunk several cups of coffee and looked ready for action, his eyes searching and penetrating the room.

'Take what you need Edward. You might want some extra paper and pens, notebooks, whatever. Better than relying on India, but David of course will know where to find whatever else you want. It's a bit late to get your shots. You'd better pick up some quinine from the dispensary though and some of that antidiarrhoeal and anti-vomiting medicine, and don't forget the iodine!' Chris hardly paused for breath or thought. 'Use it whenever you drink unboiled water and even if you drink boiled water. Use it Ed.' He tapped his pipe on the edge of the table. 'No good being laid up with a fever and dehydration. You can't afford to get sick there.

You know, during the early days of the East India Company most of the skirmishes and wars were lost and won through disease. Men wasted away like flies. That's of no use to anyone. Keep your hands clean and don't touch or eat meat. Eat mostly rice and cooked vegetables Edward. Fresh fruit is OK, but watch the skins.' Chris suddenly grinned. 'I always used to drink fresh coconut milk. You know nothing can get into it. It's clean, nourishing and you won't get sick from it. You'll find an abundance of street vendors peddling food, but you'd be better off taking your food cues from David. He's been there a while now and he'll know his way around the "do's and don'ts" of Indian cuisine. That's another thing to watch for, pickpockets.' Chris added the comment with a note of disgust. 'Afraid it's one of those things Ed. It seems the whole bloody place is corrupted. Maybe it's part of the social structure. They don't have a welfare system. How else can they live? Hang onto your wallet Ed. And don't worry about Ruth. I'll look after her while you're away. I want you to be fully alert to the situation at hand and not worrying about her and the baby. Sorry to be so frank, but you can't be pining for home in a place like India. Just be ready for whatever comes your way.'

The telephone interrupted Chris's warnings.

'Hello. Yes, this is Chris, Chris Cooke. Yes damn it man, I need to know today. Well then tell him it's urgent. If there's a plane going tonight he'll catch that one instead. Chris slammed the telephone onto its cradle. 'Is that OK with you Ed? May be tonight. Plane could leave anywhere between 9 p.m. and midnight. You'd better go and pack your things, and get those medicines.'

'Righto then. I'll just tell Ruth I'm on my way back. Mind if I take the new typewriter? It's got a better carriage return. I can't use that one if the carriage continues to stick. Mucks up the line spacing a bit. Don't want reports that look messy and unreadable.' Edward grinned.

'I don't mind at all. Good man!' Chris allowed himself to relax a little and smile at Edward. 'Like I said, raid the store and see what else you need. I'll get Jenny to make you up a box if you like.'

'Thanks Chris. Tell her I'll need dozen or so pencils as well. Heard that the are good trading material in India. The officers like them so it might make things a bit easier all round.'

'That's the shot. You won't need much warm clothing but take your suit and some casuals. Good shoes help over there. There's so much dust!'

'Ruth might be a bit shocked if I leave tonight.'

'I imagine that she might Ed. But it's better for her to face it now rather than confront you tomorrow with all the reasons why you shouldn't go don't you think.'

'That would be true Chris. I'll give her a ring and get on with it then.'

'OK. We are settled then. I'll follow up the paperwork. Jenny can help out this morning.'

Chris left the office and went in search of Jenny. She was a more than eager office clerk, keen to help the war effort, but was not the type to work in a factory or with machines. Chris liked her and put her on straight away. He had less time these days for the small everyday tasks that cluttered his work and was greatly relieved to have the space for the bigger issues of the newspaper. He enjoyed working with a small staff, compact like a family.

No-one was happier at work than Chris. He had never aspired to be the editor of a large newspaper and was satisfied with his newspaper and his lot. Being his own boss meant that he didn't have to wear political agendas or gamble time and money to win the race to the newspaper stands as the tabloids did. *"The Reporter"* was a concise and pertinent weekly. With the backing of an unexpected and large inheritance from his late uncle, he could afford to tread on a few toes and that suited him fine. The money gave him a start and enough to employ good staff. Edward was lucky enough to be around at the time.

'Just the right material' thought Chris after the initial interview. He was intrigued by Edward's seeming indifference to the war, but at the same time could see he possessed a sharp mind that capable of sifting out the issues and presenting them as ably as any seasoned journalist. Edward's concerns came through his articles and reports and Chris learnt to understand him as a man of depth and sincerity, private and thoughtful whilst he himself was rough, sociable and generous. It was a good mix of qualities. Chris was the public edge of the paper and he did it well.

Edward was far too talented in Chris's opinion for *"The Reporter"* but he refused any offers to look for a better job elsewhere. Therefore, Chris built foreign reporting around Ed. It was his way of rewarding him for his faithfulness and diligence, and a neat solution to encourage Edward to probe interesting stories that other papers might otherwise, not get their hands on.

David was Chris's backstop in India. Their chance alliance quickly grew into solid friendship and rare mutual opportunity. Chris remembered the moment well as the two of them browsed through a London bookshop; Chris intrigued by the enigma of Annie Besant and David ferreting after information on Krishnamurthi. Krishnamurthi had become a bit of a figure on the London scene, overturning the traditions of European philosophy with his revolutionary and stunning, practical philosophy of detachment and rigorous thought.

Chris had wandered into the bookshop to find David furrowing for information. David had heard Krishnamurthi talk in Bombay. Hindus, a smattering of Sikhs, Muslims and even the odd Parsi packed the audience. Krishnamurthi struck him as someone, who like Gandhi, drove to the core of religion and had the gift of mesmerising his audiences. It was not just what he said, but the presence of the man that drew people from across the vast spectrum of human backgrounds. It was a comforting and spiritual experience just to be in the gathering, the crowd of seekers willing to listen to Krishnamurthi's elevated discourses and put aside for a short time, their religious dogmas.

Chris and David were amused by the encounter and quickly formed a close friendship. It transpired that David was on leave from India and on his way to the docks. He was booked on an evening passage and was filling in time in London. They exchanged addresses and telephone numbers.

When news of Gandhi occasionally surfaced, Chris cabled David at his office for more details. Thus, 'Foreign Correspondence' for *"The Reporter"* began in India.

Five years later Chris ventured to India, intrigued by David's double life of civil servant and witness to an emergent nation. The chrysalis of an idea finally metamorphosed through sheer curiosity and the need to break the drudgery of England's long and grey winters.

Chris wanted to return to India, but the war sped towards him like an iron carriage, complete with its artillery of demands and restrictions. Still, through Edward, David could send more news of the changing fortunes on the subcontinent. Moreover, through Edward, Chris could simultaneously probe the ostentatious armour, of British rule and uncover the mystery of 'home-rule' to which Gandhi had sacrificed and committed himself. He understood David to be an invaluable ally, a man disillusioned at the petty bungling of the bureaucrats and silently sympathetic to the momentous cause of Independence that had all, but ground to a halt. Chris would use Edward to kindle David's fires and David would give to Edward what no-one could ever give him in Europe, a chance to see first hand, what Thomas had in his own way taught Edward. Chris was enthusiastic about sending Edward, sure that the moment of India's liberation was close. In a masterpiece of irony, the twilight of the Raj coincided with England's own battle for strength and survival in Europe. It was not a malicious or sadistic bent in Chris that drove him forwards, but a commitment to truth.

Chris Cooke had an innate trust in the greater scheme of things and a spark, a germ of respect for the downtrodden land that India was. India was not his home but the plucky fight of a nation wherein the majority of the population were impoverished and undernourished, struck at the core of his sensibilities and sense of justice. What Hitler was doing to Europe, England had in her own way over the centuries done to India. England robbed the lifeblood of a great nation simply because she thought she was better, superior. England had inflicted insufferable humiliations upon India and Indians because of greed as much as for reasons of race and religion, more-so even than the upper classes of India who thought they were superior to those condemned to a life sentence as 'untouchables.' Was England then, so different to the Germany that inflicted humiliations and sufferings upon the Jews and gypsies of Europe?

In Chris's opinion, there was very little. The main difference was that the yoke of British rule in India was deceivingly decorated with the colours of Indian pageantry, and as such, barely distinguishable from the customs of the Moghuls or the original Rajas of India themselves. India through Gandhi, dressed herself in the simplest clothes. Yet the British donned the fine silks and headdress of a Maharani in order to assume superiority whilst wielding the cruel and conscienceless mace of foreign rule. The sheer hypocrisy of England's menacing presence in India was obvious yet never stated. Far from fostering peace and religious harmony, Britain was stirring up secular hatreds in India no less than the anti-Semitism of Europe. It was sinister and odious, a gilded snake in the bed of English respectability.

Chris wanted Edward to expose it, to concentrate on the Hindu-Muslim alliance fostered by Gandhi and strained by the British. He hoped that India would affect and move Edward to the depths of his soul. He wanted Edward to see India through India's eyes, to touch and enter the world and aura of Gandhi's self-dignity, self-reliance and simplicity.

It was a gamble, but Chris knew that Edward was ready. Edward was tired of the war and he needed new horizons and challenges with which to sharpen his sword-like mind. However, Chris's down-to-earth understanding of change tempered his passion to expose the irony of England's territorial imperative. The realisation came slowly like a snail on a midnight course, guided by glimpses of the moon and the stars, dependent on dew to smooth and hasten the journey. India was under the canopy of a vast constellation of spiritual stars, King Ashoka, Buddha, Mahavir, and Shankaracharya, Guru Nanak, an unlimited galaxy of yogis, saddhus and fakirs. In front of him was the significant heritage of generations of spiritually minded rulers, philanthropists and holy men. Britain could not match such a constellation through a few centuries of erstwhile pirates-cum-merchants-cum-soldiers.

The economic-turned-military imperatives of England finally consolidated into a bureaucratic tangle of administrative and farcical overlords, pretending beneath the very colours that heralded the royal and spiritual heritage of India herself.

'How could England's history and heritage match India's?' Chris muttered to himself. Yet to return to the days of the Maharajas and Maharanis would in his mind, take decades. Even the kingdoms of the Czars of Russia and Dynasties of the Emperors of China could not be restored overnight anymore than the destruction of the Ottoman Empire could be reversed by another world war.

Chris breathed a sigh of relief. He could and would not wear the colours of hypocrisy parading as loyalty to 'Crown, King and Empire!' He considered himself a rough and independent man, a diamond of coarse and broad edges who had no time for fineries of custom and manner. His speech was often blunt and bold, caring less for social manners than to pierce the heart of his often, unwary subject. Royalty, admiralty and enterprise might be the engines behind England's claims to India but they were not a part of the vocabulary of Chris's life. Honour, courage and honesty were his trademarks and he wore them as any chivalrous knight would, openly and fairly. It was Britain's honour as well as his own that was at stake. It was Edward's courage and honest reporting that would represent for Chris, England's rightful place in the unfolding of a new India. An honourable defeat was, by any man's estimate, worth more than thousands of ill-won, empty victories.

The economic-turned-military imperatives of England finally consolidated into a bureaucratic tangle of administrative and farcical overlords, pretending beneath the very colours that heralded the royal and spiritual heritage of India herself.

'How could England's history and heritage match India's?' Chris muttered to himself. Yet to return to the days of the Maharajas and Maharanis would in his mind, take decades. Even the kingdoms of the Czars of Russia and Dynasties of the Emperors of China could not be restored overnight anymore than the destruction of the Ottoman Empire could be reversed by another world war.

Chris breathed a sigh of relief. He could and would not wear the colours of hypocrisy parading as loyalty to 'Crown, King and Empire!' He considered himself a rough and independent man, a diamond of coarse and broad edges who had no time for fineries of custom and manner. His speech was often blunt and bold, caring less for social manners than to pierce the heart of his often, unwary subject. Royalty, admiralty and enterprise might be the engines behind England's claims to India but they were not a part of the vocabulary of Chris's life. Honour, courage and honesty were his trademarks and he wore them as any chivalrous knight would, openly and fairly. It was Britain's honour as well as his own that was at stake. It was Edward's courage and honest reporting that would represent for Chris, England's rightful place in the unfolding of a new India. An honourable defeat was, by any man's estimate, worth more than thousands of ill-won, empty victories.

Chapter Sixteen

CHRIS PICKED UP the telephone. He needed the car now, that would take Edward to the airfield. Edward might have a wait at the airfield but that would be far better than facing an unexpected curfew at the last moment. Chris allowed his vicarious excitement to rise in his voice.

'That you Sir?' This time he telephoned the War Office directly. 'Leaving at one am? Splendid. Can we carry anything over? Two nights in Baghdad? OK then. Did you say he would be landing at the military airstrip? Understood. India? I know there are no facilities to speak of. But you have been there before sir. How do I know? Of course I know. I'm a journalist sir. I don't need to be told that the situation is tricky in India. That's why I'm sending him. Oh, righto then. We'll keep it low profile. Yes he's discreet and no he won't get people offside. I know my man. Yes, I'll make sure that all information is classified and appropriately coded. Right you are Sir.'

Chris put down the phone again. 'Goddamned cheek. Of course he knew what he was doing. That was the problem with soldier types. Always thought that they had the final say. As if Edward would stir up trouble! Pity he couldn't' Chris thought. 'But I suppose England is playing down the Congress and eager to keep Gandhi under tabs. Good. That meant that he was onto something.' They had co-operated with his request so he was happy.

'Jenny. How did you go with those items for Ed?'

'Fine Mr. Cook. They're all here packed into an overnight bag.'

'Good. I want him out at the RAF base by 5pm. How is the requisition for that car coming along? I can't imagine it would be much good Edward leaving his leaving his car at the military airfield where that lot are likely to pick the lock and take it out for joy rides. He'll need his brief typed so if you would do that for me please Jen I think we'll be organised after that.'

'Yes sir.' Jenny was efficient and polite.

Chris nodded and she left the room, notebook and brief in hand. He would make sure that Jenny did some reporting and writing and fill a bit of Edward's shoes while he was in India.

'No good keeping women at our beck and call. She is as capable as any man is.' Chris said out aloud to himself hoping that Jenny would overhear.

Chris whistled cheerfully as he thought about the plan. Edward would not mind, of that, he was sure. Edward was the sort of person who would give his right arm to help another soul. That's why Chris liked him. He wasn't the ambitious self-seeking type, always there when you needed him, reliable and conscientious. Chris closed the desk drawer thoughtfully. The top drawer was reserved for his oval tobacco tin and pipe. He often enjoyed a pipe; the rich fragrance of tobacco warming the office and filling the room with an aroma as sweet as the richness of freshly ground coffee. Tea indeed! He rolled a piece of tobacco the size of a 2-shilling piece into the palm of his hand and stuffed it into the pipe bowl. Then with a matchstick, he teased the tobacco, allowing air into the wad before lighting the pipe and drawing the smoke deeply into his lungs. His lungs reacted in a sharp and painful spasm. Disgusted, Chris spat the brown phlegm into his handkerchief.

'Damned cough!' He put the pipe aside and let the smoke curl around his head, not wanting to repeat the performance. Maybe he would eventually follow Edward and give it away all together.

Edward had found the first few months without cigarettes hard going. He was always looking for something to do with his hands until eventually his nerves quietened. Then he was able to sit and think without fiddling with a match or lighting another smoke. For Chris, it would be harder. The pipe was a part of his persona. It matched his rough manners and speech and more than once, he used it to innocently blow smoke in the face of someone he thought uppity or rude. His pipe was his way to create the silences he needed in order to collect his thoughts or to put someone off who had an axe to grind with him. Not that many people did, but it was always there when he didn't feel like using speech to put people in place.

It was nearly midday.

'Early lunch today. I feel like a walk Jenny,' he declared. 'You'll manage the rest?'

Jennifer nodded and smiled at her boss. 'I'll take any messages.'

'Thank you. It's about time you started calling me "Chris" like everyone else around here Jennifer. No good having you too timid if you're going to become a reporter.'

Jenny looked up in astonishment. 'Yes sir.'

'Yes Chris' he corrected her.

'Yes Chris.' It didn't come easily. She stammered out the words and dropped her gaze quickly to her work.

'Right oh then. See you later.' Chris walked out of the office, humming to himself. He liked the way he could do as he wanted and didn't have to put up with other people's rules. Jennifer was Jennifer, but she would soon learn to be as confident as the men in the office as long as he was boss.

The air outside was cold. The sun had a short-lived life that morning as was usual in London. The sky was depressing but also familiar and fresh. Chris pulled the collar of his Mac higher and strode into the street, not noticing city workers or shoppers, simply intent on reaching his favourite cafe at Greville on Hatton Garden, where there would be fresh coffee and steamed potatoes for lunch. He preferred and ate wholesome food. Chris was a big eater and it showed in his size, but he carried it well for his frame. He had long ago shrugged off any idea of preserving his health. 'What's the point if you aren't happy' he would always retort if anyone commented on his appetite. 'Can't depend on another life. Only got this one as far as I know.' So he would tuck into his food with obvious pleasure.

The cafe staff liked and enjoyed Chris's presence. He was unpretentious and the first to share interesting news. Today was no different. The waitress greeted him with a smile.

'Potatoes Chris?'

'Yes thanks Rose. And some of that Turkish coffee you brewed the other day. Must cost a fortune importing the stuff!'

Rose smiled and left him at his usual table.

Chris unfolded the morning paper. The news was grim. Casualties were high on both sides and there would be no breakthrough for peace for a long time yet. Churchill was a moody man, brilliant and able to predict where to send his troops. There was no doubt in his own mind that he was the right person for the job but not everyone thought that way.

'Any new news Chris?' Rose returned with the potatoes.

'Nothing you would want to hear about Rose. Except that I'm sending Ed over to India for a short break.'

'Oh?' Rose smiled becomingly, her head tilted in light question.

'Yep. Give him a break from this war business, and besides, I smell a rat Rose!'

'You always do Chris. Just as well there aren't any in the kitchen.'

Chris laughed. 'As long as they don't end up on my plate, I don't mind. By the way, did you manage to get cream this week?'

The war produced innumerable shortages and it was not every day that cream and butter were available but if it were, Chris would be the first to know about it.

'There's a bit left Chris. Keeping it for you. Mind you don't tell the boss. He might have wanted it for some of his friends.'

'Most wouldn't recognise good cream anyway. Still, they have never lived in the real world as you have Rose. Many wouldn't know a cow from a steer.' Chris smiled naturally at her. Chris respected her background and always commented on how healthy she looked, and that he thought she knew more than most city folk. Her skin was clear and fresh. Her frame was proud, her bones strong strong and her flesh muscled and toned. The farm had toughened Rose, but she didn't regret any part of her upbringing. It was a good life and there had always been plenty to eat. The city was only a place for extra income. Rose could work as hard as any man could but her father wanted her to have a secure city job and perhaps meet a good man to marry. Rose didn't think that way at all -

there would be no marriage any time soon. She wasn't interested and besides she wanted to save money to help her father on the farm. Then the war started. There was little anyone could do until the economy was stable and England safe. It didn't worry Rose. She liked working and she liked Chris. He was the person who to her, made the city a bearable place.

Chris performed his regular ritual of eating; wiping his mouth with the cloth napkin before giving Rose a satisfied grin.

'The best ever Rose.'

'Chris, you always say that.'

'No I mean it. Must have been the extra butter. Still, you might surpass yourself next time so I had better not say anymore. Got the bill?'

Chris paid and left Rose a shilling as his usual tip. She grew accustomed to his generosity. However, it was never wasted. Every penny tipped went into her drawer. She was saving to buy warm woolens. One day, she would tell Chris how his tips kept her mother in clothing throughout the war. Rose glanced after him as he walked into the cold afternoon.

The cafe always gave Chris a feeling of peace. It was a haven of familiarity and friendliness, a sharp contrast to the cold, bleakness of London and the insecurity of wartime. He wasn't in a hurry to return to the office and headed towards his favourite haunts, the inner city bookshops. Work could wait, the articles were ahead of schedule and he had no doubts about filling the pages for the next few issues.

Chapter Seventeen

EDWARD LEFT THE office feeling light-hearted and refreshed as if an entirely new chapter of his life were open. Thank goodness for Chris! And thank goodness for the fact that Chris provided him with just the right opportunity, a low-key role with an in-depth paper. Edward was no high-flier, and abhorred the life of a reporter with the daily newspapers. The pressure just wasn't worth it. Chris also preferred his paper to be well-written based on information from reliable and well-respected sources. His readers knew that each week, they could pick up *"The Reporter"* and know that they had first hand, the real 'news of the day.'

Chris readily accommodated Edward's style and insightful reporting, free as it was from 'opinion.' Edward had the uncanny knack of knowing what people thought and saw the world, England and the ward, and was able to write as if from inside their heads, from inside their fears and hopes. So he gave Edward his head, openly encouraging him to experiment with different angles in his reporting as well as fill in the gaps in his journalistic experience. The office was a 'no-fuss, no big deal' friendly set up. The additional part-time journalists, likewise enjoyed the leisurely pace at *"The Reporter,"* writing for other papers from time to time. Chris had a reputation around town of being astute and provided the acerbic voice that the politically sensitive tabloids could ill afford. His style bordered on avant-garde, but without intellectual pretension. He was generous, and could afford to be. *"The Reporter"* had fewer overheads than most papers and a regular and considerable patronage.

Edward was excited. He completed his call to Ruth whilst avoiding an unwanted display of emotion or needless drift into an explanation as to why the sudden change in plans. Ruth wanted to bring his port to the office. He would let her, why not? She would feel more connected with his trip and satisfied that he had all that he needed that way.

'I'll pack your things Edward and bring them to the office.'

'Thanks. That would be helpful. Can you make sure you pack summer shirts Ruth. From what I hear, it is damned hot on the subcontinent this time of year.'

'Shorts?'

'Might need them. Thanks.' 'Anything else darling? Ruth felt the remorse creeping into her voice.

'Can't think I'll need much more than the usual. Chris has organised medicines and notebooks and I'm about to look for something to read for the flight over.'

'I'll miss you.'

'Don't. I won't be away long enough for you to miss me Ruth. Just catch up with yourself a little.' Edward was firm.

Ruth was silent.

'Chris will keep you up to date, so there is nothing to worry about.'

'I know.' Ruth could hardly find the words.

'Well I'll be off then Ruth. Look after yourself.'

'Yes, I will Edward.'

Edward placed the receiver on the hook. 'Well at least that's over.'

Edward breathed, visibly relieved. With most of the arrangements sorted out, there was time to look around for some reading material for India. He enjoyed *"The Lancet"* and the usual run-of-the-mill novels, but this time he wanted something a little deeper. Thomas had stirred his curiosity and he needed something to familiarise himself with the mystical traditions of the subcontinent. Thomas often talked about the London and Oxford bookshops he frequented so Edward knew exactly where to go. He walked quickly without distraction for three blocks and arrived at one of Thomas's favourite haunts.

Edward stepped with excitement into a bookshop off Chancery Lane, not far from the famous Foyle's Books on Charing Cross Road. But it was a different sort of education that Edward was after, something a little less staid than he would find at Foyle's. The bookshop reminded

Edward of Thomas's library with its piles of books stacked higgledy-piggledy on top of each other, and the floor littered with loose journals as well as locked cabinet of obviously rare and precious volumes. The thrill of learning seeped out of the woodwork and into the room. Edward wondered where to start. There were sections marked "Jewish" including bound copies of the Torah, The Old Testament and obtuse manuscripts labelled *"Cabbalah."*

Then there was the "Christian" shelf with various editions of the Bible and commentaries on the Apostles and Gospels as well as compact and leather-bound copies of the Psalms. A smaller shelf occupied by a single, faded copy of the *"The Alcoran of Mohammed"* marked the "Muslim" section, and a much larger section marked "Hinduism, Buddhism and Eastern Religions" dominated the shop. The area included a variety of editions of the Gita including smaller *"Commentaries on the Gita"* with annotated text and a shelf almost exclusively dedicated to 'Oriental and Esoteric Sciences.'

This prominent section proudly displayed copious volumes of *"The Secret Doctrine"* by one Mdme H. Blavatsky and above her dedicated space in the tiny bookshop billowing with a smorgasbord of spiritual promise, was a framed photo of Krishnamurthi. Huddled and crammed into the remaining spaces on 'her shelf' were texts on Tantric Buddhism and what appeared to be the 'science' of Tibetan Buddhism. Alongside the eastern section were also numerous smaller volumes by help you chose a title.

The woman confidently marched to a shelf marked "Hinduism, Buddhism and Eastern Religions" and pulled a neat volume of *"Siddhartha"* from the shelf. 'Here, this one isn't too heavy going to start with. I have to warn you though, it won't tell you much about Hinduism. It's about the life of the Buddha. Buuut' she trailed the word meaningfully 'it is set in India so I am sure you will find something of interest. Totally new for most people in the west,' she finished triumphantly.

'Thank you.' Edward accepted the book and turned to the back cover. The book was compact and achievable. A good start indeed!

'What about this one.' The woman was becoming enthusiastic, eager to 'introduce' her customer to the esoteric truths.

Edward drew in his breath. His was not completely sure whether or not her enthusiasm was vicarious. It was. She dragged down the only copy of *"The Bhagavad-Gita."*

'It's not what you think. Look at it in the light of what you already know and you will be able to make sense of it. It's not about mythologies or gods and goddesses, but more to do with the central theme of Hinduism.'

Edward was suitably impressed with her knowledge and showed it. 'Thank you.'

The door opened and with it a welcoming draught of cold air.

Chris brushed the first spots of rain from the shoulders and arms of his coat as he stepped into the shop, grateful for the shelter and the chance to browse after lunch. He glanced quickly around the shop.

'Edward. What are you doing here?'

'Chris!' Edward was equally surprised. 'I thought you'd still be at the office.'

'I was, but I needed some fresh air after lunch. It's not often I have spare time on my hands so I thought that I'd make the most of it.'

'What a coincidence. What are you looking for.'

'Well, I could say the same.'

The woman quietly withdrew, a slight smile appearing at the corners of her mouth.

'Thought I'd find a bit of light reading for the trip. Apparently there is not too much of that here. Reminds me a bit of Thomas's library.'

'Hmm, pretty intense stuff, but a good place to browse. What have you got there old man?' Chris was instantly curious.

'The shopkeeper suggested I try these. What do you think?'

'I don't know either of them, but that one looks interesting.' Chris pointed to *"Siddhartha."*

'That's what I thought. It's about Buddha's life apparently. Not your usual *"Passage to India."*

'Uhhu. Well, you could do worse. Seems as though it might be a bit more readable than the *"Bible."* Not that I was ever a fan.'

Edward grinned. 'Never known you to be very religious Chris. I suppose that's why I'm surprised to see you, here.'

'Well, you know how it is. Let's have a look.' Chris opened the book and flicked through the first pages. 'Looks all right.'

'I'll lend it to you after I've finished.' Edward grinned.

'What? Oh, I suppose you could.' Chris felt a little off balance.

'What about this one Ed. Another of Hesse's works - "*Wandering.*"

Could be interesting and a bit easier to digest than the *"Gita."*

'Thanks. Maybe shopping for esoterica is the tail-end of this morning's lecture on India!'

'Was it that bad?'

'No, I quite it enjoyed it actually, but are you sure you and Thomas weren't involved in clandestine occult meetings?' Edward gave him a broad smile.

'Wish we were. Maybe you will have to fill me in on some of his ideas one day Ed. Could do me the world of good. Too worldly, that's my trouble. I like my food, my pipe, a good chat and putting my feet up at the end of the day. I've never been into any of this religion business. I suppose I ought to one day.'

Edward shrugged offhandedly. 'I don't know about that. Thomas never used the word 'religion.' He always referred to God as an 'It' and sometimes a 'Her.' Thomas often used to ramble on about the difference between 'belief' and 'real life' then rattle out some Hindu words I never understood, just to prove his point.

> *"You know Ed, it's your dharma that counts. It's not what you say you believe in but how you live your life. That is what it is about. It's how you treat other people and not how much you put in the weekly collection that "She'd count in the end."*

Can you believe that Chris, that *"She'd count."* 'Edward had to laugh. 'Thomas refused to fatherise God and reckoned that the old cows of India had more merit than most men on earth.' Edward moved towards the counter.

"Cows, they're not sacred for nothing. Give you milk, give you fuel, keeps a whole village alive. Most men couldn't do what a cow can do.'"

Chris roared with laughter.

'Sounds like worship of the mother goddess to me.'

'He didn't say much about the mother goddess, but he did mention Lakshmi a few times and compared her to Cybele, Isis and Mary.

"Mothers are the gateway to paradise, Ed. Without them where would we be? None of us would be here. Now you take your average village woman anywhere in the world. She collects the water, grinds the wheat, tills the fields with the baby still clinging to her breast, and then feeds the animals before sweeping out her hut with her little wicker broom. Then she'll carry the wood or collect and dry cow patties for fuel and cook the meal. At the end of every harvest, she will count out how much is left for market. If she's lucky, occasionally there will be a little extra for a piece of cloth to cover her skinny frame and perhaps for a cooking pot. There is rarely anything left over in India. The men sit around the fire and smoke bidis and drink tea and the women do all the work. Therefore, God must be a woman, don't you think, since she gives the mothers the most important work to do? The mothers are the ones who understand what god wants done. If God were a he, then men would never be idle. Since they are it means that God is a she. Sound logic Ed. That's why all the ancient religions worship the mother Goddess. You'll find it in India, in ancient Greece and Rome and you'll find it in Christianity. Look at us today. Who looks after the home and brings up the children? Neither you nor I could have done what we're doing today without our mothers and I bet we learn more from them as we do from any professor or priest. The difference is that the mothers adorn themselves with a simple apron, not the elegant robes of the Spiritual Profession."

Can you imagine that Chris, Thomas a student of Oxford University having more respect for his mother than for his own professors? Mind you, I tend to agree with him. Well what do you think?'

Chris looked perplexed. 'I don't know. I guess I don't really know. That's it isn't it. Religion isn't straightforward. I mean I know I go to Church and all that, but I wouldn't say I've ever had a 'religious experience' and nor would I recognise one probably if I did.'

'Know what you mean. About as spiritual as I get is when I listen to Bach or Handel and even then, I'm often a little mellow after dinner and a few wines. So you can't really tell.' Edward laughed self-cynically. 'Or at least, I can't. In any case, that's not why I came here.'

Chris felt like being outside in the coldness and drabness of London once again.

'Well, it is about time to move Ed. Everything fell into place like clockwork. The Old Man wasn't too impressed with me sending you off into the thick of it, but I assured him that you were discreet and wouldn't ruffle any feathers.'

Edward momentarily clasped the books to his chest. 'Thanks Chris. No I mean it. Uncanny meeting you, here. Maybe it's meant to be and perhaps I will find something in India after all apart from Gandhi, something I haven't discovered so far.'

'Let me know when you do.' Chris slapped him on the back. 'I'll wait outside while you pay for those.'

The woman mysteriously re-appeared as if from some remote signal and wrapped the books in brown paper. 'Happy reading young man. And remember, anytime you want some advice about what to read, you know where to find us.'

Edward paid her with a one pound note and waited for the change. 'Thank you. This selection looks just right. Besides, my friend turned up out of nowhere. It was his idea to try the second volume of Hesse.'

'Excellent choice. I'm sure you'll enjoy it. India you said? Well, you couldn't find a better book. Mind you, not everyone is as lucky over there.'

'Oh, you've been?'

'Of course, I have young man. Couldn't work in a place like this without having been to some of these places and seen them first hand. And besides, I'm a fan of Annie Besant's and Madame Blavatsky so of course I would want to trace her footsteps.'

'Well, that is impressive. Perhaps I'll see you when I come back.'

'Good luck.' The woman returned to her private world behind the purple curtain.

Edward watched her disappear then walked out into the street, aware that he had spent longer than he intended chatting to the woman. Chris was nowhere to be seen. 'Damn, perhaps I took too long.' Edward chastised himself.

Chris suddenly emerged from it seemed, nowhere, carrying a small packet 'Thought you might like this Ed.' It was a hardbound book, the pages unlined and empty. 'Good to keep a journal when you travel. Write down some of your impressions. I'm sure it will be useful later and you might be able to find a story or two in your own experiences.'

'Thanks Chris.' Edward was moved. 'You've really been wonderful to both Ruth and me. I can't tell you how grateful I am.'

'Think nothing of it. Are you coming back to the office? We have a few last minute details to sort out and I have asked Jenny to pack some pencils and whatnots for you. Jenny has ordered a car for 4.30. It will only take you about forty five minutes, but they want you to be there early.'

Edward stopped in his tracks.

'Would you rather Ruth took you out there? I don't want to interfere with your plans.'

'The car will be good. Thanks old man.'

'You will need to be there by five to avoid any restrictions on lights. And that will go for Ruth as well.' Chris added as an afterthought.

Edward smiled at him. 'She's packing my bag right this minute then we'll be on our way I guess.'

'You mean you Ed. You're going this one alone remember.'

'Yeah. Can't say I'm worried, but I'm glad that David's over there. Big world outside of London.'

'Don't make it sound so scary. Just keep an eye out for pickpockets, otherwise there's really nothing to worry about.'

'Thanks. Bit of an adventure then. I suppose I feel more like Don Juan rather than.

"Edward Thompson, foreign correspondent."

'Chris laughed. 'That's settled then. Let's catch a cab back shall we. Looks as though there's a spot more rain on the way.'

Chris hailed a taxi and they beat the downpour by moments. The afternoon was quiet with little traffic. Edward looked silently through the cab window into the rain and wondered how he would adjust to the searing heat and humidity of the sub-continent. England was cold, damp and depressing.

'No wonder we're always at war.'

'What did you say Ed?'

'No wonder we're always at war Chris. This place is enough to get anyone down.'

'Too right.' Chris closed the conversation, convinced that his intuition about Edward needing a change was, dead on.

Chapter Eighteen

THE RAF WAS not too concerned about Edward's presence. The Hendon Air Base was as busy as could be expected in the still, early stages of the war. There was a lot of hurrying back and forth and nobody stopped to ask what a man in civvies was doing with his travelling bags at the base. The pilot was absorbed in checking instruments and there was a cluster of air force personnel checking baggage, fuel, take off time and a myriad of other tasks.

Edward realised that in order to make his presence known, it was up to him. The focussed efficiency of the RAF was not quite as reassuring as Chris's calm confidence and but happily the opposite to Ruth's clinging and parting tears. Edward was glad to say goodbye at the office. Ruth would be a problem in this environment. Chris telephoned through to confirm that Edward was on the way and everything seemed to be progressing smoothly.

A uniformed woman walked up to Edward and extended her hand. 'Mr. Thompson. We're expecting you. I hope that you are prepared. We have less time than originally planned and you'll be taking off in half an hour. Could I have your baggage please? You'd better have something to eat at the officers' mess, only make it quick. There won't be much else to eat until you reach Baghdad.' She caught Edward's hand in a cool and professional shake.

'Thanks. Yes, I'm ready. Do you mind if I ring my wife? I just want to let her know that I'm here safely and that we'll be off sooner than expected.'

'Of course.' She deferred with a slight nod of her head. Her hair was pinned into a neat bun beneath the blue of her service cap. Without the uniform, Edward thought that she'd probably be quite an attractive woman. Perhaps she had a husband already at war.

The woman noticed Edward measuring her quietly. 'There's a phone you can use in the mess, only please don't hold up the line, it's used for back up comms.' She flushed slightly then took Edward's overnight bag. 'Put that one on the ground.

The mess boy will collect it presently. If that's your typewriter' she motioned to the shoulder bag, 'I suggest you hang on to it. There's quite a bit of rattling around in the hold.' She smiled openly, her natural friendliness taking Edward off guard.

'Thanks. I'll keep it with me.' Edward placed his bag on the ground and waited patiently for the followed mess boy.

'This way sir.' With a single swoop, he swung the bag off the ground and headed for the officers' mess.

Edward fell into step behind him, grateful for the exercise and relieved that he was no longer unnoticed. The mess was noisy and busy. Uniformed men filled their cups with tea and coffee from common pots and helped themselves to potato mash and stew, ordinary fare, but Edward knew it would be good nourishment now and better than being hungry later. He unselfconsciously joined the small canteen queue and waited his turn to fill his plate.

'You new around here?'

'What? No, I'm not one of you mob. I'm a reporter on my way to India.' 'Then you just be Edward Thompson I'm Roger, Roger Holesworthy.' He extended a free hand. 'I'm your pilot to Baghdad. Very uncomfortable and noisy and you won't get much sleep. Still there are worse ways to travel.' Roger hardly paused for breath before holding out his plate out for more potato.

'Thanks. Looks as if it's your turn. Tastes OK, but never as good as home cooking.'

Edward passed his plate to the chef, resisting the temptation to ask for less stew. The 'no meat' mantra of Chris had already infiltrated his taste buds. There was plenty of everything so he could easily leave the meat and concentrate on the potato. The coffee was hot and Edward wasted no time filling a mug and joining one of the officers at his table.

'Hello. I'm Edward. Mind if I sit down?'

The officer nodded, not taking his eyes off his food. The pilot was on Edward's heels, seating himself at the same table. Edward ate in silence. It was a comfortable and friendly atmosphere, without any social frills but warm and cheery. The men ate quickly, obviously aware of the time and pushed away their chairs to clear their plates and mugs for the next round.

'Coming with us?' The officer at his table got up.

'Yes, don't mind if I do. I'm new here so I'd better tag along with you lot.'

'We know. Petes is my name.' The officer pushed his hand out.

'Edward.' Edward smiled, amused at the rough and ready manner of the man. Petes nodded again and headed out of the mess. Edward fell in behind the group and followed them to the locker room. There was a quick flurry of clothes as the men changed into flying gear, and assembled helmets and checked essential belongings.

'Where are you off too?' Edward couldn't resist his curiosity.

'Classified information.' Petes continued to lace his boots. 'Sorry. Keep your eyes open and your mouth shut and you'll be fine. We will be with you for two days in Baghdad. You won't be able to wander around as you would like to though. Drop off in Delhi is a quick one and from then on, you're on your own old chap.'

'Lucky you're going my way. Still, it's natural for a reporter to be curious about every damn thing and it's the first time I've been to the airfield. Good luck for the first mission whatever it is. Don't envy you though I dare say.'

'You're on a free flight so you're entitled to feel lucky. Hope India gives you what you want. Mind you, I wouldn't want to be going there myself. Too many people, too many mosquitoes and too much dirt.

'Can't say I'm looking forward to that part of it myself, but then I'll be looked after so it should cushion the blow a bit.'

'It's a darned sight better than being at war. What do you have in mind over there?'

Edward was tempted to say 'Sorry, classified information' but resisted.

'I'll be doing a follow up story on that Amritsar massacre and maybe having a look at the Congress. Gandhi is still hoping to free India from our apron strings you know.'

'Is that right? I suppose he'll fast until he gets his way. Imagine that, as skinny as he is and not eating anything for ten or more days. Can't say it's my style of politics but it seems to do the trick over there.'

'Seems to have. Although I daresay, he has some other tactics going for him. He'd have to have. Gandhi studied law in England so he's no a fool.'

'Depends what you think of lawyers.' Petes was not going to be drawn. 'But then I'm not one to judge. Didn't go past third year high.' Petes lifted his head and grinned at his own joke.

'But you're an officer! You must have something going for you.' Edward smiled broadly.

'Reckon it was good luck more than good management. Seem to have a natural talent with the men. Things just progressed from there. Plus, I like the technical side of things so they have stuck me in comms. Not that I am at liberty to say much about that. Well, we'd better get a push on. The engineer's about to crank the old bird up and we'll be off.'

Edward felt the faint thrill of excitement once again. It was really happening and in a strange sort of way, he was looking forward to the trip. It would be uncomfortable no doubt, but then not everyone got the chance to travel courtesy of the RAF.

Chapter Nineteen

THE ENGINE DRONED incessantly and Edward drifted in and out of a fitful sleep. From time to time he would wake and be surprised to find himself fastened in by the three-way harness that prevented him from shooting to the metal shell of the plane, every time it hit an air pocket. It was uncomfortable, but safe; safe enough for him to lapse once again into sleep. His mind was completely dissociated from the reality of London, the familiar wartime hum of the city, the clinking of coffee cups and smell of fresh buns, the sudden last minute flurry to file stories for *The Reporter.* He struggled to capture his thoughts and anchor them in the here and now, in the fuselage of the plane setting its course to Baghdad. Instead, fresh dreams flooded into his mind, dreams that were unreal, disturbing and dangerous, as if he witnessing someone else's and not his own life.

Edward forced himself into wakefulness, head throbbing with the effort and blinding noise of the engine. However, before he could construct a solitary thought, sleep tugged him back into unconsciousness. Then, his mind was flooded by another lucid scene over which he had no control. Finally, the struggle was too great and Edward succumbed.

The dreams flitted backwards and forwards, Thomas, Rome, and Mussolini. Then he saw Thomas's grave, Hitler's face over the Vatican - in his left hand - the swastika poised like an ancient weapon, ready to hurl at the image of Christ imprinted in a vast mosaic on the floor of the Basilica.

The same woman who had once appeared in his dreams was before him now, her face semi-shrouded by purdah, soft, haunting, her eyes deep and dark like onyx and her mouth a gentle in a soft expression of comfort; half-opened, tender, calling him. Edward's eyes turned to meet hers. She extended her hand towards him and Edward, stepped onto the vast plains of India, his hand caught in hers. Her fingers, subtle, exquisitely sensitive and intelligent, offered him ethereal gestures of pure love. The vision drew Edward's eyes into hers surrounding him in an unexpected cloud of compassion. Then she receded behind her veil, her full-length gown swirling around her in a dance of coyness; concealing her beauty then revealing her innocence; untouched, like an ancient goddess.

The throb in Edward's skull intensified forcing him into wakefulness. Edward held his head in his hands, surprised by the tears streaming down his cheeks.

'You all right there? Got a bit of a headache? Here, have these.' Petes handed Edward some tablets. 'Happens often. It's the fumes, the engine and the low air pressure. Can't take too much of it if you're not used to it.'

Edward held his hand forward and accepted the canteen of water Petes handed him. He drank thirstily, washing the tablets down with the first gulp.

'That's better. Go back to sleep. We've still got a long way to go.'

Edward wasn't so keen on the idea. The dreams disturbed him and he couldn't cope with the loss of control over his mind. However, he did sleep. The tablets acted like a sedative until his sleep was still like the waters of an, Himalayan lake. The dreams started again but this time, Edward felt deeply peaceful as if he had found something for which he had been searching for a long time.

She came to him again, this time, only her eyes, deep pools of black and around the eyes, pearl white. *"Midnight Pearl, Midnight Pearl."* The name repeated itself in his mind. *"Midnight Pearl,"* a solitary jewel in the darkness of a strange and unfamiliar land. Her eyes closed momentarily before they opened again, the long lashes dripping with tiny teardrops.

Edward rose to wakefulness to find the tears welling again. 'I wonder what that was all about? *"Midnight Pearl?"* ' Edward heard himself say. Strange. The most beautiful eyes he had ever seen; compassionate, and then filled with anguish and pain. Perhaps that was India. Thomas had endlessly praised this *"Mother Goddess."*

Perhaps this was she, beautiful yet beyond his reach. It was impossible to consolidate the image into corporeality, the gossamer-light touch of her hand, gentle, as if the flesh had no substance. There was nothing sensual about her, nothing he wanted from her, but something far deeper attracted him to her, as if she knew him in his pain.

Edward moved in his seat. There was not much cushioning him. The plane suddenly hit an air pocket instantly dropping five or so feet. His head was completely unprotected, save for the harness. As Petes warned, the ride was bumpy, rough and uncomfortable. He glanced around him. The other men were silent, motionless apart from the buffeting caused by occasional air pockets catching the plane off guard. Some of them were sleeping, head resting on sweaters, some were gazing straight ahead, as if lost in the world of mothers, sisters, daughters and wives. Who knew? Perhaps this was their last journey. Like any wartime journey, no one knew whether they would come home or be caught in the false homage of premature death in an unfamiliar and hostile land? Edward was shocked, saddened that some of the men were so young - years younger than he. Yet, from the lines under their eyes and the weary slump of the bodies into their harnesses, he could tell that they were also more seasoned and hardened than he would ever be. Edward had become familiar with the harshness and savagery of the war from the constant stream of disturbing reports and photos. He did not have and would never have the face-to-face combat that these men had. He had never had the shock of the sudden and brutal death of friends in front of his own eyes, leaving a legacy of shattered and permanently damaged in both war and peace. In these men he could see resoluteness, resignation to their share of the horrors and perhaps become heroes. In reality, Edward knew that the horrors outweighed the heroism. And, more than often, the sentiments, the sheer terror and the disgust at useless death, the initial shame and shock of killing another human perfused the reports like dirt on toilet paper. The picture was never pretty. Never. In Edward's mind, there was no glory in war. War was a dirty job that someone had to do. The sooner it was finished the better.

The plane lurched on its left wing then righted to the centre.

'Harness tight?' Petes turned towards Edward. 'Brace up now. We're in for a bit of rough stuff.'

Petes was right. The plane bucketed and swung in the clouds and Edward had to fight the fear of the violent motion flinging him against the roof. Then there was the embarrassment of losing the contents of his stomach. No one else looked as sick as he felt. Perhaps they were simply used to it. He held his seat well and kept his mind focussed on a distant point in the plane to manage the nausea. It worked a while and then he would be once again, overcome by the desire to vomit. Sheer pride kept him from being sick. Eventually, the plane levelled and he was able to loosen his grip on his senses and lapse once more into a welcome and restful sleep.

Chapter Twenty

Iraq

THE SHARP IMPACT of the wheels on the earth jolted Edward back to reality, snapping him out of sleep and the indefinite world of the sky and dreams.

'Thank God.' Edward muttered under his breath, the harness still tight as the plane taxied towards the parked jeep.

'Good man. I'll let you know when we can unbuckle and move out.' Petes was keeping a close eye on him. He was not about to take any risks. The plan was to usher Edward to the mess and keep him occupied with cards and magazines for the next couple of days until it was time to fly out to Lahore. All being well, there would be no complications. Petes had business with a couple of senior officers in Baghdad, and could not afford a stranding without an exit route. The plane would leave only when he was good and ready.

Edward had heard snippets from Chris about British and American intelligences during the war, but it was the one topic about which Chris was usually closed-mouthed and it looked as though Petes intended keeping his trap shut also.

Petes unbuckled both their harnesses then dropped out of the plane urging Edward to follow.

Edward was tired, but grateful to feel the earth beneath his feet. He looked quickly around the airfield. There was nothing much to see, except a cluster of metal hangers, a few scattered jeeps and at the far end of the field, a windsock. The dust rose around them, settling on their baggage and mixing in with his perspiration.

Petes grinned.' Not as friendly as home!'

Edward nodded and managed a smile. He was weary and unsure how he had come to this palpably hostile place in the desert. The angry eyes of the man heaving their baggage onto the dirt fixed on him as if Edward had just robbed Ali Baba's cave. The shimmering horizon threatened to refresh the waves of nausea in his belly and he suddenly missed the familiarity of London's grey drabness, pocked- marked by the intrigues of the European war.

'Don't worry about this place Edward. We won't be here too long and the base is a little more interesting than out here. Jump in man.' Petes slung a leg over the half- door of the Jeep and positioned himself firmly next to the driver. 'Give me that.' Petes grabbed the handle of Edward's typewriter case. 'You're in the back.'

The engine was already kicking over as Edward hoisted himself over the tailgate into the jeep. At least the wheels would stay on the ground this time. The field was surprisingly smooth, but Edward kept a tight hold on the passenger strap. He was unwilling to subject himself to further buffeting and, at worse, a rude ejection from the metal bench on which he was sitting, onto the floor of the jeep.

There were plenty of armed men at the base, but no sign of women. Edward briefly wondered whether *"Midnight Pearl"* was from Baghdad. He imagined it would be impossible to meet her here anyway with Petes almost following him into the john! The sky was dusty and hazy and there was no discernible outline of the city. The dust clotted into his nostrils and inside his shirt, prickling under his arms.

'God, London was dismal at the best of times, but this wasn't much better. A wash would be welcome if that were part of the deal' he muttered.

Edward wondered about breakfast. Turkish coffee? He grinned to himself. Chris would love it here, a timely sample of exotica to break the monotony of war.

'This way Edward.' Petes returned with a scrap of paper in his hand. 'Our room is the third on the right. I'll catch you there in half a mo.' Petes pointed to the first of three bunkers.

The metal roof looked ominously hot in the haze, but the floor was concrete and no doubt contained the temperature to bearable levels. Four or five huge fans circled slowly in the corridor and the absent clanging of a distant door reminded Edward more of a prison sentence than a couple of nights 'courtesy of the RAF.' Still, it was better than a tent under a tree that wasn't even there!

A few shirtless men, dressed only in trousers and with shaving bags in hand, tousled for first place in what was obviously the communal washroom.

'At least that's fixed.' Edward thought. 'That's where I'm off to.'

The room was basic; two single bunks on either side with a collection of metal hooks for hanging clothes or towels. The fan was silent and Edward adjusted the setting. The fan whirred slowly into life, slightly off centre and swinging dangerously for a few seconds, before righting itself on the horizontal plane. The first wave of air caught Edward's forehead. He turned his face upwards, taking in a few deep breaths. Then the angry-eyed man knocked metallically on the still-open door. Edward turned in surprise. The man held his bags in one hand, the other hand clenched, knuckles glistening with sweat and grime.

'Thanks.' Edward pointed to one of the bunks. The man snarled and took a step into the room. Edward stepped back as the porter flung the bags through the three remaining feet of the room onto his bunk. Edward gave him an instinctive half- salute and smiled briefly, taking in the figure of the man. He was over six feet tall and filled most of the doorway. His hands now hung loosely by his side, the fingers separated by meat, the fourth finger on both hands strangled by a broad band of gold. The man pulled off his neck kerchief and held it in both hands, his eyes glazed as if by a distant memory. Then the sound of the jeep engine coughing distracted him for a moment.

Edward moved swiftly to the door, pushed it shut and secured the safety catch in one movement. He breathed heavily, the sweat forming on his forehead, his palms sweaty and hands slightly trembling. Petes hadn't warned him about this one. The rest of the men seemed relaxed and happy enough, so perhaps this was just the routine 'welcome' to Baghdad. He turned to his luggage and quickly searched for his towel and shaving bag. Ruth had packed his belongings with her usual sense of order. The medicines wrapped in a smaller towel. He dropped them onto the bed. There were pain relievers as well as the antidiarrhoeal and iodine tablets. He pulled the top of the painkillers and popped a couple in his mouth. The rest could wait. He urgently needed a wash, something to remind him of normality and decency.

The sun assumed a potent and unkind glare by mid-morning. The haze thickened and it was impossible to see anything except a moving line that was the airstrip. The power had temporarily failed and the fans were now still, the air languid and oppressive. Edward turned on his bunk, trying desperately to sleep and forget the heat and the sweat dripping from his frame, sapping his will to fight his fears.

'No wonder the Bedouins wear oceans of cloth. The bloody sun. And dust!' Edward thought. 'English clothes were just not made for this climate. Even in war, this mob wears robes to keep cool. Wouldn't mind one of those long tea towels on my head just now.'

'One soaked in icy water would do just fine.' It was Petes, who broke the silence, also unable to tolerate the heat, sweat and dust any longer. Petes was lying on the bunk next to him, flipping quietly through the pages of a manual. 'Feel like going shopping? There's a bazaar in town where we could pick up some iced drinks to cool off a bit.'

'Thought we were here for the duration.' Edward remarked dryly.

'We are, but I have a pass to go to the bazaar, as long as only two of us go at anyone time. What do you think?'

'Why not. Better go now before the sun gets up any further.'

'Bring your camera.'

'Will that be all right.'

'Sure. You're a tourist. You'll see something different here to Bouverie St.'

'How do you know that's where I worked?'

'Don't you still?'

'Yes I do. But how did you know anyway.'

'We know Chris pretty well. He's been around the traps a long time, otherwise there's no way you'd be here now.

Edward took a long look at Petes and shook his head. 'Well since you know Chris so well, perhaps you can help me find him something interesting at the bazaar; some trinkets or dates or whatever.'

Petes grinned broadly. 'We'll find you something Ed.' He heaved himself off the bunk and ripped a shirt off the hook. 'Give us a minute. I'll just get rid of the shadow on my chin.' Petes was out of the door in less than a minute, whistling softly to himself.

Edward could hear the splash of water as Petes went about his business, clearly unfazed by the trials of a strange place. Perhaps though, this was not strange to Petes. When he returned, Edward had pulled a fresh shirt from his luggage.

'I need to change this shirt. It's dripping already.'

'Don't bother. It will dry in the wind and there's no point getting another one soaked and covered with goddamned dust.'

'Well, at least he was still English!' Edward felt relieved. He wasn't used to the discomfort of the heat and smell of his own sweat. It was earthy and salty, not like the soapy cleanliness he wore to the office. He rarely extended himself in physical work and even if he had wanted to explore the streets of London or, when they travelled to Oxford to visit Thomas, it's intriguing lanes, Ruth was too delicate to manage the distance. Petes on the other hand looked at ease with himself, despite the discomfort.

'Maybe I do need roughing up a bit.' Edward remarked to Petes.

'Bring your hat. It will keep you cooler.' Petes was concerned only with essentials.

They set off in an army jeep. The driver was unconcerned about their presence and drove as if his singular mission were to break the axle. The pitted road was poorly kept. Edward kept one hand firmly on his head to stop his hat from flying off and the other gripped the seat in front of him.

'Nearly there. Don't mind the ride. They're all like this over here. Never been to India? Well, you'll find life much the same there. More people in India though. They travel around in bullock carts or those pedal-powered rickshaws. Not many cars here and those that have them usually have drivers, although not as adventurous as this one. Look. There's the bazaar.' Petes tapped the driver on the shoulder and pointed to the edge of the bazaar. He signalled his watch pointing at two p.m. 'We have a few hours here. Plenty of time to nose around and do a bit of shopping.'

Edward was relieved to get out of the jeep. His legs felt wobbly but he quickly regained his composure, and gave Petes a direct and cool look. 'Petes? Does everyone call you that?'

'That's the way I like it. No need to know anymore and best that you forget you met me later on. Safer that way.'

Edward looked at Petes with disbelief. 'You mean you're one of those intelligence chaps.'

'Petes it is; no more and no less.'

Edward felt distinctly uncomfortable and was grateful for their entry into the bazaar. Petes seemed to know his way around and took him directly to a tiny shop bursting with hand-woven carpets and silks. The shopkeeper was a wizened and shrunken man, his eyes alert and watchful, sparking with the prospect of a sale.

Petes gave the old man a casual greeting. 'Hello Wahid.'

'Mr. Petes.' The old man smiled genuinely and grabbed Pete's hand, shaking it up and down until Petes pulled himself free.

'Wahid, this is my friend Edward.'

'Ah! You look for something for your missus? Eh?' The old man took Edward's hand and dragged him to a pile of neatly folded cloths.

'Steady on there Wahid.' Petes intercepted. 'He just wants a small item, something for the office, for the bossman.'

'Eh? Oh. You want small carving, something precious, with jewels?'

'Something simple Wahid. And inexpensive!' Petes had the situation in hand.

'Lot of good stuff here Edward. Pity some of it is so bulky. Wahid will find you nice carving you can pack into your things.'

Edward fingered one of the rugs in amazement. 'Pretty fine detail. I wonder how long it takes to make one of these?'

'Kids do a lot of the work in these parts. Sit there in the same spot working all day. Get nothing for it and after a few years, their eyesight is shot. That's the law of survival. If you want to eat, you have to work.'

'Good God. I thought child-labour was outlawed.'

'You haven't seen much old man have you.'

'Guess I haven't. Makes me sound a wet behind the ears. I suppose you've travelled a fair bit Petes?'

'Here and there. I'm quick to pick things up.'

'So it seems.' Edward remarked.

'They don't like you to loiter here. Get a bit jumpy. Best we push on to one of those food shops. Hope you like fresh nuts and dried fruits? Chris might like a few.'

'Wahid. That one will do.' Petes grabbed a brass piece, a bowl with a long and slender stem curved upwards to a mouthpiece and stuffed some notes into the old man's hands. 'Cheerio then.' Petes jerked his head at Edward and moved quickly through the small doorway and into the blazing light.

'Give this to Chris to stuff his tobacco into. Compliments of Petes.'

'Will do. Thanks.' Edward had to laugh.

'Want to sample the food?'

'Good idea Petes. And I'm still looking forward to that icy cold drink.'

It was four in the afternoon by the time they arrived back at the mess. The driver was waiting for them at two p.m. and Petes decided to take the long route. 'Just to see the sights and take a few extra precautions.'

Edward remembered the ominous face and beef-like hands of the man at the base The 'sights' amounted to a caravan of camels and tents loosely assembled and tethered to stakes in the sand. The camels were content to lie in the heat, some fortunate to be under a grove of palms and others, long lashes closed to the heat and dust, dozing peacefully. The 'well' was a low structure of roughly hewn and lain stones; clearly precious and guarded by a man with a curved sword attached at his waist. The man nodded in quiet recognition of Petes then signalled a peddler to where the jeep had parked. The peddler produced a tray of dates, almonds and dried apricots.

'These are the best you'll find anywhere Ed. Take your time.' Petes took one of the dates and popped it into his mouth. He took a swig out of an invisible flask and the peddler gave a low whistle at one of the camel drivers. The man appeared with a goatskin of wine and handed it to Petes. Petes took a long draught of the cooling liquid and handed it to Edward.

'You won't find anything as sweet as this in London Edward.'

Edward looked at Petes and then at the man with the sword then put his head back to let the nectar flow down his throat, cooling and soothing his gullet. After a few seconds, he pulled his head up for air and smiled at Petes.

'A good drop Petes.'

'That's my man.' Petes grabbed the flask, took a quick swig and handed it to the man with the sword. The flask was handed round and finally to the camel driver. Petes fished into his pockets and pulled out a wad of greasy and crumpled notes. He counted out four or five then passed them to the sword man and turned abruptly on his heel.

'Time we left Edward. Leave them to sort that out amongst themselves.' Petes wasted no time getting into the Jeep and the engine sparked into life, the wheels spinning in the dust before they headed out of the camp.

It was impossible to talk above the sound of the engine and Edward needed all his strength and concentration to remain seated as the wheels bumped over rocks and holes on the road and skidded around sand dunes. When they finally caught sight of the base, Edward was relieved for the stark ugliness of the bunkers and the gleam of metal in the ferocious afternoon light. The jeep slid to a sudden sideways halt, the breaks jamming beneath the driver's foot.

Petes leaped out, clearly fresh and untroubled by the ride. 'I suggest you have a kip a few hours Edward. Afternoon is the best time to rest while it's still hot then there's a game of poker tonight with the lads.'

'Sounds good, thanks the tip.'

The evening was pleasantly cool with a light breeze fanning the officers' mess. Edward excused himself early from cards. The pungent smoke was overpowering him and he wanted time out to gather his thoughts. The company of the men was welcome, but after a couple of hours, the game became intense and the men, clearly intoxicated from a succession of mixed drinks, began to increase the bets. Petes appeared preoccupied and from time to time, left the game to smoke outside. He was the only one, Edward noticed, who did not drink, his cold sobriety and blue, steady eyes, a reminder to Edward Petes still had his eye on another game. Petes noticed Edward get up from the game and nodded quietly as Edward slipped back to his room.

Edward could feel Pete's eyes watching him as he made his way out of the bunker, cold, calculating but oddly friendly and comforting. He felt a wave of relief as he shut the door behind him and flicked on the light. The beds were slightly ruffled and Edward looked quickly around the room. Strange, he was sure that his bags were under the bed and not to one side as they now were. He pushed them under the bunk with his hand, noting that the catch was open. There was nothing he could do. He would tell Petes about it later. Then, perhaps Petes had taken the chance to have a quick rifle through his belongings. "*Siddhartha*" was lying on the side table where he had left it, the pages undisturbed and inviting.

Edward picked up the book and opened the cover. It seemed light enough and he was grateful that he would not have to use all his concentration. This was new territory and he didn't want to wade in out of his depth. The light was semi-dim, but sufficient for reading. He lay on his bunk, boots off and shirt half open to catch the semi-warmed air fanned from the ceiling. He flipped open the book to the first page. The story was simple and appealing, the themes and characters easy to identify with.

An hour slipped by and he absorbed himself journeying with "*Siddhartha*" throughout Ancient India. Then the moment of "*Siddhartha's*" trial arrived. Edward could almost see the beautiful woman in the forest tending his thirst and hunger. He stopped, catching his breath in a coarse cry.

"*Midnight Pearl!*" She was unnervingly similar, the innocent temptress in his dreams! The memory of his dream was suddenly lucid and present. Even with the memory of her so clear in his mind, Edward could still not catch hold, of her. Her body dissolved into the pearl-like eyes, flecked with compassion and kindness. This time, she awakened in him, his desperate need to be loved, and his need to be understood and healed of the hurt Ruth had so thoughtlessly inflicted. Edward cried in pain at the revelation. He put the book down.

'Ruth!' Ruth was the one who had led him into relationship, but through her own neediness was depriving him. Edward inwardly remonstrated to himself. Ruth could not be his mother any more than he could be her father. The awakening worried him. How could he have not seen himself?

'But then,' Edward eased his rationale 'His family background was secure, he had a good job a sound sense of self esteem' so it was less possible for him to admit his neediness and vulnerabilities. It was far easier to observe the weakness in Ruth - Ruth the fragile flower - translucent, attractive, and disarming. Now his own vulnerability was chillingly clear. Perhaps Thomas had seen in him what he could not discern within himself. Even Chris convinced him that he need a break from the office, time to think, time to learn. Yet, both men respected him sufficiently to say nothing directly. Perhaps that's what Chris meant when he said "*Inside Ed, you're a real loner,*" Edward mused. At the time, he was startled by the comment and brushed it aside, thinking that Chris was referring his capacity for deep thought. Now, Edward felt shocked and vulnerable. Exposed to himself, he felt isolated at some outpost of civilisation, without friends, without the comforts of his own culture and without Ruth. This wasn't being 'on the job,' it was time dedicated to soul searching whilst the guards on his consciousness were down.

Edward stared up at the ceiling, the fan whirring slowly, as slowly as his own heart beating painfully against his chest and terrifyingly rhythmic movement of his breath. He wanted to scream to break the silence or to fill it with the comfort of Chris's chatter and Ruth's nervous laughter.

Petes walked in, smoke in hand and beer in the other. 'Feel like a drink old man? Don't want you to miss the fun out here all on your own.'

'Thanks.' Edward sat up and took the beer, grateful at its coldness and Pete's presence.

'Everything all right? It's not good spending too much time alone out here Edward. A man can lose his soul in the desert.' Petes paused and sat on his bunk, drawing deeply on his cigarette. 'It's the sand and sun you know, everything here is amorphous. Even the trees begin to lose their shape and become wavy lines on a hazy horizon. Heat affects you that way, can mess your mind around if you're not careful. Keep the fluids up Edward and don't go off anywhere on your own. Still, could be worse. We're not in the First World War out here. Pity those chaps. Petes kicked off his boots and swung his legs onto the bunk. He stared absently at the ceiling, still smoking, the ash falling unnoticed onto his shirt. 'Sleep Edward. Tomorrow's another day.'

Edward breathed a sigh of relief and decided that Petes was right. It was no good brooding. Perhaps the heat that made him read more into the book.

Chapter Twenty One

THE PLANE TOOK off at 0700 hours. Edward awoke at 6am to find men moving around gathering their belongings into kit bags and hastily gulping coffee and biscuits. 'There you are Edward. I was just on my way back to see you. We're out of here within the hour. The first haul is to Quetta for refuelling, then straight onto Delhi. Have to move on so you'll be in Delhi sooner than planned. Top secret I'm afraid so you won't be able to give David a reason other than *"business completed earlier than expected."* That's all. Understood?'

'Understood.' Edward raised his eyebrows but thought better of pursuing the matter. He fell in with the other men in the washroom. The sensation of clean and cool water splashing onto his face was the best remedy for a fitful sleep, plagued with wakeful moments of self-doubt and dreams of an endless expanse of desert, stretching to the shores of Britain. He felt like coffee so hurried through the wash and pack routine to leave enough time to drink and relax before take-off.

The plane lurched off the runway in a cloud of dust. Baghdad merged into the early morning haze below. The whites of open rooftops melted into solitary stream, like an ancient river reflecting in the early morning sun. The mixture of dust and the glare of the Middle Eastern sun, worse than Edward had reckoned. India would probably be no better.

The flight was noisy, the fumes penetrating and infusing the cabin with a raw reality, but Edward felt more settled and adjusted. He unbuckled his harness, but Petes cautioned him against it.

'Never safe in the air Edward. Keep it on. By the way, do you think you'll come back via Baghdad?'

'Not if I can help it' Edward had to smile.

'Not welcoming? Still, there is a bit of British history there and you might feel like doing a story on it one day. Let me know after the war is over. Might feel like it myself and I know my way around. Could do with a holiday rather than business.'

'I'll definitely think about it. Thanks Petes.' Edward was relieved at the change in his tone. The cool and disciplined 'intelligence officer' was now the relaxed and good humoured 'guide.' Edward was quizzical at the change, an eyebrow betraying his surprise.

'They all know me at the base. Just say you want Petes and they'll know where to find me.' Petes said casually.

'You read my thoughts.'

'Keep your head down in India Edward' the discipline crept into his tone 'bit of funny business I hear. Don't look obvious and don't tell anyone you came with us. If they ask, just say it was arranged in advance, and you came on a routine flight.'

'Will do. How do I contact David?'

'They'll radio through when we're about two hours out of Delhi. Keeps it simple and there are fewer questions asked by the civvies. Don't forget to ask David to tee up the return flight before you leave. Can't leave too much to chance or you'll be catching the slow boat home.'

'Thanks for that. Chris reckoned I'd be there about three weeks. Could be longer though.'

'There are a few flights, but not many. The RAF can't afford to do a shuttle service in the middle of the war so keep your wits about you.'

The throb of the engines drowned out any chance of further conversation. Edward resisted the temptation to drift into sleep, occasionally peering forwards to catch glimpses of the cockpit. The crew were well trained and obviously liked what they were doing. It was better than sitting around waiting for the call to action. At least they were in the air and focussed on the job at hand. The pilot was an ex-engineer. He was grateful for the chance and was pulled into pilot training at the beginning of the war. His navigator joined straight after school and was reaching eighteen years of age at the most. He looked competent, if not too young for the responsibility. Edward wasn't convinced that war was the best way to turn boys into men, but there was little choice at present. Now they were thousands of miles away from home. Soon, they would be over Iran, edging the great sub-continent and crossing the Indus valley, the ancient seat of Indian civilisation, before heading into the world dominated by two of the worlds great religions; Hinduism and Islam.

Edward tried to trace with his mind, the history of the subcontinent he had gleaned from Thomas's impromptu discourses. At the time, he was intrigued with stories about the ancient civilisation, the gradual division of families, kingdoms and land into a messy agglomeration of small Rajas and feudal landlords. Thomas had wised him up on the milieu of innumerable minor gods, goddesses, mythologies and tales that was India.

Then he related the gradual evolution of India's main religions including Jainism, the lineage of the Saints, Sages and Gurus. Thomas used to speak with amusement about the rich social and cultural history that the gurus brought with them. They were ready apparently, to challenge the greedy and often warlike and bloody manners of the Rajas. Thomas was more serious however, about the development of Christianity, the plight of the Sikhs at the hands of the Muslims and the exodus of the Parsis from Persia into India upon the loss of their homelands. Then there was India's political history to trace; the invasions of Alexander the Great along the northwestern reaches of India, finally halted at the banks of the Indus River. No less colourful were the aspirations of Genghis Khan to claim the riches, beauties and mysteries of India as his own, uncannily intercepted by a visionary dream.

Later India suffered incursions by assorted Muslims until they too had an immovable foothold on the spiritual, political and literal landscape of "*Bharat*." For a nation with its fair share of 'pacifists' and 'vegetarians,' they mustered extraordinary courage and military skill along with sheer determination to protect their homeland. But destiny it seemed, also provided the unwilling Hindus with a combination of impenetrable mountain passes and a mass of religious power in order to dominate and defeat the military might and ambition of Alexander, Genghis and others.

Finally, India succumbed, to the Moghul Empire from the west, and with it, accepted an overlay of anti-idolatry onto the mosaic of spiritual belief that had united and breathed life and rhythm into the nation for millennia. Faith was the pulse of India. With the determination of their own faith, the Moghul's also brought with themselves into India, an impressive array of architecture and administrative skill; eventually to be eroded by greed following protracted dealings with the Portuguese, Dutch and British during the 17th to 20th centuries.

India was a nation in disarray rendered a no-man's land by the British merchants cum soldier-pirates, a nation of acute and unbearable oppression of individual human dignity, a nation struggling to reassert its historic, cultural and religious traditions. None of the Sikh, Muslim nor Hindu leaders could now call India solely their own. India was now land of the dispossessed ruled by an oppressive British bureaucracy that had disenfranchised both the Hindu Rajas and Moghul Kings in its zeal to claim the Peacock Crown and all the wealth inherent in that throne.

India, the *"Jewel in the Crown"* of the British Empire was indeed, a haven for of merchants, looters and military autocrats.

'God, and I have to mix with the bloody Raj.' Edward wondered whether the history of India could sustain the presence of the overbearing British. In both Chris and Thomas's estimation, the British Raj were no better than the Indian robber- merchants, only more practised in aloofness and insensitive to the sentiments of a timeless land and its noble people. How was it possible that five major religions - held together in a dynamic yet tolerant co-existence - could be comprehensively shattered and dismembered by Britain? The subtle threads of history and religion were cleverly unravelled by British rule, then tangled together into an impossible knot in order to increase England's claim to sovereignty in a land that did not even belong to her! Surprisingly, the threads of British administration, the rail and postal system brought new life, communication and transport within India, building new bridges and prosperity in the Empire. It was the attitude of superiority that did the damage. Although the British fared well in India, there was no promised decrease in poverty through granting land ownership and power to the otherwise landless poor.

At least Allan Hume, according to Chris's deliberations, had abhorred the obvious injustices inflicted by the British and in 1885 set up the Indian National Congress in an attempt to give Indians representation on nominated councils. Congress nevertheless favoured the middle classes. Gandhi smelt the rat and tried to turn Congress into a movement for the masses, uniting all Indians in a common cause - Independence.

'Not all the British are bad.' Edward tried to bargain with the inner dialogue dominating his thoughts. 'They weren't planning a united India but at least the Muslim League had the stated aim to imbibe in Muslims loyalty to the Crown.' Edward felt the need to defend his national purpose. It was true that the League bolstered Muslim sentiments at the end of the first war. Something had to compensate for the severe curtailment of the Caliph's powers and Congress decided to support the movement to demonstrate Hindu- Muslim unity.

Edward wasn't so sure. Chris felt strongly that the British earmarked the Muslims for division from the Hindus long before Gandhi took up the cause of religious unity. Now, Jinnah, the 'heir-apparent' to the League with the careful support and encouragement of the British, opposed Congress. Gandhi was caught in the middle with the difficult task to temper and humour Jinnah whilst encouraging Hindus and Muslims to live as one.

'Well our war has certainly made things worse for India.' Chris's parting comments stuck in Edward's brain.

> *"Independence is off the agenda and Britain as usual, is using Indian armed forces and wealth for her own war effort."*

Thankfully, the war was a unifier, but word had it that the Indians were rebelling, wanting the same status as their British counterparts. Good for them! However, the situation rapidly became more complex with Japan's entry into the war, posturing in the Pacific and engaging Burma in conflict in her quest for territory and supremacy. The USA, according to Chris's sources, would inexorably be drawn into the debate for Indian

Independence and since the northern airfields were needed, they would presumably support any Muslim demands for partition.

'Perhaps that's what Petes is about.'

'What did you say Ed?'

'Petes! Just thinking aloud.'

'Don't think too much, it hurts when the air pressure is so low.' The plane jolted as if struck by lightning. Edward lurched forwards and upwards, held only by his harness as the Dakota dropped like a hawk into an airless vacuum.

'Hold onto your hat old fellow. We'll be through this one in a sec.'

Edward did not feel like responding, the impossible headache, the pain searing like a tight band across his forehead, visiting him once again.

'Surviving old man?'

'I think so.'

'Wait for this stuff to settle and I'll have at something for you.' Petes rummaged under the seat for a small kitbag. He pulled out a makeshift medicine kit and found the remaining painkillers. 'Got your canteen Ed? Swallow these. God, anyone would think I'm a bloody doctor.' Petes congratulated himself with his trademark grin.

Edward reached across for the tablets. 'Sure you can spare them?'

'Just take them. You look awful.'

Edward managed a weak grin. 'I feel it. Never mind, these will do the trick.'

Pete's grin widened as he let Edward swig the tablets down. It would be several hours before they were set to land and refuel at the fuel dump. Within half an hour, there would be a change of pilot. Then they would be back in the air for the long haul to Delhi. Petes knew the now, well-established route from London via the Middle East to India like the back of his hand, and he knew that Edward would suffer unless he played 'nurse-maid.'

'That's the trouble with civvies,' Pete's resisted the impulse to think aloud, 'no tolerance. Too soft and silly for my liking.' Pete's impressed upon himself to exercise a little patience and at least get his charge to Lahore in one piece. He settled deeply into a mood of humoured resignation and closed his eyes.

Chapter Twenty Two

Quetta, Oman

THE TRIP TO Quetta was uneventful apart from the smell of fuel and the constant throbbing of the engines. The plane came in for its final approach and dropped safely onto the airfield. The wheels locked for a fraction of a second as they hit the earth with a distinct thud and then bumped and rolled over the uneven surface. The engine screamed, wing flaps tortured by the sudden impact of air. The Dakota slithered and skewed sideways before coming to a definite halt.

'Rough ride eh? The pilot's good. He's been everywhere this one. Wouldn't be an anywhere he couldn't put this bird down.'

'Glad you feel so confident. Not exactly my cup of tea.'

Petes laughed. 'You civvies! You haven't lived. There was an earthquake here about five years ago. Amazing anything remains of the base or the airstrip for that matter.'

'I always was one for having my feet on the ground if there is any left that is.' Edward added ruefully. 'Anyway, can't thank you enough Petes. Where are you going in India?'

'Have to wait and see. My mission takes me north. We might cross paths, you never know.' Petes wasn't giving anything away.

Edward discreetly untied his harness and followed Petes to the rear door of the plane.

There was very little left, of the base, just sufficient to service the plane and air crew. Edward was grateful for the reprieve of solid ground, a toilet and tea. Then they boarded again and the Dakota wheeled, nose eastwards and towards the ancient civilisations of India.

'Look, that's the Indus below. We must be getting close.'

The river snaked like a cord from the mountains towards the sea. It reminded Edward of a mother's womb, the umbilical cord trailing behind a newborn child.

'That's the Indus Valley. Valley of the long lost civilisation of Mohenjo Daro. Oldest civilisation in the world Ed. They were, quite advanced you know, civil engineering works, public bathing areas, plumbing to the houses, advanced agriculture, you name it! Really makes you wonder. In any case Edward, when you see the Valley you have your reference point for the whole of India.'

'Historically as well as geographically it seems Petes.' Edward remarked. Petes raised an eyebrow and cocked his head at the scene below.

'Perhaps you are right. From the upper Indus Valley, we fly towards Delhi. Not long to go now. Think you can last the distance?'

Edward nodded, still reluctant to waste energy on speech. He was grateful to Petes for his practical support and cheerful nature. Chris had some good friends and Edward was glad that they treated him with the same respect as they would Chris. Edward leaned his head against the impossibly ribbed fuselage. He felt tired and old. Then there were the thoughts of Ruth creeping into his solitude, nagging and worrying him.

'I shouldn't have left her.' He was unable to suppress the self-recrimination.

'You're better off where you are Ruth. I dare say you'd be able to tolerate the journey and so far, it's been a men thing all the way.' Edward had to smile. Comforted by reason, he allowed a broken sleep to command his mind. Better than worrying. Besides the headache would make hard work, of any conversation.

Petes handed him a jacket. 'Stick this under your head. No use making the damage worse.'

Edward felt like a sissy, but didn't bother covering his shame. Embarrassed or not, he was not travelling well. He would feel happier when the plane touched down. He took the jacket and gave Petes a last nod before drifting into semi-sleep. Petes kept watch. Civvies were always a worry. The trip was basic and rough, a far cry from the comfortable cabins of the steamers or the luxury seats of the Empire Air Services, the Sunderlands. Wartime was wartime and Chris wanted the job done. The man looked OK, obviously from the city, a bit drawn and pale as if he had been through the mill. Petes would make sure his car was at the airfield before he himself left for quarters. India was India and he would find it tough, but perhaps the man could do with a change.

The final leg was an hour longer that Petes anticipated. The Dakota circled around the city before climbing into a long, upward spiral.

'Something must be holding them up.' The pilot yelled to Petes. 'There's a lot of chatter on the radio. Got some chaps flying out. They want the field clear until they're on their way so we'll have to hold out I'm afraid.'

Below, the scurrying of cars and men martialling, and refuelling planes, resembled a nest of frantic ants before a storm. There was obviously something urgent happening and the Dakota had no choice but to circle overhead, as if she were a dying vulture sapped of her strength from want of fuel. Finally, the makeshift airfield cleared and the cars and men miraculously disappeared into buildings, and once again, out of sight.

'OK. Our turn now, we're going down.' The pilot confirmed.

Petes gave him the thumbs up and shook Edward's shoulder, jerking awake.

'We're going down Edward.'

'What did you say, we're landing?'

'That's right. Our turn now. Hold on, we'll be there in a few minutes.'

The plane circled and began a slow, winding descent to the airbase. The pilot looked out of his window, absorbing the vastness of the plain below them.

'Can't see much from here' Petes announced. 'This is India.' Petes grinned. 'It will take about one hour for you to reach the David's residence. He has an errand to run as I understand before you get there. Not that it's far from the airfield to the British Compound. You won't mind old chap will you.'

'Not at all.' Edward hid his mild confusion.

'He will enjoy your company Edward so go along for the ride. Might be a change of pace to play host to a recalcitrant journo from the homeland!'

'Is that the word that's around?' Edward was surprised.

'Something like that. You've come here to sniff out the Amritsar story and then what's going on in Lahore I hear. Murder of General O'Dwyer. Not a safe time for an Englishman to be in India.'

Edward smiled. Probably Chris had stirred the pot before he had even left London. 'So I won't get the posh treatment,' Edward laughed.

'David will look after you well. He doesn't really like the razzmatazz of the Raj, but he's an excellent host. I can personally vouch for him.' Pete's softened his tone.

'You know him?'

'Yes, and I know *about* him.' Petes smiled, carefully watching Edward's reactions.

'I guess you'll be reading my cables to Chris, Petes.'

'Didn't say that I wouldn't! Things are pretty hot around here so I expect you'll have lots to write about.' Pete's grinned broadly.

'Have to wait and see about that. Chris wants me to travel around a bit.'

'Good luck then. Don't envy you. There have been some riots recently. Stay with our lads and don't go wandering off, alone.'

'I'll keep my nose clean.' Edward crossed his heart in mock promise.

Chapter Twenty Three

Delhi, India 1940

EDWARD AWOKE TO the peaceful clattering of metal on metal. The local woman was adjusting pots on a small gas burner, preparing rice, dahl and roti. Her movements were quick, accurate and timeless. The rhythmic rolling of the chapatti pin momentarily mesmerised Edward as he passed the kitchen. Her work reflected an almost religious attention and dedication as if she were cooking for her god. The woman's eyes didn't leave her small rolling board, even though she must have heard Edward near the door. Instead, she continued to squat in dutiful absorption, from time to time, turning the widening circle of dough on her board before kneading a fresh piece into a small triangle and dabbing it with oil. Then she started the whole procedure all over again. The old woman worked with obvious peace and contentment.

Edward wondered how it was possible that such a land could produce clearly masterful strokes of art in the kitchen and at the same time, the chaos that ruled the village market places.

'Ah, Edward, there you are.' David strode towards Edward, linking his arm in his own before leading him away to a small sitting room.

'That's Shanti. Wonderful cook. The food is always just right, not too much spice but just enough to warm the palate. Wait until you try it. I hope you don't mind a light curry?'

'Not at all. It could be quite a pleasant change from mutton and veg.' David laughed. 'You won't get much mutton in these parts, or beef for that matter. The Indians over here are still pretty much vegetarian. They think that we've come to corrupt them to our barbaric ways; you know, wine, women, meat and song.'

It was Edward's turn to laugh. 'I suppose that's why Gandhi wore his cottons when he went off to England for the Round Table Conference.'

'It's a bit more than that Edward. Surely, you of all people would understand the significance behind the dhoti?'

'The dhoti… oh… that loin cloth?'

'Yes. That was Gandhi's clear statement that India was not going to tolerate English cloth. Undermining home rule and all that, and besides, Gandhi preferred to represent the poorest of the poor, the landless farmers and Harijans, most of whom have little more to wear than a dhoti - if they're lucky.' David added as an afterthought.

'I remember Churchill's reaction. Incensed by him if I recall. Quite beneath his class to deal with a half-naked fakir!' Edward laughed heartily.

'I can see you're a convert to the cause of Khadi already.' David remarked soberly.

'I do remember David, Gandhi visiting the Lancashire mills. Quite a sporting attitude really. They were losing their livelihoods as well, especially after Gandhi burnt the cloth.'

'It doesn't finish there,' David cut in. 'Britain controls the Egyptian cotton industry which is part of her reason for allowing Mussolini through the Suez and into Abyssinia. Isn't it absurd Edward, it isn't about national identity, it's about money and power. As for Wallis Simpson and Edward, don't even ask! They want to increase their interests in Italy - cotton. Hitler is a diabolical kettle of fish but the Prince of Wales working to bring Mussolini and Hitler together is another thing altogether. I'm sure it's the influence of Wallis. Funny business in Hong Kong so I believe. Imagine Wallis and Edward being seduced by Hitler and all the while he has his eyes on the British Crown. They attend his parties you know, and they accompanied him to one of Wagner's operas.'

'Wagner?'

'Yes, Parsifal. You've heard of it of course. Based on Wolfram Von Eshenbach's work *"Parsifal - The Grail Romance?"*'

'My late brother in law Thomas, mentioned it as a matter of fact.'

'I'm sorry about Thomas, Ed. Chris mentioned it to me before you arrived.' David looked saddened.

'Thanks David.' Edward was surprised at the sudden tears smarting. 'Thomas had his own views on the British throne and its spiritual significance as well as political power hence the threats posed by Hitler.' Edward felt suddenly better as his thoughts locked onto Thomas's philosophical musings, his emotions cooled for the moment.

'Apparently Hitler is besotted with the whole theme. Sees himself as Klingsor the black magician. He probably thinks that he's the reincarnation. Anyway, you know how the story goes. Klingsor steals the Spear and wounds the King of the Guardians of the Holy Grail. Perhaps to Hitler, that represents the Allies. Well, the legend of the Holy Grail is still alive in Britain and Hitler clearly sees himself as the one to seize the *"Spear of Destiny"* as it's known. In Picasso's depiction of Parsifal, Picasso sees himself as the holder of the Spear and Hitler as Klingsor, intent on ruining Europe. Hitler is also apparently well versed in the occult. Eckart and his Thule Society was Hitler's mentor. Possibly, also the Blood Lodge of one Guido Von Liszt. You've heard of them?'

'No. You're saying that Eckart and occultism was breeding ground for the Nazi Party?'

'Quite so. People refer to Eckart as a great philosopher but in fact he was a pure Satanist and as such, adviser to Hitler.

Imagine the man said,

> "Follow Hitler! He will dance, but it is I who have called the tune! I have initiated him into the "Secret Doctrine," opened his centres in vision and given him the means to communicate with the Powers. Do not mourn for me. I shall have influenced history more than any other German."'

"The Secret Doctrine!" Edward was momentarily stunned.

'Apparently. Why? Does it mean something to you Edward?'

'Well no, I mean yes, it does. The woman in the bookshop said something about Annie Besant I think. It's a work by some Russian woman, a Madame Blavatsky. It was a bit heavy for me to carry though and probably to read by the sounds of it. The woman in the shop seemed to think the world of Blavatsky and Besant. Thomas mentioned them too from time to time.

'Annie Besant was the President of Congress for a while.'

'Good god. What an extraordinary coincidence. Thomas never mentioned that.'

'I'm very sorry about your brother-in-law Edward. You have lost a philosopher as well as a friend. Chris also told me about your wife. I hope you don't mind.' David spoke softly in humble deference to Edward's loss.

Edward raised his eyebrows. 'I guess not. Even Petes seemed to know enough about me.'

'Petes?'

'The chap from the Airforce. All very hush hush. He seems to know about you David. A bit of a mystery really. Disappeared in a flash when we arrived in Delhi. Although he did say we could catch up after the war and do a story on Baghdad. Mind you, I'm not busting my gut to get back there.'

'I see. And Thomas?' David deftly changed the subject.' He seemed to have quite an influence on you.'

'I guess he has - had. It's quite interesting and funny enough; it seems that although Thomas isn't here any longer, the conversation picks up every so often where he left off. As though I am still learning from him even though he is dead.'

'Dead? Well I guess that's one way of putting it. After living here for a while, you in believe all sorts of things. But I suppose that's a bit insensitive of me Edward.'

'Not at all. I have to admit,' Edward opened cautiously, 'I have become more curious about reincarnation and past-lives since meeting Thomas. But that doesn't really explain Hitler and his connection to India.'

'Oh, it's fairly well known Edward. Hitler studied eastern occultism and mythology. He was especially interested in Tibetan esoteric sciences. They're all connected; the Tao, Tantric Buddhism, yoga, Mithraism, the ancient cult of Isis, not to mention the Cabbala, Gnostics and the

Grail Romance. Intricate study. Then you get into the fringe sciences Edward, astrology and the myths of Atlantis. Mind you, most of the people associated with these studies have been persecuted in one way or another. Look at the Parsis right here in India, only a handful of them left! Driven out of Persia by the Muslims. You can't blame the Muslims for everything though.

Even we 'Christians' instigated the so-called *"Holy Inquisition."* That was basically a witch-hunt.' David paused for a moment as if lost in another world. 'The Gnostics carried some of the more secret wisdom handed on through Christ that the rest of us weren't privy to so of course, the 'powers-to-be,' in this case the Church, weren't going to stand for it. If you go into it a bit, there's a connection with the first Templar Knights that protected King Solomon's Temple and the body of wisdom that they held. Through the centuries, the Knights were linked to the original Nazarenes who saw Jesus as a man only, not as a god.'

'You seem to know as much as Thomas David.'

'Oh? Guess it's just a natural interest of mine. You can't help it out here. Surrounded by the stuff as it were. Well these Nazarenes held fast to their belief that Jesus' birth was natural, not 'virgin,' as the Church would have us believe. The Nazarenes also saw the Gospels as unreliable and not the true precepts of Christ. Altogether, they must have appeared nothing short of heretical to the establishment.'

'Nazarenes? Can't say I'm familiar with the term.'

'Not surprising. They are known out here as the 'Nestorian Church.' They broke away from Roman orthodoxy in Persia along with what is now the Egyptian Coptic Church. The Nestorians are a minority but there are links with the Knights Templar and it seems with the Merovingians who claim to be the blood descendants of the House David into which Jesus was born.'

'I didn't know that Jesus had or could have any descendants.' Edward was stunned. 'The Templars have their centre just around the corner from us at *"The Reporter."*

'Oh. Well that is a coincidence. Imagine if Jesus had survived on the Cross then the latter descendants could claim the Throne of David and along with that, the 'right to rule' Europe here and, now Edward.' David paused thoughtfully.

'Dagobert II would presumably have created altogether an entirely different destiny for Europe if that were truly the case. Instead, we have Hitler posturing for the crown with his 'master race' of so-called Aryans and at the same time after the artefacts of Jesus. Actually, Hitler even aligns himself with the *"Order of New Templars"* and dresses himself up in full armour as a *"Grail Knight."*

'And at the same time he thinks that he's Klingsor!' Edward shook his head. 'God knows what is in the man's mind!'

'I don't think I want to know. I thought Nazism was a simple case of economic revival for Germany, *"Plant trees with the Hitler Youth."* Pretty sinister isn't it.' David shook his head in a sideways almost Indian acknowledgment of the seriousness of mixing the occult with politics.

'Hitler undoubtedly sees himself as the *"Messiah"* of Germany, albeit a black Messiah carrying his bloodstained and as such, consecrated swastika. You know Edward those 'nuptial rites of the flags' at his Nuremberg rallies are nothing short of perverse. Sick, absolutely sick. It's as if he is impregnating the youth of Germany with his warped ideologies. I wonder what the Mahatma thinks of him, corrupting India's symbol of wisdom and wealth?' David sounded as incredulous as he felt. 'And along with that, he practices a host of other black magic and pagan rituals. Hitler is in fact, nothing short of an indecent minister with his SS 'priesthood' of Teutonic Knights. Well, he's siring a sick and black society Edward.' David paused for thought. 'Strange thing is that Napoleon defeated the Knights of Malta and until Nelson restored Malta, he also held sway over the ancient traditions. The Knights are even more rigorous in their heritage than Hitler is with his Aryans.' David reached for a glass of water. 'Are you not glad you're in India Edward!'

'I'm not so sure. Not with Annie Besant and bent swastikas. Might as well be Europe!'

'Don't worry. He can't get you over here. This lot are pretty mild by comparison. They simply perform their morning ablutions followed by innocent rituals in the temples and I haven't seen any of them waving black swastikas over India. At least I hope not.'

'I hope you're right David. I heard Congress has attracted some fundamentalists. Who knows what Independence will spawn.'

'You're not wrong there. But do you want to hear the rest of the story about the Nazarenes?'

'I suppose I do. It has to fit in somewhere.'

'I am sure the gaps will be filled in for you Edward. What with your brother-in- law hovering above you.' David's eyes lit up with amusement.

Edward laughed. 'I haven't much choice then have I!'

David chuckled. 'There is a link with India. Jesus's brother is believed to have taught Nazarene beliefs in a few places including Persia, Turkey and India. Essentially, it's a monastic tradition so it would fit well into a place such as India with its heritage of yogis, ascetics and Saints. He could easily hide himself away and be unnoticed as a Nazarene and the yogis would undoubtedly accept him.'

'You're not a closet Knight Templar are you David?' Edward could not resist.

'No, nor a Freemason. I'm simply a humble clerk, remember?'

'Of course.'

David continued, 'As well as the swastika, the Nazis use the double 'lightning' rune which was a 'sig' or power rune, used by ancient Germanic tribes to represent Thor and Donar. Makes your blood curdle Edward. Perverse and dangerous people. Nevertheless, you have to wonder about us also. Churchill would make a perfect *"Grail Knight"* himself, don't you think? He looks fit to enter any chivalrous order. By the way, did you know that the Maltese Cross fell off King George's coffin?'

'No, I didn't.'

'Pretty spooky. Rather like a bad omen. Especially with King Edward abdicating. Leaves England in a vulnerable position. It weakens our position over here too of course. The British crown is seen no longer to be immortal and indestructible. We are very much as mortal and vulnerable as everyone else. King George was a good man. Gandhi dropped in on him for tea!'

'Yes I know. Thomas met Gandhi at Oxford. He often used to talk about the impact Gandhi had on his Professor Thompson. *"Not since Socrates has the world seen his equal for absolute self-control and composure,"* if I remember rightly.'

'Very Oxfordian Edward. Speaking of which, would you like some tea?'

'Yes, I would, very much thank you.'

'Chai or English tea?' David pre-empted his request, smiling as if the answer contained some ageless wonder of India.

'Chai will do nicely.'

'Shanti, Shanti.' David almost sang the words. 'Do chai dunyavaad.'

'You speak Hindi?' Edward deferred.

'No, not really. You do learn a few words and phrases here and there. So long as you can say *"namaste"* and *"dunyavaad,"* you will get by.'

'"*Dunyavaad?*"'

'Thank you.' 'Oh, I see.'

'But don't worry. If you like, I'll set you up with a guide to do all the translating and take care of the money side of things.'

'Dunyavaad.' The two men laughed.

'Well then Edward, where were we?' 'The mortality of the British Crown.'

'Yes, very much under threat and not just by the Nazis. You know the story of the Kohinoor diamond, the *"Mountain of Light"* - now part of the Crown jewels as it happens.'

'The annexing of the Punjab to British India and Dhuleep Singh's abdication to England?' Edward offered.

'Yes, sad isn't it. Well the Kohinoor is something of a *"Spear of Destiny"* for the Indians. Probably more authentic than the Spear that they dug up, and a good deal older! It originated from Africa. Magnificent piece of work. It's one of the largest and most beautiful diamonds in the world. In any case, the Kohinoor came into the hands of one King of Malwa who was besieged by the Sultan of Delhi, around

AD13 I think. At that time, Delhi was administered by Qutab-ud-Din Aybak. He's the fellow that built the famous tower *"Qutab Mnar."* You'll have to visit it.' David reached for his pipe, idling on a mahogany side-table.

'Delhi's hardly recognisable now,' he continued. 'It's been rebuilt four or five times by the Muslims until it was finally moved to the ancient site of Indraprastha. That's precisely where we are now.' David struck the match to the tobacco and sucked deeply on his pipe. 'Indraprastha is the ancient city of the Pandavs in the *"Mahabharatha."* 'He paused for effect, blowing a plume of blue smoke towards the ceiling. The fan caught the plume and buffeted it for a few seconds before expanding and descending the smoke into the room once again. 'Thomas must have told you something about the epic. From the Gita?' David prompted.

'A little, but it hasn't all sunk in yet.'

'No doubt. The significance is that the Kohinoor passed from Hindu to Muslim hands and stayed with the Moghul emperors until in 1813 when it came into the possession of a Sikh, Ranjit Singh, the so-called *"Lion of Punjab."* By that time, the British East India Company had well and truly, overplayed its hand with the Moghul rulers. All they had left was a monopoly over China Trade, mostly in tea. The Company's charter was up for renewal and the monopoly of London-Indian trade was finally broken. The challenge came from the British manufacturing industries.'

Shanti walked in with the tea.

'Ah, there you are. Right on cue-but this time, Indian tea and not tea from China! Dunyavaad Shanti. Chai chayiee?'

'Nay, nay.' Shanti backed quickly out of the room. David smiled.

'What did you say?'

'Asked her if she'd like a cup of tea.'

Edward looked embarrassed.

'I like to do that sort of thing. Totally against the rules of course. Not supposed to treat any Indian like us and especially one from a lower caste such as Shanti.' Edward looked at David with growing amazement.

'Nothing wrong with it. I don't go along with all this caste stuff. It has its place, but when that means that you have to hurt someone's feelings or offend their dignity, then I make sure that I do the opposite. A bit tricky at times though. You have to be careful you don't give them the impression that they can put it all over you.'

'I see.' Edward felt confused.

Shanti returned with steaming bowls of dahl, a large dish of vegetable curry then returned with a plate stacked with an assortment of pooris and rotis along with what appeared to be stainless steel savoury plates. She expertly placed her commission on the table between David and Edward.

'Thank you Shanti. We'll eat in a minute. Leave it here for now,' he instructed her in English.

Edward looked hungrily at the food.

'You want to eat now?' David slapped his thigh.' Good. Well, tuck in. Be careful with the curry if you're not used to it. Just take little bits with a wedge of roti, like this.' He spooned several helpings of curry into a compartment on his plate then tore off a small piece of the flat bread before cornering some curry and rice and popping it into his mouth. 'Mmm. Tastes good. Try some.'

Edward scooped the curry into a similar compartment on his plate, using the pieces of chapatti to spoon it into his mouth.

David grinned. 'Better than English stew. Here, try the dahl. It's best with a dollop of yoghurt. Well. Let's see now. The British East India Company came to a sorry and inglorious end. It was pressure from the Lancashire *"cotton kings."* Cotton once again! In any case, they wanted a share of the action and couldn't sell their goods in India. Manchester was demanding full employment so the Company could no longer protect the traditional Bengali weavers. Much like that beautiful cover on the couch.' David pointed to a coarse, brightly woven cloth. 'The Company had had a 213 year monopoly and that, in the opinion of the British industrialists, had to end. At least they managed to preserve the tea trade with China for the next 2 years. It was worth 3 million pounds per annum and that represented almost one tenth of England's total revenue.

About the same time, our Raffles of Singaporean fame opened free trade with opium. Indian opium. There you have it Edward.' David reached for some dahl. 'Opium was the largest commercial British export to China. Opium. The seeds of Hong Kong were the opium poppy. Just as Bombay and Calcutta were founded on British greed, so too was Hong Kong.'

Edward looked at his plate. There were little piles of curry, rice, dollops of yoghurt and wedges of chapatti torn and stuffed under the rice.

'The Company always had its, fighting ships, but it was the pirates who finally propelled the Raj along its current militaristic lines.' David seemed for a few minutes, more interested in his curry than talking.

Edward observed him closely, watching the impeccable manners yet easy grace of the man. He neither took too much, food nor ate, too sparingly, clearly enjoying every mouthful, as if blessed for his consumption.

'So much for merchant beginnings. In any case Edward, when Lord Auckland was Governor General of India, he was accompanied by a lady called Emily, who boldly sketched in the Kohinoor onto her painting of Queen Victoria. Perhaps it was a prophecy. Dalhousie was next in line for the Governor Generalship and as such, he annexed the Punjab to British India. That is where all the trouble with Colonel Dyer started and now Sir Michael's murder. Part of Dalhousie's deal with the Maharaja was that the Kohinoor Diamond be presented to Queen Victoria as a gesture of goodwill. It came into the hands of John Laurence, who thought nothing of it until Victoria demanded it from him. The British, love their luckless souls, cut it in two, and then from 187 glorious carats into barely 19. Now part of it's in the British crown jewels.' David paused, silently swirling pools of thought into his chai. 'By this time your Dhuleep Sing, the real heir to the Punjab, moved to England and later supported Britain over the 1857 Mutiny. How easily India's soul was stolen!' David sighed and leaned back against the elegant curve of the sofa.

'Perhaps I should have brought the Kohinoor with me as a gesture of goodwill.'

Edward said wistfully.

'I am not sure that it would make that much difference now Edward. The Indian's are in no mood for parleying with us I'm afraid. But if you could convince the 'King Emperor' that India needs her wealth for herself and not for the war effort, then that would be another thing altogether.'

'I'll do my best but I don't fancy my chances.'

'The Indians are magnificent fighters. Couldn't have done without them in Africa.'

'And the Caliph?'

'Turkey? Can't really blame Jinnah then, can we. Even that part of his personal ambition fired by Nehru's insults.' David added as an afterthought.

'Have you met them?'

'Nehru yes. Jinnah keeps himself to himself. Always has. Hid away in England for the most part, but they all come out of the woodwork when the pickings are ripe.'

'You sound cynical David.'

'I'm not. I'm realistic. Even the Aga Khan was a part of the plan for the "*Federation of Princely States*" and to boot, he's supporting Hitler and his grab for the British Crown!'

'We can't get away from Hitler then.'

'Not even at the League of Nations. And all the while, we are as divisive as the worst of our own enemies, playing on religious sentiments and caste distinctions to keep India in pieces.'

'You believe in religion David?'

David laughed. 'I didn't say I did.' He pushed his plate away with his free hand, the cup of chai in the other.' Churchill has the power to wreak more havoc than the 1857 mutiny. Gandhi represents everything that he despises. He is anti-Empire, anti-Monarchy, unpretentious, simple and probably insolent. Gandhi is fighting a lone war. So many of them advocate violence - Bose, Azad and Nehru. In addition, we know it. We'll use the existing divisions in India to drive wedges into the peace process. Extraordinary though how Gandhi's war is primarily a religious war, fighting for the 'truth' as he sees it. But that's quite different to the occultism we were talking about.'

'You sound defensive of the old man David.' Edward took a shot.

David smiled humbly.' The spinning wheel is Gandhi's symbol, not the swastika. Over here Edward, symbols are a part of daily religious life in one form or another. Amazing how the corruption of the wheel means something else entirely.' David sipped the chai.' Nothing as good as Indian cooking. The Indians take their religious symbols quite literally. You have to be careful not to offend their feelings Edward. Well, there's plenty of evidence for that already isn't there!' David finished.

'I'll be careful not to wave any swastikas whilst I'm here.'

'The Buddhists use it. Symbolises the footprints of the Buddha.'

'"*Siddhartha*" you mean?'

'You've read it?'

'Reading it more like it. That's the one I did pick up at the bookshop. A bit lighter than the Gita and definitely not as dark and mysterious as the Secret Doctrine.' Edward smiled mischievously.

'You're an enigma Edward. Really, I thought you were the mild journalist on a holiday in the east. Mind if I have a look?'

'It's in my bag. I'll haul it out after dinner.'

'Thanks. I like Hesse. When I can get my hands on him.'

'I have another one of his with me. Would you like it?'

'Thanks. I wouldn't mind.' 'You were saying David?'

'Oh, about the Buddhists? Yes, they took the swastika to China and Japan. It's a pretty ancient symbol really. Thor used it on his hammer. The swastika is on all sorts of archaeological artefacts, including those of the American Indians and the Mayas of Mexico. You'll find it on mourning ceramics of the Greeks and also in early Christian and Byzantine art. Believe it or not, it was even a sacred symbol of the Jews! Actually, I think it was Guido Von List, who suggested it be used as a symbol for anti-Semitism. That's how the National Socialist Party in Germany came to appropriate it around 1919 along with the adulterated Protocols of Zion as an anti-Semitic weapon. The same year, as your Amritsar massacre.'

'Nineteen nineteen? Not a good year then.'

'Not a good year. We British were doing in India what the rest of the world was trying to recover from. Unbelievable really. Dyer was virtually acquitted in England and nobody except the young Sikh has ever held O'Dwyer accountable. Natural form of justice I expect. Dyer thought that Gandhi wanted to cause a revolution so they introduced the Rowlatt Act especially to nail him. It was nothing short of suppression of human rights. Murder really. Well, now we've got Eckart and Hitler cooking up racial genocide for Europe and Britain has already condoned - or turned a blind eye to - her own actions. Perhaps Gandhi was wise in choosing the spinning wheel rather than the swastika. So much for art Edward! Do you like Hitler's version?'

'No I don't. Do you?'

'Hardly. Now that he's got the Spear of Longinus as well, who knows the fate of religion in the world.' David threw his hands into the air. 'Napoleon was the last person to have had the Spear in his personal possession. Nostradamus called him the *"First Anti Christ"* and it looks as though Hitler will be the next with his new religion of black magic and paganism. That is, if all the stories about the Spear are true! No doubt the Spear's reputation is more potent than the Spear itself. Did you hear that Charlemagne was possessed the spear?'

'No I didn't.'

'Perhaps Charlemagne imbued his own power into the Spear.' David grinne mischievously. 'This may be nothing more than a *"holy war"* that some other force has roped us all into. The real worry of course Edward, is that our chaps were duped into thinking that a Hitler-Mussolini alliance would be a good thing for Europe, *"to control the spread of Bolshevism."*

'I see your point.' Edward was thoughtful. 'How is it that you're so up with all of this David, and living as you are so far away from the heat of the action as it were?'

'You're not wrong there Edward. That the cables come and go from London and India is important to the war effort, so one way or another, we are privy to information that you blokes might not always have access to. Besides, there's a bit of the mystic in me.' The smile flashed back onto David's face.

'Looks as though Thomas is following you around too. On the other count, I thought Chris had a pretty good line to the top?' Edward said dryly.

'He's well trusted around the traps.' David remarked colourlessly.

'So when do I get to meet Gandhi?' Edward found it hard to suppress his curiosity.

'Yes Edward, we are indeed here and now in India!'

'I can't help but be fascinated by the man. And as you say David, he's fighting a different war.'

'Oh, don't get me wrong. Issues of freedom are on the agenda, not just Gandhi's love for the Old Man and compulsion for religious unity. Although he does dress the Independence issues in the convenient cloth of *"Truth"* and *"Non-Violence."*'

'But already there's been so much violence surrounding Gandhi.'

'That is so Edward, but let's not judge prematurely shall we. Gandhi would see it himself as more of a *"purging,"* a holy purification if you will. Besides, he is the ultimate disciplinarian and discipline is needed with the current political climate of this country. As I said, wait and see. When you meet him, you will form your own views.' David was emphatic.

'OK. I must admit I feel a bit of trepidation. Maybe he'll see me as yet another British interloper on the precious soil of India.'

'No doubt, you will feel so. Gandhi likes the British. He has no axe to grind apart from *"leave India."*'

'And I've just arrived.' Edward laughed.

David joined in. 'We'll make you feel welcome whatever it takes. The evenings here are lovely. Feel like a short walk to shake off your stiffness?'

'Thanks. I would. I haven't travelled with the RAF before. Good chaps though.'

'Petes' looked after me pretty well.'

David looked into the remnants of his tea.

'Anything wrong?'

'Tell you one day. But for now, let's go for that walk.'

The two men left their makeshift dining table and strolled into the soft Indian evening. The crows were already circling above the rooftops, alerted to the opportunities of the dusk.

'It's not like Bombay.' David noted Edward's mild alarm at the crows. 'The Parsis leave out their dead for the crows to pick off the flesh. Part of the religion. Mind you, makes a lot of sense when you see the crematorium and burial grounds. Most of it seems to go into the rivers on funeral pyres. Pretty basic by our standards, but then, it could also be a good deal cleaner. Leaving nothing behind I mean.'

'Oh, I see. Have you been to a funeral here?'

'Observed one from a distance. Lots of wailing and carrying on. They really do it in style with the sandalwood incense, garlands of flowers, priests, the works. The pyres are impressive. I think though, that the sandalwood is to protect the departing soul as well as cover the aromas as it were.'

Edward was silent. Odd land, yet strangely beautiful. How Thomas would have enjoyed the ceremonies and rituals in his boyish, enthusiastic way.

'Thomas was buried at Oxford?' David enquired innocently.

'Yes. The funeral service was quite extraordinary. It was as if there was a spiritual feeling in the atmosphere. Ruth looked positively glowing. It was special.'

'Funerals can do that to you. Here? It is almost eerie, as if you can feel the soul watching its own funeral. Perhaps it does.'

They reached the gates of the compound, David leading the way into the widening streets. It was quieter than the morning rush through the crowds and busy activities of daily life. Women in soft saris sauntered past with children scampering behind and playing with bits of tin and wire. The smells of cooking and the lilting sounds of banjans filtered from nearby homes, taking the harsh and brutal edge, off the reality of poverty and death. There were few men on the street, except for the occasional rickshaw and peddler hoping to lure a few extra rupees from the stupor of dusk.

'It's rather wonderful Edward don't you think? Such a gentleness in these people. Their home life is important and although they aren't nearly as advanced materially as England or USA, many of them are just as intelligent and refined; more so really. Most of the chores are still done by hand. It gives the place a more measured and rhythmic flow.

Much like a cow turning a mill or a waterwheel feeding the crops.'
'You sound very lyrical David. Has this place got into your bones?'

'No.' David was quick to reply. 'I like it. That's all. Look, try one of these.' David pulled out a couple of annas and purchased two green coconuts from a vendor. The vendor slashed the tops with a machete-like knife and motioned them to drink. Then he took the husks and scooped out the soft meat with a broad-blade curved knife. The flesh resembled raw strips of salmon in texture, only creamy white and subtle to the palate.

'Do you like it?'

'Yes. It's quite different, fresh.'

'I'll arrange for your currency tomorrow Edward, then you'll be free of me and able to experiment a bit as you move around.'

'No hurry. The service is pretty good.' Edward shot his host and companion a grateful grin.

'Good for you. Enjoy while you can. You'll have to keep your wits about you as you head into the Punjab. Not that they're any different to people in Delhi, but you'll be on your own there. So, watch what I do for now. You'll get the hang of it. There's plenty of poverty here Edward, no doubt about it, but don't get caught up in personal crusades.'

'That's Gandhi's basket no doubt.'

'His revolution is very deep. Gandhi would like to see the whole of India spinning to restore cottage industries for villagers. He demands all members of Congress wear *Khadi*.'

'I like the feel of homespun.' Edward offered. 'It's much softer than our cloth.'

'That it is. In fact, Gandhi won't allow Congress to wear machine made cloth, even if it has been made in India.'

'Adamant?'

'You'd better believe it. That's not all. He insists that all castes take part in cleaning the latrines.' David grinned at the memory. 'He also allows the untouchables into his ashram in Ahmedabad. That caused quite a stir let me tell you. He carries his beliefs through to women. Gandhi would have all women out of purdah if he could and of course, abolish child marriage and "*sati*."'

'Sati?'

'Bride burning. Edward, this country is very different to England.' David touched his arm. 'Here, there is absolutely, no form of social welfare. Families depend upon themselves to survive. So if the man of the house dies for some reason, who is going to support the widow? She is just another mouth to feed. With no income, if there is no cottage industry from which she can earn a few rupees to buy her flour and oil, then how will she eat? It has become a sort of religious ritual where the widow is expected to hurl herself onto her husband's funeral pyre.'

'That's simply barbaric!' Edward was beside himself.

'Happens all the time. Even if it is outlawed, there is enormous pressure on the widow to commit. Gandhi wants to stop all that.'

'I see. What's his view on the war?'

'Gandhi blames Hitler but I don't see that he sees the link between social suppression in Germany and the rise of Nazism. Gandhi's a socialist at heart but his model of reform is self-cleansing, not racial cleansing.'

'A bit austere?'

'Very definitely Edward. That's Gandhi's style. He's moralistic and at least he has the grace to extend some of his moral fibre to support Britain in principle. But he won't raise the army or police to defend the country, not even to suppress religious rioters - Hindu-Muslim rioters.'

'And that's "*complete non-violence?*"'

'So Gandhi thinks. A sort of obstinance that old men allow themselves if you ask me. On the other hand, Congress is ready to support Britain in the war, more than likely because of the chances of early Independence.'

'And Gandhi?'

'Won't have a bar of it. He's adamant that India's Independence is a totally separate issue to the war effort.'

'What if the Japanese cross into India from Burma, or the Chinese for that matter?'

'See it this way Edward. Gandhi understands power. He wields enormous power, but he won't use it unless absolutely necessary. Any show of power is violence in Gandhi's view. Therefore, he would not ever persuade India to rise to her own defence other than to set an example of moral poority. He is a fanatacist in his own way.'

'You mean fasting?'

'More powerful than guns, mightier than the sword and even swifter than the pen in reaching people.' David looked into the sky.

'The crows are coming lower. Maybe they can smell the curry in our pores.'

'Charming. They wouldn't attack people would they?' Edward was slightly unnerved.

'Not unless you're already on the heap old fellow. Still, it's a practical solution in a land like this.'

'No room for sensitivity and niceties.' Edward lifted his eyebrows.

'They only make matters worse Edward. Look at us with all our British manners. At the end of the day, we are as bad as the average man, only perhaps a little more unscrupulous.'

'Then you think we could never be the measure of the man that Gandhi is.'

'Don't get me wrong Ed. There's nothing wrong with most of us. Take the Viceroy for example, good chap, but too loyal to the King to understand India and Gandhi.'

'Have you told him what you think.' Edward laughed.

'What, me?' David's amusement spread into his eyes. 'He'd have me for the crows if I did.'

'You think they've already got the scent David?'

'The crows or the Viceroy?'

'The Raj.' Edward sobered.

'I wouldn't be surprised if they do. I must say I won't be sorry when all this business is finished.'

'You sound bitter.' Edward said mildly.

'No, but I'm in love with an Indian woman.'

'Oh. Well that's bound to create a division of loyalties.'

'Not really. I have no qualms about where my personal life ends and professional life begins. And besides, I like Gandhi.'

'Think you can follow his morals? I thought he practised abstinence.' It was Edward's turn to be amused.

'That's not the point really. Gandhi doesn't expect others to follow him. In any case, he has stepped away from Congress. Gandhi is leading his own crusade of spiritual, social and moral unity for India through his own sheer willpower and stubbornness. It's about some obscure *"Ramraj"* and nothing to do with the mundane politics of Congress. And nobody can dissuade Gandhi when he decides that he will fast.'

'"*Unto the death!*" Who's leading the way with Congress then?'

'A literal fight unto death it seems, between Jinnah, Bose and Nehru. David became quiet.

'Do they listen to Gandhi?'

'Perhaps.'

'They aren't loyal to him?'

'You sound like a reporter.' David slapped him on the back. 'To be fair, no. The answer is no they aren't and Gandhi wouldn't expect it either. He is a bit like a father with sons quarrelling over the inheritance. Besides, his standards are far too high. Moral pooritan. Of all of them, Nehru seems to be the one most deeply influenced by the old man. Gandhi's very much his father-mentor.

'What about Jinnah?'

'Like it or not, Jinnah's loyalties are firmly Muslim identity and nationhood.'

'Jinnah is not a Gandhian then.'

'Jinnah was affronted by Nehru and so I wouldn't be surprised if his actions aren't partly fuelled by competitive hatreds so he would hardly side with the ally of his enemy.'

'Good God. Nothing sacred in the liberation movement.'

'Nothing. Well, come on then. We'd best be getting back. It's getting late. Keep the crows wondering shall we.' David turned them back.

'You were right David. The walk has done me the world of good and I feel quite safe with you.'

'Good. I know my way around here and people get to know you too. They're not all bad, but neither are we, just different.'

They fell into step, passing the vendor's cart now obscured by the fading light.

'Your quarters are very comfortable David.' Edward opened.

'You like the cottage?' David was pleased.

'Very much.'

'Good. Then stay a bit longer.'

'Thanks for the offer. Did you say that Gandhi is around?'

'He is and he isn't. I'll track him down for you.' David was pleased that he had Edward's company and conversation. It was refreshing to discuss his thoughts with someone equally intelligent and thankfully, not stuffy like most of the British he met on a day-to-day basis in India. He could give Edward no guarantees about Gandhi, but he would try. If Gandhi were in a mood for fasting and solitude or was simply being obstinate, then that was that. If there were prayer meetings, at least Edward could attend and see the other side of Gandhi. Perhaps they could go together. It would be a welcome change from his normal routine.

It was not to be. Gandhi was 'temporarily indisposed' and David suspected he was testing Edward's willingness to step into Gandhi's world to meet him on his own ground. Then Gandhi could also wait. Maybe it was better for Edward to see a bit more of India first-hand. Then he would appreciate the man in a different light. It was a bit awkward for him coming straight from London and with no sense of the people and their problems. Perhaps that's what Gandhi was after when he enquired about Edward's plans. Test the real mettle of the man - that was Gandhi's style for sure.

David broke the news gently to Edward. 'Edward, it's probably the right thing at this stage. Once you've been to Amritsar, you'll see India differently. You'll get a much stronger sense of the Sikh, Muslim and Hindu identity of the country and see for yourself where Britain fits in. Our oppression of the Indian is not so visible here, but you won't miss it at Jallianwala Bagh. See the evidence for yourself first-hand.'

'I'm sure you're right David. I do want to see India through India's eyes. Maybe Gandhi will warm to me once I've rubbed off a bit of my *"civilised veneer."*

David chuckled. 'I'm sure he'll like you whether you have or not. You're not frightened of him are you?'

'He leaves me a bit in awe I must admit.'

'Don't let it sway you. He's every bit a man just as you or I.'

Edward kept his own peace. He would form his impressions later on his return.

Chapter Twenty Four

THE TOUCHDOWN ONTO the dusty piece of ground at Amritsar that served as an airfield was an awakening. Edward felt more at peace with the vast and chaotic land that had invaded his senses and psyche than he ever had in Britain. Nevertheless, he entered the Punjab with a sense of trepidation and caution. The British were not popular in India, especially now that Britain was deliberately stalling the process of Independence. Twenty two years after the atrocities at Amritsar, the memories were as fresh as if Colonel Dyer had stepped onto the *bagh* and opened fire on thousands of defenceless citizens. Now, the mere sight of an *Angrezi*, an Englishman, was more than enough to stir emotions. Edward understood this much at least. Oppression and murder were neither noble nor honourable and from oppression came Gandhi's renunciation of wealth and the conjugating of himself and his people to poverty - to free India from Britain. There was nothing in Edward's opinion, noble about poverty.

Gandhi was able to sustain the appearance of a life of poverty yet in reality it was a far cry from the desperate and dehumanising impact of endless days with scant food and precious little fuel for cooking and heating. On top of that, the Indian people continued to endure marginal accesses to polluted village streams or wells that provided the essentials for washing, drinking and sanitation.

Edward was aware from the war reports, how the human will was severely sapped when the body was undernourished and how fatally morale fell when the essentials of human dignity were stripped bare. How could it be possible for poor people to mete out an existence, let alone produce extra for the markets when their less-than-subsistence life did not even afford them the status of animals? The grinding pain of toil accumulated over the centuries and the burden of population and poverty exaggerated the pain of a continent broken, then destroyed by foreign greed.

From the tired fields, the dust swirled in untiring eddies of emptiness and fruitlessness. India, was a land with a humbled and dying soul. The rural communities of India fared badly under the Rajas; they did no better under the Moghuls and continued to suffer under the British. What could Gandhi do? In all likelihood, the landowners would seize power and opportunity to entrench their advantage, driving the poor deeper into debt and despair. Gandhi had at least, the noble ambition to free the rural millions from the yoke of suppression; no matter the guise of their masters and overlords. Gandhi wanted a vast network of cottage industries throughout India, he wanted to restore and rebuild village life, to equip them with clean drinking water, adequate sanitation and infuse their people with pride and independence. His vision of an Indian *"Shangri-La"* was a sophisticated and culturally sensitive version of Tolstoy's vision for self-sufficiency. *"Clean up India"* was closer to Gandhi's heart than any Hindu, Muslim or Sikh sentiment. But that meant he had to address the ultimate failings of the human spirit and start within himself, the mammoth Mahabharata, the unlimited battle of the self over the self, the conquering of the maya, the expunging of the weaknesses and impurities within.

Edward began to gain his first glimpse into the massive battle being played out in the Indian heart and soul.

Amritsar was a case in point.

The British, eager to control and discipline the emerging Independence movement sweeping across India, created and almost instantly enforced a punishing piece of legislation that was aimed squarely at 'sedition.' Less than a month after the cunningly contrived martial law, the *"Rowlatt Act"* was signed, the English Colonel Dyer, launched his unilateral attack on unwitting Indians, gathered as they were to celebrate a Sikh religious festival and at the same time, protest against the arrest and removal of two political leaders from the Punjab. Innocent, non-violent and harmless, the primarily Sikh celebration that welcomed the presence of all religions into its midst, was for Dyer, a symbol of insolence, rebellion, sedition.

Furious at the growing influence of Gandhi and his power to mobilise vast numbers of people to the cause of Independence, Dyer acted swiftly and decisively to curb and incarcerate the Indian spirit of through bullying, bloodshed and intimidation. To add insult to great injury, Dyer then enforced his own special form of humiliation, *"The Crawling Order"* where, local residents were forced to crawl on their bellies through human excrement and dirt past the point of a crowd attack on a British woman, the missionary Miss Marcella Sherwood, who was beaten with fists and sticks in a range of India against England after the slaughter of innocent citizens riling against the removal of their liberties.

Miss Sherwood survived the attack, rescued by Hindu residents and returned to England, her honour intact, India's soul then brutalised by the *"Black Act"* as they called the Rowlatt Act, Dyer attempted to contain self-determination, Independence and the freedom of every Indian from dominance by their English overlords.

At Amritsar on that day, Sikhs, Muslims and Hindus suffered a collective, and murderous fate. Colonel Dyer's brutal punishment of the Indian community irrecoverably scarred the soul of India. Closing off the only exit from the sunken ground that served as a gathering point for the predominantly Sikh Indian community, Dyer meted out personal revenge upon the rebellious Indian souls determined to shake off British brutality as much as they wanted their freedom from British rule.

Defiantly assembling in their thousands in the face of martial law, the residents of Amritsar and surrounding villages gathered to vote on a series of resolutions to restore their liberty, to free their leaders from incarceration and to object to the needless slaughter of innocent people.

Colonel Dyer had another idea altogether. At 5.15 pm when the meeting was almost at its conclusion and the tens of thousands of people gathered together had the least idea of his intentions, Dyer order his fifty Indian troops to open fire on the crowd. There was absolutely no warning to anyone to disperse and leave the compound.

Sixteen hundred and fifty rounds of ammunition later, almost four hundred lives were directly lost to the shooting, and another thousand lost to from the panicked stampede as the crowd desperately tried to escape the bullets or from injuries sustained during the massacre; people left wounded and bleeding overnight because of Dyer's curfew. And amongst the people of Amritsar not caught up in the dying was a single young man, Udham Singh who witnessed an event that would change India forever.

At his trial, Dyer unwittingly admitted to planning an armoured car attack. Only that the opening into Jallianwalbagh was too narrow, were more lives not taken by the cold brutality that masqueraded as 'order.'

The atrocities of Amritsar gouged a lasting well of abhorrence into the heart of India. The British were not gentlemen; they were barbarians hiding beneath polished manners and boots. Behind the *"Black Act"* was the unmistakable and sinister note of racism, the suppression of human rights, importantly, the right to gather and the right to object. And object Gandhi did. For Gandhi, the massacre at Amritsar was the final spur into determined action to shake loose the British bonds that bound India to servitude.

Gandhi's response was the true launching of the *"Satyagraha"* movement, the conscious statement of non-violent opposition to British Rule. Within months, Gandhi proved his charismatic influence over the Indian population, gathering hundreds and thousands of people to protest against the British in India.

Chapter Twenty Five

EDWARD FELT GUILTY and uncomfortable on his arrival in Amritsar. He was acutely conscious that he was an impostor, another British 'intruder' on this timeless land. No matter how many excuses he made to himself that he was a 'journalist reporting' on an incident of some 21 years ago, the harsh reality of the unresolved crime jarred on his conscience and clouded his journalistic senses. It would be easier to merge into the dusty Indian plains, unnoticed in this land than be visible as the "*Angreezi* "reporter that he was.

He pulled his hat forward to rest on the edge of his forehead. He felt safer that way; hidden, unobtrusive, unknown. Edward had already decided to be discreet, yet behind his caution, was an unexpected fear of meeting the victims of Dyer's death trap; of facing and confronting eye to eye their relatives, friends, descendants. He imagined pretending innocence; a Britisher 'holidaying on the subcontinent' rather than be for the people of Amritsar, a vicarious memory, a reminder of past atrocities, a hot knife searing an ever-open wound.

There could be however, no hiding the memories soaked into the soil of the Punjab or the stories imbued into infinite particles of dust swirling across the physical and psychological landscape.

April 13th became a day of national mourning for all of India and, here he was so soon after the murder of General O'Dwyer, so close to the anniversary of the brutal acts of Colonel Dyer. Originally intended as a day of Hindu-Muslim unity, "*Baishki Day*" was now the day to commemorate the oppression of millions of Indians by the British. It was the day that Gandhi used as his springboard for the free India campaign, the day that signified more potently than any other in India's rich spiritual calendar, that freedom and self-determination was the foundation of self respect. It was ultimately only self-respect that would remove the barriers of race, religion and caste and unite all Indians as Gandhi had always wanted.

"*D-Day*" for India was close at hand and Edward felt like a lone reed breaking in the torrential monsoons of bitter torment. It took less than a flicker to spark an explosion of passion in India. News moved as rapidly as currents in the ether, unbounded and unhindered by time and space. The natural daily intercourse of culture and commerce assured that sentiments would rise and fall in a matter of moments or hours. India was predominantly a social continent, a vastly interconnected network of religion, caste and creed.

Edward knew that could not escape notice, not here, not in India. He felt a dozen pairs of curious eyes assessing and following him as he cautiously alighted from the plane, watchful and mindful of the proximity and protective shield of the car. David insisted that he go 'straight in and straight out' to the compound, to avoid being inadvertently entangled in preparations for the anniversary celebrations. He also knew that his curiosity would inevitably draw him to the heartland of the Sikh community, the Golden Temple but for now, to the compound, Jallianwalbagh.

The car was the frontier for his flight from national hatreds. Edward stepped quickly and carefully towards the open door feeling every second as if on a knife's edge. The air was hot, still and suffocating. India in March was a tin-shed climate with rising temperatures constantly infusing will-sapping heat into the atmosphere. There was no relief except the promise of the cooler and distant hills. On the plains, the dust would not settle and without rain, it gritted into the margins of doorways, windows and of sanity. He grimaced inwardly.

India was well and truly telling on his meagre reserves of tolerance. As well as the physical climate, the shift of social norms, the lack of gentility to which he had become accustomed and predictable behaviours, robbed him of his sense of security and safety. The culture of India was complex and subtle with vastly deeper layers and far more intricate rules than he could fathom. As much as he would try, he understood that the ground would shift beneath his feet as imperceptibly and defiantly as Gandhi faced the 'Raj' and shot his arrow of 'self-rule' into the pupil of British beliefs. Nothing - could hide the air of bitter resentment that dropped like the final curtain on the lingering act of the Empire. It was not yet over and the air hung heavy and hostile over this airfield also.

The driver waited in quiet acquiescence and, at the command, darted towards him, grabbed his luggage and hoisted it into the very English car boot. He then ran at the double to close Edward's door behind him and stood to attention as Edward positioned himself in a semblance of comfort and respectability before running to the driver's side and turning the engine. At the command *"Cello, cello"* the car sped from the formality of the airfield towards the dishevelled edges of Amritsar.

'Punjab. This is where it all started. David briefed you I imagine?'

'Yes he did thank you. My name is Edward, Edward Thompson.'

'Robin. Robin Allen.' Robin stretched a hand over the front seat and for the first time, Edward was able to catch a glimpse of a slightly ginger moustache sitting deftly atop a softly smiling and upturned mouth.

'It's wonderful to be met.' Edward was genuinely grateful.

'That's all right old chap. Do the same for anyone really. Not much fun in these parts. Since Gandhi started to stir up the disobedience campaigns and *"hartals,"* there isn't much joy in being British. Class us all in the same boat if you will.'

'Yes, I expect that would be the case. Feels fairly tense here, not like Delhi. Delhi was completely chaotic, but this is different, as if there is a brooding feeling in the air.' Edward looked to Robin for an explanation.

'To be expected I suppose. Look out!' Robin grabbed the driver's shoulder as he narrowly missed a small group of school children neatly dressed in pinafore blues.

'Damned stupid these drivers. Can't teach them a thing. Where were we? Oh yes, the tension. Well, it's not long until the anniversary celebrations. Always a difficult time. We keep a low profile and let them get on with it.'

'It's that bad?'

'Oh yes. There's no doubt about it, passions rise to the surface and if you're unlucky enough to be British, then expect to cop your fair share of insults. We are careful though, not to antagonise them.'

'You must have heard about O'Dwyer's murder?'

'Everyone did. Created quite a riot. Not a literal riot, but since a bit of British blood was shed for a change, it makes revenge seem sweet.'

'Hope everyone here is all right.'

'There isn't a problem directly, but you don't know old chap, when things can flare up, especially in the next few weeks. We British are the only people who think that Dyer did the right thing. Totally different view over here.'

'It must leave you feeling quite edgy.'

'At times. I thought you might want to go straight to Jallianwal Bagh. Have a look for yourself. Did you bring a camera?'

'Yes I did. Does your driver mind?'

'He gets a few rupees for the trouble so I'm sure he won't think too much about it.'

They swung into a narrow lane. The driver struggled with the wheel for a few seconds then pulled the car to an abrupt halt.

'Here we are. Let's have a look inside then shall we.' Robin briskly opened the door and stepped quickly outside into the lane and walked towards the compound.

'Righto. Thank you. Dunyavaad.' Edward decided to be polite to the driver and nodded briefly, touching his dust-caked hat and followed Robin into the blinding afternoon light.

Robin quietly lead Edward from the car parked at the end of the compound towards the opening where Colonel Dyer had once stood with his troops and opened fire on tens of thousands of innocents.

Edward followed dutifully, counting the steps as if each one was a painful journey into a past he did not really want to think about. He pulled the hat further over his eyes to protect himself from the cow dung fire smoke hanging in the atmosphere as heavily as the memory of the massacre. His throat felt tight and he wanted to instinctively cough, but he suppressed the feeling as the mood of sombre silence surrounded them.

Robin had clearly been here before. He walked boldly forwards into the compound, keeping an even gait, untroubled and unswerving. There was nothing Edward noticed that was arrogant about Robin's movement, only a quiet reverence for the ground that was once soaked with the blood of so many defenceless citizens.

Edward faltered. He could not understand why, but he could not take another step into the compound. Then he saw their faces, the faces of women, torn with desperate fear. He saw the images of the past race in front of him in slow motion; the people running in panic, blindly towards the edge of the compound, bodies falling as the bullets found their mark, a huddle of women tumbling, falling it seemed… he looked up and saw a solitary man standing by what appeared to be a sort of sunken part of the field, a well…

Edward stopped dead in his tracks.

A young man was watching Robin walk quietly towards him, reaching out his hand, catching the young man's hand in his, putting his arm around his shoulder, talking and nodding, looking into the well that the man seemed, wedded to as if rooted to the past.

Ravinder took Robin's hand. His friend. Every now and again, he would visit the compound and each time he would feel more sure, more reconciled with the horrible past; the night when he lay across his grandfather's body as he lay dead and his baby cousin died as he reached out to her. Every now and again he needed to remind himself that it was real, that the 13 April 1919, nearly twenty one years ago now; happened. Every now and again he wanted to look into that horrible well and remember the single head trying to push above the dead bodies and her voice crying out to him, *"Meri madada karo, madada.."* He tried to imagine each time what it would have been like if he had tried to help her, to save her. Then he would console himself, that he was only a little boy, eight years old and there was nothing he could do. There was nothing he could do and no-one ever asked him to do anything differently from what he did then, to hide against his grandfather's chest, to reach out to his baby cousin, to tear the turban from the dying man's head and push it with all his might into the seeping wound in his thigh.

There was nothing he could do then and there was nothing he could do now, except, accept Robin's hand of friendship and remember that there *were* good English men, that not all men were like the military man that murdered so many of his Ravinder's own family, their friends and their neighbours and that their lives taken for no reason at all.

For a moment, Edward breathed a sigh of relief. Robin looked towards him and nodded. Edward hoped it meant that they were leaving the compound, but it wasn't to be. He was still stuck in one place on the compound, his mind seared with images he had no control over. Like a procession in hell moving with agonising deliberation - one by one - the faces from the compound flashed across his vision and haunted his aching conscience. There were women and children all scrambling over the top of one other to reach the wall and climb out. For a moment, the present calm of the compound stilled Edward's mind. Then, the latent mood of unanswered questions and unresolved grief, the bubbling undercurrent of the violence of mothers losing children, of fathers losing their sons and brothers; was sobering and quieting. Then he heard it, the echoes of screams and shrieks of wild terror and rage scorching the atmosphere.

Edward stood and gazed at the wall for a moment that felt like eternity. The whitewash was cracked and peeling like pieces of skin from a flailed body. The wall rose in an interminable defence of a spiritual heritage that India observed as diligently as morning prayers. Across the surface, flecks of the past spattered in gruesome displays; brown smudges, long rips and sharp holes that testified to the wall's cruel twist of purpose. Once the guardian that offered timely and safe homage to the collective spirit - the wall was now a tortured memorial trapping the will of ancient rituals in an unscaleable fortress of betrayal, death and destruction.

Suddenly, Robin was beside him, an arm loosely draped across his shoulder. 'Awe inspiring sight.'

Edward snapped out of his trance.

'It certainly has an atmosphere that never changes Edward.' Robin remarked soberly.

'Can I look more closely at the well?'

'By all means Edward. That young man is Ravinder. I see him here from time to time.'

'Oh?'

'Yes, he returns here as if this is his pilgrimage place.'

'Was he…'

'He was here yes, during the massacre if that's what you mean.'

Edward looked across towards Ravinder but the young man was already leaving, moving towards what seemed to be a hidden exit at the far end of the compound.

'He was only eight years old you know. He just survived by virtue of his grandfather's body shielding him from the bullets. But his mind will never forget the sheer horror of it all, especially at the well.'

'He talks to you about it?' Edward was incredulous.

'We have become friends of sort.' Robin said evenly. 'It is good for him to talk about that day and night.'

'He can't forget.'

'No, he can't and he won't. So this is how he deals with the memory. He looks into the well and hopes to see something different each time, something new, something that says life and not endless death and horror.'

'Robin…'

'It's OK Edward. I need to remember also. Don't forget to take photos of the wall.'

'Thanks. I nearly forgot.'

'This place does that to you. I don't know anywhere else in the world where there has been such a deliberate killing of human beings in a confined space and time as this.'

Edward shuddered. 'Are you sure that the British won't change their mind about Independence?'

'Not while the war's on old chap. Mother won't allow her precious resources to be diverted for anything; or anyone for that matter.'

'I see.'

'Independence is important, but there *is* the other side.' Robin kicked the loose dust under his boot. 'If India decides on her own course, then she'll be fully equipped with army, navy and airforce.'

'Does that matter?'

'Well, you've seen the way that it's done over here; the military are the face of power and control. Give India her rights and power and then we British are threatened. For now, the Indian forces are a part of the Empire, no more.'

'And after Independence?'

'Precisely. Who knows the implications.' Robin threw his arms into an illusory sky. 'Even Gandhi doesn't have complete control over the will of Indians. They don't all agree with his policies either.'

'So I've heard.'

'So what do you do with armed groups of people that aren't used to power and force except under another's command?'

'I see your point. In the current climate, anything could happen. Hindus murder Muslims, Muslims murder Hindus. What about the Sikhs?' Edward added.

'This is Amritsar after all. It's the heart and soul of Sikh territory. The Punjab still belongs to the Sikhs despite Muslim claims to the contrary.'

'A bit of Israel in India.'

'You could say that Edward. A lost city for a lost tribe.'

The wind picked up handfuls of revengeful dust and hurled it against the brim of Edward's hat, which could not now and could never shade his eyes from the vision of carnage. He winced. There was no mistaking who he was. He was simply glad that he had come to Amritsar now, to witness the killing field himself, to be here and yet gone in enough time before the anniversary of the massacre on that unforgettable *"Baisakhi Day."*

'Got all you need Edward?'

'I think so. Glad I will not be here in April. What date is the anniversary?'

'April 13. I won't be here either. We'll stay well away this time. O'Dwyer's death is just enough to spark the whole thing off. I'll point out the Lane where Dyer set up the *"Crawling Order."*'

'That will be interesting.'

'It's one thing to rule this mob, but to publicly humiliate them - not a safe game to play.'

'Does this sort of thing still happen Robin? I mean - the liberties and indiscretions of power?'

'Of course. Every day. But you won't see it. Most of the time it's well and truly hidden. Strange how the civilised man becomes such a brute when he's out of his own cage.'

'You mean the English outside England?'

'Edward, there's a very strong socialisation factor at play. Has to be. But out here…' Robin made a long and broad sweep in front of the windscreen with this free hand. 'Out here, the opposite happens. The cork is suddenly popped out of the bottle as it were.'

'Malabar caves revisited.' Edward mused.

'So don't be surprised if you find yourself teetering on the edge of *"what is real and what isn't real"* if you understand what I mean.' Robin glanced quickly over his shoulder at Edward.

'So it isn't just the heat Robin.' Edward smile was tinged with resignation and experience.

'No it isn't. There's a timeless pace about this place. People flow in an endless tide of birth and death and at either end, there is acceptance as if an unbroken cord connects them to their destiny. For us, life is a series of short events punctuated by courtesies and formalities. Our reality is simply a few sacred seconds, threaded on the journey from babyhood to death. That's all. We just don't have the same sense of the eternal and immortal that these people have.'

'The *"Immortal Throne."* Isn't that the name of the Sikh temple?'

'We'll visit it later Edward, when the mood takes us. The "*Akhal Tahkt,*" seat of their religious belief and political power is as sacred as any Hindu temple or Muslim Mosque.'

'How do they all survive together?'

'Ask Gandhi. That's his quest. You haven't met him yet I take it?'

'I want to yes. Absolutely. David said he would try and organise something for me.'

'Good. You'll like him Edward. There's nothing quite like meeting the real thing, the Mahatma I mean. These temples are wonderful but not a bar on Gandhi himself. I tell you, he's a walking vision of Sikhism,

Christianity, Islam and Hinduism. Go to any prayer meeting with the Mahatma, pick any faith and you can be assured that Gandhi will fill your soul.'

'He's really an inspiration then.'

'Inspiration? Gandhi is the well that never dries.'

Robin fell into a gentle silence, content with his contemplation of the barefoot Saint.

It was Edward's turn to look worriedly at the narrow alleyways. All the time he was conscious that Sikhdom loomed larger than life in the magnificent presence of the Golden Temple. He wanted only to look into the huddled landscape of buildings formed by almost lightless alleyways, as if watching a movie, and not touch, feel, listen or grieve the torment of India. As they turned into the Lane, Edward faltered. The exposure at Jallianwal Bagh impressed deeply upon him with its sense of collective grief and shame, shame that belonged to his English past.

Robin understood Edward's unease. Neither of the men spoke. After two or three minutes, Robin moved them away from the vision of the Lane and back towards the car. Enough for one day for the erstwhile reporter from London who was clearly quite out of his depth on the Subcontinent! He needed something softer for his sense and that would be the timeless beauty of the Golden Temple, its majestic sweep across the landscape a luminous reminder of the once great Sikh community and its remarkable leaders. Robin signalled with a grand sweep, of his hand towards the Temple, a fitting gesture in the aftermath of the grotesque monument to British insensitivity and the tragedies of the past.

'There Edward, is Sikhdom for you in all its glory. We shall pay a visit, you and I and my beautiful wife Marion.' Robin grinned cheekily at the thought.

Chapter Twenty Six

ROBIN AND EDWARD walked back to the car. It was mid-afternoon and the heat was intense. It was not a good time for further sightseeing and in any case, Robin always made a point of resting in the afternoon.

'Let's go home Edward, to Marion and my cottage. You will feel totally safe there.' Robin said intuitively.

'Thanks old man. I am feeling a bit out of sorts.'

'I am not surprised.'

'The compound..'

'No need to explain.' Robin said quietly. 'In any case, it's time for a nap. Habit of the Indians and a darned good one at that.'

Edward laughed. 'Looks as though India is well and truly under your skin Robin.'

'Let's enjoy a cool down and then rest as long as you want. I'll get my servant to wake you for dinner.'

Edward nodded graciously and let *"servant"* rest on his thoughts before shutting and closing his eyes. It was a steep ascent to climb the cultural divide. *"Servant"* in India did not quite equate with *"maid"* in Britain. There were worlds of difference; rights, pay, opportunity, future… but it required too much effort for him to continue to examine and assess the differences in caste and status that India rudely threw in his face.

Chapter Twenty Seven

England

THE BRITISH PRESENCE in Amritsar was as neat and orderly as Edward had expected. The thought briefly crossed his mind that this was where Colonel Dyer and General O'Dwyer had once lived. He shuddered and shook off the thought in case it became a bad omen. There were good British men, just had Ravinder had described Robin.

Robin, like David, had his own cottage. He was a married man and lived in inordinate simplicity. Edward thought that was probably, to appease his conscience at the excesses of the Raj. The tone of the cottage was nevertheless welcoming and soothing.

Robin opened the door to his home and sanctuary to Edward. He walked inside calling to his wife.

Marion emerged from the living room and greeted her husband with a quick kiss on his cheek.

'Edward, meet my wife Marion. Marion, this is Edward.'

'How do you do.' Edward bowed slightly, resisting the impulse to say "namaste" and laugh at the extraordinary coincidence of names.

'Edward, how lovely to meet you. David told us about you. You must be courageous to brave the wilds of India on your own.'

'Thank you Marion. But I feel as though I have been thoroughly looked after.'

Edward smiled broadly, relieved that the ordeal of the Compound was well behind them.

'Good. Please come in. You're tired I'm sure. After tea, Amrit will show you the bathroom and where you can rest.'

Marion was the perfect hostess, attentive yet not overly so. She poured the two men tea and herself a cool lime drink.

'I don't like tea. I drink limewater instead. It's better for my health.'

Edward smiled and accepted the tea. He drank quietly and then allowed himself to be led by the unobtrusive Amrit to the bathroom.

The water was deliciously cool. Edward poured streams of the cooling liquid over his head and shoulders, lingering in the sensation and illusion that the water felt and eased both his emotional and physical pain. He let the water wash away the dust of India and the ominous feeling that India still had more in store for him.

He towelled himself dry and stepped out of the bathroom. A coarse cotton bathrobe was draped on a large brass hook on the bedroom side of the door. He gratefully pulled the robe around his body, completing the luxury wash and feeling dazed by his luck. There were hotels and hotels, however, they were hardly a match for this delightful, British-Indian hospitality.

Chapter Twenty Eight

SLEEP CAME EASILY and painlessly, his mind settled by the even repose of the English household. There was little noise and the shuttered windows provided a much-needed, tranquil recluse. Edward was curiously aware of how sleep had become the refuge from unaccustomed trials. Yet the dreams continued the intrusive thoughts of pressing and urgent realities that not even sleep could disguise.

Fortune had immersed Edward in the maelstrom of Indian sentiment and unbridled passions. His unconscious mind toyed with the brooding difficulty of reconciling the lingering British presence. The subcontinent survived with implements as primitive as the water wheel and hand plough yet yearned for the rewards of industry, administration and order.

Edward's delicate emotions were challenged and confronted by the invisible hostility that penetrated his consciousness, making it impossible for him to disconnect from the private tragedies, the atrocities, poverty and suppression that dismembered Indian lives from a noble past.

There was little room for Edward to heal his own deep hurts over Ruth's infidelity, whilst his mind fought to form an objective view of a dying nation, struggling for rebirth through the promise of 'Independence.' Yet the storm of impressions and exposure to the raw realities of exploitation somehow cleared his own intense pain, born in a climate of English 'restraint' and the polite burial of anguish, grief and torment.

Edward could imagine himself covered in the grit and dust of foreign soil, unshaven and clothed in crudely woven cottons that revealed only tortured and strangely open eyes, piercing the landscape with a kind of savage inner truth. The brutality of the landscape was at one level, scalding water over a softly shawled soul and on the other, the cynosure, and the brazen truth that Edward thirsted. The harsh and unrelenting comfort of the decaying images allowed him for a brief moment to relax his guard and feel the aching grief of Ruth's betrayal. The broken earth burst in gusts of wind and caught in the edges of Edward's eyes, catching his shocking tears in perfect sympathy and burying them in weary sands.

Edward blinked, but only the gritty remnants of restless sleep and the rude awakening to his inner pain greeted him.

'Ruth.' Edward groaned like a dying man. 'Ruth, why did you do it?' Edward started to weep, at first with awkward control in order to prevent himself from feeling the storm of emotions and then with long rasping breaths that tore aching sobs from the depths of his being. The storm rose and flooded his awareness with her betrayal, his guilt and an inconsolable anger towards his manhood. How could he blame her? He had never accepted how much of a child she still was, that she had never fully matured to womanhood wanting not a husband, but a father. Ruth was not his wife; she was a waif looking for security and stability. He gave her what she wanted and in return, she invested her sacred, womanly feelings in another man.

> "Drunk! I don't believe you Ruth." Edward almost shouted aloud. "You must have known what you were getting yourself into. There's no such thing as an accident, god damn you! You knew Ruth; you knew but could not admit consciously your need for a man and not a father."

So, that was it. Edward the paternal guardian for the society orphan lost in sick and meaningless circles. She was easy prey. No wonder you had to do it drunk. You would never be able to face me otherwise. Edward's grief turned to hate. "At least if you were woman enough you would have told me you wanted out. Innocent? My foot. You're a reckless coward." Edward stopped in embarrassment, aware that he no longer could hide behind his work, or even the working holiday to India.

Robin suddenly appeared, hovering diplomatically near the door with a long glass of soda water. 'Sorry to intrude old man, thought you might like som refreshments.'

'Thanks.' Edwards snapped back to the present. 'Robin, I am so sorry. I've made such a fool of myself. It's my wife.'

'Did you sleep?' Robin solicited.

'As a matter of fact yes. I didn't expect these feelings to surface though.'

'Don't worry. You're probably over-tired. I'll leave you rest a bit longer. Won't mention a thing. Marion is at the market, so there's only Amrit and myself here at the moment.'

'Thanks awfully.' Edward was calmed by the relative privacy of male company.

'Don't mention it. After dinner, I think we should look at your plans for visiting the Golden Temple. It's really a must see Edward before we leave for Lahore.'

Edward nodded and took a long sip of the soda water. There was no point in fighting the flow of feelings and momentum of events into which he was unconsciously cast. If there was such a thing as 'unconscious.' The soda was slightly sweet and soothing to his aching throat. Marion had her own version of cool drinks, especially adapted for the hot and uncomfortable summer of the Punjab. She was as gracious in her generosity as she was in her manner - quite a woman.

"Ruth, you could learn a thing or too I'm sure. Perhaps I'll bring you to meet Marion one day."

Marion was mature and unaffected by her husband's status. She was earthed, compassionate and practical. By contrast to this wonderful and sane soul, Edward became acutely aware that Ruth lacked older women in her life. Perhaps that was why she flung herself into the social set. *"Not a good way to learn. Wrong people altogether for you my dear."* Edward felt confident that he finally had a grasp on Ruth's out-of- character behaviour and determined that he would spend time introducing her to new people and separate her from the lecherous grasp of the 'do-gooders' of London.

'That reminds me, I must cable Chris.' Edward's thought jogged him into the present. He pulled out his notebook and pencil from the briefcase and jotted a few notes and observations.

"Weather stinking hot. India no picnic. Gandhi indisposed at present. Amritsar a nightmare of imperialism. Will make my pilgrimage to the Golden Temple, then visit Lahore before resting up in Srinagar and flying to Karachi.
Edward."

That would do. Chris would not want much more than 'touch base' communication until he had written a full report on Amritsar and had developed a more informed view of the direction of Congress. Edward folded the note into his pocket to give to Robin after dinner. The cable would no doubt go via David and onto Chris.

Edward toyed with the idea of sending a message for Ruth and decided against the idea. *"I'll let you stew for a few days Ruth - it will do you good."* Edward had to admit to himself that his feelings were more than just grief. There was anger, the anger that arises from searing hurt and betrayal.

Chapter Twenty Nine

England

IT WAS 3.30 AM. Ruth lay awake wondering where she had gone wrong. 'So soon my little one.' Ruth ran her hand across the slight roundness in her belly. It was hers; the child belonged to her! She had lost Thomas, but now; Ruth allowed an absent hand to caress and stroke her unborn child.

"Ruth... "

Ruth awoke and looked into the dark room.

"Ruth, can you hear me?"

'Thomas! I thought you'd gone.' Ruth was bewildered and delighted.

"Ruth, it's not my time. It's too soon. I have to leave now. I'm sorry."

He was gone. Again, he was gone. The faint apparition receded into the woodwork.

'Thomas, you wouldn't do that! You can't just come and then disappear like that.'

Ruth sat up in bed and switched on the lamp. 4.15 a.m.

'Oh no!' It was too early and she had hardly slept. She wanted to slump back into the pillows but the spasm in her belly caused her to crouch on her knees and double over with the pain. Ruth shrieked in agony. This time, she was alone. The pain accelerated into nauseating and excruciating waves that tore at her sides, wrenching her in half. Her breath compressed into her lungs intensifying the pain as she rolled onto her side, rocking and hugging her legs to ease the agony.

'No! No. You can't come yet!' Tears streamed down Ruth's cheeks. 'Not yet.' The pain relented and for a few short moments, Ruth gulped for air, her mind panicking, questioning then understanding. 'Dr. Anderson!'

There was hardly time. The pain was intensifying and closing in on her. Ruth forced herself onto the floor and into a crawling position. She made it as far as the stairs then collapsed onto her stomach. The telephone was in the hall downstairs; it could have been in America. She was not going to be able to make it down the stairs.

"Come on girl, you have to try." It was Thomas again.

'Thomaaas. Help me Tom.'

"Come on Ruth. Try. For God's sake, try."

'I can't. I can't.' Thomas was gone.

'I can't. I don't want to.'

"*Then don't Ruth.*" This time the voice came from inside. Edward. Edward with his ice-cold logic forced her to see herself. Edward, the man she had betrayed snapped her back to her senses. She had no choice. If Edward could cope, then at least she could try and not leave him with a dead wife as well as a dead child. She grasped the banister and heaved herself onto the step. The pain stabbed, into the small of her back. Her stomach heaved and she caught her mouth to repress the urge to vomit. Again, she heaved herself onto the next step. It was easier, but she was beginning to lose blood.

'Oh my God. Not yet. Please, not yet!'

Frantically, Ruth pulled herself down another few steps before she lost her grip and fell. The last few stairs caught her under the ribs, winding her and robbing her of precious breath. The pain now seared into her lungs and Ruth felt dangerously close to dying. Then suddenly, just as her mind verged precariously on unconsciousness, it cleared. She felt herself floating outside her body and looking down on its crumpled doll form, the toy blood oozing through the nightdress onto the floor. The lungs fought for air and breath came in rasping gasps. The hands lay like lifeless porcelain sculptures by her sides. It was over. It was all over.

"*I'm dead. This must be what it's like.*" Ruth's thoughts were loud, but felt far away, as if it were someone else thinking aloud. Then the loud throbbing in her ears water pumping through a narrow pipe and in a second, the throbbing turned to a roar. Ruth felt herself being tugged into a dark space. She fought to regain consciousness, but the tugging pulled her with an urgent momentum towards a narrow tunnel. The sound increased and her ears filled with the rushing of air moving past at a million miles per hour. Then blackness - complete blackness - darkness, death. Ruth was aware, aware of the darkness, that she had lost touch with her body, with life and had reached death. Ruth was totally at peace, her mind clear and strangely accepting, of the finality of life. Then came the light - the soft, golden light.

"Ruth, it's not the right time. Go back to Edward. He'll need you. Go now Ruth, you haven't much time."

The light disappeared and Ruth found herself looking down on the crumpled rag doll of a body one more time. A dread and sickening feeling washed over her in an unwelcome tide and she was pulled back into her body.

Ruth awoke, bleeding and in deep pain. 'Oh my God, what do I do now?' Ruth struggled for a moment with the desire to die and slowly forced herself into a sitting position. The hall table shifted slightly with her weight, but was firmly wedged against the wall. She yanked at the telephone cord pulling the telephone to the floor beside her. Her mind was reeling and eyes barely able to focus, but she dialled, agonisingly slowly.

The telephone rang for an interminably long time. 'Dr. Anderson here.'

'Dr. Anderson, it's Ruth, Ruth Thompson. The baby...'

'Ruth, are you all right? Stay where you are, I'll be right over.'

'I've lost the baby.' Ruth could hardly speak.

'Ruth, open the front door when you hear the siren. I'll send the ambulance ahead. Better still open the door now. You might faint. I'm coming over.'

The telephone went dead. Ruth dropped the receiver and sobbed into the wall. There was a deepening pool of blood staining her nightdress. The flow frightened her. There was nothing she could do, nothing. She lay curled like a child into herself and let the pain rack her body.

"The door. Open the door." Her mind pressed her urgently. It was too hard. She couldn't make it.

'Come on Ruth, you must.' Ruth shouted aloud. 'Open the door!' Ruth responded to her own urgent command and crawled to the front door. It was easy. It was as if some superhuman force had taken possession of her body and hauled her into a kneeling position. Her hands found the chain and lock and with almost masterful accuracy she slipped the chain free of its guard and un-snibbed the lock. She felt she could stay on her knees forever, buoyed by her newfound strength of spirit. Then, just as the lucid image of the Virgin Mary slipped into her mind, she collapsed into a huddle on the floor.

Chapter Thirty

CHRIS PICKED UP the telegram from his desk tray. The paper was unfolded as if it had just arrived and hastily placed where he could find it.

'Edward! Well. You're all right then.'

He read the cryptic note and smiled to himself. Good show. Edward had survived as far as Amritsar. There was no doubt in his mind that India would absorb him into her womb and in time, the recent problems with Ruth would resolve. That was the thing with Edward, he was just as sensitive as his wife, only he would never admit it. 'Well, that's all under control.' Chris placed the telegram to one side. The second telegram looked identical to the first, except that it was marked:

> *"Confidential– Editor only"* and signed *"David."*
> *"Chris, all's well. Gandhi not available for another two weeks. Will make sure Edward meets him. Do him the world of good, apart from writing some fresh gossip for "The Reporter." Good to hear that you are still afloat, despite the war. Regards to the staff. David."*

'Gossip!' Chris laughed. It was true, Independence was purely speculation until the new Indian Constitution was in place and Britain had formally withdrawn her sovereign claims to the ageing kingdom of outmoded and decadent rulers. The Muslim League, Congress and fledgling political parties were hardly representative of the Raj in any case. The new regime would be interesting to observe close hand. Well, that's why he wanted Edward on the scene. The pressures of Europe were felt worldwide. It was no longer possible to confine conflicts between nations or even within regions. The tentacles of the Empire spanned the globe, and practically every continent on earth. As Britain withdrew into the lair of *"Commonwealth,"* Asia would no doubt feel the impact. Indeed, India had benefited from Britain's presence. That much he knew. The gradual putting together of essential services and a far superior administration in his estimation was worth gold. But that would not help the Indians in their cause for Independence. Chris tapped his fingers impatiently. The pressure on him to send reporters closer to the lines was mounting, but he was reluctant to do so. Edward was not ready for that sort of action. Not that any other man at war had an option, but at least Chris had the luxury of choice. It was easy to legitimise Edward's presence in India, and thus explain the absence of reporters closer to the western front. Chris admitted to himself that he would hardly recover if he lost 'his man' to the Jerry and was content at the compromise to send him to the steamy and emergent drama being staged on the subcontinent.

The telephone interrupted his thoughts.

'Yes.' The voice barked. 'Christopher Cooke?'

'Yes that's me. What can I do for you?'

'This is Dr. Anderson. Ruth Thompson's family doctor.'

'Oh? Is anything wrong?'

'I'm afraid so. Mrs. Thompson miscarried at about 4.30 this morning. I'm sorry to say she's lost a lot of blood. We'll have to keep her in hospital for about a week. I understand you employ her husband Edward?'

'That's right. Just received a cable from him. He's on assignment in India.'

'I see. Well could you please pass on the news to him.'

'Thank you. Yes, I'll cable him immediately. I am sure that he will want to come back as soon as he can. Please pass on my condolences to Ruth. Is she all right?'

'She'll be fine. She was asking after you. You can visit her tomorrow if you wish. Might cheer her up.'

'Thanks again doctor. Will you be there tomorrow?'

'I do rounds at the St George in the afternoons. I'd be happy to meet you.'

'Righto Goodbye then.'

'Goodbye.'

Chris put down the phone. 'Christ. As if being pregnant wasn't enough.' He went to brew fresh coffee and to collect his thoughts before cabling Edward. 'How on earth will I put it.' He had forgotten to ask Dr. Anderson how Ruth came to miscarry in the first place. Poor child. Ruth was just that. At least she had by all accounts, a good doctor to look after her. Chris selected a chipped and off-white cup and filled it with steaming coffee. Maybe it was just as well she had not gone to India after all. Chris couldn't imagine the difficulties of losing a baby in India. That was the whole point! Life on the subcontinent was so cheap, no one cared, and no one batted an eyelid at the obscene levels of infant mortality, yet, in Britain, one lost baby was almost a national tragedy. It didn't make sense. It wouldn't help either Edward or Ruth worrying about the futility of life and death in India.

He sat at his desk and penned a carefully worded and sensitive note to Edward.

> *"Edward. Received your cable. Glad all is well. Ruth unwell. Sorry to report she lost the baby early this morning. Will see her in hospital tomorrow. Dr. Anderson caring for her. Are you coming home? Chris."*

Chris re-read the cable and placed it in the 'Urgent Out' tray for immediate dispatch. What a turn of events. Perhaps Edward would be unable to see Gandhi after all!

Chapter Thirty One

RUTH LAY IN a white coma. Her body was wasted and thin, her eyes pulled back into their sockets in anguish and pain. The baby was dead. She had hardly become used to the idea of being pregnant, and now… What had she done? There were no more tears. After the first screams of pain, Ruth went into deep shock. Her body shivered and convulsed as it fought to expel the child from her narrow frame. How could the body reject its own creation? How could she have not heeded the warning to rest and nourish herself? She had barely recovered from the loss of Thomas before she threw herself back into the whirl of social engagements, this time, without the comfort of alcohol to numb her insecurity, isolation and fear. Edward was gone. He accepted her display of independence and infidelity with the staunchness of a protestant aunt, but now she had to face him with her lost womanhood. She had lost the baby! It just wasn't fair. She felt robbed, robbed of her one chance to have something of her own. Yes, Edward would become the child's father, but it was not his child. It was *her* child. The sobs that wanted to rise to the surface hardened into a knot of shame and defeat at the pit of her stomach. She felt nauseated and wretched.

Dr. Anderson had comforted and consoled her, but not even, he could compensate for the loss of her child.

Chapter Thirty Two

India

'WHEN IN ROME, do as the Romans do!' Robin delicately placed two golden pooris next to the bed of rice on Edward's plate. 'And, enjoy.'

Edward had to laugh. 'You're right I suppose. No point in pining away for the homeland. Incidentally,' Edward turned to his hostess, 'Marion, where did you learn to cook all these wonderful delicacies?'

'Oh no, not I, Amrit. You would be surprised at the talents that Amrit has hidden beneath that innocent shawl he wraps around himself.' Marion looked amused.

'Amrit? He cooked these?'

'Amrit is as ancient as India and, has the culinary skills of the Savoy Chef. Besides, you aren't a part of this culture until you've sampled at least fifty different dishes.'

'There are so many?' Edward gulped down another *poori*.

'Oh yes, and more. This is just part of the cuisine of the Punjab. Mind you, I think it is the best! Of course, I am totally biased having Amrit as our cook. Wait until you travel around a bit more. You'll be pleasantly surprised. If you can turn a blind eye to the intrigues of Hindu-Muslim amity or the lack thereof, and focus on the food, then you will have a story.'

Robin helped himself to another pile of pooris and mixed together some rice and vegetables.

'Mind you, Gandhi won't help you if take that angle. Not much mileage in the starvation diet of a great Saint.' Robin roared with laughter.

'Perhaps that's where Gandhi has gone wrong. Maybe he needs to eat more food to unite the masses, not the other way around.' Marion joined in the hilarity.

'But Gandhi would not be able to make friends with the English that way. Imagine, the Mahatma being served mutton chops.'

'I see. Or a good Scottish haggis.' Edward joined in.

'Some more Edward? You know, only the Punjabis can get their pooris to rise so beautifully. It's the yoghurt. They mix yoghurt into the batter and it comes out completely differently and also gives them this golden colour.'

'Well, you've sold me. Is it the same in the north?'

'Much the same, but there are always local variations, just as there are in dress, dialect and so forth. Eat up!' Robin waved a hand encouragingly at the steaming pile of pooris. 'Incidentally, there is greater European influence in the south so the food and dress can at times be very un-Indian. And, they speak English!'

'This is far more interesting. It's the real thing Robin. Do the Muslims also eat like this?'

'They eat halal meat as well as the usual variety of vegetable dishes, dahl and rice. Meat is definitely a source of contention for the Hindus. This land was once pure vegetarian and some areas are still completely devoted to the traditional Hindu lifestyle. All that has to change as soon as you introduce new cultures. Look at England. Our entire cuisine changed with the spice trade.'

'Indeed, mysterious alliances of exotic spices have blessed the British Crown Jewels!'

'That came a lot later.' Robin corrected.

'Then the Punjab has had a strong historical as well as culinary influence on Mother.' Edward began to understand the story.

'You might say that. Tell me, what you know about Ranjit Singh?'

'Very little really Robin, except that he was the last legitimate owner of the Kohinoor diamond.'

'Correct. Singh was quite adventurous with the diamond. He wore it as an amulet, sometimes in his turban and then he attached it to his horse's harness. Can you believe that? A diamond of that size!'

'Quite an impressive good luck charm!'

'Quite so. But the luck diamond has many facets.' Robin tapped a little more subji from the spoon onto his plate.' Apparently, Singh died and shortly afterwards, the Sikh army went on to fight the Chinese in Tibet before challenging the British. That was 1845. The British naturally retaliated and through Lord Dalhousie, the Governor General of India at the time, annexed the Punjab to British India. A band of three, call them the *"Three Musketeers"* if you like, proceeded to 'demand' the Kohinoor as part of the deal. Eventually, the diamond came into the possession of her Majesty, but never into the hands of the heir to the Punjab, Dhuleep Singh.'

'The Kohinoor was thus destined to grace the Jewels?' Edward began to draw the connections.

'Indeed it is, or a part of the diamond more precisely.' Robin added.

'I see. One would think the British administration would have returned the diamond by now.'

'Ah, the secrets of the crown cleverly buried in a climate of India at war with herself.'

'Do you attribute any power to these artefacts Robin?' Edward was curious to explore Thomas's revelations.

'I wouldn't call the Kohinoor diamond an artefact exactly, but yes, it has its own power and significance.' Robin demurred.

'If it came back to India, into whose hands would it fall?'

'Good question. By rights, it belongs to the Punjab, the Sikh community presumably. But then, it was originally a priceless piece of Hindu worship.'

'And now?'

'Who knows Edward. Look at the Maharajas and Princes of India. They have sold off so many of their jewels already to fund the First World War. You understand why Britain wants a system of princely states in a new and independent India, and it is probably easier to control from a distance. A better return on their investment so to speak. From that point of view,' Robin paused as if muddling over the treasury of the entire subcontinent, 'the Kohinoor would become the property of the ruler of the Punjab. However, that creates its own problems with Jinnah hoping to separate the Punjab into Hindu India and Muslim Pakistan.'

'You can't cut the diamond in half.'

'A further desecration indeed - and it can't belong to the Punjab if the Punjab no longer exists in its entirety.' Robin was acutely aware of the imminent prospect of the growing divisions.

'I see your point. India will suffer the same fate as the princely diamond and be cut and divided from her original glory?'

'That's Britain's hope, but if Gandhi has his way, there will be no more 'princely states' as such. There will only be a united India, which includes an undivided Punjab and no 'Pakistan.' If India resists partition, the Kohinoor belongs to the people of a united India, the Sikhs, the Muslims, the Parsis, the Buddhists and the Hindus.'

'And the Christians?'

'One would hardly give the Spear of Destiny to Arabs in the Middle East.' Robin remained firm in his argument.

'I suppose not. The diamond does therefore, have a spiritual as well as national history?'

'Definitely. If you take it purely in the spiritual context, then it is a Hindu relic. But Edward, this is no longer Hindu India, this is a Muslim-Hindu nation with a fair smattering of the other major and minor religious groups.'

'Doesn't Gandhi realise that it's impossible to unite the religious sentiments of people?' Edward was feeling slightly exasperated.

'He does and he doesn't. That's why his prayer meetings appeal to all faiths.

'Indian unity' means just that.' Robin could not, be swayed in this reason.

'Well, I wish him luck. And from what I've seen of Amritsar, the memories of the British should help him in his cause.'

'Yes, a sobering sight Edward. Perhaps we British ought not to leave after all!' Robin lightened his tone.

Edward laughed. 'That will send poor Gandhi to an early grave.'

'Robin, do you think Edward might like to stay with us rather than return to the drab fold of *"Mother."* 'Marion chipped in with light banter.

Edward looked to his hostess and gave a slight bow.

'Pardon me Marion, I am sure you are right. India is both charming and colourful and your warm household is no less than the best of India.'

Marion laughed. 'It is getting late. Tea Robin?'

'Thanks.' Robin shot Edward a glance then smiled broadly. 'The honourable gentleman must be by now, be satiated with the intrigues of the subcontinent as well as Amrit's superb cooking.'

'Amritbhai, Amrit.' Marion called him with her singsong voice. 'Amrit, do bring some chai and *ladus*.'

'*Ladus*?'

'That's a sweet Edward' she said, turning to her guest. 'Although, not strictly a Punjabi sweet, it is one of my favourites.'

'Thank you. I'm delighted. And Marion, I'm sure that you are right; the warmth of India far outweighs any of the side-scenes of religious enmity.'

'Ah, Edward, we can see that you are already a convert to the great land. Then soon you must venture into the Kashmir. What do you think? Can you survive without us?'

'I'm not sure.' Edward teased. 'Perhaps I need a guide.' Edward's eyes twinkled. 'May I steal Maid Marion for a week?'

'No chance!' Robin interrupted and swiftly placed a free arm around his wife's shoulders. 'Marion is devoted to her King and being with child, unfit for the rigours of the life of a vagabond and rogue.' Robin raised his imaginary glass. 'To our little Robin Hood.'

'To Robin Hood.' Marion and Edward replied in mock jest. 'And congratulations to Marion. You both must be thrilled.'

'We are excited,' she replied demurely. 'Actually, Robin wants to call him Lance, after Lancelot.' Marion burst into peals of laughter.

'And you?'

'Definitely Robin. But if it's a girl, Gwenhwyfar.' Marion beamed.

'To Lance and Gwenhwyfar!' Robin toasted.

'And Marion.' Edward was quietly serious. Edward looked deeply into his lap his hands folded gently in a gesture of quiet acquiescence to a fate he had not expected, far less wished for. Marion's unbounded joy of pregnancy, the intimacy of their shared moment was not lost on Edward.

Robin caught by his mood stopped in mid-stream. 'Everything OK old chap?'

'Oh, I'm sorry.' Edward paused. 'My wife is also pregnant. Her first child.'

'Congratulations old man.' Robin slapped him heartily on the back.

'It isn't mine. The child isn't mine.' Edward felt the choke in his voice.

'Oh, I'm dreadfully sorry Edward. You must be so hurt.' Marion intercepted her husband.

'I suppose I am. I hadn't thought about it that much until I came here and the feelings suddenly surfaced. I am sorry, I didn't mean to ......'

'Not at all. In fact, it's a good time to reflect. You're away from home and the break will probably do you and...'

'Ruth. Her name is Ruth.' Edward looked straight into Marion's eyes; tears just touching the curve of his lashes.

'The break will probably do you and Ruth the world of good.' Marion patted Edward's hand gently.

'Of course.' Edward dropped his gaze for a moment.

'Still, shan't let that interrupt a wonderful meal. Are those *ladus*...?' 'Edward looked towards Marion.

'Ladus? Yes that's right. Here they come.'

'Indeed Marion. I'll have to watch Amrit. He'll steal you away from me.' Robin's attempt to soften Edward's blow was well timed and perfectly pitched.

Edward smiled and accepted the tea and sweet.' Maid Marion - the entire Kingdom will bow to your tastes.' Edward made a flourish with his teacup.

'I am honoured Edward. Perhaps while you are on your travels you will meet Maid Marion's Indian counterpart.'

'Oh.'

'Yes, Dropidy. Destined to capture your heart. So beware.'

'Strange you mention it Marion. I kept seeing images of an Indian woman on the way over here. I was totally mesmerised by her. Those eyes

- totally magnetic - like two pure pearls only the colour of a midnight sky.' Edward turned towards Marion. 'Somehow, she looked straight into my soul, as if she had been there before.'

'You know someone over here?' Robin teased.

Edward laughed shyly. 'I don't as a matter of fact. Strange isn't it. You let your defences down for a minute and it's all there in front of you.'

'All there?' Marion questioned.

'A beautiful woman. I've always loved Ruth dearly Marion, but this woman was quite different, extraordinary really.'

Marion raised her brows at Robin. 'We see. Perhaps India has already captured you Edward?'

'Does it happen like that?'

'It does. Usually it is a little subtler than simply a woman. No offence meant of course to the more fey amongst us! '

'It's often a sensation you feel in your bones, as if your history and heritage is linked somehow to the ancient Maharajas and Maharanis of India.'

'And now you are Maharaja Robin and Maharani Marion.' The atmosphere exploded in delight.

'So perhaps we will receive the Kohinoor my King and bring it home to this wondrous land.'

'The Holy Grail my Queen, belongs to you alone.'

'My Lord and King.' Marion quipped, raising her glass.

'Lord and King,' the men enjoined.

'And now, let's plan the holy war.' Robin attended the practicalities.

The evening was pleasant and a welcome release for Edward's aching hurts. Somehow, the acute shame he felt over Ruth's actions dissolved in the good- natured company of Robin and Marion.

'I must ask her again about Dropidy.' Edward noted.

Chapter Thirty Three

ROBIN POSTPONED SRINAGAR until early the following week. The weather was unseasonably cold and bitter as Himalayan winds swept across the airfield, making the prospects of a safe and uneventful journey less than likely.

'It's fortuitous Edward. I'd like to show you around. You'll have plenty of time now to visit the Golden Temple and there's a meeting in Lahore coming up of the All-India Muslim league. Definitely worth a visit.'

'You're probably right Robin, and no doubt there'll be something to flesh out my report for Chris.' Edward was enjoying the company and happy for extra time.

'Undoubtedly. It's a critical time for India and will test Gandhi to his limits.'

'Are the Sikhs involved in the division?'

'Can't really say at this stage. Sikhs are an important part of the Armed Services, but that's only from the British point of view. Whichever way you look at it, they are bound to suffer whether or not India remains united or is divided along the Punjab. Someone has to be the loser in this Edward. The Sikhs are wonderful people in their own right, but I hardly think the All-India Muslim League will see it that way. They broke away from Muslim suppression centuries ago, understandably, there is a certain animosity between the two sides.'

'One wonders if their gods have a hand in the whole affair.'

'If so, then on whose side? If you're a Muslim, the Garden of Allah belongs to you. The catch is that disbelievers are destined to die under Islamic law. If you are a Christian, then the latter-day interpretation of the Bible means that if you believe that Jesus died on the cross for you, and you are entitled to eternal salvation. For the rest of us it's - well - hell.' Robin smiled broadly.

'You don't believe that Jesus died on the cross for you Robin?'

'Didn't say that I did. If you're a Hindu,' Robin continued, 'as most Indians are, it's simply a question of absolving your karma and improving your destiny next time around.'

'Quite a medley of beliefs! I wonder who is right?'

'Are you sure this is a good time to test your beliefs Edward?'

'My skin is white.' Edward regressed to the familiar.

'Ah, then you must be Christian.'

'Yes, but there are plenty of Indian Christians surely?'

'The great Saint and disciple of Jesus Thomas made sure of that. Still, you might like to convert to Hinduism.'

'And burn Ruth on the pyre of my grief?'

'A neat solution altogether.'

'Robin, you and David really are quite a challenge. There's not much distance, between skin colour and the inner world it seems.'

Edward found a frame for his feelings.

'Ah, Edward you are observant. That's the whole point. You can wear anything you choose, but there's nowhere and nothing to hide in this land, especially from yourself.' Robin looked reflectively at his wedding ring. Perhaps we should visit the Emperor's Sheesh Mal, The Palace of Mirrors in Great Royal Fort in Lahore!

Magnificent. The vision of yourself, the "*Swadarshan*" may become clearer to you though the Islamic eye.'

'You mean, you can see me and I can't see myself Robin?' Edward was mortified.

'You might say that. Perhaps India has the same problem herself, unable to resolve the puzzles of her karma and destiny, no matter how many mirrors, how many "*Manserovas*" she glances upon.' Robin twirled the gold band on his wedding finger. 'It is in her nature, in her psyche to be the innocent victim of her own passions. India is a spontaneous cauldron of sentiment forever bubbling on the fire of belief. Not to mention the *"ignition factor"*; the continual search for cultural and religious identity.' Robin paused.

Edward was silent, still coming to terms with the implications of his lack of knowledge of himself.

'What bothers me Edward, is that in a country with such a deep and tested religious history, Indians continue to indulge in childish retaliations. In fact, we English only survive by virtue of our thin veneer of superiority and civility. As you have seen in the case of our Colonel Dyer, a very thin veneer indeed! How easily the crust breaks to expose our gross inferiority complex. Sheer brutality Edward. There is no excuse for it in any language or any guise that protests 'God.' Even the 'Empire' is an insufficient god in my view to sanction the oppression of another human being. We haven't set any sort of example for the Indians! Then how can we challenge the 'divine right' of the Muslims to kill the Hindus or even our prerogative to smash the Hindu's 'gods' and 'goddesses' in the name of Christ Edward. You see my point don't you?'

Robin knew that Edward was open to the irony and continued with barely a moment to allow him, doubts to set in.

'So why do you think the Sikhs picked up the sword? The Muslims were slaughtering them!! Even the Parsis, bless their innocent souls, were tortured for their faith. Is there any religion on earth that does not hate and despise all other religions!' Robin knew that he had made the point.

'Gandhi is the only living example I have seen of brotherhood. Gandhi is the Christ of the Hindus and a better example of *"love thy neighbour as thyself"* than any, Christian I've met. There would be no British India Edward if England were truly Christian and loved her god and her fellow man. We would never have set a foot, off the Isles in the first place if that were the case; in pursuit of greater lands we've exploited, suppressed and murdered. There would have been no ship Tyger without Elizabeth the First's greed, no British East India Company, no Bombay and no battle for Bengal. Greed, murder and division Edward. That's both India and humanity's recent and present story.'

'I see Robin. To state it mildly we are no better than they.'

'Yes.' Robin nodded. 'Are we not also from the fabled Aryan stock now genociding the rest of Europe? Put to one side the Celts and Druids, many of us have descended from the Scandinavian pirates and merchants! Perhaps that is the true stock of the East India Company now plundering and oppressing the Indian. Merchants Edward. Even the Christians discovered England through the trading routes. So from where did they originate? The Aryans I mean. Hitler might think that his Germanic stock, are the true Aryans, but others who would beg to differ. The roots of the true Aryans lie here in this very land Edward, right where you and I stand.'

Robin pointed through the window to a grand array of aerial roots hiding the invisible trunk of a banyan tree.

'Sure enough, the jewel of history is right here under your nose. Because we stand amongst the branches, we cannot see the tree in its entirety. Take the perspective, of the seed, or the overview Edward and you'll see it all. Britain is fighting over this dustbowl of humanity, the Punjab, and yet if you take the lesson from that old and convoluted tree, we are destroying our very own roots. Perhaps that is the real issue here; there is no longer any dynastic trunk in India. The ancient kingdoms are as dead as the Emperors of China or the Tsars of Russia.'

'Wouldn't keeping the princely states solve the problem?'

'Not the way they are at present Edward. You have seen the wealth of the landlords and the poverty of the rural masses. They're just as blinded by their pomposity and greed as we are by ours. It wouldn't change a thing! What India needs is the complete restoration of her soul as well as her kingdoms.'

'Another fallen civilisation.'

'Fallen, yes, but not forgotten. At least the British have been a little less blatant in India than the Spanish Conquistadors in the Americas. Greed Edward. A powerful and potent poison! Put the dust of gold in front of the average man and he will no longer have the sense to till the soil. Then the earth decays, lost to summer winds and winter monsoons and along with the earth, civilisations fall. It's all very well to have magnificent jewels and stunning palaces adorned with fine ladies, but if you forget the basics of tending the land and all its creatures, then your kingdom will inevitably crumble.'

'Nothing could persuade *"Siddhartha"* to remain in the palace.'

'You like the story Ed?' Robin reverted to the familiar.

'There is something attractive about his journey.'

'You find some parallels?' Robin's eyes sparkled.

'Temptation?'

'Ah, your purdahed beau.'

'Quite. Although I wouldn't say that I'm here on any kind of search for the Holy Grail nor any knightly conquest to save maidens.'

'No of course not.' Robin's mirth bubbled in his eyes.

'What do you mean Robin!'

'Of course not Edward. Like all of us, you are the contented, civilised and well-heeled Englishman.'

'Well I wouldn't put it quite like that.'

'Then?'

'Maybe you're right. Maybe I am looking for something, only I don't know it.'

'You will know when you have found it Edward?' Robin looked sympathetically at Edward.

'It or her! I suppose I am still looking. I've hardly been here a few days and so much has happened. It feels as though all my cultural threads and chords have completely unravelled then tangled themselves into something I don't quite recognise.'

'Or something in between Edward. Perhaps this trip to Kashmir will do you good. This is a powerful land as you have already experienced. You've been flung into the depths of a rich and all-all-encompassing history Edward. There's no going back. Not if you want to remain sane that is. You just have to go along with the flow of humanity here and everything that, that means and is. Don't fight it and you will discover the sweetness of India.'

Edward felt relieved and laughed. 'I think I will stick with you and Marion for a while if you don't mind Robin.'

'No hurry. First, I'll see if we can't attend the final session of the Muslim League.' Robin ushered his guest towards a lightly furnished drawing room. 'Quite an impressive gathering so I hear. Jinnah will call them to prayer outside Emperor Aurangzeb's beautiful Mosque. It will be a great stage for one of the most compelling, moments in India's history. No doubt about it.'

'Oh?'

'Very symbolic. Housed within its great sandstone walls is a relic of the very Holy Prophet himself.'

'I see. Jinnah bows to history and his fore fathers.'

'Appropriately so Edward. Alternatively, he aligns himself with them! In any case, if you want to build a nation, then you must firstly build, or claim monuments that underline your cause, your constitution and your courage. Jinnah chose as his backdrop, no less than The Royal Fort constructed by the very Akbar the Great himself and suitably enhanced by every Moghul Emperor of India thereafter. In Jehangir, he finds great solace, as well as appropriately, inspiration for greatness. Jinnah is smart enough to seek the blessing of the greats before him, the vision of the Imperial Mosque invoking clearly, none less than Allah and Mohammed into the foundations of the new Pakistan!'

'Then he must, by definition of history and the Almighty succeed.'

'Who could stop the man? Who would come between Allah, Jinnah and his new Pakistan?'

'Gandhi?'

'Gandhi can do nothing in front of the might of such a person as Jinnah. Jinnah's will is paramount. Jinnah believes anyway that Pakistan is Allah's will.'

'I see. Have they not tried to prevent him?'

'Yes of course, however now you have the Muslim League driving the wedge in before the signing of the Government of India Act.'

'Britain at work once again.' Edwards said flatly.

'There are many intrigues Edward, none the least being Jinnah's personal vanity.'

'Ambition o'er leaps itself and falls on the other!'

'Precisely. Actually, at Lucknow three years ago, Gandhi more or less acknowledged that Jinnah would go to war. At that stage, the differences were irreconcilable between the Muslim League and Congress.'

'Is there any other course apart from war?' Edward felt weary to the bone.

'The Chief Minister of the Punjab wants to avert Partition, to maintain a united India. But not even Gandhi could find it possible, or pertinent perhaps, to give time to Sikander.'

'You know him Robin?'

'Of course. We are here after all. Sikander is a good man in my opinion, but, also prone to act to protect his own interests. Who would not be Edward? However, he is right on the mark. He feels that the Muslim communities do not want partition, but Jinnah does.'

'A private war you think Robin?'

'Just days ago Sikander suggested a loose Federation but Congress will not co-operate and now Jinnah has also marked his man. He wants to destroy Sikander and partake of the Punjab at the same time. Britain does not seem to be able, or willing, to act otherwise.'

'Dangerous alliance of hearts Robin?' Edward felt the rising tension. 'Linlithgow has in my opinion, simply fallen into Jinnah's hands. Muslim interests secured through a separate state and then punish Congress for Satyagraha and non co-operation during the war.'

Edward chuckled. 'So I have not left fascism behind at all! Without India, Hitler lives on.'

'Edward, the Muslim feeling has caught the imagination of the Viceroy and the Congress is simply unhelpful at this stage in the cause for a united India.'

'That's blackmail Robin. Surely!'

'Blackmail or not, Congress must have been too single minded not to realise the greater liberation of India more or less depends upon co-operation with England now, as we speak.'

'Then history has already signed the fate of India Robin.'

'History will carry on without doubt and in my view, partition is a stake through the heart of this land but a stake nevertheless.'

'You and Marion? What then?'

Robin smiled gently.' Do you smoke?'

'From time to time. Ruth doesn't like the habit.'

'Marion also is too pure to enjoy the subtle aromas.' Robin pulled some pipe tobacco from his pocket. He smiled amiably at Edward, stuffing the pipe loosely but firmly. 'There isn't much here to remind us of home. I enjoy the simple pleasures of life. Sometimes I wonder about Marion. I mean, there are few friends for her and the shopping is not exactly, well, London. Oh, we do have our shops, but it's quite an adventure to go into the market place, especially for an English woman.'

'I'm glad I didn't bring Ruth.' Edward thought that Robin had neatly evaded the topic of leaving.

'For you Sahib.' Amrit walked in with a note on a silver platter.

'Home?'

'Must be from Chris I expect. Probably wants to know when the real stuff will come through.' Edward picked up the telegram and read it slowly, the colour draining from his cheeks. He took a deep breath and placed the telegram quietly on the side table.

'Is everything all right Edward?'

Edward felt as old and tortured as the banyan tree in the courtyard. 'It's Ruth. She lost the baby, Robin.'

'I am so sorry Edward.' Robin placed a hand on Edward's forearm. 'I don't know what to say, what to feel..'

'Thank you Robin. I don't either.' Edward confessed.

'Today Edward, we shall walk into new territory, into a new family where we can sample the true beauties of our wonderful Sikh brothers and sisters.' Robin was careful to avoid all reference to Jallianwal Bagh.

'Oh?' Edward still smarted from the loss of the child that was not his, stunned into solitude and silence by the intense trauma of being married to the wayward soul that was his wife, Ruth.

'You need a balm for the eyes and for the heart Edward. The Golden Temple will do that and much for you and more, I promise.'

'Thanks.' Edward said grabbing the opportunity for Robin's company before it slipped out of his grasp.

'Do you like architecture as much as your brother-in-law did?'

'That's a question I dare not answer Robin. Thomas was, well he seemed to have an uncanny ability of feeling the history of a place, of somehow sensing....'

'It's soul perhaps?'

'I guess you could put it that way Robin. I was never much good at existentialism.'

'Existentialism is a form of humanism is it not?' Robin probed further.

'True. I suppose for Thomas, buildings are a direct extension of the human mind. In India that clearly reflects the past Emperor's visions of grandeur.'

Robin laughed. 'Or the colonial masters!'

'Your humble cottage! That does bring me back to earth somewhat Robin.'

'Hearth and home are at the core of religion no doubt Edward. Your home...?'

'Very important to Ruth and me. But I still can't quite see myself embracing existentialism or humanism as my core belief.' Edward referred only to himself.

'The abstract is still way beyond me I am afraid.'

'Perhaps so Edward. But you have quite a way with words though from what I hear.' Robin slapped him lightly on the back.

'Thanks.' Edward raised a single eyebrow. 'David?'

'Small world out here Edward. David keeps me posted. There are too few of us not to keep an eye on one another.'

'And also on your visitors.' Edward felt better already.

'I hope that you feel safe and that we are looking out for you.' David patted Edward's arm.

'Yes. Truly.' Edward breathed out a sigh of relief.

'Wait until you see it, the Temple. Its people are mendicants for any travel-weary war correspondent.'

Edward felt himself laugh. 'Sounds as though I have walked straight into another conflict Robin. What does it mean? *"Amritsar?"*'

'Tell me Edward, can you keep a secret?' Robin laced his voice with humour. 'Yes. Why?'

'Then let the Temple herself tell you her secrets and hidden meanings.'

'You mean, just as Thomas could plumb the depths of architecture, I can too?'

'Ready Robin?' Marion returned wearing a sunhat.

Edward smiled. 'You look lovely.'

'Thank you. Shall we?'

Chapter Thirty Four

THE TRIO WALKED into the morning light towards the holiest shrine of Sikhism, the gold-leaf embellished *'Harmandir Sahib.'* It as though they were walking through time, culture, religion….

'Ah. This is what a man needs Marion. A good walk.' Robin breathed in the intoxicating air.

Marion laughed. 'I am safe under the blessings of Nanak and in the company of two strong souls.'

'Do women visit the Temple Marion?' Edward was genuinely curious.

'Of course. Sikhism is the cultural and architectural bridge between Hinduism and Islam. Women are revered in Hinduism - in fact Durga's Temple is close to Harmandir Sahib. Women are also protected, veiled from vicariousness, in Islam.'

'A little extreme don't you think?' Edward had a fleeting image of *"Midnight Pearl."*

'Hmm. I am not sure Edward. I for one am still toying with both sides,' Marion glowed with joy, 'whether to enjoy goddess status amongst my brothers or to simply hide myself under the purdah, shielded as it were, from the travails of the modern woman.'

'Marion!' Robin chided. 'Poor Edward may take you seriously yet.'

Marion said nothing, her head slightly bowed beneath the straw hat, her chappelled feet, obediently walking the path.

'Robin, I think that Marion is serious. Perhaps she is much better off under the sari or veil.' Edward teased Robin in return.

'Well, I suppose we would have many more chances to enjoy the beauties of the Mosque or Durga Temple.'

'Or indeed, bathe our souls in the sweet Amrit at Harmandir Sahib.'

'You see Edward. I am not sure whom I have married in Marion. I may yet have to undergo conversion and follow, in my wife's footsteps, as any devoted husband would.'

Edward laughed openly. 'Oh for your wisdom Robin, and Marion's penance.'

'The penance is all his I can assure you.' Marion piped up. 'Look, the Temple.'

Marion's face lighted up reflecting the pure sheen of the Temple face, shimmering in the sunlight.

'It's beautiful.' Edward could not help himself.

Robin, fully aware of the awesome beauty of the Mandir remained respectfully silent, allowing Edward to become absorbed in the enduring monument to Guru Nanak, the magnificence of the moment, overwhelming and extraordinary. Marion stopped, mesmerised by the beauty of the Mandi, captured in its ethereal spell. Robin walked casually beside her and stopped, taking off his shoes. He pulled a large handkerchief from his pocket and placed it, over his head. Silently, he gave a second handkerchief to Edward. Edward followed Robin's lead. Marion, still captivated in a world apart from them, took off her hat and pulled the long scarf loosely draped across her shoulders up and over her head. She slipped off her golden chappals and smiled radiantly at Robin. Robin inclined his head slightly, then bowed in reverence to Marion's unexpected bliss. He led the way, slowly, walking towards the magnificent white building with its gracious Hinduistic curves styled to please the eye and pacify the heart; the twin emblems of temporal and spiritual authority.

'Akhal Takt Sahib, Throne of the Almighty.' Robin whispered.

Edward gazed along the pure white curves, noting the perfect arches and twin parapets atop the building. 'Fitting.' He thought quietly, 'To anyone's God.'

Marion continued silently and single-mindedly along the causeway towards the temple, sitting majestically at the centre of the pool. Edward drew in his breath, captivated by the reflections of splendid beauty in the water. They crossed over, and Marion continued, like *"The Lady of the Lake"*

- magnetised by more than white marble and gold - towards the ornate clock tower that overarched the main entrance. The dizzying yet harmonious blend of styles immediately impacted upon Edward. He felt disoriented, unsure of whether this was Hindu or Muslim India, the extraordinary presence of Moghul architecture, yet the subtle and graceful arches of Hinduism, or something else altogether. Marion looked upwards at the clock tower, reminiscent of her heritage, comforting, in this most extravagant, yet obviously mystic vision of spiritual beauty and belonging. She ascended the stairs, then seemingly floated, into the sanctum. She smiled enraptured and clothed in the shimmering light that emanated from the gold lotus dome inverted over the temple in its homily of protection.

Edward wanted to weep. The sheer monument to faith, the magnificent arches, the gentle supplication to the heritage of the India that was as ancient as time itself, the comforting womb encased in pure marble, glittering and eternal gold. There were no words necessary, no thoughts present to jar the sublime supplication to his heart and soul. This was it. This was supreme feminine beauty that transcended the masculine creation; etched in intricate patterns onto the inner temple walls.

Robin watched quietly the submission of Edward to a history far greater and more powerful than the British, in this land that simply absorbed.

Transported by the moment in eternity, they returned to the Guru's Bridge, the naked causeway linking the Temple and the city. Marion once again led the way, Edward at her heels and Robin, starkly obedient in his bare feet and covered head, silently following, content to linger in the memory of timelessness and immortality.

Chapter Thirty Five

LAHORE WAS, AS Robin promised, a cynosure for the eyes. They descended quietly in the Dakota, overawed by the sudden appearance of the glorious spire of the Garrison Church of St Mary Ami adjacent to the airfield. With Robin as his able companion, Edward quickly immersed himself in the beauties of the ancient Moghul Empire. Lahore fort rose from the plains in silent sympathy with the greatness of the once-were emperors.

'From here Edward, you can travel to Karachi and from Sindh, trace the ancient trade routes back to the Middle East.'

'The Silk Route?'

'Yes. Alexander the Great almost came this far. He was reportedly after the riches of the Empire.'

'But he didn't make it. India could have become part of the Hellenistic tradition.'

Edward's comment was as dry as the evening air.

'No doubt. There is however a reversal of fortunes with the arrival of Emperor Ashoka. You'll relate to him Edward. Ashoka virtually turned India into a Buddhist dynasty then took his missionaries along the trade routes to Persia and into the western world taking the *"message"* as it were, with them. They also went into China incidentally. Buddhism before Ashoka, only had a faint hold, even in India. You can imagine the resistance a 'Christ-like' figure would meet in the Brahmin Priests of this land.'

'You equate Buddha with Christ?' Edward was more amused than amazed.

'Why not. Both loved the poor, were compassionate, loving, gentle, shunned wealth and were renunciates of, let's say, the passions of the flesh.' Robin smiled broadly, slapping his companion on the back.

'You're teasing again.'

'Edward, I don't mean to intrude on your private life, but at least send your wife a telegram.'

'You make it impossible for me not to Robin. What would Buddha or Christ have done? Is that what you're saying?'

'Well?'

'And I'm being tempted what's more.'

'Are you?'

'I hardly think so. Besides, I haven't even met this *"Midnight Pearl."*'

'So you have given her a life already Edward. Don't you think it's a case of the pot calling the kettle black?'

'Robin, I know I sound so priggish, but to have an affair with one of those charity nerds. You know what I mean.'

'No. I don't.' Robin said simply.

'They're all the same. So full of themselves, dripping with wealth.'

'You're jealous.'

Edward gasped. 'What! Jealous of some creep.'

Robin remained silent and cast his eyes along the long line of the fort. 'Beautiful isn't it Edward. Shall we have a closer look?'

'I guess we might as well. Perhaps you are right; I had better stop sulking over Ruth's affair. Who knows, it could happen to any of us.'

'Or more pertinently, to you Edward!'

'Robin!'

'Come on then. Let's go in.'

The two men walked towards the fort, Edward mildly in awe at the grandeur and sheer, architectural elegance of the building.

'Puts Buckingham Palace in perspective.'

'You're quite right there. Look. Imagine their archers in the turrets.' Robin pointed upwards.

Edward followed his gaze, suspended, for a moment, in the timelessness of lost kingdoms. His foot slipped off the bottom step and he reeled backwards into Robin.

'Hold on there old man. Don't want you cracking your skull on the threshold of a whole new life!'

'Thanks.' Edward gasped and hurriedly searched for a handkerchief.

'Here. Use mine.' Robin handed Edward a spotlessly white handkerchief. 'Are you alright. You look as if you've seen a ghost.'

'Oh my god, Ruth.'

Robin sat Edward on the step to recover his composure.

'Ruth. What's happened to you.' Edward felt as if he could die.

'Here, drink some of this.' Robin handed him a metal flask. 'It's only water. I never drink during the day.'

'Thanks. Oh my God. You're right Robin. I should have sent her a cable.'

'Well. It is not too late, you know. What happened just then? You look like as white as a sheet.'

'You wouldn't believe it if I told you.'

'Try me. Here, drink up.' Robin was determined. 'Can't have you collapsing on me. Wouldn't look very British would it.'

Edward managed a smile. 'Thanks again Robin. I feel so silly. Been nothing but trouble to everyone since I left England.'

'Don't mention it. But I'm still curious.' Robin put a strong hand under Edward's armpit and hauled him to his feet.

'Steady. Still a bit dizzy.'

'Dizzy?'

'It's gone now. Must have been the shock.'

'Shock? Come on man, out with it.'

'My brother-in-law, Thomas! He was standing in that turret waving to me.'

'I see. Did you know he was coming to India?'

'You know that he is dead. It happened when he slipped on the steps of St Peter's in Rome.'

Robin took a step backwards. 'You very nearly just did the same Edward.'

'My God. But surely… Thomas…' Edward's voice trailed away.

'Maybe he just wanted to remind you about Ruth Edward. She's just lost her brother and now her baby….' Robin's voice trailed away.

'That's it. I should go home.'

'Cable her at least. Even if it wasn't your baby, she is your wife after all.'

'And I suppose I'm not much of a husband.'

'That's for you to judge my friend. Now, do you want to go in or shall we go back?'

'There's no need. I'll be fine. Let's enjoy it while we're here.' Edward recovered his resolve sufficiently to enjoy the rest of the day with Robin.

On their return, Robin, with the smooth efficiency of a diplomat arranged immediately for the cable.

'Jot it down Edward and I'll have it sent off this afternoon.' Robin flung his hat onto the hatstand and simultaneously switched the ceiling fan to high. 'I'm sure that will be a weight off your mind and no doubt your wife's.'

Edward retrieved his pencil and notebook and hastily scribbled a few lines.

> "Ruth. So sorry about the baby. Are you all right. Tell me if you want me home.
> All my love, Edward."

He handed Robin the scribbled note, the relief his face palpable.

'Good man. You'll feel better when that's on its way.'

'I certainly feel a lot better. Can't imagine why I didn't want to do it in the first place.'

Chapter Thirty Six

Lahore, India, 23 March, 1940
IT WAS DAWN. The new awakening to himself and the sense of humanity and history far greater than he had ever encountered or imagined, set Edward's senses tingling and his mind buzzing with enthusiasm.

Amrit arrived at four in the morning to prepare an early breakfast for Robin and his guest.

'Mr. Edward. You drink tea?' Amrit enquired with a polite knock.

'Thank you. You are here early.' Edward remarked.

Amrit nodded his head sideways, beaming with pleasure. Robin had insisted that they bring Amrit with them to Lahore.

'He understands our ways Edward. Can't do without him.' Robin had explained quietly.

'Yes, thank you. Is Robin awake?'

'Oh yes, oh yes. You are leaving early today for the Gardens then afterwards Jinnah's park.' Amrit looked a few degrees less pleased. The corners of his mouth dropped slightly and his eyes betrayed a sense of disapproval at the unfolding of events in the Iqbal Park.

'It seems so Amrit. Thank you. Shall I come at what time…'

'In fifteen minutes will be very fine Mr. Edward.' Amrit grinned again.

'Accha.' Edward remembered a singular word of Hindi.

'Bahot achha.' Amrit beamed.

Chapter Thirty Seven

'MAGNIFICENT PLACE ROBIN. Can't say that I blame the British for not wanting to leave.'

'We do love it here.' Robin surveyed the opening panorama of the Shah Jehan's magnificent vision of heaven. 'Marion finds India very romantic. Wait until you see the Shalimar and botanical gardens. From another world, not just, another era.' He chuckled.

'Better than in Britain?'

'Their concepts are most amazing. Commissioned by Shah Jehan, they follow strict geometric and cultural laws.'

'You follow Islam?'

'Today, the Quaid-i-Azam will determine the future of all Muslims in India and certainly that will earn him some privileges in Bahist.'

'Bahist?'

'This is not quite the complete heaven, but as close to structured beauty as you will find anywhere. You should see it at night time, light reflecting from the water, the sound of rain falling in pools, marble cascades….. simply beautiful!'

'It is.' Edward whispered.

'Place of perfect protection for the nobility, Saints and those as fair as Marion.' Robin gazed along the high wall to the first of the watchtowers. 'As safe as anywhere could be in India.'

'It does feel peaceful.'

'Let's walk. I wanted for us to have some space and fresh air before the opening session.'

'Do you think it will be a little claustrophobic Robin?'

'You could say that. Besides, sometimes the dignitaries come here for a reception or early morning walk themselves.'

'Jinnah?'

'Maybe. It would be good to see the other side of the man if you know what I mean. Not just the future statesman, the political broker wheeling and dealing lives for the sake of nationhood.'

'Or fighting his private war with Nehru.'

'Shall we?' Robin began to walk along the promenade adjacent to one of the long, rectangular pools. One wonders whether the Khalifat movement isn't the only fallout from the First World War. Are you ready for it Edward? The opening session?'

'I am. Something also with a bit of substance for Chris than just Edward's *"travel notes."*'

'Good. Gird your loins man, there'll be close to a hundred thousand of them.'

'Good God. What chance does Gandhi have of stopping it.'

'Jinnah has garnered a considerable force in his followers. But Gandhi knows Jinnah quite well and in his unique and manipulative way, he will try and twist the Muslim arm towards a united India.'

'Gandhi manipulative?'

'The prerogative of age Edward. When you're confronted by a sheer wall of numbers, fired by religious passions and the forceful arrogance of youth, then, an old man has his ways.'

'You think that Gandhi can stop Jinnah?'

'No I don't. But I think he'll give it good shot.'

The two men found precious moments of practical peace as they walked side by side past the pools constructed almost 300 years ago by an Emperor who clearly enjoyed beauty. The birds fluted the first tunes of the day. The sun glanced over the sides of the garden walls. The atmosphere was heady with fragrances of a late summer and the air was alive with pregnant hope for the new day. The gardens were soothing a reminder for Edward of his own noble heritage, the glorious springs and late summers he enjoyed with Thomas on the banks of the Oxford River.

'England is not as mystic as this Robin.'

'Aah. You've discovered the soul of the Sufi Edward.' Robin affectionately slapped Edward on the back. 'India is far richer thanks to the Shah Jehan's creative imagination. Look at the Taj! Who could not say that it has not enhanced the soul of this noble nation? Yes, the Emperors were great, but in my heart, I feel that it is the mystic in the Muslim, that makes him the creator of great wonders.'

'They appear every bit as developed as a Greeks.'

'Every bit. In addition, you will be surprised to discover, just as the Greek civilisation was emerging, the Aryans settled the Kashmir. Two thousand years later, at approximately the same time as the sacking of Damascus and Jerusalem by the Persians, the Prophet Mohammed was born. The Muslims in turn persecuted the Persians. History has a way of settling scores it seems. But I must agree with you, the Moghul Empire was every bit as grand as that of our Greek ancestors.'

'What about India? There doesn't seem to be much in the way of monuments to her past. Surely, they were not simply pastoralists?'

'There are of course numerous temples to the deities, but there isn't much knowledge about the deities themselves except through their legends.'

'Strange don't you think? A civilisation without a history.'

'Hard to say Edward. Look at Ancient Greece and Rome. Very little remains, a sunken visage in the sand.'

'Nebuchadnezzar?'

'Yes. And I wonder whether Jinnah can see the parallels.'

'He would hardly be receptive at present.'

'All that will remain, of Gandhi will be a broken spinning wheel.'

'Not a crooked swastika Robin.'

'Not at all Edward. I quite like Gandhi's Tolstoyian sentiments. There's something very endearing and enduring in humility.

'Perhaps you could set the swastika spinning like a wheel.'

'Now there is an interesting image, a sort of wheel of enlightenment, a token to India's self-perpetuating mythology and nationhood. But the wheel would have to spin clockwise not anticlockwise like the Germanic-Aryan swastika.' Robin turned towards the watchtower, mindful of making tracks to the car.

'So you really believe Aryan roots are in India.'

'Why not? Migration happens.' Robin was philosophical.

'Along the trade routes. And Lahore was the hub of trade ages ago.'

'And still is. History in the making! Right here and now Edward as we stand and speak, Mohammed's devotee Jinnah is entreating his Allah, the One and only God, for this land the Punjab for himself and his people.'

'Formidable.'

'To say the least. In addition, an old man scantily wrapped in his homespun dhoti does not want Jinnah to proceed. He wants them to exchange vows of brotherhood and non-violence, to bend in mutual *"namastes"* and share the cracked earth that ultimately belongs to no-one.'

'You sound philosophical.'

'Live in this country long enough Edward, and it speaks for itself. The Punjab doesn't belong to Jinnah or to Nehru. It can't be divided like an apple with its seed wasted on the ground. This land is as sacred and holy as St Paul's Cathedral in London. The land creates its own history, not the other way around. Jinnah might get his way, but it won't be, an easy peace. It won't become his Punjab alone. Not even *"Pakistan"* is sufficient to command secular claims over the hearth of three of the world's greatest religious communities. They all belong here - not just Jinnah. Jinnah will lose the blessings of India if he cuts her to the core with his territorial knife.'

They walked under the tower gate and into the almost blinding light of the true Punjab, scant of seclusion, devoid of the protection of high walls, and absent of luscious gardens and marble waterways promising eternal paradise.

'Are you ready?'

Robin waited patiently for Edward to adjust his clothes and tie a neck kerchief.

The atmosphere was hot and slightly oppressive.

'It's just as well that Marion isn't here. I don't want to take any risks with her and the baby.'

'I quite understand.'

The driver arrived looking somewhat subdued. Edward felt as though he were going to the gallows. The roads were empty, as if in early mourning to the death of an incognito empire. As Robin imagined, the Mosque was filled to capacity. The two men were ushered unshod, to their seats. The atmosphere was overpowering and almost awesome. Robin strongly warned Edward against bringing a camera.

'Edward, bring nothing, nothing to write with and no camera. Just bring yourself. We're going as observers.'

Chapter Thirty Eight

EDWARD WAS SURPRISED at Robin's veracity, but as soon as they neared the Mosque the overwhelming oppression of belief and purpose stilled his mind into silence. A fierce tranquillity filled Iqbal Park. The silence contrasted sharply with the intensity of the new Muslim nation being visibly birthed in the gathering. Inevitably, there would be a cost. *"The Land of The Pure"* demanded, immense sacrifice.

Jinnah consciously spurned, Mother India.

Edward sensed the overpowering aura of patriarchy, manifest, yet superbly disguised under the flowing garb of religious and national identity. Then who would Jinnah honour as the mother of his new nation? India? England - the surreptitious *"mother"* who had spawned and nurtured the Muslim League? Did the infant Pakistan not, by virtue of birth, have a direct relationship with the *"Mother Goddess,"* Ancient Bharat, now burnt and sacrificed on the pyre of his ambition? What of his spiritual brother - the absent Jew? Did not the same father, if not mother, seed them both? Was not this womb of Pakistan also the field of the death of India? An entire nation conceived, birthed in stone, devoid of the mother, purged, cleansed of the feminine; a hundred thousand men, the great Badashi Mosque beckoning Jinnah towards new nationhood.

Adjacent, the great Royal Fort of Emperor Akbar the Great and his Moghul successors, built on the mud foundations of Hinduism, was the silent witness to the Act.

'If India could weep Edward, it would be now.' Robin broke into his thoughts.

Edward observed in detached fascination as the All-Muslim League of India passed the resolution to create a new and separate Muslim nation. United India was no more. The synchronous bowing of wills to the unquestionable destiny of the Punjab, was the final note, the tolling bell for millions.

Edward felt afraid. It was not fear for his life or for Ruth, but a chilling fear that struck the chords of his humanity. Whether or not he liked it - his values were challenged - he was completely exposed, isolated in this gathering that valued a God not so different to his own, but that listened to feelings of division, of death.

The totality of one hundred thousand men bending in unison at Jinnah's command completely stunned Edward. For the first time, he realised the powerlessness of intellect in front of religious and national fervour, in front of irrecoverable destiny. It was not even a question of choice, the resolution was pre-determined, fait accompli.

The Quaid-I-Azam's eyes lifted over the gathering and for a brief moment, Edward felt the cold thrill as their eyes locked together. Culture meant nothing - absolutely nothing - in front of Jinnah's singular and omnipotent determination.

It was ultimately Fazalul-Haq, the Chief Minister for Bengal, who moved the Lahore Resolution and on March 24 1940, Pakistan was born.

India was destined to division.

'There's no going back Edward.' Robin was resigned. 'In my estimation, there will be a bloody war and England will quietly withdraw to the sidelines. Jinnah has more than Gandhi to contend with. He has his bone to pick with Nehru and pick it dry he will, as dry as Parsi bones after the crows have consumed the last remnants of flesh. This is Jinnah's private war as much as it is the death of the Indian and British Empires. Jinnah will use England every bit as much as England used Jinnah. He's astute. Mark my words Edward. I don't think the Hindus with their vegetarian ways are any match for this man. One day, both history and Gandhi will grieve for India.'

Chapter Thirty Nine

THE FLIGHT TO Kashmir was predictably easier than the long haul to India from London. The Dakota was no less comfortable than on the previous sojourn. Robin behaved like an excited schoolboy, gawking through the pilot's window whenever the opportunity presented itself.

'You know Edward, these old birds, are the wings of the Empire. Imagine; cross over *"The Hump"* and you reach Burma. Fly a little to the north and you have access to the wastelands of the Chinese dynasties then onwards and you encounter a nation mourning their grand Tsars. In addition, here in the middle of it all are we, robbing India of her Rajas and Rajinis. Incredible isn't it?'

'You mean we are plunging India into mediocrity if we leave and robbing her of her right to rule if we don't?' Edward reflected on Robin's lofty perspective.

'Perhaps. Could be worse though. Imagine India under communism or fascism.' Robin noted dryly.

'Stretch of the imagination isn't it Robin? I mean fascism. Isn't Gandhi anarchistic?'

'Don't be naïve. I mean we're fighting fascist Germany with all her trappings and symbology of inverse Hinduism.'

'True. And in India?' Edward conceded.

'Fighting all the trappings and symbology of Hinduism and at the same time, creating a climate for the fundamentalists, the Hindu fascists of India.' Robin was resolute.

'You don't mean that surely?'

'I certainly do. Look what 'Independence' is spawning. You now have the Hindu *"Mahasabha,"* the Hindu communalists and the *"RSS."*'

'The *"Rashtriya Swayamsevak Sangh."* Edward remembered. 'Sounds ominously like the SS.'

'Well they are Edward. The RSS is rooted in Nazi ideology.'

'Hitler youth in India?'

'Doesn't make a great deal of sense does it. We leave India and Hitlerism moves in. Hitler perverts Hindu mythology in Europe and Britain goes to war. Here, the swastika is set in stone so Britain exploits the same power of mythology to make bloody sure all of the past, present and future brings India's wealth home to the Motherland.'

'British crown obviously does not like any one else's myths.' Edward struggled with the complexity.

'And King Arthur?'

'Ah, well, there's a different story altogether.' Edward recalled the quips of Marion.

'Can't see that it is Edward. What's better about the mythology of Britain?'

'Well, who is this *"Dropidy"* woman that Marion mentioned.'

'Trust a woman to sympathise with another woman.' Robin smiled.

'Dropidy isn't a woman of repute surely?' Edward persisted.

'She had five husbands.' Robin chuckled.

'Oh!' Edward smiled.

'In a manner of speaking. The legend is that the *"Pandavs"* were expelled from the kingdom to the jungle for 13 years. Dropidy was their sole female companion. But in the style of all great tales, the Pandavas, the five lads as it were, were not jealous of one another.'

'Impossible!'

'It's true.' Robin believed the story. 'Actually, something the United Kingdom would never be able to do is to keep the peace amongst rival husbands, not of the Dropidys of India nor for that matter, the assorted concubines and wives of Persian and Indian Kings.'

'Robin, you do shock me.' Edward grinned.

'Yes, it appears my friend that somehow, we have missed our calling. Wonder of nature is that a Muslim man can have two or three wives and that they can live together in semi-marital bliss. In that, there is little difference between the husbands of Hindu's Dropidy and the wives of the Muslim man, except of course, Dropidy had the upper hand.'

'You mean, they don't have any reason to fight one another. Just share around the women!'

'Do you think you could do that Edward?'

'You have got me there. And I'm jealous of Ruth's whoever-he-is and I don't even know his name.'

'Well then, there you are. We cannot be as emotionally or as spiritually advanced as India can we now Edward, if we can't tolerate a little jealousy.' Robin's tone was mild and humourous.

'You win. But does that make the Hindus and Muslims better than the British?'

'I didn't say that Edward.'

'But surely you don't agree with child brides Robin and this, this "*Sati*" business.'

'Sati? No of course not. Put yourself in their shoes for a minute. Natural form of social welfare. That's it. You have one less mouth to feed and the children stand a better chance to become strong. Besides, sati is rather romantic don't you think?'

'Romantic! I hardly think so. Do the husbands ever do it for their wives?'

'I am afraid not.' Robin said soberly.

'You sound like a fan of the Deutschland.'

'I am. Who needs any of this mothering stuff.'

'Robin! You're about to have a child.

'I'm winding you up.' Robin stated laconically. 'But you're right Edward. It stinks. India is a testament to the "*Great Mother.*" Why do you think they worship so many goddesses? Mother Bharat. Why not a little humility like the average Indian? The men love their goddesses. They worship their "*Lakshmi*" every day - the businessmen do in any case.'

'Lakshmi? Is she another Dropidy?' Edward felt overwhelmed.

'Wait until you meet her Edward, "*The Goddess of Wealth,*" she'll guarantee you lasting fortune.' Robin burst into laughter.

'I'm not sure that I want that.'

'You might need her. Not to mention *"Durga."* Where we're going, unless you have the *"courage of the lioness"* - you might as well turn around and head home.'

'I'm not entirely sure whether to believe you or not Robin.' Edward decided to stand his ground.

'Believe it! This is the place of warriors. Some of the more militant Sikhs and Muslims would as soon cut you in half as give you the time of day.'

'Perhaps they have *"Ghurkha"* blood.'

'Perhaps. However, it's more than that. We are, British after all. The tribesmen here don't respect British cloth; our military colours if you like. You're in different territory here Edward. Put a foot out of place and you are history.'

'Surely not that serious. Is that why you came with me?'

'Let's just say it's safer this way.'

'I'm enormously grateful.'

'Don't mention it. I need a break away too. You know Marion was so young when we married. I sometimes wonder whether she was ready, whether she married the right person.'

'Not you as well. But you both seem so perfectly matched.'

'Oh yes, we are. It's more to do with maturity. Imagine being a Hindu and becoming a child bride. How could you possibly make the right choice at that age.'

'Aren't the marriages arranged?'

'Many are. Some, indeed before conception of the child. It's a cultural and caste requirement and it makes one wonder how on earth they stick it out.'

'Are Hindus allowed to divorce?'

'Unheard of. Both sides of the family would disown the wife. The shame falls squarely on her shoulders, not the other way around. That's only part of the burden. Look at how poor many of these women are. If they are not lucky enough to have been born into caste and wealth, they often have hardly enough to eat - even when they're nursing a child.

If they're lucky enough to own a cooking pot, there's rarely any such thing as clean water. If you value your privacy, then a communal or even non-existent latrine would hardly suffice. You would not want to live as a villager in India for very long. It is a hard and harsh life, although of course, it does have its rustic beauty and simplicity.'

'We do forget how lucky we are.'

'Yes, but our fortune will not solve India's problems.'

'I'm getting used to these landings.' Edward yelled over the roar of the engine.

'You must tour the Indian airfields next time. Quite a history in itself.'

'No thanks. These few will do nicely for now.'

The Dakota made an undramatic entry onto the airfield and both Robin and Edward were relieved to touch the ground.

'You won't find it as volatile as the Punjab Edward, but I'm sure you'll find it more colourful. There aren't as many British here. There are incidentally, proportionally a higher percentage of Muslims in the Armed Services than either Sikhs or Hindus.'

'Oh. Any reason?'

'None that one can pinpoint, except that the British helped to set up the Muslim League after the collapse of the Ottoman Empire. The British have clearly maintained their relationship with the Muslims since the days of the Moghul emperors.'

'British-Muslim alliance!'

'Muslim-British India would be undoubtedly be suppressive of the Hindu population.' Robin added.

'It hardly makes sense of World War One. How do the Turks take our alliances on the Subcontinent?'

'Curious isn't it. One day they're the enemy and the next, we're seeking to subvert them for our own ends. Subversion is after all, a form of war. Just a little subtler I suppose. The Muslims have the bargaining power here. With the concentration of trained personnel at the northern frontier, Britain has very little choice except to accede to Muslim demands.'

'And Kashmir?'

'It's the case in point Edward. Kashmir is the territory between two warring factions. Jinnah wants it as a part of his homeland and the Hindus want Kashmir for India. It's all a bit murky at present. Apart from which there is still a lot of wealth in the region.'

'No doubt Mother will be interested in that.'

Robin raised his eyebrows. 'Well, we might as well move on.' He cast his eyes around the airfield. 'These airfields are hell. I wouldn't want to arrive in the dark.'

The support vehicle wheeled smoothly to the wing of the Dakota, ready to whisk Robin and Edward into hubbub of Srinagar.

'Edward, I'll be on official business for the next week.' Robin tapped the bowl of his pipe against the car door. 'Let me know where you want to go in the city or even further afield, Ladakh if you like. I'll arrange a driver for you. Since the Resolution, we're looking seriously at the implications for Kashmir. Jinnah is unlikely to settle for just the Punjab and Sindh.'

'Anything I am allowed to know? Chris would appreciate whatever he can get his hands on I'm sure.'

'No, I'm afraid not. Not at this stage anyway Edward. Let's see how things develop but you understand how sensitive the situation is at the moment. But he would have received your report on Lahore by now.'

'True. Perhaps I can play sightseer for the time being.'

'Excellent idea. The beauty of this valley is unparalleled anywhere Edward. If you are looking for the Garden of Eden - then here it is.'

'It's definitely far more than I expected. The mountains are almost ethereal set against the lake.'

'I see Srinagar through similar eyes. Only at the moment, one can almost see blood flowing into Dal lake.'

'Point taken. I'll leave you alone to get on with things.'

'Good man. I'll need to put my mind to the job. Now, if there is anything you need from the hotel, just call for Bashki.' Robin gripped, the bony shoulder of a grinning youth.

'Bashki?'

'Haji.'

Robin laughed.

'He likes you already. Ready to serve you Sahib! OK. I'm off then. See you in a week old man. Look after yourself.'

Edward shook Robin's hand and let Bashki take his bags. He felt strangely comfortable in his aloneness. The far outreaches of the kingdom were oddly peaceful and hospitable. The hotel room was clean and offered magnificent views of the lake. Trees adorned the water's edge and the faint pink of reflected flowers caught the fading light. A small assembly of houseboats hugged the banks in uniquely Kashmiri heritage. Edward wondered whether it would have been better to stay on one of the intriguing houseboats, but Robin had insisted on 'dry' accommodation.

'There's plenty to see Edward.' He had remarked. 'In any case, you'll have plenty of chances to go boating.' Robin had also accurately estimated the value of 'time alone' for Edward. The city was overflowing with beauty and serenity. The Hazrat Bal promised to be more splendid than the Mosques of Lahore and as well as the monument to the Prophet, there were wooden Mosques to visit, unique in their style and setting. 'Emperor Akbar,' Robin confided, 'is definitely in competition with Durga in Srinagar. The people revere Durga here as much as the great Prophet. Even Shankaracharya has his place on the hill in Srinagar. So I'm sure my friend, that you'll be soon immersed in a spiritual if not architectural extravaganza. Look after the body as well as the soul. You are not destined to leave us here.' Robin warned.

Srinagar was both fascinating and disturbing. Deep in the heart of northern India, the people proved to be unpretentious, almost simple. For the first few days, Edward lazily explored the city. The 'holiday' Chris planned for him, finally arrived. The romancing with ancient emperors, their kingdoms and Gods, was refreshing and uplifting, not to mention the overwhelming power of the mountains, providing a distinct frame for exquisite flowers and the immaculately kept Shalimar Bagh Moghul gardens. The Hazrat Bal was challenging, and Edward felt, totally tomb-like. He shuddered at the thought of the power of the past rulers and wondered if the early Judaic and Christian emperors were as daunting.

'Then I must go to Shankaracharya Hill.' Edward remarked aloud. 'At least I can pay homage to King Solomon and perhaps remind the Jinnahs of Srinagar of their heritage.'

The car and driver were omnipresent in Edward's daily routine. The driver was happy to sit inside the car until *"Sahib"* was ready to be driven. Edward felt embarrassed. As if Bashki's solicitations weren't enough to remind him of his Englishness. Then, if Robin had insisted he have a driver, it was probably better to acquiesce. The challenges of India proved to be multi-faceted. It was all very well to have to tolerate the heat of the plains, the dirt, lack of sanitation, the enmity of the nationals towards the British and innumerable other corrosions of his British civility. It was quite another matter, cast into the vast web of spiritual and religious heritage of India. He had no control and very little understanding of its history, purpose and effect.

All the prompting and priming by Thomas had not prepared him for the shock. If only he had listened to Thomas and taken his spiritual life more seriously. It was not until Thomas's death that Edward realised the rich inheritance of wisdom and the quiet assurance Thomas provided for his inquiring mind. To Edward, Robin was as intellectually challenging as Thomas was. It was however Thomas, who held the soft light to tend to and at the same time, gently bend one's beliefs without breaking them. Robin, was more inclined, to jest.

The sun was setting over the lake. The view was expansive and stretched Edward's imagination beyond the towering Pir Panjal range. Reverberations of Alexander's onslaught and the throng of civilisations moving to and from Kashmir thundered into the silent evening. On the edge of time and history, the brief sojourn of the British into an ancient land appeared both puny and insignificant.

'If only they knew. If only they realised that their war toys were meaningless out here.' Edward caught himself speaking aloud. He would have to keep his thoughts to himself. The driver was watching him closely.

The car drew into the base of the monument. Edward absently lit a cigarette and gave it to the driver.

'Stay here. I'm going for a walk.'

The driver nodded. Edward wondered if he had understood. He would not, on fear of losing his job or even death, abandon his charge to the wilderness of Kashmir.

Edward walked. He had not had the chance to stretch his legs properly for days. After the cramped conditions of the plane, he wanted to step out. The tourist route although interesting was never enough for Edward. He was in his heart a man of the hills and of nature. Only when he was alone near mountains had he felt a deep inner peace, a peace that, defied the turmoil of relationship and the eroding inner self-doubt that nagged at the value of his work. Here, close to the bosom of civilisation and Throne of Solomon, none of that mattered. Ruth was safe and Chris was not expecting much of him whilst he was in India. Edward breathed long and deeply. The air was clean, refreshing, and tinged with the subtle fragrance of late almond blossoms. A light breeze pinged with the crispness of dusk and sharpened Edward's step. He was unaware of where he was going, but sure that the path would lead him further from his fears and worries towards a place of meditation and solitude. At last, he had found a welcome interlude in the business of newspaper reporting, even whilst 'on holiday.' The unease of Britain at war was ever present and even here in India, he felt the underlying tension of Britain attempting to exert her influence and retain power over a nation with much more pressing needs. The subcontinent India, and most probably in the coming years Jinnah's new Muslim nation, was grappling with mind blowing poverty, overpopulation and a communalism that was tearing at her heart. Here, at the very Throne of Solomon, Edward could sense a tradition of spiritual primacy that far outshone the petty bickering of kingdom builders. He wondered, if The Buddha had ever walked this path?

The path came to an abrupt halt at the saddle of the mount. The monument rose in quiet repose against the evening sky. A series of open steps gave the building the feeling of the ancient Ziggurats. Edward climbed the first group, hesitating with disbelief at the unmoving and unmistakable memorial to the past. Another group of steps led to a stone canopy capped by a tiny dome atop an impressive tomb-like structure.

'This could be anything, Jewish, Islamic, Christian or Sikh. And even the *"Throne"* looks like the home for a Hindu goddess.' Edward reflected.

'Sahib?'

Edward started. An old Sikh gentleman, his turban wound in curious beauty around his aged head, attended the Throne.

'Sahib, you sit.' Edward felt unsure, but obeyed in muted respect and sat where the old man signalled. He could feel the coldness of death in his limbs and realised that he could not stay here long. The monument was a solitary reminder of his mortality, stark, naked and silent. Nevertheless, the view captured him in its magnificence, tearing his thoughts away from the concreteness of life and death.

'My God Ruth, if only you could realise the beauty outside your little charity world.' Edward sat motionless, unmoved by his wayward thoughts.

The sun settled on the far shore of the lake and shed long rays across the waters. As he turned to view the panorama below, Edward could discern the defined edges, of houseboats with their pinpricks of light briefly playing and merging with the fading light of dusk. Soon, they would burst into the darkness as if switched on by the call of night time. The pinkness of the sunset flicked at Edward's pupils, turning the surrounding wilderness into a garden of rose-like beauty and softening the edges of the landscape into the subtle evening light. A cascade of light billowed and like a waterfall, plummeted into the lake as the dying sun broke through the canopy of clouds. The atmosphere stilled and subdued into a semi-sleep.

Edward relaxed into a shawl of gentleness and peace. The air wrapped around him in delicate tendrils and caressed his face with infinite tenderness. His mind filled with the consummate beauty and, an awe of oneness, an all-embracing and eternal love that ached into his heart. Then, like a forgotten mother, the evening mist fanned and rested on the crown of his head.

In the soft evening embrace, Edward badly wanted to sleep a sleep that would last centuries, a sleep that was free from dreams and thoughts of yesterday, today and tomorrow. The numbness in his limbs deepened into a lightness and freedom. He felt as if he were out of his body, flying over the vast landscape then hovering like a bird over the quietened and illuminated water. The lake felt as though it were a dizzying distance below, but he could feel the light chop and dance of wavelets as they tried to catch at his mind. The lake pulled at him with a magnetic force, a plumbless vortex that longed to wrench him into its dark depths.

Edward struggled, his mind gasping for light as his lungs, sodden with the struggle, gasped for breath. He pulled back from the water, defying its gravitational hold on his life and death and searched frantically for the familiar territory of his own body.

'Edward, relax. You're safe with me.' The voice was soft and echoed in pulsing waves through his consciousness. 'Edward, it's not your time. Relax. You are not going anywhere, not yet. A little journey for now, but no further. Look around, what do you see?'

Edward ceased his struggle. 'Who is it? Who are you?'

'You know who I am.'

Edward remained silent.

'You've been searching.'

'No, I haven't. I'm here on holiday.'

'You're here to find yourself. And I'm here to help you.'

Edward was aware of a tugging sensation, a sickening feeling as if the voice would rapidly disappear into the night.

'Don't worry. You've left your body for a few moments and you're about to return. The body will be cold. Look after it.'

'How do you know me?'

'I know you. This isn't just the birthplace of the dynasties of India or the spiritual realm of Buddhists and Muslims. This is the throne of your own religion.'

'The Throne of Solomon?'

'Abraham, Moses, Solomon. All passed this way.' The voice was softly humorous.

'No, not possible, Moses?' Edward puzzled over the implications.

'Why not? The Promised Land.' The voice began to fade.

'Am I supposed to believe you?'

'This is the Pathless Mount where all find homage, Abraham, Moses, Solomon, Buddha, Jesus, Mohammed. All knew me here. You too will find your way.'

'Oh?'

'Return to Srinagar.'

The word 'Srinagar echoed in his mind like a bell tolling over an ancient tomb. For a moment, Edward saw the fleeting image of Abraham holding in his hands, seeds, and scattering the seeds over the waters of Dal Lake. The waters rose and expanded over the Middle East and Europe, the seeds flowering, bearing symbols of Islam and Israel. Edward hesitated, unsure of the meaning.

Then before him stood a wizened and old man, prayer wheel in hand, his eyes sharp, glinting hidden truths.

'The monks will guide you.'

'The monks?' Edward startled himself with his own voice, aware that he was 'back' in his body. He started to shake violently, his body racked with cold. The air was numb with an ominous chill. It was getting dark and the monument felt strangely close, a silent sarcophagus, open, beckoning.

Time to return. He did not want the driver to come looking for him. Edward felt his way carefully down the steps and searched briefly for the path. It took twenty minutes to return to the car. By the time he opened the door and climbed in, the driver was well and truly asleep, his head resting on the wheel.

'Sahib. No sleep!' The boy jolted upright as Edward slammed the door shut. Edward patted his arm and nodded towards the hotel. The boy struggled with the implications and sparked the engine into a rushed but comforting drone. Edward rubbed his arms and thought about a hot chai and long bath. The driver picked his way slowly down the mountain under the looming presence of *"Takht-i-Suleiman."*

Chapter Forty

THE DESCENT FROM the Throne of Solomon was a return to the corporeal from the transcendent. Edward felt his legs; they were as real as the smell of petrol and the metallic 'ping' of small rocks flying from the wheels into the undercarriage of the car. He wasn't sure whether to believe it himself, here he was, transported as far away from London as he could possibly be, then elevated to age-old scenes that curiously connected Thomas's illuminating tales.

He smiled to himself. No wonder Thomas spoke to him as if he had found the lost treasures of the Ark! His was an intoxication of a wealth far greater than just the jingling of absent coins in his pocket. So this was it, the watershed of the world's greatest religions and something, someone, had confronted him with time and belief upon the pinnacle of life and death. The promise of a heritage far richer than he had known filled him with a sense of majestic depths within his own soul, a resonance as real as the daily reports he filed in London.

Edward cast a sombre glance towards the driver, but the boy was holding onto the steering wheel with all the strength in his frame. The wheel fought him, as if to alter their destinies with the hewn rocks strewn on the road. Edward looked through the rear window at the looming mountain overshadowing his descent. The gall rose in his throat. He wanted to scream in rage at the mountain, at the voice that moved in on his private world. He felt robbed of the illusion of his mortal security, the sanctuary of his well-shaped beliefs and the fragile shell of his relationship with Ruth.

'No!! It was not going to be like that. No one, not even *"God,"* whoever or whatever that was, could shatter his soul with untimely and uninvited intrusions into his psyche. How dare anyone or anything destroy the sheltered bliss of this lost paradise with the rude shock of his vulnerability; of impermanence?

Edward's rage clasped his vocal chords forcing him to gasp for air and free him from the grip of his exploding sanity. As he breathed, he inhaled the foul fumes of bidi smoke coming from Bakshi's mouth. Edward gagged, dangerously close once again to being overwhelmed by nausea. There it was, he could take it or leave it. He could accept the higher wisdom of his solitude and the challenge to his very mortality, or he could reject it in a moment of shocking defiance. Edward chose the former, not wanting to expose his cultural resistance to the greater flow of destiny, the unravelling fabric of textual beliefs, which in fact shrouded more intricate and carefully woven truths. The driver's coarse dress reminded him of the grinding reality of poverty, the painstaking moments, that fed and housed millions of families across India. The blatant truth presented him with the choice of gratitude, or a path of obstinate crudity and brutality that so many other English in India had chosen. It was too obvious, too stark to ignore.

He pulled his head in and silently acknowledged the lessons of life and death. There was no going back, he was forever, transformed and transfixed.

They arrived at the hotel late and tired. Edward felt both grateful and humbled by his experience, but more so, by the apparent and present indications of normal human life. The power of the mountain had sobered sense into his naive English soul and the words *"The body will be cold, look after it,"* rumbled into his thoughts.

The hotel was a bubbling hive of activity; insects dancing close to the naked and hanging bulbs and the aromas of burning oil and steamy rice mixing into the smoky light.

'Mr. Thompson Sahib. Where you been? Outside too cold.' The hotel owner looked concerned. 'Come Sir. You sit here.' The little man hustled Edward into the warmth.' Chai? Chai OK Sir?'

Edward grinned at the bony and child-like man. 'Chai, very good. Thank you.' He had never felt better than with the attentions of the gesticulating and fussing hotelier.

'Come. You sit and drink chai.'

Edward followed him into the hotel dining room and sat smilingly at the table. Bakshi brought chai, hot, spicy and sweetened to a heart and life-warming pitch. Edward wrapped both hands around the crude china and lifted the cup to his mouth. The steam blurred his vision and caused his nostrils to stream but the liquid restored his inner fire, lighting the burner of his heart and his soul that came so close to death. In that moment, Edward knew that there was nothing better than the warmth of human company, no matter how annoying, how ridiculous and how very Indian.

'Sahib, you OK now?' It was the hotelier.' You take bath now. Hot bath? Bahot accha. OK?'

Edward nodded in quiet relief. A bath would be perfect and then some food. The coldness of the *"Tomb"* come *"Throne"* of his enigmatic ancestor was sufficient to chill the remnants of worry and self-pity into permanent death.

Chapter Forty One

THE MORNING LIGHT over Srinagar was to Edward a holy shroud soothing the darkness of his soul. The lake stilled into a calm that mirrored the resting, timeless limbo of eternity. The movements of the early morning vendors and boat people could barely ruffle the surface of either the lake or the majestically curtained atmosphere. The backdrop of mountains walled in any hope of journeying into the distance. It was here and now. Edward could not imagine that anything existed outside this Shangri-La of ancient civilisations and religions. Of all places on earth, there could be none other as beautiful, as mystical or as completely enchanting.

Edward wept quietly into his towel. He allowed the grief of his brother-in-law's death to surface. Here in this land that Thomas would have adored and breathed into his very bones, it was impossible to suppress. He knelt by the bed, his head cradled in his arms and resting on the softness of the quilt. Edward quietly yearned for the mature and wise counsel of Thomas. Yet, the only sound of solace was the lilting call of the morning cuckoo, resounding and echoing persistently into a vacuum of time and space. He allowed himself to drift into the space occupied for so long by the spirited discourses of Thomas. Thomas's full and melodious voice, which for so long, enriched and caressed his soul. Nothing. His mind felt the void, the edgeless surface of emptiness that was neither the birthplace nor tomb of thought and feeling. Thomas was 'gone.' Adrift in the ocean of fathomless loneliness, Edward felt the shockwaves of torment wrack his body. Breathless and his stomach knotted in grief, he gasped for strength as his lungs ached and fought for breath. There was no loosening the tight hold of grief. Almost at the limit of his endurance, the pain suddenly eased and Edward lifted his head to find a strong figure shadowing his bed.

'Oh my God. Who are you?'
'Hello Edward. You've come to the right place.'
'What on earth… '
'Don't ask. Have you forgotten?' 'Forgotten?'
'It's Easter.'
'What?' Edward pulled himself onto the bed to ease the torture of his belly and lungs.

'Easter. I thought that you might be praying.' The mouth curved into a gentle and compassionate smile.'
'Actually, I was thinking about my brother-in-law.'
'Oh? Not about the Resurrection?'
'I suppose you could say that, if you believe in the life after.'
'And you don't?'
'I'm not really sure. Who are you anyway?'
'You don't recognise me Edward?'
'No I don't. And how do you know my name?' Edward was becoming impatient.

'Not many do recognise me, but then I'm hardly flesh and blood.'
'You look pretty real to me.'

For a moment, soft gold, haloed the figure. The hands, palms outstretched and held high as if to catch the morning sun as it streamed through the window, entranced Edward's eyes. The palms folded in a quiet namaste. Edward noticed the perceptible white ray passing through the palms as if from the ether, a lance to bind the hands together in lasting prayer. The figure looked like the ascension, surrounded in divine light and an aura of total, peace. Edward felt like collapsing into the arms of light, his mind enclosed in a womb of motherly softness and grace. The moment of Grace felt like forever and Edward began to breathe quietly in his inner nakedness. Yet, he felt neither fear nor shame, simply a sense of surrender and inner resolve. The words were as gentle and profound as he had ever heard. The sounds merged into his subconscious. There was no time to conceptualise or crystallise thoughts and impressions. Edward sighed and laid his head once more on the bed, this time entering a deep and restful sleep.

Chapter Forty Two

THE TIME PASSED without concern. The Srinagar day unfolded like so many others in its lilting assembly of human voices, bird calls, the restful ruffling of the wind through quiet leaves, the lap of the lake at the side of boats and houseboats. Edward slept as he had never slept, unaware of the passing of the hours or the unfolding rhythms of the primordial town. He awoke feeling refreshed and somehow deeply eased from his burden of pain and loss. Ruth flashed into his mind and for an instant he remembered. It was Easter! He had forgotten that she would be spending it alone, childless, and husbandless.

> *"Resurrection Edward? No, not possible. Resurrection would mean that matter was immortal like the soul. No Edward, only the soul is immortal, not matter. It may be possible that the "soul" reincarnates, but definitely not the body. If the elements of nature were immortal like the soul, then we would still have Aristotle and Pythagoras walking amongst us today. However, you don't see them do you! You don't even see Jesus. So if he appeared before the Disciples then he must have been either flesh and blood or a bloody vision my friend."*

Thomas's discourse reverberated into his thoughts. The play on words slightly shocked Edward. Yet, Thomas's brutal logic jolted his mind free from the veil of myth and blind faith he was long accustomed to, ingrained by the recitations and repetitions of hymns. Edward looked at his own palms. There were slightly sweaty and pink. He wiped his hands on the towel and then his face.

'God Edward, how can you do this to yourself. Thomas was the scholar, not you. Here you are so far from home and you aren't even aware that it's Easter. For God's sake man. Get a grip on yourself.'

There was nothing to grip; there was no sense of the rational in this far off place. The fragrance of spring was like intoxicating nectar that rendered the intellect senseless and heightened the aesthetic; the intangible, invisible and evaporative beauties denied him in England.

Edward's senses felt more acute, not to the jars and crashes of human weakness, but tuned to the beauties of nature and the slow wonder of days that seemed to stand still.

'You must be dreaming man.' Edward admonished himself. Edward looked at his watch. It was midday and he had neither eaten nor washed. It was time to make a move. The guide had promised to take him to a relic or tomb.

'Must be an Islamic Saint. A pity indeed Thomas that you couldn't be here.' Edward bargained. 'No use Edward. He won't come back. You'll have to do the searching for Thomas now. Finish it off as it were.' Edward surprised himself with his clarity and reasoning.' Finish it off for Thomas?' That was a bit presumptuous. Then a lot had happened since he had arrived in Kashmir. With Robin otherwise occupied, there was no one to talk to. There was no escaping that he was in at the deep end. Thomas always warned him it one day, would happen.

> "One day good man, you'll be out of your depth and you'll have to swim. You see Edward, if you don't swim, you'll be so overwhelmed that you will lose the power to know the real from unreal, imagination and fantasy from hard facts. It does that to you. You have to stay afloat, to discern the mystic from the spiritual and the spiritual from the mundane, because if you do not, you run the risk of teetering over the edge into the abyss of insanity or disbelief. That's the real hell Edward. It is the not know ing that destroys your mind, not knowing what is real and unreal. It is the not know ing your own mind Edward. It is not knowing how to bring the mind into line with logic and reason and set you on the path of true wisdom that matters. That is hell, when the mind is un-reined, when the intellect has no control over thought or feeling.
> Equally Edward, unless truth and humility tempers experience, it has little value.

That's what wisdom is. The Hindus call it self-enlightenment or self-realisation. That's what you are after. They use the chakra, the wheel of self-knowledge as the symbol of truth. Without it, your thoughts will be spinning out of control and there is no way that you'll be able to hold them steady or on course. That's when you lose your mind, when the wheels are off the rails of reality; your mind spins like Arjuna's chariot without the driver. Take note my friend, when the spokes break, your sanity goes with them and truth is merely a broken arrow in the hands of a child. Look after your mind Edward. You need to temper your beliefs with reason and experience, but don't allow yourself to become cynical either otherwise you will never taste the sweetness of the life."

Edward caught his reflection in the mirror. The shadow of the morning looked strangely soft in the light. 'Perhaps I should grow a beard. I wonder what Ruth would think?' Edward stroked his chin. 'Shouldn't hurt.' The trembling of his chin reminded him that he had not fully recovered his composure. He wasn't sure whether it was vulnerability, whether he was missing Ruth or that his visitor humbled him. The snapping of twigs alerted him to the world outside the hotel room and he dressed quickly. The air was still crisp and sharp although warmed by the noon sun.

The hotel seemed quiet as if content to rest in a midday slumber. Edward searched for the hotelier wondering if it would be possible to eat before setting out to visit the tomb. There was no one around except for the guide.

'Sahib. Waiting long time. You ready Sahib?'

The guide looked faintly impatient, but ingratiated himself to the prospect of a few hours of touring around the old city and showing the Englishman its secrets. He was strange for an Englishman. Most of them wore uniforms and were sharp with him but this man was more introvert and unsure of himself.

'Sahib. You come this way please.'

Edward checked his wallet and followed the man into the courtyard. The sun was surprisingly warm and for a moment he was tempted to leave his pullover behind but still remembered the sudden coldness of the mountain.

The car felt its way into the maze of tiny streets and Edward suggested they walk. The guide would hear nothing of it. Cars were a rarity in the village and he was on this occasion, able to show off his standing by taking the Englishman through its impossible alleys and streets.

The car came to a sudden halt and the driver lunged towards Edward's door.

'Rozabal Sahib. This way.' The guide set off on foot.

Edward, anxious not to lose him stepped smartly to keep apace. Soon, they were confronted by an almost Japanese-style building with three roofs and carved arch- windows. The grounds were tidy and clean and a few local people lounged near the entrance.

'You like Sahib? This tomb to Yuz Asaf.'

'This is a tomb to an Islamic Saint according to the hotel.'

'Sahib, you come quickly inside, please.'

The guide led Edward towards a small entrance and into the larger rectangular building. Inside, there was a wooden shrine and the guide took Edward through a narrow opening into the burial chamber. 'Here Sahib, this grave to Saint Syed Nasir-ud-Din and this,' he pointed to the larger gravestone, 'this Sahib, is grave to the great Saint.' The guide pushed Edward towards a tiny opening where he could look below the gravestone onto a sarcophagus. It was covered with a worn cloth and oriented perpendicular to the north-south facing gravestones. 'Sahib, you see, you see!'

Edward froze as if suddenly cast into the floor alongside the gravestones. His heart missed a beat as he desperately tried to deny the flow of his thoughts. Ed ward felt shaken and bewildered. Did he believe in the resurrection! There it was in front of his eyes; proof of great Saints buried in Kashmir. The guide could not answer any of his questions. He must be mistaken. For a fleeting moment, he felt the calming presence of Thomas.

'Sahib, you ask the monk. The monk, he knows everything. I take you there?'

'Take me where?'

'Hemis Sahib. Hemis bahot accha monastery. Monk there, very wise. Know everything Sahib.'

Hemis? How far away was Hemis? Today was Easter Sunday. There was less time to reach Delhi. Chris wanted him home by May 10 at the latest and Ruth was already in trouble.

'*Hemis?*'

The hotelier was all smiles. 'Hemis too far Sahib. Dangerous journey. No car, no car. Very big mountain.' The bony man pointed to the mountain range.

'Himalaya too big to climb without porter and guide - and the weather Sir - sometimes very bad. You not look too, strong mister. Sahib, you not make the journey today.' The hotelier waved his hands in mock disapproval at Edward.

Edward stared back at the little man with the quizzical look on his face. "*Ask the monks!*" The voice on the mountain had said.

'Ah, Sahib, I see you very interested. I tell you where you can find a little monastery. Chalo! Chalo!'

The hotelier called loudly to the guide, all the while madly waving his arms and shaking his head at Edward.

'Himalaya too far mister. You not go there today.'

Edward had to suppress a laugh. Here he was in the middle of nowhere with this incredible little man, at once giving him hot tea sending him off for a bath in the next! It was unusual, quaint and strangely comforting. Even in England, Edward had never experienced such concern, comical thought it was, nevertheless, underscored by a sense of humble respect and noble protection. Edward's heart warmed to the little fellow and he gave him a hearty slap on the back.

'Bravo Sahib!'

The hotelier looked at him in mock surprise and continued with his arm waving. Edward decided to eat then retire to his room to read. He thanked the guide and handed him a few coins.

'Tomorrow, early!'

Tomorrow, he would call and arrange the flight to Karachi.

Srinagar was hauntingly beautiful and temptingly attractive to his eyes and soul. He could stay here forever if he were able to do so. The days would roll by and he would soon lose himself in the majesty of the mountains and the magnetic pull, of the lake. The monastery could wait. Tomorrow would come too soon and there would be little time after that for rest.

Edward lunched alone and then returned to his room, grateful to be away from the peering eyes of the guide. He stretched out on the bed letting out a long breath of completion and satisfaction. So much had happened in such a short time. He still wanted to digest this morning's experience and the visit to Rozabal, and as Thomas warned, temper his experience with reason. *"Siddhartha"* lay on the bedside table. Edward picked it up and absently turned to the page bent at the corner. The words blurred in front of his eyes. It was an effort to refocus. Then he mustered sufficient concentration, to complete the remaining chapters. The book absorbed, Edward drifted into a light doze until the bell for dinner sounded.

The hotelier awoke him at 6.30am to take the call. It was Robin.

'Edward old man. Are you ready? There's a plane leaving at lunchtime for Karachi. Make sure you're on it. There isn't another for a week and I don't want to have to worry about you wandering off into the hills. Have you heard back from Ruth?'

'Nothing. And thanks. Thanks for trip.'

'Don't mention it. Had an interesting time?'

'Interesting, you could say that.'

'Hotel comfortable?'

'The hotel is first class. Quite a profound place Srinagar.'

'Why do you say that old man. Altitude isn't getting to you is it? Never mind. We'll have you out of here by noon. Beautiful though. You are right there. Srinagar is a place of gods. It is a wonder that they let anyone into the valley, but of course, they need us here at the moment.' Robin's voice echoed strangely on the line.

'Right. How is Marion?'

'She's fine thank you. I will arrange for someone to meet you in Karachi. Is there anything else I can do for you before you go? Any messages for home?'

'No thanks. I'll cable David from Karachi. However, there is one thing. Do you know of any monks in Srinagar?'

'Monks. No. There is an old man at the market place. He's often there with his prayer wheel. You won't have that much time this morning. Be quick if you do. Rightio. Have to move on now. Catch up with you next time. You are coming to Amritsar again, I take it.'

'Thanks. I'd love to. Love to Maid Marion.'

Robin laughed. 'Will do.'

Edward heard the parting click in his ear and replaced the receiver onto its hook.

Breakfast was a hasty affair. Edward settled for five pooris and a dob of yoghurt. The chai arrived in a steaming teapot. He drank four or five times out of the tiny cup before calling the hotelier.

'How much Sahib?' he joked.

'Sahib, you very polite man.' The hotelier bowed slightly.

'No mention Sahib. This do?' Edward handed him a generous wad of notes.

'Too much, too much. You keep.'

'You keep.' Edward replied. 'You keep. For your missus. Buy her new sari huh?'

'Thank you Mister. She wear punjabi.'

'Good. I will need a car to go to the airfield for 11.30am. Make it sharp, and in the meanwhile I will need a guide.'

'Guide? Oh, you go out now?' The man sounded disappointed.

'Yes. I want to go back into town.'

'OK, OK.'

The hotelier disappeared and returned with the guide who was decidedly sleepy and unkempt.

'He too much drinking Sir.' The little man looked dismayed.

'Not to worry. Do you think he can make it into town in one piece.'

'Yes, yes. He ready.'

Edward walked back to the courtyard, the guide trailing behind him.

'Here. Have something to drink first. Ten minutes, OK?' Edward pushed him back into the hotel and went to collect his camera. As he crossed the courtyard, a withered man with fading robes stepped into his path. Edward stopped and stared at the apparition.

'Are you the monk?' Edward was amazed by the coincidence.

The monk stared silently at Edward then swung his tiny wheel into the wind. For a few moments, it spun idly, ribbons trailing like unfettered flags. The wheel chat- chattered then abruptly died as the monk tucked it back into the safety of his robe. His eyes penetrated Edward and Edward had the uncomfortable feeling that the monk knew all about him. The monk turned quickly on his chaffed and bare heel and disappeared into the morning light.

Chapter Forty Three

England

RUTH AWOKE IN the hospital feeling tired, but relieved that the baby was gone. Her mind searched for answers. 'Why, why this? Thomas dead? Now the baby! It couldn't be.' Her feeling of restfulness and relief at the diminution of the pain, dissolved into heart rending grief. Her child was lost before it was born. Confusion washed over her as she clutched emptily at her pillow, but the tears would not come. A deep anguish at having failed herself, of having failed the child filled the void normally relieved through her tears or drink. Why? Why had the child died? And Thomas - Thomas appearing and telling her that it was too soon, that it was not his time. The child? 'Thomas?' Ruth gasped. 'Perhaps…' The thought lingered, 'but if reincarnation were true, then why so tragically, why not the clean equation of birth, death and rebirth? Not this way Thomas, please, you couldn't.' Ruth's mind whirred with pain. What would Edward think and how could he ever understand or console her? Edward who coolly dismissed the possibility of reincarnation as nonsense, was unable to accept Thomas's wisdom.

> "Nonsense? My dear fellow, what more elegant explanation exists than the concept of karma and reincarnation? If I were to die tomorrow, then do you think that I would go to heaven? Heaven? Where is heaven Edward. Do you think that there is a need to resurrect these somewhat tatty clothes? Come, come Edward. Your mind must learn to embrace greater truths and deeper wisdom. Surely my friend, your reporter's instinct tells you that reality lies beneath the 'so-called' and apparent truths."

Thomas's logic was appealing.

'Of course, you must be right Thomas.' Edward replied. I only see what I choose to see and even that is only the view of others.'

"That settles it then. You must search for yourself my dear brother. There is no time like the present. When you find the time, dip into this." Thomas placed a copy of "The Light of Asia" into Edward's hand. 'It's about Buddha. I'm sure that you'll appreciate the language if nothing else.' However, Edward had put it aside and forgotten about it.

Ruth turned to her side. Her belly ached with trauma and the dull ache of loss. She was still losing fluid, but at least the large clots of blood and flesh were no longer tearing from her womb into a cruel puddle onto the floor. She wondered whose flesh it was, hers or the child's. Did it matter? A part of her was gone now anyway, her hidden life that she had never wanted Edward to see. Why did she need to hide from him? Edward knew too much about her and there was never any room for her own privacy. Edward had a life and she wanted a life as well, a life that he could not reason into logical order and sequence, a life that allowed the spontaneous and unexpected. But not this. There was no joy now in her brief flirtation with motherhood was warming, fulfilling. She had felt contented, but now, now, it was gone, taken away from her as easily as the pregnancy started. She groaned. It would be a long time before she could forgive herself. Not for herself, but for the child. Next time, it would be different. Edward could not love her in the way a husband should. Not yet. He still protected her like a child. But she had grown up now and wanted to be free from the cage of childhood. The pains in her gripped her belly and held, forcing Ruth to tuck her knees into her chest and rock in despair.

'I thought this was over, there's nothing left' she protested.

'Mrs. Thompson, are you all right?'

'The pain.' Ruth gasped.

'Where is it hurting dear?' The nurse reached her bedside and pulled back the sheets.

'All over, like an ache from under my ribs all the way into my legs.'

'Are you hot? Let's take your temperature.' The nurse whisked the thermometer out of its casing. She tucked it deftly under Ruth's left arm. 'There. Don't move please. Three minutes, then we'll know.'

Ruth groaned. Three minutes was a lifetime of pain as Ruth allowed herself to sink into a semi-stupor, frozen by the agony of her tortured womb.

'Dr. Anderson's here to see you Mrs. Thompson.' The nurse jolted her back to the present.

Ruth opened her eyes, the room spinning and blurred in front of her.

'Hello Ruth. How are you feeling? Dr. Anderson smiled broadly as he approached his patient. 'Did you sleep all right?'

'Dr. Anderson.' Ruth wanted to cry. 'Thank you for coming. I'm so sorry…'

'Think nothing of it Ruth. I'm here for you. Now, where's the pain?'

'I'm aching all over.' Ruth was still nauseous and slightly dizzy.

'I see. Dr. Anderson took the thermometer from the nurse and held it to the light before shaking the mercury down again. 'It's way up I'm afraid Ruth. I'm worried about infection. I'll need to take a swab for the laboratory. I hope you don't mind but it's not worth the risk.'

'Risk? Is anything wrong?'

'I'm not sure yet Ruth. But I want to play safe. Edward won't be impressed to come home to find his wife sick from lack of her doctor's care.' Dr. Anderson smiled protectively.

'Edward? He knows?'

'Yes. Chris Cooke sent him a cable. I expect that Edward will answer within a couple of days. Do you know where he is at present?'

'He was going to Delhi then to Amritsar, but that's about all I know.'

'We'll find him.' Dr. Anderson's said briskly. 'Meanwhile young woman, I think you need to sleep and recuperate. I have asked the nurse to make sure you eat and drink properly. You lost a lot of blood last night and you'll need the strength.'

'Oh? I didn't know it was that bad.'

'As I said, you lost a lot of blood and it will take time for you to build your strength. I'll be back again this evening Ruth. You might have news of Edward by then.'

Ruth smiled as Dr. Anderson closed the door behind him. Her head sank into the pillow and she breathed deeply. She looked at her hands, pale and white on the bed cover. The skin looked stretched and old as if she had aged ten years in one night.

'No charity work Ruth.' Ruth felt the resignation in her thoughts. She could sense the change in herself, as if the child passing through her womb changed her life and opened the door to a new beginning. She loved Edward, he was stable, predictable, affectionate, but she needed room to move. Guilt immediately invaded her thoughts, pushing away her sense of self. *"Somehow, she would make it up to him."*

It was Friday. Ruth had been in the hospital for four days, and still there was no word from Edward. She slept, ate and waited, waited for the message that meant that he loved her; that he had forgiven her. No message came, nothing. Dr. Anderson continued to console her and even Chris came to the hospital to comfort her. He arrived looking sheepish and somewhat guilty.

'Chris. You did the right thing. Edward needed a break and probably one from me also. How were you to know that this would happen? Besides, he is probably travelling somewhere.'

Chris remained silent. He had received Edward's report of Amritsar but there was nothing from him for Ruth. 'You are probably right Ruth. I'm sure that he's caught up in events in India and perhaps the cable is waiting for him at the hotel or some such thing.'

Then it arrived. In a rush of concern, Edward wrote.

23 March 1940
'Ruth. So sorry about the baby. Are you all right?
Tell me if you want me home. All my love, Edward.'

Chris called her the moment the telegram arrived on his desk. 'Ruth. There is a telegram waiting for you from Edward.'

'Oh Chris. Thanks.'

23 March 1940. Today was March 27! It had taken four days to reach her.

Finally, Ruth returned home. *"Oh God, Edward, I feel so guilty. How could I. How could I do this to you, to us!"* Nevertheless, deep inside, she was relieved. Edward was OK and he had heard his news and responded to her with his telegram. Loving, supportive, ready to abandon his work of all things and come home to her. It was clear that Edward was concerned, but this time, the decision was hers. Ruth walked to the kitchen to make herself a late breakfast. As she stirred the coffee, her anger welled into rage. 'No, no. I don't want you any more. I hate your little world you creep.' Ruth stormed upstairs and grabbing her diamond brooch and pearl necklace flung them through the window into the street.' There, I don't want you fancy charity world. I don't want to know. I don't care anymore. It's not worth this!'

She pulled her robe around her stomach and leaned against the dressing table. Her dishevelled hair hung in soft strands to her shoulders. Her eyes looked deep, still shadowed with dark rings of sorrow and worry, her mouth strangely lifeless without lipstick. There was nothing beautiful in her appearance. Not any more, Ruth looked at herself with amusement. *'Oh Ruth, you used to be so attractive. Look at you now. You're no good to anyone like this!'* As she tore at her hair with the brush, disgusted at the image challenging from the mirror, she nevertheless saw the glow, the faint glow of contentment on her cheeks, the same soft glow that edged her cheekbones in pregnancy. She was a real woman now - she had been with child for a brief, wonderful period of time. What did it matter that the child did not reach term? It was *her* child. That was all that mattered. The grief felt the same as losing a living baby birthed through her womb. Who could tell her now that the child was not real, that it had not lived like any other child? She had felt the baby inside her. Her womb stirred for precious moments with new life and now it was gone. In spite of the overwhelming grief that washed over her, her wholeness of self persisted, a fullness that was connected to the cycle of birth, life and death. Even in death she felt the strange sense of completion, that in loss and grief, there was also fulfilment.

Nothing and no-one could touch that feeling of wholeness, not even Edward. Something told her that Edward was only a part of, and not her whole life. Oh, she loved him and he her, but she now knew, that she no longer needed his ready arm or kind words, the gentle pats on the hand, the solicitous words that gave her the sense of security she had so desperately yearned for. Ruth looked with amazement into her own eyes. 'Yes, that's it Edward. I'm no longer a child.' Her words echoed in the stark room as Ruth pushed her hair back and swept it into a high bun. Her cheeks bloomed with life and her mouth curved into a full and natural smile. Although she was thin and a little pale from the miscarriage, she felt strong. She dropped her robe onto the floor and pulled a sweater and trousers over her limbs. She added a thick cardigan and headed back downstairs, humming quietly to herself.

'Edward my love, you'll be surprised when you come home.'

Chapter Forty Four

THE PEARLS AND diamond brooch lay in an impossible cluster on the edge of the gutter. The weak morning sun glinted fortuitously on the diamonds, reflecting the gay abandon reminiscent of their erstwhile owner. Feet scuffed on the coarse roads continued determinedly towards the promise of work. The slow and scant early morning traffic, moved in a sleepy procession towards the city; numbed by the stupor of disbelief that temporarily immobilised wartime Britain. Mothers, hasty with concern, hustled children in grey coats towards the safety of schools in the full knowledge that "security" was now illusion. The shops opened their doors; the baker and news stand attracting the early morning trade.

The morning air was sharp and a cold wind lingered on street corners. Winter slowly gave way to the first signs of spring, the early blossoms still shy and yet to burst into their showy proclamation of the changing seasons.

The young Indian girl Mani walked along her street in distracted wonder. She felt strange in this land. It was not just that the weather was different sort of cold, but the city lacked the familiar buzzing warmth of Rome. She ached for the quick moods of the markets, the rough embrace of uncles and aunts, the gay taunts of young neighbourhood men and the delights of steaming bread sold by street vendors. London was dismal, dreary and dim. She could not imagine how this could be better than home. Even her mother Ami felt it. At least in Karachi, there was a pulse. Here, the streets were deathly quiet, like stagnant arteries. War! Ami shivered despite herself. She wept internally at the thought of England's mercilessness and how it had wrenched her family apart, flinging her and the child Mani far from their home in Karachi to foreign shores; cold and uninviting.

Chapter Forty Five

India

IT HAD HAPPENED one morning, when their lives were untroubled by the regular hum of baking, of chappaled feet chattering on the pavement outside their shop door, of customers pressing and winning a bargain, of the carefree songs of their daughter Ami as she skipped between them both - her mother Ami and father Hanif - as they sold there home-baked wares. Hanif announced he was going to war.

'It is time Ami. I must go and join our cousins and brothers and join the fight. England is at war.'

'But Papa,' Mani protested, 'England is not our home. You must look after us, not her!'

Hanif lightly touched his daughter's head. 'I must go child. It is my duty to support England and many of our cousins have joined the war effort.'

Mani doubted her father's sense. Deep inside herself, she knew her Papa had already left them in his heart. She cried tears filled with torment, tearing at her dress and hair.

'Tomorrow,' he announced, 'I leave.'

Ami wept and cried, not as Mani had with a child's distress and fear for the future, but with the aching dread that only women know when their men are lost to the futile furnace of war. 'No Hanif. You can't leave the bakery. Who will bake and sell your bread?' Ami pleaded and wrenched at her clothing with anguished hands. 'Hanif! You waste yourself in this way. What will become of your children and grandchildren? What kind of man are you that you run from your wife and home to this madman's war? Do you hear?' Ami squared her vision on her husband, distressed, tearing at her clothes in her grief and rage.

Hanif remained transfixed turned to stone by the vision of his wife ripping her apron, his eyes unseeing, his ears unwilling and unable to hear.

'Go then, go and fight with your brothers, cousins uncles and friends. Live and die in each other's blood and remember that your wife and children starve while you roam the battlefields like wild animals lusting and thirsting for the kill. You are weak. You are no man spending your prime on death. Do not return home to this wife.' Ami screamed. 'She won't recognise you nor open the door to one stained by the blood of stupidity and foolishness.' Ami banged her cooking pot on the table and stormed out of the kitchen, flinging her torn apron onto the floor.' If you have no shame husband, then I too have no shame. I will no longer look after your home. Find me as I am in front of your brothers and uncles. Perhaps then they will see that their sister has no protection while they are at war, and her rape is on their conscience.'

Mani tearfully remembered the scene between her parents, how her father, at first shocked by her mother's display, became cold and distant from them both. He had followed her mother into the room that served as bedroom, living room, and storeroom - cluttered as it was with wooden chairs, hand-woven beds and baking implements that hung from the ceiling on long hooks.

'Woman, dare you speak those words!' Hanif's anger was cold and harsh. 'No woman in this house is without her honour. Obey me before you shame us in front of my brothers and uncles.'

For a terrifying moment, Mani thought her father would kill them both, but instead he caught his wife and twisted her arm until her hand covered her face.

'Your name is cursed woman and you curse the name of my father and his father.'

Ami gasped in horror, yet defiance raged in her eyes.

'Go to your sister and stay there. You are not welcome in your own home. And take the child.'

Ami, sobbing, grabbed Mani, pulling the child desperately to her breast.

'Go then. Go to your war, but you will not find me at my sister's, or her sister-in- law's home. I'd rather you find me dead than live in your lie.' She screamed.

'Enough!' Hanif yelled after her.

Ami slammed the front door shut, running into the street with tears streaming down her pale face and hair open, flying in the morning breeze.

Hanif returned home late in the evening, his dark eyes brooding and dangerous.

'You are going to London Ami, with the child.'

Hanif kept his distance and held his tongue, but he would not change his mind. That night, he packed their belongings and did not escort them, but sent them to her Aunty's house. Then a short note arrived.

> "Your uncle in London will provide for you. You will be safe and well looked after. The child can will go to school in England where she will receive a good education. It is the best way."

Ami opened the letter, her eyes narrowing with humiliation and anger. She screwed the letter into her hand and let it drop onto her sister's floor.

'Ami, what is it?'

Ami remained silent, sorrow pulling the corners of her mouth and tears smudging face.

Her sister picked up the letter, hastily scripted in their local dialect. 'Ami, you can't go to London. Stay here with me.' she implored.

'No sister. You have enough mouths to feed without two more. I will go. I will go to my uncle just as Hanif says. If Hanif or his brothers die, then it is Allah's will, but at least he won't have to return to a wife who has no love or respect for him or his war.'

'Ami, not in front of the child!'

'Aunty, it does not matter. Mama is just worried, that is all.' Mani piped.

'That's right child. Allah will protect us.' Ami smiled affectionately at her daughter. 'We will not think of home. We must not think of it. Uncle will be waiting for us and you will go to a new school. It will be better for us to live where you will have a good education. We will be with our family and that is what matters.'

Chapter Forty Six

England

WEEKS LATER, AFTER a long journey by sea, they landed on the English coast. Ami's uncle greeted them with more warmth and affection than she had known for a long time and hurried them to their new home in the middle of London.

Mani felt the fierce winds of change pull at her dress and the rain torture her sandalled feet. How could this be better than Karachi? The grey skies, the sooty buildings, the neatly paved roads. Even her mother longed for the lively madness of her beloved home. How could she bear this dull place? If she had known that London was as lifeless as market fish, then surely she would have defied her father's command? It was no use thinking. Her mother warned her not to think. They were in London and that was that.

Mani kicked at the road with her impatient foot. For a tiny instant, the glint and sparkle of light on glass caught her eye. She squatted to the ground, her childlike curiosity stilling the pain in her stubbed toe. For a moment, she was unsure. The shattered glass from broken lay in a lonely cluster on the ground. She had suddenly and without warning, come across the pile of glass glittering at the roadside. The broken glass looked more like a sprinkling of jewels than a shattered window. It was not something she should be afraid of at all! A brooch surrounded by a string of - they must be beads - lay next to her foot. She picked up the brooch and hung the delicate string across her hand. Quickly, she turned to see if anyone had noticed her and jammed the treasure into her school satchel. Perhaps, perhaps these would be the treasures that would take them home to India, home to Karachi.

Chapter Forty Seven

RUTH SETTLED INTO her morning routine, breakfast with strong coffee and the paper. After a long battle with stomach cancer, New Zealand's Prime Minister was dead. The reviews of Vivien Leigh in her unimagined role in *"Gone With the Wind,"* continued to draw readers' interest and Australia's Joan Hammond had appeared on London's Queen Hall stage. Despite the war, the world continued to revel in its creative and artistic heritage and wealth.

Her eyes wandered lazily over the articles. She was happy. Edward was away and she had for now, precious time for herself and her thoughts. She sensed her unfolding maturity, her innate womanly wisdom surfacing to tame otherwise reckless moods. She felt an inner wisdom, distinct from the pleasant and reassuring consolations of Dr. Anderson or the robotic platitudes of Edward. Her emerging connection to life and new understanding, was far deeper and stronger than any comfort she drew from charity balls, velvet and jewels.

The jewellery! For a moment, she had forgotten her precious jewels, cast into the street in a moment of hatred and self-disgust. Ruth bolted to the front door and threw it open to the wind, her hair flying in a suggestion of madness. Frantically, she looked up to the bedroom window, estimating the arc of her throw and tracing the line to the road. Then she scrabbled through the fallen leaves and swept litter at the roadside, but there was nothing there. The jewels were gone! Shocked by her foolishness, she stumbled indoors.

Chapter Forty Eight

India

HANIF CAREFULLY SORTED the grains in his shop to still his mind from thinking about the coming problems in his hometown Karachi.

'Array!' his brother announced. 'India is not at peace. Imagine the killings when the British go.'

Six months training in the army left Hanif homesick for Ami's cooking. Since the birth of the child, he had lost interest in family life. At least this child had survived, weak though she was. The first, like an omen of Karachi's future, brought them pain, death and grief. After the birth, Ami could hardly move, her strength sapped by the deep infection that festered within the womb. The mother was wasted and weak after bleeding and the months of fever that ebbed and flowed like a tide of curses through her failing form. Then when Mani was born, she had no milk and it was her sister Kahina, who nursed the child, herself full with milk for her own infant. For once, the children came before the men, the mothers grateful for a reprieve. Hanif turned away. Subdued by destiny, he turned his attentions and energy to his shop and Allah.

The sisters, Ami and Kahina were happy with the new arrangement. At twelve years old, Kahina's eldest child Sesheta, proved that she was a born mother, adoring the infants as if they were living dolls sent to amuse and entertain.

'Sesheta, put the child down before you drop her!' Kahina was terrified. It was enough to watch her own infant without having to worry about Mani in the unorthodox care of her older cousin Sesheta.

'Mama, the babies need holding and besides, you don't have eight arms.' Sesheta protested.

'Nor do you Sesheta. Now put her down!'

'Mama!'

Kahina relented, exhausted by feeding both babies. She watched helplessly but was grateful to her assistant.

Sesheta as precious as a china vase, was perfectly formed, with delicate features far too beautiful to hide beneath the purdah. Her father, entranced by her precise and graceful movements and hauntingly deep eyes, did not believe the child was his.

'Kahina, this child is not mine. She is not from Shah stock.' He shouted, overcome with resentment, rage and rejection. 'Whose child is this one woman?'

Kahina, too shocked by the outburst to remain near him, sought shelter with Ami and Hanif for the first year of Sesheta's life whilst Hanif and his brothers pleaded with Dada to let the matter rest.

'Dada, you are much older than any one of us,' they implored, 'but this child is yours. Let the woman be. She is distressed enough and needs none of your jealous fears. Think of the child.'

Dada had softened sufficiently to cool his anger and Kahina finally returned home. Ami was relieved. Her house was small but Kahina never forgot their kindness and took Ami and Mani in when the child was born.

Hanif eased his grief with hoarse and hollow sighs, his chest inflating and deflating like a pair of bellows. He had lost his heir at birth and now, Ami and the girl child. Dispossessed by circumstance, he solemnly vowed to leave the war. *"Jihad"* no longer held any meaning except to conquer the evil lurking within his own heart. His wife's insults cut deeply yet he mourned her. He felt humiliated and enraged, but acted only to protect them from impending bloodshed in the province.

Ami had no choice but to retreat behind a curtain of silence, pregnant revenge in the face of Hanif's solitary and stubborn decision.

Hanif hated himself, not his wife or their child. He hated himself, his weakness, his anger and his impotence. He loved Allah and in Allah's love, he found the solace that no man or woman, not even his brothers or his wife could provide him. Like his brothers, he could and would sacrifice in a moment, his life. Yet in this hour of need, he could not bear the thought of raising his sword. He stretched his weary legs to relieve the cramps. 'It's the cold nights Saadi, sleeping under the midnight sky, watching the stars rise and fall and all the while, we wait. By Allah, there will be a time when the whole of the Kashmir will belong to us and we will roam the hills, as free as the Saints and Sufis.'

'Hanif, you dream only.' Saadi's tone was dry, dismissive. 'Your long-suffering Saints are dead.' He spat on the stony ground next to Hanif, his eyes fixed on a distant star falling softly and dying within the black void of night. 'Go then. Go to the hills. This war is for men and not poets.' Saadi's disgust was open.

Saddened by his brother's contempt, Hanif said no more. He had lost the lust for blood and land and not even his faith and love for Allah could kindle the fires of passion.

'Hanif, you are not like us Don't stain your soul with war. You are like Kabir.' Saadi persisted, sensing the dismay in his brother. 'Leave this war and enter the Mosque.' It came as an instruction. 'Send your wife and child to stay with her sister. Now that you won't fight this war, at least learn and teach.'

It was a good suggestion. Ami would hardly return to a man who wanted nothing of her. Saadi was right, this war was not for him. He would seek out the Imam and pray for Allah's grace. Hanif knew he was not ready yet, not for the Mosque. He had the shop to run and his niece Sesheta to teach. She too craved the Sufi tales and poems. Even as a child, she loved Kabir, caressing the pages of poems as if scribed in gold. Then at fifteen, she insisted that he teach her to read and write.

Saadi was shocked. He demanded that Sesheta learn to sew and cook and when she was ready, she must marry. Hanif pleaded with his brother to leave her be and let her learn. Finally, Saadi relented. So Hanif applied himself to the child's education as if Allah gave her into his care.

Ami was amazed. 'Hanif, you don't have such regard for our own child' she admonished.

'Ami, our child Mani is still young. She is far too tender to learn anything of literature and poems. Let her dance. It is better for her that she learn to dance and maybe to sing.

Ami agreed readily enough. The child was weak in memory and her body needed building. So Ami found her a teacher and the child took to her dancing lessons as if it were born into her.

For Hanif, it was far too late to wonder about the fate of his child and her mother. He brooded for weeks before finally deciding to seek refuge in Allah, the Imam and the Mosque.

Chapter Forty Nine

England

AMI SHUDDERED. The mornings without Hanif were at first, cruel and lonely. In Karachi, it was better that the men lived in their own world with their Allah, but England was different and she felt more alone. Where was Allah now? What God would let a woman suffer the jealousy and rage of her husband? What God would lock his daughters into goals and hide them from the world? Allah was a man's god and she was a woman. The Allah of men was the Allah of greed and wars that had nothing to do with keeping a home. Could anyone's God spill blood or sow seeds of suspicion and punishment? Was this the same one who stole her husband each week? And did the same Allah create wars in other nations? Hanif, her husband like many other men, prostrated himself on Allah's hearth each week, hoping for what? A home, a wife, a family? They had all that and now they wanted more; a war, a war that would take life from life and husband from home. Who was this Allah then, that made men pay homage to a lifeless womb? Who was this Allah who allowed market places anywhere to sanction men to look at another man's wife or want their child daughters? She Ami, wanted to talk to this 'God' that destroyed homes and families.

At least her Hanif was pious and pure of heart and would never harm another, but she Ami had now lost her Hanif to his ideas of fighting with his brothers and to his Allah. Hanif had never put his hand to her in all their years together. For that, she was grateful, for that and his humble nature. Hanif read and sung the *"Suras"* as if it were he, who had written them to his God. He was strong and constant in faith. Although he respected and loved his Hindu neighbours, he could not join with them, to sculpt and worship stone idols of gods and goddesses. It was

Allah who was sacred to him, not lifeless forms of stone. The market men openly loved "*Kudah*," the imageless one, and yet, they watched and worshipped the vision of young maidens blossoming like lotuses in their own towns. Sesheta was such a living idol, a visible goddess manifesting before them as if sent from "*Bahist.*" Her mother Kahina, covered her with the veil before the men came and took the child from her. "*Al-lat.*" Perhaps she was that one, a sacred jewel, more beautiful than the midnight sky, her hair as plentiful as the flowing River Indus as it rushed into the Arabian Sea.

"*Princess of the Night, my niece, a priceless pearl that no man may touch.*" Ami chanted it again and again as if to secure and protect the destiny of the child. She did not need the Shariya Law to protect her niece or daughter. She needed the wisdom of the women of Karachi; their long experience, and a mother's natural foreboding of the loose eyes of, no-longer, pious men. So it was that the women conspired to keep Sesheta hidden at home, safe from the grasping gaze of the market men.

Chapter Fifty

THE PLANE TOUCHED down in Karachi on a beautiful and dazzling spring afternoon. Edward felt sufficiently experienced and acclimatised to enjoy the flight without mentally withdrawing from the physical discomforts. The metal bird circled like a Phoenix, wings dipped towards the ocean and catching the reflected rays of the sun. The harbour sparkled with newness and freshness, belying its ancient origins. From Srinagar, they had followed the Indus and its great tributaries, appearing as outstretched fingers arising from horizons of the Himalayas and opening towards the azure sea. The image reminded Edward of the outstretched palms of Jesus on the cross, open to receive the grace of God as the great rivers flowed from the sacred lakes of Tibet towards the oceans, some through the heart of India and some, merging with the waters of the Arabian Sea.

Perhaps that's what civilisation was; the nail that crucified nations, spilling their lifeblood into the oceans. When India was just herself, long before the British arrived; the rivers *were* life, delivering vital nutrients to hungry plains and the populations they housed.

The day was too brilliant to think of the wars of the west and the damage wreaked by the industrial revolution. Indeed, if the Hapsburg dynasty were not so powerful, war would never have become as mechanised and effective as it was, and, Edward knew he would instead be travelling overland or spending months on the open sea following the ancient trading routes.

Karachi was itself a testament to the power of trade and travel. A jewel cast in a resplendent empire. Even the wonders of the modern world could not erase the tantalising beauty of the ancient caravanserais.

From the air, Edward studied the stretching artery of the Indus, reaching along the valley and towards the exploding mountains. At its mouth, the Indus suddenly swung eastwards and Karachi lay like a solitary diamond, stranded by time and geography from the great river and her fertile plains. Below, the deserts of time were expansive and desolate. Israel could never compare with the isolated beauty of this holy port, tucked out of sight from mainstream European and Middle Eastern trade. Karachi's history was as tangible as an aged and priceless relic, the port a quietly pulsing testament to its glorious past.

Chapter Fifty One

THE MAJESTIC DESCENT of the Dakota onto the timeless land mesmerised and enthralled Edward. The wings arched away from the body of the plane, claiming the air and the airfield as a king would sweep and claim the panorama with his gaze. The great bird tipped its wings in the final seconds of a perfect flight. The plane hung effortlessly above the airfield, motionless, timeless, and observant. Then it settled like a feather on the forgotten land.

Edward sat silently in the unexpected excitement as the metal bird trafficked towards the fuel dump. The plane paused and came to a standstill with imperceptible ease. Without even a jolt, the journey ended. Edward remained motionless, his composure intact in the awareness of the completion of his flight, his journey. The parallel, the consummation of his experience and new belief had lifted him to new heights and then delivered him safely onto the sure ground that was his every enquiring, ever patient mind. Pacified and stilled by the vision of this new land, his heart opened in a burst of acceptance and spontaneous love towards the Arabian Princess that was Karachi. Karachi - delicately and purposefully placed at the edge of civilisation, balanced at the threshold of mystery - immediately entranced, and enthralled him. Edward knew that within the precious days that he would spend in this ancient city, he would taste the intrigue of long-ago kingdoms that brought rulers and visitors from far with a constant tide of wares, precious jewels and cloth.

Karachi was timeless.

Despite the enchantment of the land, his mind was sharp and able to discern the realities of ground transport, the familiar blur and movement of uniforms and buzzing of porters. Time merged into the reality of measured movements on the airfield, heightening his sense of peaceful observation.

Chapter Fifty Two

'YOU'LL BE STAYING in the city old man.' The Major slapped him jovially on the back.' There's quite a colony close to the market places and it will be far more interesting for you than the military outposts. Give you a feel for the land and people. There's nothing in the world as fascinating as the markets here. Buy anything you want, and if you can't find it, they'll find it for you. Ancient, modern, you can't miss. The food is the best! Try what you like, especially the nuts. First class.'

'Thanks. I will. I expect there's not much happening this afternoon?'

'What? Oh, not really. Just the usual. Pretty quiet I imagine. Take the opportunity to look around if you like.'

'Thanks. I understand that there are more Muslims here.' Edward suggested with caution.

'Pretty friendly lot really. We never have any trouble with them in any case. You'll mostly see the men though. Women are kept away a bit if you understand.' The major gave him a sidelong glance.

'I understand.' Edward remained impassive.

'They're not all Muslims here you know. There's a fair smattering of Hindus, Sikhs, and Christians of course.'

'The works of Thomas.' Edward reflected.

'Yes, so I believe. First Christian into India and he came through these parts, into the Sindh. Quite a few Indians are Christians here.' The Major swung the steering wheel to the right and then back to centre. 'Pothole.'

'Oh?'

'You wouldn't imagine that India with her pantheon of goddesses would tolerate a patriarchal God, and especially the *"Golden Son"* strung like a living mandala on a cross.' The Major was for a moment lost in thought. 'The Hindu image of Kali is really most horrible, but the Crucifixion is not everyone's cup of tea either. Still, they sacrifice animals in these parts. Goats, as it happens.'

'Goats. They kill goats for worship?'

'Probably a range of other animals as well.' The Major was whimsical. 'Mind you they used to fling themselves into the well at *"Kashi"* until our lot arrived. Imagine, impaling oneself onto a sward of upturned swords in the name of your God.'

'No, I can't.' Edward looked through the etched glass of his side window, the market place softened by its effect. Men continued to walk slowly and aimlessly as they had in Delhi. The same bullocks drew heavy and ancient carts with goods along both sides of the street. Old men, heavily turbaned and with voluminous robes squatted together to share bidis and steaming pots of tea. Stray dogs howled and slunk from stall to stall looking for scraps all the while avoiding the abuse and kicks from the stall owners. The dirt and water from a roadside vendor flowed into the makeshift gutter, defying the dryness of the air and facade of cleanliness.

The atmosphere was more suppressed than Delhi, but at the same time, cosmopolitan and vibrant. The urgent and serious thrill of competition buzzed through the market place reaching crescendos of coarse cries as jealous street vendors jostled for custom and, bombastic traders with their tiny galaxies of exotica, fought for attention. There was a sense of excitement, a sense of a bargain and the opportunism of wily and sharp businessmen.

'That's it!' Edward exclaimed. 'There are fewer women here.'

'This is the Islamic quarter.' The Major's tone became more formal and contained.

Edward withdrew into quiet introspection watching and waiting as a prisoner looks through the bars onto a land that was once his, but now possessed and inhabited by scores of others. The robes swirled and flowed in a massed choir of colour and intensity. The numbers increased and swelled as the car probed deeper into the marketplace. Suddenly they were surrounded by a hundred men, hostile with peering eyes, clothed as one. Edward could see the faint image of the Mosque hanging over the market from a distance, its shadow throwing an ominous and pregnant command over the busy toing and froing of shalwar kameez.

'Is that the Mosque?'

'One of them. You might like to visit it sometime.'

'Yes I would, that's if they don't mind.'

'Probably won't let you inside my friend, not unless you undergo the conversion.'

'To the faith? Edward looked at the faces around him, Indian, but here, there was something else he could not place. 'Are these people all from India?'

'Most are. But you get your smattering also of Persians, Afghans and Turks if that's what you mean.'

'There's something different here that's not in Delhi, or even Amritsar or Lahore. The people there were friendly, almost innocent, but this is different, as if there's a storm brewing.'

The Major looked at Edward, raising an eyebrow in open query. 'You haven't heard anything have you old man?'

'No, nothing at all. In fact, Robin was very close-mouthed about official business. I did not even see him in Kashmir after he dropped me off, not until he rang to say goodbye this morning that is.'

The Major whistled softly. 'Good. The situation here is a bit delicate at the moment. Nothing official old chap, but we're expecting trouble, between the Hindus and Muslims.'

'Really. What sort of trouble.' Edward did not want to lose his mood of contentment.

'The Punjab may divide. A bit of fighting might go on I'm afraid.'

'I thought Gandhi wanted them to work together.' Edward could not bring himself to absorb the implications.

'That's Gandhi's dream, but others might see it differently.' The Major stated with largesse.

'The British you mean?'

'I'm not at liberty to say. But you attended the session at Lahore.'

'You know about that?' Edward was slightly aghast but also mildly amused.

'Nothing goes unreported. We're here to do a job as much as you are.' The Major gave Edward a reassuring and faintly smug smile.

'Of course, it's just I didn't realise that the news was passed around so quickly.' Edward rose to the challenge.

'Radio connection up this way is fairly clear. Don't want you walking into trouble, but then with Robin, you will be well looked after.'

'And David?'

'Ah, David. You warmed to him I take it?'

'David was very hospitable and helpful.' Edward responded carefully.

'Indeed he is, one of the best, but his views are a little, shall we say Gandhian?' Edward looked at the Major with an open and humorous grin.

'The intrigues of the sub-continent. David is an anarchist?'

'Anti-establishment indeed, but clearly and thankfully for all of us, not anti British.' The Major slapped his thigh and pulled a packet of cigarettes from his pocket. 'Smoke?'

'Thanks.'

The Major flicked the packet towards Edward before pulling a cigarette from the box into his own mouth. 'Matches are in the glove box.' He nodded towards the passenger side. Edward opened the glove box, fastidiously arranged with notebook, flask, matches and a wad of currency. He took out the matches and closed the glove box with a neat click. Edward lit his own smoke then passed the match across to light the Major's. The Major drew deeply, inhaling the first lungful of smoke before settling his head back against the seat. 'Edward, between you and me, I want to be free of this place as much as any of us do, but none of us have much say when it comes to the Viceroy. It's his game and we more or less go along with what he wants. As I understand, he's had a few discussions with the Home Office and England can't afford to let Gandhi have his way. There's too much at stake. Look at the war man. India can't consume us making this and that demand when all our efforts are necessary for the home front.

'So Independence and Gandhi has to wait.' Edward's tone was non-committal.

'Independence has to wait. Besides, we need India's troops.'

'Another fallen Caliph Major?' Edward's tone was slightly acerbic but he had mellowed whilst in India to be well short of critical.

'Yes, we owe the Muslims a favour and a debt from the First World War. And yes we need them on our side so Gandhi and his idealism at present serve neither India nor England.'

'How can it not serve India.' Edward was unconvinced.

'India is no longer the India of pre-Moghul times Edward. Nor is she the same India of ten or twenty years ago. She is an emerging nation, a nation of six religions and three hundred million souls.'

'But that's precisely what Gandhi is talking about; religious unity and especially at the time of nationhood.'

'Gandhi is talking about an unworkable ideal.'

'An unworkable economic ideal Major.' Edward's voice was once mildly accusative.

'That's not for me to answer. You'd have to speak to the Viceroy. We aren't privy to the same information out here. Our instructions are to keep the peace and wait until negotiations are completed.' The Major slipped into his smooth demeanour. 'Besides Edward, you're here on holiday, not to solve the problems of the fledgling Muslim nationhood.'

Edward retreated into a quick silence shocked by the Major's careless revelation. The market whisked out of view and suddenly, they were travelling past rows of stone and whitewashed homes.

'Ah, Edward, here we are. The people here are friendly and the food is good. Take a guide and visit Clifton Beach when you have the chance. It's especially refreshing early in the morning.' The Major whistled a quiet tune under his breath cheerful and confident that the sights and wonders of the city would distract Edward. 'There's a party tomorrow night,' the Major broke in,' would you like to come? A bit of English company might do you good after your long sojourn in the Kashmir.'

'Yes, thank you. I'd like that. Mind you, I don't drink much these days.'

'I quite understand. In fact, I'll order extra soda.' The Major killed the engine and opened the door. He stretched towards the expansive sky then flicked imaginary dust from his lapels.

Edward alighted and walked to the Major's side of the car. He smiled and lightly saluted the Major. The Major returned him an honest and friendly smile and saluted in response. Then he summoned a porter to collect the luggage and waited until Edward was safe inside the hotel. Edward heard the rough choking of the engine and the soft crunch of gears as the Major disappeared back towards the Muslim market and onwards to the safety of the military quarters.

The hotel was pleasantly cool and clean. The foyer was virtually empty, barring the inevitable assortment of porters, the hotelier and strangely, an old woman dragging herself along the floor. Edward tried to look more closely without causing her offence. She was the cleaner! Somehow the cunning old witch, edging determinedly towards his foot, was a part of the rags she used to wipe the floor. He stepped politely aside to allow her to continue her slow, but definite path. She passed by him without looking up and continued to the main door, before turning on her haunches to retreat backwards into the hotel foyer, all the while dragging and wiping her rags over the polished floor.

Edward watched distractedly for a few minutes before feeling slightly irritated by the lack of attention from the hotelier.'

'Anyone here?' he half shouted.

The hotelier continued to sort through chits on the desk and suddenly turned to close himself into a small office.

Edward looked in exasperation at the closed door. This was unreal. Here he was probably the only guest for months and this man was deliberately ignoring him.

Edward coughed, powerless, as the anger welled to an uncomfortable tightness in his chest. The man continued to ignore him. Edward could hear the slight chink of money as he counted his takings behind the closed door. 'Ah, so that's it!' Edward announced. He pulled an envelope stuffed with greasy and crumpled notes from his pocket and loudly slapped a few onto the counter. The man emerged from his hole and smiled with mock kindness at his guest.

'Sahib. At your service. I hope you had a pleasant trip?' The man's eyes were watchful, carefully assessing and probing his guest for cracks and opportunities.

The old woman brushed at Edward's ankle and looked briefly into his eyes. He felt her silent victory burning deeply into his rage. Edward was neatly trapped between the filthy rags of the old woman and the hotelier's smirk. He shrugged and lifted one foot to let her pass. The man's eyes narrowed in quick expectation, obviously displeased by Edward's gambit.

'Of course, for the best room, it will be extra.' The hotelier lanced, hoping for a quick kill. Edward deliberated, wondering whether to telephone for another hotel or to give into the little shark's manipulations. He casually looked at his watch and turned to the hotel entrance.

'But for you Sahib, only the best will do and at no extra cost.' The man was all smiles his hand spread in an expression of generous defeat.

It was settled. The atmosphere clicked into activity. A porter appeared, jostling space and time to carry his bags and the little man, keys strung on his belt took Edward's elbow with expert ease.

'This way. For you Sahib, the best room. From here, you see the market place, and ah, the girls.'

Edward did not break step. They reached the top floor and he wondered whether the hotelier had any more surprises for him. Perhaps there would only be 'ah, water, for you sahib, at a reasonable price,' or perhaps, rats in the room. One thing was clear; they would fleece him of rupees at every step!

The room was surprisingly clean and Edward remembered the contemptuous eyes of the old rag hunched over the floor. There was a marble table under the window and a four-poster bed, deeply slumped in the middle. At least there was no evidence of rats. The hotelier showed him the bathroom. It was equally sparse, but clean.

'Hot water Sahib?' The man showed him how to adjust the heat. 'OK. You eat?'

In fact, Edward felt like vomiting, but said nothing. Now that he had landed, he felt a certain deep unease in Karachi. Despite the Major's tacit warning to remain 'on holiday,' Edward was tempted to gauge the mood of the city more closely. The market was close and convenient to the hotel. The prospect of exploring was far more attractive than tolerating the moodiness of the hotel staff. He could not imagine a hotel 'dinner' would bring him anything except discomfort. Despite the protestations of the hotelier, he set out without a guide, to sample the 'wares' of Karachi. Girls aside, there would be much to see.

'How dare he,' thought Edward,' insinuate that I want a woman!'

Chapter Fifty Three

THE INSULT WAS hardly reason to stay holed up like a rat in the hotel. Robin's choice of accommodation far outshone that of the Major, but perhaps that was the nature of Kashmir. The street was dusty and narrow and provided Edward with the illusion of privacy he longed for. There were a few people moving through the lane, including the occasional purdahed women. The women hesitated, huddling to the wall and allowing him sufficient space to pass, veils drawn to observe, and shut out unwanted stares. Edward was aware of their measured and conscious reaction and relieved to catch sight of a cluster of saris coming into view, obviously adorning married and unpurdahed women. 'These must be Hindus.' He remarked to himself. There was at least, a remnant of normal male-female interaction here. The women smiled briefly at Edward and swept past him, chattering in a language he could not place, softer and more lyrical than Hindi. He was unable to discern the casually flaunted words and could sense their eyes turning to watch him as he passed.

'Namaste' the oldest of the women briefly raised her hands in salutation and then the loose knot of women passed.

The interlude reminded him of Ruth. At least these women were civil. However, that was hardly fair on the purdahed flock and their keepers, chained by tradition and suspicion to a life of secrecy and hidden truths. No doubt, the presence of Muslims in India brought higher levels of modesty and poority of religious practice. From what he could gather, the Hindu version of worship bordered on the obscene and irreverent to say the least. The Muslim on the other hand, was restrained and mindful of a lawful Allah in practical life. Whether life was different behind closed doors was another matter, but here in the market, the open modesty and shyness of the women was pleasing to the eye and refreshing for the soul.

The market place came into view and the dominant throb of male voices drew him into the warm expectation of a bargain, much like the sounds of an auctioneer priming the pump of impulse, hoping for a quick sale. Edward glanced around and noticed the alert, yet quickly dropped gaze of a dozen vendors, conscious like vultures of his presence. They would pretend innocence, blissfully unaware of the catch until, the single crime of curiosity cursed him into commitment. Then money would flurry from hand to hand and it would be over as quickly as it started. The catch this time was perfect and promised good dividends all round.

Edward, off- guard, snared, walked determinedly to a grain store for quick refuge before the numberless hands clutched and grasped from beneath the moving margins of their shalwah kameez. As he entered the shop, he caught his breath, overwhelmed, by the trays of produce, lentils, beans, grains, nuts and freshly baked breads. The air was sweet, scented by the delicate fragrance of incense, hard work and honesty.

'Dada.' A woman's voice called from behind the patterned curtain dividing shop from home. 'Dada, Angreezhai.' The pitch heightened slightly.

'OK child, one minute.' The voice was lilting and mellow. A man stepped through the curtain and trailing behind, the fleeting wisp of a blue purdah followed him into the shop. 'Sesheta, wait.' The grocer spoke English.

Edward noticed the young woman's hesitation, as if to defy her uncle with innocent curiosity. He deliberately avoided looking at her to protect them both from embarrassment. The soft scent of rose caught his attention, distracting him momentarily from the market place and the grasping vendors waiting for him to reemerge from the quiet firmness of the grocer.

Edward fixed his gaze on the trays of produce. The nuts merged into a coalescence of amber on brass. A collection peacock tails in intricate and mesmerising designs patterned the counter in exotic and unexpected colour. Edward drew back in disbelief. The illusion of reality superimposed upon the giddying dance before his eyes exploded his senses. Years of careful English training and repose melted into the sensuous metalled beauty of lost and far-flung kingdoms. The illusion of bowed purdahs, soft voile shimmering in the breeze and bejewelled bangles on slender wrists and ankles awakened an image of a thousand queens of the orient. Edward fought to focus his eyes on the almonds but instead, his eyes opened into the sensitive and dark eyes meeting his from behind the half veil. Her eyes searched his with a softness and compassion that he had encountered only once in his life. Her pupils were like drops of liquid obsidian encased in honeyed almonds. This was her, *"Midnight Pearl,"* set into the perfectly sculptured form of a living goddess.

The grocer turned suddenly to witness the extraordinary meeting between his niece and the foreigner, now transfixed like a statue.

'Sesheta, continue with your reading.' Hanif commanded her quietly.

'Yes uncle.' She answered in English.

'What are you reading?' Edward blurted out.

'Kabir' she replied spontaneously.

'Kabir? May I see.' Edward smiled, unable to separate his eyes from Sesheta. It was too late. She handed Edward the book as innocently as she had met his gaze. Edward extended his hand and in barely a second, crossed a thousand years of culture and training. Their fingers touched briefly on the hard cover of the book and Edward felt the embossed lettering slide against his fingertips. He reached with his other hand and caught the book before it dropped to the floor.

Sesheta blushed. 'I'm sorry.'

'No matter.' Hanif intercepted. 'Do you like Kabir?' He turned to Edward, and smiled disarmingly.

'I haven't read anything of his. I've just finished *"Siddhartha."'*

'Perhaps you could show my niece. Is it in English? I would like her to learn to read and write properly in English. She's a keen and excellent student.' Hanif gave a slight bow.

'I can bring it to you tomorrow.' Edward entered the moment with perfect manners and a deliberate touch of restraint.

'Thank you. Uncle?' Sesheta stepped into the conversation.

'That will be fine. Meet me here tomorrow. Is four o'clock convenient for you?'

'Yes, that's perfect, I mean I don't think that I have anything arranged for then.'

'Oh, then you are here on holiday?'

'I am here to have a break, that is correct. My wife has been seriously ill and I am to return home soon.'

The girl's eyes did not flicker. Somewhat unnerved Edward searched for the masculine reassurance of her uncle.

'You may be able to help with a guide' he asked the uncle. 'I'd be delighted Sir… ah?' Hanif waited for the introduction.

'Edward. Edward Thompson.' Edward placed his hands together in reverent respect.

'Hanif. And this is my niece Sesheta as you have gathered.' Hanif returned the namaste.

Edward deliberately did not look at Sesheta until he became aware that he still had her book in his left hand. 'Oh, I'm sorry. Have you read all of this?' he questioned her lightly, touching the sentence with the gentle respect that her uncle had shown him.

'Yes. I'm reading it for the fourth time. Uncle is very generous, but it is difficult for us to find good books in English.' For the first time, Sesheta dropped her head coyly. Sesheta looked to her uncle.

Hanif was busy selecting almonds. He gathered a few then placed them gently into Edward's hand. 'Try these. Karachi is famous for its produce.'

'Thank you.' Edward warmed to Hanif. He put one into his mouth, instantly delighted by the perfect and rich flavour of the full-bodied almond. 'Wonderful. How much are these?'

Hanif said nothing and looked kindly at Edward. 'No, I couldn't.' Edward protested.

'Be my guest. Is that not how you English like to do it?' Hanif smiled openly.

Edward relaxed and looked around the shop. Sesheta had disappeared behind the curtain and the two men were left together.

'You seem impressed by my niece.'

Edward was caught off-balance. 'No, it's not that.' He was unsure how to express the truth.

'You certainly had an instant liking for one another.'

'Oh. I do beg your pardon. It's nothing like that I assure you, It's just…' Edward hesitated.

Hanif looked at him intently, but without accusation.

'It doesn't matter. So many things have happened since I came to India.'

'So many things?'

'I've had all sorts of dreams and almost, well, visions I suppose. But I never expected to meet one of them.' Edward stammered awkwardly.

'Sesheta in a vision?' Hanif looked amused.

'I'm afraid so. At least, I'm not sure. They are the same eyes. I am sure of it. They are exactly alike.'

'As?' Hanif persisted.

'As, well as the eyes I saw on the flight from London. Only your niece's eyes are somehow gentler, although just as pure. The eyes I saw on the plane penetrated my soul like, well, as if they knew me from beginning to end. It later struck me that such eyes could only belong to a goddess.'

'Her mother and aunt protect her as if she is the crown princess.' Hanif threw his hands into the air.

'Oh. Then she's not married?'

'She won't marry. She's already insisted on that. *"Uncle"* she says, *"Uncle. I want to study. I don't want to marry and become like the other women, hiding their fears and resentments behind embroidered hoods."*'

'Quite a strong girl!' Edward remarked.

'She is hardly a girl, that is the problem. Everyone insists that she should marry. You can't imagine the fight I've had with my brother to keep her out of wedlock. He would rather see her off and forget about her.'

'Then what is to to become of her?'

Hanif raised his eyebrows. The conversation was becoming too intimate for his liking. 'Be careful when you go outside. Show them this bag.'

Hanif filled a bag with almonds and walked Edward to the door of the shop. 'Just a moment. Wait here.' He moved a few paces into the street and motioned a rickshaw to come to the shop. Hanif lost himself in conversation for a few moments with the rider then stepped back into the shop. 'Where are you staying?'

'On the other side of the market.'

Hanif handed the boy a few coins. 'Don't pay him anything else.' It came as an order, more for the boy's sake than his. He spoke quickly, his language lilting and melodic. 'He'll pick you up again from the hotel at nine in the morning.' Hanif nodded in the boy's direction. 'I've instructed him where to take you. You will see the best sites tomorrow.'

Edward stepped gratefully into the tiny carriage, aware that the vendors and shopkeepers were keenly observing them. He wondered whether the boy would be able to pull his weight, or whether they would grind to an excruciating halt before they had left the lair of marketeers. Edward turned to wave to Hanif.

'See you at four.' Hanif waved and retreated into his shop.

The rickshaw lurched into action. The boy applied his full weight to each pedal until he had sufficient speed to coast through the narrow and winding alleyways, his bell ringing and warning stray dogs, cows and women to stand out of his way.

Chapter Fifty Four

THE MORNING WAS fresh and strangely quiet. Edward wondered whether the city was living in the past only coming out for business and the occasional religious ceremony. Cool air dropped over the city in sharp reminder of Kashmir, but the morning sea breeze soon whisked away memories of the mystical mountains.

The boy arrived on time and had clearly not anything in mind except to do his master's bidding. "*Whatever that was!*" Edward thought aloud. Hanif was altogether too kind and Edward was surprised and grateful for his new friend's courtesy and unexpected generosity. Perhaps that was it; Seshetsa's uncle was keen to make sure the meeting was a "once off affair." Edward recalled the extraordinary moment. The vivid impression of their eyes meeting evoked in him a slight sense of fear. Of what? Was it because Sesheta possessed a power over him, over which he had no control? Or was it because temptation drew him like the unsuspecting *"Siddhartha"* where nothing, not even his English poise could protect him?

Under the expert guidance of the boy, the rickshaw moved patiently through the tight laneways and onto the broad promenade at the ocean. Already, the water stirred into a rhythmic swell, barely above the line of the ocean, but sufficient for the occasional wavelet to lift its head in soft sprays of sea on air. The breeze was more marked, carrying its load of salt and stories of long journeys across the Gulf.

Edward breathed deeply. Here, there was no feeling of the clamouring oppressiveness of the market place or the odious slyness of the hotelier. The breeze fanned the rickshaw. He felt the full temptation of the Major's suggestion. The boy nodded towards the beach. It seemed a good idea. He would not abandon his charge or leave him stranded, prey to the wandering vendors. For now anyway, the open beauty of the Arabian Sea was far more compelling to Edward than any market.

Feeling unburdened, Edward stepped lightly onto the coarse sand. He was acutely aware that his polished British presence contrasted starkly with the earthy assembly of camels and vendors. There seemed little distance between the frantic pace of Karachi and the endless possibilities spanning the sea to Africa. Edward sensed the ocean between the continents, connected as they were, by strong threads of history, trade, slavery to common colonial masters and no doubt, similar aspirations to be freed from the yoke of foreign rule. The pulsing rhythm of Africa's soul remained deeply buried beneath an oppressive and brutal regime long before Gandhi's struggle for the rights of Indians in Africa.

He looked along the length of the beach. The curve of sand appeared more beautiful than the smooth curve's of Ruth's face. The softly lapping ocean was more peaceful than a child's breath gently heaving its breast. Even the sun was soothing, gently dropping its long rays over the water, smoothing the land and sea into one distant horizon of the past, present and future. The sight stilled Edward more than a thousand lullabies. He was aware of the strength of the landscape and his impotence against the constancy of nature. His feet connected loosely with the sand as he embraced the morning.

At thirty-five years of age, Edward exercised minimally and knew that it would not be long before his body lost its youthful edge. Ruth was oblivious to his ageing, but Edward could feel the approach of maturity, not only in experience, but also in his soft and unused body. The sand slowed his pace, forcing Edward to look up for fear of losing balance. Then with the same suddenness as his entry onto the beach, he found firm and pebbled ground. His muscles relaxed and adjusted to the surface, steadying his body and quickening his pace. He felt good. The sound of the ocean was like a mother's lullaby sustaining him. No matter where he was, Edward found that the sea air was always the remedy for a worried mind and tired body.

The ocean waned from the shore with its continuous, slow yet powerful momentum. Edward could imagine setting sail from Karachi, filled with adventure, free from care and looking to new shores with renewed spirit. Perhaps that was how he should return to England, regenerated in strength and spirit. God knows he would need it! The war hinted at being, long and telling. Chris was right to send him now. The days and months to come would be strained and frantic, despatching the fortunes of England like tantalising yet nutrition-less food on throwaway plates.

A yellowed cart stalled on the beach, written into the scenery like a final verdict of sand over the sins of man. At least the coconut milk was sweet. Edward drank and handed the husk back to the vendor.

The mix of India and Islam provided a lingering reminder of his own origins. The raw honesty and innovation of poverty was a welcome change to the fashions of Europe. Not that Karachi was unfashionable. The saried women with carefully swept hair and the subtle hints of jewels on wrists and ankles told Edward that they were just as conscious as women in the west were. A flutter of cloth temporarily veiled his vision of the sand, beach and ocean. Edward turned to observe a group of young women exercising as if in military drill, their unusually masculine garb ordinary, yet different. A few of the women wore a soft scarf across their shoulders and tied in a knot between their shoulder blades. Some had let the ends of the scarf loose to fly in the breeze as they went through the rhythm of their morning drill. This was what had caught his attention. A scarf flying in the breeze, strangely juxtaposed against the enthused discipline of the exercise routine the women were patiently performing. He had witnessed a similar happy assembly, the tidy lines of chattering schoolgirls in Delhi. But these young women were mostly older than school girls; orderly, yet serene. Compared with this scene, the purdahed women suddenly appeared in Edward's mind, suppressed, hidden, robbed of freedom and the ability to express their innate beauty as Sesheta had so innocently demonstrated. The women folded and stretched like egrets bending to feed, elegant, graceful and unhurried.

Their poise matched the tranquil air that surrounded them. These were clearly not Muslim women.

In an instant, Edward's silent observation was shattered as a young woman approached him, confident, smiling, her voice soft and welcoming. She spoke in English.' Hello. Do you like this beach?' Her peace and sense of quiet authority temporarily stunned him.

'Yes, I do. It is very peaceful here.'

'Good. We think so too. Come and join us at Satsang at the ashram tonight if you are free. Someone will show you the way.' With that, she turned and moved with ease back into the group.

The morning continued without further event and Edward enjoyed his 'guided tour' of Karachi, although he could not help but feel sorry for the boy. The bicycle rickshaw seemed far too big for him and Edward was no sparrow. The hills were long so Edward insisted on walking on the steepest sections. He pulled the boy up at a cart filled with sweets and at another overtopped with mangoes and refused to continue until the boy had eaten, more than Edward had himself could manage. The boy ate quickly before his fortune expired, then stepped back onto the rickshaw, grinning and wiping the last of mango from his mouth and chin. By three thirty in the afternoon, he was tired and so Edward alighted from the rickshaw and walked beside the child. As they approached the market, the boy became scared and insisted that Edward ride in the rickshaw for the last hundred yards or so to the market.

Chapter Fifty Five

IT WAS FOUR in the afternoon. Hanif quietly waited at the shop door for Edward and the boy.

'Was the boy all right?' he looked intently at the young driver.

'Perfect. Not a hitch.' Edward patted the side of the rickshaw. The tinselly doll waved and bobbed on its string and the boy grinned toothlessly at Edward.

'Good.' Hanif handed him a note. The lad's eyes widened in disbelief and he hopped onto the bicycle and pedalled off before his employer changed his mind.

'Good lad.' He spoke to Edward. 'His father is training in the army with my brothers and this one has to provide for himself and his sisters.'

'So young.' Edward murmured.

'Yes, so young. Did you have a good look around?' Hanif seemed slightly strained.

'Yes I did, thank you. The rickshaw was the right answer Hanif. How much do I owe you?' Edward reached into his pocket.

'Please, no.' Hanif placed a restraining hand on his arm. 'It is my pleasure. Really. Perhaps, you have brought the book for my niece.' Hanif spoke lightly and courteously.

'I have.' Edward pulled the book from his bag. 'And your niece, is she here?'

Hanif looked away. Edward could sense his discomfort. 'She is studying at her mother's today.'

'Oh. I see. Please send her my best regards Hanif. My name and address in England is inside the book in case you ever come to London.

I would be glad to return to you the favour anytime Hanif.' Edward smiled openly.

'Thank you. Indeed, I will make sure that Sesheta looks after it properly.' Hanif placed the book beneath the shop counter. 'Edward is there anything else I can do for you?' His tone had become slightly cool and distant.

'You have already done far too much Hanif. Thank you. Only do you know where the ashram is?'

'The ashram?' Hanif looked surprised.

'Yes. I met somebody on Clifton Beach who said to join them at Satsang this evening.'

Hanif laughed. 'I know them well. They were business friends before they started the ashram. I will take you there myself, only later, after the shop has closed. Eat at the hotel and I'll pick you up at half past eight.'

'What a coincidence Hanif. But I suppose you must know a lot of people here.'

'I wonder about sending Sesheta to the ashram to study. But her father would not think of it. Once they go to the ashram, they won't marry.'

'Oh, I see. And Sesheta?'

'She is as pure spirited as the best of them, but she cannot join any ashram. Her father would kill both of us.'

'It's that serious Hanif?'

'No man, no matter his religion, likes to lose control over his daughter and it is enough that her father has allowed her to study with me. He would not hear of anything further. Perhaps when they return from the frontier, he might see things differently.'

Edward had no answers for Hanif, only a dull sense of danger for Sesheta.

'Don't be late. I will send a message to the ashram to let them know you are coming.'

'That's very civil of you Hanif. Thank you. The Major invited me to party tonight, a cocktail affair I think. I would like you to accompany me, if you can.'

Hanif remained wordless, as if a thousand thoughts were drifting through his mind.

'Go to the party, after the ashram. You will see many things differently after that.'

Hanif's enigmatic comment left Edward wondering more about Hanif, than any other experience he had, had in Karachi.

Chapter Fifty Six

THE PARTY PROMISED to be a delightful escape into English life. Edward dressed carefully and conservatively, matching the colours to draw attention only to the elegant tie. It was a present from Chris fitting for the occasion. Ruth would love to be at such a party. 'Hardly with her husband,' Edward thought. He caught himself before a mood of resentment and jealously set in. Besides, she has suffered enough without him added salt to her wounds. 'Pity, she might appreciate the change of scene and the military set could prove to be far more fascinating and intriguing than, the boring and useless chatter of charity charmers.'

Edward put his feelings aside and took his time arranging his hair and brushing the flecks of cotton from his jacket. The party would provide 'light cocktails' only, and he felt like a proper meal. He slammed shut his case and locked it.

'Too many prying eyes and loose fingers in India,' he muttered, then turned onto the landing, locking the door behind him. The hotel was quiet, the slight hustle of regular staff busying themselves in the foyer. He stepped quietly onto the stair case and moved softly, keen not to arouse attention as he moved towards the dining room. The room was set with the basic necessities; arrangements of dishes on a side table and local linen on the tables. The attempt at westernising the hotel was half-hearted. Edward sensed that it would be better to eat 'Indian-style' as Robin and Marion so clearly enjoyed. The menu consisted of a simple, but tasty selection of delicacies and Edward picked slowly through the food, as though it was the Last Supper. The hotelier presented as both chef and waiter, fussing unnecessarily with unwanted detail. Edward resigned himself and smiled at the man.

'Do you have any cool water.'

The man gave a slight bow then disappeared into the kitchen. He returned with a stainless steel pitcher topped with slices of lime, sprigs of mint and a few misshapen ice cubes.

'Thank you.' Edward was genuinely surprised at the delicacy of the presentation. Then he remembered the warning *"Drink only boiled water."* He poured a glass from the pitcher then suggested as an after thought 'Chai?'

The man bowed again and removed himself at the double to prepare the tea. Edward hastily took the pitcher and emptied half into the dusty and abandoned rubber plant propping open the dining room door. He returned to his seat, breathing quickly and absorbing himself in his meal. The waiter returned with the chai and Edward breathed a sigh of relief as the warm sweetness laced with cardamom touched his lips.

Chapter Fifty Seven

HANIF ARRIVED, ON time, dressed in a clean and pressed shalwar kameez. His hair freshly washed and combed back gave him an air of refinement and authority. A subtle hint of sandalwood followed him like an invisible aura.

'Hanif, will you join me for tea?'

Hanif shook his head gracefully. 'Thank you Edward, but I have already dined. We must leave in order to be on time for the Satsang.'

'Of course.' Edward summonsed the hotelier and asked that the meal, be charged to his account, then followed Hanif into the courtyard.

The car was waiting, engine purring and duco gleaming with fresh polish.

'The car belongs to the Imam.' Hanif said simply.' He lent it to me for the evening.'

'Did you tell him where we're going?' Edward was mildly alarmed.

'Of course. Swami Rajika and the Imam are old friends. The Imam is of course bound by the laws of the Book and the customs of the Mosque, however, he is a gracious and broad-minded soul.'

'Then you're not getting yourself into unnecessary trouble Hanif.' Edward needed reassurance.

'On the contrary. He was delighted and asked me to send his respects to Rajika.'

'Then that's settled.' Edward accepted the open car door and stepped into the passenger side.

Hanif closed the door and returned to the driver's seat. He pulled the door gently shut and moved the car into gear.

'Swami Rajika is well known in Sindh Edward. Apart from a regular following of wealthy women and visiting dignitaries, she is welcomed in both royal households and religious circles.'

'Is that so?'

'Her talents as a teacher are famous. But she has of course, now entered the life of hermitage.'

'She did not look like a hermit to me.' Edward felt surprised.' She was with a considerable group on the beach.' Edward recalled the tranquillity of the scene.

'In India Edward, when you reach a certain age you renounce the world and seek hermitage from the company of family and business friends. In Swami Rajika's case, hers is an inner hermitage. As you observed, she is in an active community.'

'Does that qualify on a spiritual journey?'

'More so. You see if one simply run into the hills and seek quietness and solitude in a cave, then one does not face the challenges and illusions of the mind. Over here, we call it Maya, I think you use the word Satan.'

'Oh.' Edward became thoughtful.

'Like your *"Siddhartha"* Edward, once you renounce the pleasures of the flesh, then Maya, will tempt you like the medusa.'

Edward felt a sharp pang of guilt. He knew Hanif referred to the meeting with his niece. Edward could not find the words to either apologise or protest his innocence.

'Of course, Sesheta is a goddess in her own right and one could hardly imagine Maya working through her.'

Edward let out his breath. 'Of course not.'

The men travelled the rest of the distance in silence. Hanif kept his eyes on the road, carefully watching for side laneways that could produce vagrant dogs and cows. Edward sat quietly, studiously clasping his hands and, from time to time, absorbing the unfolding panorama of stars from behind the deepening dusk.

They arrived without incident and Hanif parked the car, a distance away from the building. A saried woman greeted them at the door and signalled to leave their shoes at the entrance. Edward felt mildly embarrassed at the exposure of his English stiffness and bent to untie his shoelaces.

Hanif softly kicked off his chappals, followed her into a furnitureless room and sat on the floor where she indicated. He waved Edward forwards to sit next to him.

'Don't worry Edward, it's quite comfortable after a few minutes.'

Edward sat next to him, thankful that they had left their shoes outside the room. The coolness of the floor was refreshing and the room, soft and inviting, the floor covered by cotton cloths on thin cushions. Edward desperately wanted to study the faces in the room but restrained himself.

'Were these the same women who earlier performed physical drills on the beach?'

He tried to concentrate on the figure on the low cushion-chair in front of them. It was the Swami. The eyes greeted his quietly then looked into the gathering, beyond as if fixed on far distant point. From time to time, she would turn her gaze closer, settling for a few moments, on the open eyes of the people sitting cross legged on the floor in front of her. They were still and silent, as if absorbed in another world.

There were several women and two or three men present, apparently content to return the Swami's wordless greetings with equally long and totally silent gazes. The soundless lecture was unusual and somewhat disconcerting for Edward, used to the quick chatter that entered uncomfortable social silences. He caught the drift of the exchange and looked at the Swami as the others did.

Suddenly, Edward felt a rush of warmth, a shower of love as the Swami looked straight into his eyes. Edward wanted to look away, acutely shy and conscious that he was the centre of the teacher's attention, in that moment. But she held him in her gaze. Edward could feel his armour melting. He wanted to cry and like a small child, run into the lap of a parent. He fought to hold back, embarrassed by the tears that pricked at the corners of his eyes. The sense of love became intense and Edward felt himself becoming smaller and smaller, contracting into a solitary point, as he had at the Throne of Solomon. Then the eyes reappeared, gentle, reassuring, loving, as if they knew him intimately, deeply and then were gone.

Swami Rajika was looking in another direction leaving Edward numbed and unsure. Hanif nudged at his elbow. The other people in the satsang were pulling themselves to their feet.

'Come.' The young woman who had greeted them at the door was beckoning them to move. 'Swamiji will want to meet you.'

Half an hour later Edward and Hanif left the ashram. As he started to put on his shoes, an older man walked past them. He smiled fondly at Hanif, then turned to Edward,

"*You must call her.*" He said simply. The man was gone in a moment.

Edward felt a wave of dizziness wash over him.

Hanif quickly caught him at the elbow.' Edward, I will join you and go with you to the party. We can go together in the Imam's car. I know some of these people and you look as if you are somewhere else at present.'

'Thanks. I would be grateful Hanif. Do you come here often?'

'When I can. I have to be discreet. My brothers don't think that it's proper for me to spend time at the ashram. After all, the people here once had considerable influence in the community as Hindu merchants, and now, well you know the story.'

'The Major mentioned something about Partition.'

'He would. The British are trying to appear fair to the Muslims, but I don't trust them. Pardon me Edward, I don't doubt your sincerity, but after you've lived here for a while and seen certain things…' Hanif's voice trailed off.

'I quite understand. Are you a teetotaller?'

'How did you guess?'

'I can't quite see you as the drinking type. The Major said he would get in some extra soda. Will that be all right?' It was Edward's turn to be hospitable and courteous.

'That will do nicely. Oh, Sesheta gave me one of her poetry books for you to read. It is written in Persian, so you won't understand it, but I'll read this one out for you if you like.'

'Thanks. I'd like that.' He felt a strong brotherly warmth towards Hanif and his smile reflected his sincere affection for the man who had looked after him so well in Karachi.

They sat in the car as Hanif repeated the verse.

"I may be clapping my hands, but I don't belong to a crowd of clappers. I'm neither this nor that. I'm not part of a group that loves flute music, or one that loves gambling, or one that loves drinking wine. Those who live in time, Descended from Adam, Made of earth and water, I am not part of that. Do not listen to what I say, as though these words came from an inside and went to an outside. Your faces are very beautiful, but they are wooden cages. You had better run from me. My words are fire. I have nothing to do with being famous, or making grand judgements, or feeling full of shame. I borrow nothing. I don't want anything from anybody. I flow through all human beings. Love is my only companion. When Union happens, my speech goes inward, towards Shams. At that meeting, all the secrets of language will no longer be secret."

Edward sat quietly, struggling with his thoughts and emotions. 'That's quite beautiful Hanif. Who wrote it?'

'Rumi, after his few fruitful years with the Shams of Tabriz. It was a sort of divine introduction. Shams eventually died in an ambush by the community of Rumi, a case of spiritual jealousy it seems. After his death, Rumi flowed with poetry. It's very inspirational don't you think?' Hanif said with boyish enthusiasm.

'Beautiful.' Edward was astonished at Hanif's depth.' Are you a Sufi Hanif?' 'I am a Muslim, a Mystic, a Sufi, a Hindu…'

'A Buddhist, a Parsi and Christian too.' Edward chipped in.

Hanif smiled and retreated into himself, the hum of of poetry still echoing in his thoughts.

Chapter Fifty Eight

THE PARTY WAS in full swing when Edward and Hanif arrived. The women floated in and out of the room like zephyrs trailing their extraordinary and expensive gowns. Some of the women, eyes turned endearingly to loose and attractive men, showcased the most exquisite and delicate jewellery Edward had ever seen.

'Steady on old boy,' Hanif mocked with his open grin. 'Don't gawp or they'll be over here in a flash. Look that at that beauty.' He pointed to a silver brooch with flutters of diamonds on filigree fronds arranged as if drops of dew on a mountain fern. The woman wore it on her left shoulder, pinned flagrantly to exaggerate the sheen, drop of her green, and expensively, silk gown.

'At the woman or the diamonds?'

'Oh?' Hanif smiled.

'I mean the diamonds.' Edward repaired graciously. 'That brooch looks so much like the one Ruth wears.'

'Really? I don't know whether any of the jewellery of the Sindh have reached as far as Britain, but you never know. Of course, there is the diamond in the British Crown Jewels.'

'It must be worth a fortune?'

'These trinkets are worth...' Hanif let the sentence hang.

'So little compared to inner bliss.'

'You are quick to understand.' Edward's discernment pleased Hanif.

'Does Allah patronise the ashram?'

'There they call God by a different name. However, Rajika assures me it is the same one as our Allah, our Kudah. We have much in common. We think upon a God without form.'

'Without form?'

'Yes. Quite different to either the Hindu or Christian concept where they like to see God as a little boy or as a man.'

'Oh, I see. Then how can you, see your God if there is no body?'

'You saw Rajika's eyes? That's how you see your God. Through inner contemplation.'

'Edward! You're here and with a friend I see.'

'Major. This is Hanif….' Edward's voice trailed away.

'Yes. we know one another well. Good to see you again Hanif.' The Major slapped Hanif lightly in the back. The Major slid expertly beside Edward and extended his hand. 'Come, meet my wife. Laura.' He grasped Edward under the elbow and nodded for Hanif to join them. He steered them towards a small circle of women.' Laura, this is Edward, Edward Thompson and Hanif you know of course.'

Edward extended his hand. "A pleasure to meet you.'

'The pleasure is mine I am sure.' Laura reciprocated with a slight bow of her golden head.

'A drink Hanif?' The Major asked smoothly.

'I think Hanif and I would both prefer soda thank you Major.'

'Call me Stephen. It's much more pleasant, particularly at a party.' The Major attempted disarmingly. 'But you're late Edward. Did you go somewhere first?' he probed, carefully eyeing Hanif.

'We did go out, but not for dinner.'

'I see.' Stephen moved stiffly towards the drinks cabinet.

'He can see that you are not the same as you were when you first met, Edward. That's why I thought I had better keep you company.' Hanif explained lightly and dispassionately.

'The Major does seem somewhat at sorts.' Edward felt momentarily off balance.

'I hope you don't mind that I'm here Edward. Perhaps I'd… I'd better go. There's the shop accounts to attend…'

'No. I won't hear of it Hanif. You stay with me. Besides, I feel, well, it somehow doesn't seem that important to be here after all. All these women, their fancy clothes and jewels and the Major with his self-importance.

'Ah. Then your time at the ashram has affected you after all.' Hanif laughed.'

Good. Then we must look the part. Let's go and talk to those women. You can ask her about the brooch if you're brave enough.'

Edward and Hanif accepted long glasses of soda from the Major. The liquid was cool and refreshing garnished with fresh mint and a slice of lime.

'Edward, I'm sure you'll be happy to know that almost everyone here is anxious to return home. Especially now that the war is on, no one wants to be away from his or her family.' The Major looked expectantly at Edward.

'If it were all right Major, I would rather like to send my wife a cable. Can I do so from here?'

'Yes of course. Come at eight tomorrow and we'll send the message for you from the base. Are you staying a few more days?'

Edward looked to Hanif but Hanif was looking deliberately into his glass, carefully avoiding Edward's eyes.

'I think I will be here for another day only. Then I must get back to Delhi. David will be wondering if some Indian beau has not whisked me away.'

Hanif lifted his head and caught Edward's shoulder. 'Your wife must be waiting to hear from you. If I may, I'll send news with you to my family in London. Sesheta's cousin and Aunty are there and they too must be homesick.' Hanif rescued Edward with aplomb and grace that was completely lost on the Major.

'It would be an honour Hanif.'

The Major turned sharply surprised by Edward's obvious respect for Hanif. 'I see you've made good friends of our Muslim friends Edward. 'The Viceroy will be pleased.'

Hanif raised his brows in jest and lifted his glass to his host. 'To the British in India. May you keep her treasures safe.'

'We will keep your jewels safe Hanif. Long live the treasure's of India!' The Major raised his glass and rallied his men. 'Long live the treasure's of India.'

The women turned to see what the fuss was about.

Edward caught the sudden dazzle of diamonds on green silk. 'Shall we?'

Hanif nodded towards her. 'We shall.'

Chapter Fifty Nine

England

THE CHILD MANI returned home excited, yet afraid. Her mother would want to know why she hadn't eaten her lunch, then she would have to tell her about the treasures in her satchel. She had lost her appetite, worrying about what her mother would say, and at the same time, she was excited about the prospect of going home, home to her father, her uncle and his shop. Throughout the day, Mani was careful to keep her satchel closed so that the other children in her class would not see the diamonds and pearls, peeping from under a clutter of crumpled papers, her lunch wrapper and doll. She was scared that her teacher would find out and then, Allah forbid the police! Who knew what would happen? Her mother would never forgive her for stealing! She had never in her life stolen anything. Nothing! The trinkets were just lying in the gutter waiting for someone to pick them up, anyone! It had just happened to be *her*, Mani, on her way to school, bracing the coolness and unfriendliness of the London morning.

Sometimes their parents held fears that bombs would catch the children on their way to school. But London was already used to the bombs, its children trained to scurry for the shelters and tunnels and hide from death falling from the air. They would huddle together in the damp underground until the wailing of the sirens had stopped. When the last of the dust had settled and the engines of the German planes were nothing more than a distant drone, the Air Raid Wardens would shepherd them back onto the streets. Them, Londoners, dazed and weary, would start over wherever they had left off before.

Mani was used to the routine of hiding, huddling with the other children and then running free again when all the fuss was over. Her school shoes always seemed to be dusty and cuffed by running through the debris of buildings and broken bits of whatever was in the path of the bombs.

It was Ami who could never become used to the sound of the sirens, the wailing of women, the crying of children and the thud of bombs hitting the ground, buildings and roads, shattering the peace and any sense she had that this was a safe and happy home. She continually fretted and bemoaned their life in England. Oh how she wanted to return home to their bustling and beloved Karachi. 'I would rather die in our homeland child than be buried in the rubble of the bombs in a land we don't belong in. Here, we live like rats, hiding in the tunnels and dugouts.'

Mani had no reply. She did not understand the world of adults any more than they understood hers.

This morning was special. No bombs, no sound of sirens or running for shelter, and no swapping scarce rations with other children to break the dismal routine that was their daily lessons. Today, Allah had granted her mother and her a way home to their beloved Karachi. The jewels hiding in her school satchel were their way home to see Papa, their chance to leave this life of loneliness, of war and bombs and their only chance to leave behind the cold and grey of London.

Mani pushed open the front door of their flat. 'Mama, Mama.' She stepped inside; cautious yet eager to tell her mother before she discovered the brooch and string of beads herself. 'Mama?' Mani felt more scared now.

Ami had the habit of taking her daughter's school satchel and emptying its contents on the kitchen table each afternoon. Usually, she searched for tell tale signs of forbidden sweets swapped for her home made breads and chapattis, or notes from Mani's teacher about forgotten homework or the next round of bomb drills - when and where they would be held. The city had built underground shelters for the children who remained in London. So many were sent to the country, far from the chaos, the noise and the danger that was the war. Already, England had lost so many men that she dared not lose her children also. So she built more shelters and stuffed them with food and blankets to keep the children fed and warm.

It was enough for the children to hear the sirens blaring and teachers' whistles blasting them to urgently assemble. That was enough without having to spend hour after hour hiding below their schools until the *"All Clear"* siren brought them back into their classrooms.

'Mama.' Mani felt desperate.

'Child. What is it? Put your satchel down and come for your milk.'

'Yes Mama.' Mani dragged her feet into the kitchen her enthusiasm waning.

The paint was peeling off the kitchen wall and the stove was cracked on one side. The sink was little more than a tub, with a pipe leading into a large metal bowl to catch the drainwater. Mani sat at the table and placed her satchel cautiously by her side on the floor.

'Mani, do you have any homework today?' Ami was matter of fact.

'No Mama. There is nothing.' Mani said sheepishly.

'Nothing? No homework? Let me see your case child.'

'No Mama! No, you cannot…'

Ami laughed.' What is the matter child. Give me your case.' Ami reached down to pick the satchel up from the floor.

Mani slid off her chair and plucked her satchel from the floor, clutching it to her chest. 'No Mama. There is no homework tonight.' She shook her head vigorously causing her plaits to swing from side to side.

'What is wrong with you Mani? Did you leave your books behind?' Ami softened a little.

'No Mama, no.' Mani's eyes were wide with the prospect of being smacked. 'Mama…'

'What is it child. Show me your case.' Ami reached towards her.

'I found something on the way to school. I didn't want…'

'You found something?' Ami waited patiently.

'It's nothing.' Mani rushed her words, her resolve and courage dissolving into tears. She held the satchel tightly to chest and backed away from her mother.

'For the sake of your Papa Mani, give me the case!'

Mani let the satchel tumble from her arms and onto the floor. Then, in a flood of tears, she ran from the kitchen, fear shaking her tiny body as she headed for her bed.

'Child, tell me what happened.' Ami stood at the bedroom door.

'Mama, I need to…' Mani clutched at her dress.

'Come on then.' Ami lifted the little bundle of her daughter and carried her to the bathroom.

'Don't forget to wash your hands. Then I want you in the kitchen.'

'Yes Mama.' Mani was relieved that a call of nature had saved her from a beating. She thought the better of locking herself in the bathroom. The tinkle of water from the tap was soothing and for a moment, she lingered, her hands playing under the stream. Her mother's command echoed in her ears and she quickly dried her hands before peering into the half-light of the kitchen. The smell of hot milk and fresh pooris comforted her. For a moment, she forgot about the jewels in her school case.

'Would you like some milk Mani?' Ami smiled at her daughter, amused by the performance.

Mani nodded sat carefully at the table, her eyes fixed on her mother. Ami poured her milk and placed two steaming pooris on the plate in front of her. She watched silently, as the child gradually became absorbed in the warmth of the milk and pooris.

'Have you had enough Mani? More? Or can you wait until dinner?'

Mani suddenly remembered the treasures. Too scared to speak she shook her head her plaits once again swinging from side to side.

'Good. Time for your homework and to do your reading.' Ami wagged a finger at the wide eyed child sitting in front of her.

Mani made good her escape and ran to her bedroom before her mother changed her mind. She felt safe here, among her dolls and toys, the photos of her cousins and torn letters from home. But it was difficult to read her book. The words blurred in front of her eyes and she wanted to crawl under the covers and think about her treasures and hope that they more than just broken pieces of glass and cream coloured beads carefully threaded on a hidden string.

Ami breathed a deep sigh of wonder. The jewels that Mani had hidden in her school satchel lay across her hand. The light from the stove highlighted the perfectly cut facets of the diamond brooch. The smooth edges of the pearls caressed her hard worked fingers. Ami had never seen anything quite so beautiful in her whole life. The child had clearly found something precious. They could not be just trinkets lost somehow in wartime London, shaken loose from grip of frightened woman as she ran from the falling bombs. The broach and pearls were prized by someone, belonged to someone. Ami knew that they could not keep the jewels. The owner, whoever he or she was would want them back. She would pin a notice at the corner store or take them to the police. For now, she would hide the jewellery from the prying eyes of relatives and neighbours; from her her uncle and from Mani so that the child would forget all about them. Ami took the jewels, wrapped them carefully in an old piece of black cloth, salvaged from torn curtains, and hid the parcel in the corner of the kitchen cupboard. She closed the cupboard door and returned to the stove. It was time to prepare chai for herself then the simple dinner they would both share in their tiny London kitchen.

Chapter Sixty

India

EDWARD RETURNED TO the hotel after a most extraordinary evening. The experiences at the ashram had awakened him to himself. He felt both fragile and strong, vulnerable, and at the same time, trusting. The exposure to his own weaknesses was strangely welcome. He longer had to hide from himself and in that moment of intense love he had felt at the ashram, he also felt acceptance. The cocoon of emotional and spiritual safety had provided him with momentary shelter from the rigours of his travels, the cacophony of recent experiences in India and at the same time, relief from the cold and isolating cloak of his English sensibilities.

The company of Rajika and Hanif had somehow stripped away the layers of pretence that guarded his soul against his hidden and inner fragilities that he had not even betrayed to his wife. In a few moments, all that he had built to form the character he identified as 'Edward' had vanished and along with it, his careful composure. More than once, he had teetered dangerously close to dissolving into tears, and finally, succumbed to a love greater than he had known in his life. Rajika's presence and magnetic eyes had lanced his well constructed English armour.

Nothing in *"Siddhartha"* prepared him for this. In the aftermath of the ashram Edward could see his own life, his insignificance in the tide of humanity that was India, his powerlessness to face the enormous unfolding of the Second World War. The grim history of Europe lay before him and yet, what affected him now was the kindness of the people he had found in India; David, Robin, Hanif and now, at the the ashram the overwhelming sense of love and acceptance. Edward looked at himself in the cracked mirror, humbled, yet more aware, in touch with himself than ever before. He was alive! He had never felt so alive. All was gone in an instant of death; Thomas, and now Ruth's baby! Everything was lost and yet, nothing was lost.

The mirror blinked in the morning light. Edward saw his own eternity in the glistening shadows on his chin. For the first time, he noticed a rough handsomeness in his face. He wondered whether Ruth had ever seen him like this; alone, at peace, savage in his independent strength. He stroked the surface of the mirror, running his fingers over its sharp and unforgiving edges. Unlike the mirror, there were no margins at the edge of time. Time flowed as one, a myriad of moments forming into pools of eternity, from where all life emerged. Edward gazed into the mirror unaware that blood splashed from his fingers onto the marble floor. He snapped back to the present and cursed himself.

'Fool man. Pull yourself together!'

The blood collected into small blotches on the grey-white floor. It would stain if he did not wipe it down. He looked around quickly for a towel or cloth in the bathroom; but there was nothing. He swore, quietly and carefully, somehow grateful for the reminder of his physical mortality. He contained the blood from his finger with a crude dressing. He did not want to draw attention to his carelessness - another crack in his faltering English composure. Edward had assumed David's customary wariness of the relationship between the Indian and Englishman, aware that slight indiscretions would jeopardise his precarious authority. It was only the colour of his skin and his dress that allowed him to assume superiority. Who could tell when the Indian psyche, fuelled by centuries of foreign dominance, would rebel?

It was time to go. Edward dressed, gathered his belongings and packed his bag. It was a pity that he would not have time to see Sesheta and Hanif again. However, she had his copy of *"Siddhartha"* his name, telephone number and address carefully written inside the front cover and he had Hanif's package, safe inside his suitcase. For the time being, Edward desperately did not want anything to remind him of India's *"Midnight Pearl."* Ruth would be waiting for him and his brush with the purdahed goddess was over; finished. He knew that he could not afford to allow himself to look into Sesheta's eyes again. His mind drifted back…there was more to her than just her physical beauty and he still could not fathom the dream, the dream and then meeting her…. "*It was more than that.*" Edward tried to tell himself. "*How could mere coincidence have drawn them together?*" He could not allow these thoughts! Were not these the thoughts that dragged a man to the edge of insanity? Had Thomas not warned him that thoughts could and would destroy a man?

Chapter Sixty One

THE TRIP TO the base passed quickly. Karachi stretched out before Edward in a smooth and uninterrupted line of buildings. Houses, shops and Mosques were all jointed at the seam by the ever shifting spiritual and national identity of India - Hindu, Muslim, Sikh, it mattered not. The flowing robes and saris, the bobbing heads, turbanned or purdhaded - all formed the throbbing pulse that was India. The parade of buildings gave a sense of form and structure to belief; an architectural expression that was uniquely India, eternal. All that was now threatened by the greater architecture of Jinnah's ambitions. Edward was grateful to be in the car, whisked away from the hubbub of cultural watersheds and towards the more acerbic, yet predictable levels of the British base.

The car door slammed firmly shut on the past as the Major opened the door to let Edward out, and then shut behind him. Edward stepped forwards towards on the airstrip towards the aeroplane, his jaw determinedly closed to stop the tide of thoughts about Sesheta erupting into words. He tried to think of Ruth and remember the words of the older man at the ashram *"then you must call her."*

Edward's thoughts swerved towards his own pressing future. *"Ruth, how could I leave you!"* He had not realised how much he cared for and loved Ruth, how his paternal protection of her masked a much greater love that he had dared not admit even to himself. Ruth was everything he had wanted - the flame that warmed his heart and fired his passion for work and friendship. Without her, he would never have had the confidence to forge such a close relationship with Chris, his now trusted mentor and friend. Without Ruth, he would never have met Thomas, never enjoyed ambling along the paths of inner inquiry and spiritual pursuit. Without Ruth, he would have never have had a home life, a life that was as dear to him as his professional prestige and performance. Ruth was the seed, the flower and the fruit of his inspiration and it was only through his jealousy that he had allowed her to wilt and nearly die.

'Ruth, Ruth, my poor Ruth.' Edward murmured. He desperately wanted to reach out and touch her.

'This way Sir.' A young officer opened the car door.' Your bags are on the way. Please come with me. The Major requested to send your cable immediately. There is not much time I am afraid. The plane is due to leave in under the hour. Would you like some coffee brought to the desk?'

'Thank you. Thank you.' Edward pulled himself together and folded his hands to hide the rough bandage but the officer had already noticed the white of torn strips of handkerchief.

'Cut yourself Sir?'

'Oh it's nothing really. Did it while I was shaving. Should have been more careful I suppose.'

'I will get it seen before you take off. Medical orderly could dress that for you in a minute.'

'That would be very helpful. Thank you.' Edward clicked into his familiar English tone, respectful yet commanding respect from the junior officer. The formalities of rank provided him a perfect backdrop to readjust his thinking and more noticeably, to reset his feelings. The icy coolness of military protocol was welcome. Edward noted all transfers were smoothly executed and the only effort required of him was to present himself at the communications desk, to drink coffee and acquiesce to the quiet attentions of the medico. The superb detachment of service relieved his sense of disquiet about Ruth and nagging guilt aroused by Hanif and his friends at the ashram.

The cable was ready within two minutes. Edward handed the sheet to the officer, who read it, and re-read it quickly.

'Sir, you have forgotten the date.'

'Oh. You're right. How remiss of me. Time seems to be a different out here.'

'Yes Sir. That is so. But I'm sure Mrs. Thompson will want to know where you are when you are there.'

'Quite so. Thank you.'

Edward adjusted the cable and inserted the date, April 1, 1940.' He re-read the cable.

> "Ruth darling. Are you OK? I trust that Dr. Anderson is looking after you well. I am so sorry about the child Ruth. Please don't worry - everything will be all right.
> I'll be home soon. All my love, Edward."

He folded the cable and marked the outside 'Confidential' then handed it to the officer.

'Thank you. How long will it take to reach London?'

'About two days Sir. Depends on Comms whether they can get a clear line or not and whether it needs to go via Delhi. If all goes well, it could be in your wife's hands by this evening, but is not usual, I'll have to warn you!'

'Wonderful. Thank you. I imagine you want me on the plane in ten minutes or so.' Edward grinned, relieved that the worst was over, his natural humour surfacing for the first time since he had left for India.

'Five Sir.'

'Five it is then.' Edward saluted cheekily.

Chapter Sixty Two

'EDWARD, EDWARD, IS that you?' David urgently called. 'Edward don't leave the airfield just yet. It's better that you wait for me to arrive. There's already been a few riots and we need to get you out of there safely.'

The flight from Karachi had been absolutely smooth and exhilarating. The dull throb of the engine matched the pulse and rhythm of the blood pumping through his body. As the plane climbed above the dusty plain Edward's spirits soared. He wanted to go home. He was ready to make the journey back to his wife, rejuvenated, refreshed and he was going via Delhi where he knew David would welcome him like an old friend. The plane flew a steady and untroubled course, marking the miles between great and ancient cities. The landing was however, more difficult and the pilot faced a tricky manoeuvre to avoid rioters mobbing on the side of the airfield. There were a few tense moments, and then the police came, the sight of their sticks sufficient to quieten the mob.

The signs In Delhi were bad. It was clear that tolerances were torn and there was no telling when tensions would erupt into violence David was concerned, dutiful and anxious to move Edward to the compound as soon as possible.

Edward felt in total command of himself. The situation did not look good, but he felt totally calm inside. The plane taxied closer to the mob, the pilot peering all the time anxiously through the porthole. The sticks waving over their heads could have been band batons, but they were not. They were crude yet effective weapons if wielded with the anger that was about to spill throughout India. The pilot knew that an enraged crowd, would quickly turn feelings into a frenzy of bloodletting. Their defiance could soon turn to real power and the presently unknit mob could suddenly knit into unified action to storm the helpless batons of the police.

Edward saw the beginnings of panic in the pilot as he realised in a slow and awful instant, that there was no turning back. It was too late, the plane taxied into the most vulnerable position, stranded and prone like a vulture on a desert. The plane shuddered to a sudden stop. The mob was upon them in no time. The pilot frantically waved his arms from behind the safety of glass, gesticulating innocence, hoping they would go.

'Angreez, Angreez' he shouted.' Angreez!'

Edward was now the main defence. The pilot pointed to the rear of the plane and horror struck at once on their faces. If the Englishman were hurt then nothing, nothing would prevent recriminations, public flayings and possibly death. To defy the police, Indian police, was one thing, but to put in danger the life of an Englishman - everyone knew the consequences. Amritsar was not only a memory; it was the philosopher's stone, the Aladdin's lamp of grisly and certain outcomes in the hands of the easily insulted and mortally offended British Raj. The mob withdrew into a loose array. None of the men wanted defiance to turn into their own certain deaths.

Edward caught himself breathing quickly, the blood pumping into his heart and expanding in his temples in short thrusts of pain. He remembered the unpleasant headaches that accompanied him on his flight from England. Quickly he assessed the situation. The uncanny calmness of nerves and presence of mind restored in an instant, as if someone had dropped a stone into his brain. He could feel the 'ping' of awareness. The plane seemed a fragile and useless shell - thin metal protecting him from certain death. Yet it was still a shield and god willing, could fly out of here if they needed to. The engines were still humming and the pilot gathered both shaking hands onto the rudder and forced forwards, wheeling right on the airstrip. His eyes widened in sheer hope that the mob would dissipate and allow him to taxi to - to anywhere that was safe. Edward sat like a rock, immovable, completely aware of the danger, yet strangely at peace. At the centre of the storm, there was only silence and total calm, predictable and constant. Death could not touch them. Of that, he was sure. Suddenly, the danger was over. The mob dissipated. Edward's English presence had doused the inflamed Indian mood as quickly as it had ignited. He looked at his wrist watch and noticed that the entire scene had passed in less than a few moments; his precarious life in the balance along with that of the pilot and his crew.

The plane taxied to a standstill and Edward was quickly ushered to the air base. David spoke urgently yet quietly and Edward understood and obeyed the command. A porter brought him a chipped, opaque glass filled with water and offered it with a gnarled and crooked hand. Edward looked into the glass. Then as by destiny, he accepted and drank the water. Edward could not believe he was doing it. Everything inside him said "*NO*" yet he still stretched out his hand and accepted the glass and drank the water. The water was cool, slaking his thirst as single drops formed a river of life that flowed into his stomach. He watched as if from outside of himself as his hand passed the glass back to into the porter's grimy hand. The hand grasped the glass and shoved the glass back inside his dirty tunic. Then he turned to Edward, eyes privately satisfied, mouth turned upwards in a malicious and cunning grin. Edward felt and heard the sound of every thought "*That was a mistake!*" But it was already too late, the curse of disease already working itself into his system.

David arrived looking decidedly more flustered than his usual composed and aloof self. Events in Delhi warned of the potential for unprecedented conflict. It was not as if the tensions went unnoticed. The combination of the festering hatred between Muslim and Hindu fundamentalists and the suppression of Independence in a climate of European war was explosive to the point of volatile, stretching his sense of security and sanity beyond breaking point. Not even the Saint-like Gandhi had the power to suppress and transform the cauldron of revolt. Neither Gandhi, nor the administrative wisdom of the British masquerading behind the farce of superiority, could contain the outrage of India. There was nothing more brutal than imperial sentiment oppressing the powerful emotions of the Indian. Ultimately, India would cast aside, the shroud of the British Raj like death's cloak, to reveal the crumbling bones of a war-torn, corrupt and status-conscious Empire. England was no longer, in the eyes of India, the 'civil' master. She was the thief in the night, the deceiver parading wealth, position and power, commanding obedience to hide her own ineptness of culture and falseness of character. The soul of England had long ago sold herself as a cheap slave to her fascination for wealth, the tantalising trinkets of the Subcontinent and exotic spices, but above all, her insatiable lust for power.

David was amongst the first to notice the signs of the decline, not of order, but of faith. India no longer had faith in the capacity of *"The Empire"* flaunting her brutal hold on power, to bring peace and stability to the thronging millions of souls who were India. India's cultural roots ran far deeper and were infinitely more enduring than the thin cultural veil displayed by the pompous Raj.

When he arrived in India, David quickly shed his aloofness. He was at his core, a hardy and honest soul, kindly disposed towards his unwilling servants. Once in India, David quickly met himself fairly and squarely. In that moment, he was instantly able to appraise his power, his ability to adapt and to step into the present and pressing need. He knew that he had to encounter and deal with the Indians on a one-to-one basis, moment by moment. This was as much a war of winning the confidence of the individual as it was Gandhi's war of persuading the masses to remain orderly and peaceful. Through a humble and respectful nature and attitude, through attention to the needs of individuals, David achieved the genuine acceptance and respect of his Indian hosts and servants alike. When they were with David, they simply forgot to hate or resent his kind, the British.

David approached the Base with sober awareness of the situation. The rioting had unnerved the British and there was a sense of having to move fast to settle their affairs in India rather than enjoy their customary, leisurely authority. The Viceroy was prepared to savour his station until at least the end of the war, but this unprecedented violence was not part of the plan. The British were clearly losing control. Yet for David, it was a doorway to freedom.

Chapter Sixty Three

'HELLO OLD CHAP. Had a good time?' David greeted Edward cheerily.

Edward nodded, unable to speak.

'Are you OK. Not feeling under the weather are you?'

Edward was tempted to remain silent to contain the already sharp pains in his belly, but forced himself to smile and rise to David's handshake. 'The trip has been wonderful David. Quite extraordinary really. Thank you so much, for everything.' Edward said sincerely. 'I am feeling a bit queasy though.'

'Haven't been eating out of the shops have you?'

'I've been careful believe me, but I am wondering about the water.'

'Water?'

'The porter. He handed me a glass before I could think about it.'

'You drank it!' David was alarmed.

'I'm afraid so.'

'How long ago' David placed a palm on Edward's forehead. 'It couldn't have been more than half an hour ago.'

'Hmm. Seems a bit soon for a stomach upset. Usually takes at least 48 hours.'

'I am sure you are right David. Perhaps it was the shock of the crowd at the airport. The funny thing is that I felt totally calm, uncanny really, as if I were in complete control of events and knew that I would be safe.'

'Oh?'

'Have you ever felt it? As if the world stands still and you observe from the outside. Magnificent Feeling.'

'I am sure Edward. But let's get you home and a doctor to see you.'

'Thanks. Any news from Chris or Ruth?'

'There's a cable waiting for you. I thought you'd prefer to read it when you arrived back at the compound rather than have to read it at the base.'

'Anything wrong?' Edward was mildly concerned.

'I haven't read it Edward. But in view of what has happened, Chris sent me a forwarding note and asked especially that you be at the compound to receive the cable.'

'Chris?'

'Seems as though he has been keeping an eye on Ruth.

'Good chap. I knew I could rely on him.'

'I've some good news for you from my end.'

'Really?' Edward was relieved at the opportunity to steer the conversation onto something else.

'I'm getting married Edward.'

'Congratulations. Who's the lucky woman?'

'You will meet her when we arrive. Her name is Meera.' 'Meera? Sounds pretty.'

'She is. Very.'

'Good. I'll look forward to meeting her.' 'We're having a traditional Hindu wedding.'

'Oh? Something the Raj has arranged for you?' Edward smiled.

David laughed heartily. 'There are a few Anglo-Indians in Delhi, but I am somewhat out of sorts with the status quo. Not really the done thing at my level. But then that's love for you.' David looked quickly at Edward, alerted by his withdrawal into silence. 'We will be there soon. Hang in there old man.'

Edward nodded. He found it difficult to resist clutching his stomach and stretched his legs to relieve the pain. The driver noted his weakening passenger and taking David's stern glance as his cue, began to dodge and skirt around the potholes rather than drive through them. Edward was grateful for the tiny reprieve. The deadening pain in the base of his stomach and growing nausea absorbed Edward's full attention. There was no space and energy left for small gratitudes.

David intuitively gauged and respected Edward's need for self-containment and busied himself with his own thoughts and plans. First, he would settle Edward into bed and make sure the bathroom facilities were accessible. Edward would need a bowl. Once severe gastroenteritis took hold, if that what was happening, it was difficult to make the distance to the bathroom. Vomiting was often rapid in onset and almost impossible to control.

The telegram could wait until when Edward was stable. Ruth's decision to divorce would be painful enough without him being laid up in Delhi. She came to a rapid conclusion and Chris was concerned that guilt more than reason drove Ruth to want to leave her husband. He had pleaded with her to wait for Edward's return, but Ruth was adamant.

'Ruth, it can wait. Nothing is as important as your health at this moment. You are hardly over Thomas's death, and now you have lost the baby! So for God's sake, don't think of anything else for now. Give yourself a chance Ruth. Give yourself and Edward a chance before you do anything rash.'

Ruth did not want to listen. She felt strong enough to face life without Edward and was sure that it was time he was free from her neediness. Edward wanted someone mature, steady and reliable, of that she was sure.

Chapter Sixty Four

DAVID BODILY LIFTED Edward from the car. By the time they arrived at the compound, Edward was doubled over in pain, groaning and in a semi- stupor.

'Call the doctor.' David ordered an officer. 'Here, help me with him. There's a good man.'

The officer ran to the telephone as David successfully commandeered support. Edward could feel himself sliding further and further away, feeling the nausea rack his body and the waves of dizziness sweep over him. It was a struggle to hold onto consciousness, but eventually he let go. The faint came as a dark and overpowering cloud imploding on his awareness.

David stumbled under the sudden weight of the collapsed man. He fought to regain his footing and support Edward's head and shoulders. The officer picked up his feet and together they carried Edward into David's cottage.

The room was as he had left it, neat and orderly with the bed an invisible comfort for the prone and unconscious body.

'Bring the bowl from the bathroom. Put it next to his head. No, not there, on the floor. I will need two or three towels and find out when the doctor will be here. There's a chap.' David barked the orders but softened his tone as the junior man's eyebrows shot up at the change in his manner. David felt Edward's limp wrist hoping to find the pulse. It took a few seconds before he could detect a weak, irregular and racing pulse. He felt again at the neck, forewarning of dangerously falling blood pressure. Edward's pallor and unconscious state was more than a simple worry. Medical help was always close at the compound, but there was always a risk.

Edward moved slightly, a soft groan emerging from blue-pale lips. 'Ruth, Ruth…'

'Shh. Don't worry now Edward. Ruth's OK. Just sleep for now. You're going to be out of action for the next few days.'

David wetted a folded towel and wiped the sweat from Edward's forehead and then his hands. The body began to shiver.

'First signs of fever. This is going to be a long one.' David said it aloud, more for his own benefit than the semi-comatose Edward. He sat on the bed next to Edward and looked at the pale, but strong face. The man had changed. The trip had done something to him, something that not even David had seen happen in India. It was as though the illness stripped away all the layers of British culture, the facades diminished to reveal the transparency of his being. The body was in good shape, fit, not overweight but precarious in the grip of dysentery. David wondered whether he should roll Edward to one side, in case the vomiting started.

'Hello David. Is this the man?' The doctor walked in without introduction and placed his bag on the bed next to David. 'Don't mind if I have a closer look?'

David got up quickly. 'Not all all. Please go ahead. I am so glad you could come quickly.'

'Looks as though your patient is in for a rough time. Do you know what happened?'

'Can't say. He was fit when he left here. He had some water at the airfield, but it was only half an hour later that he started feeling off colour. Bit strange really. Usually takes 48 hours I should have thought.'

'That's right David. Can't be the water then. Dysentery takes longer to set in.'

'He was nauseated and dizzy in the car. Had trouble holding himself together.'

'When did he lose consciousness?'

'He was doubled up in pain and groaning a bit when he was in the car. When we lifted him out of the car, he slipped into a faint. That was about 15 minutes ago.'

The doctor remained silent and felt for the pulse then took Edward's blood pressure. He placed a careful hand over the abdomen and pressed gently under the ribs. Edward's eyes remained closed, but the telltale reflex guarding of the abdomen under the doctor's expert fingers guided him in his provisional diagnosis.

'Liver. Has there been any vomiting or diarrhoea?'

'Not yet. I have put a bowl near him though. In fact, I was about to turn him on his side.'

'Good idea. Can't say what will happen in the next 12 hours. He has a fair temperature coming on. Keep him warm when he gets the shivers. You'll also need a fan in here and call me straight away if his skin becomes loose or his eyes turn.'

The doctor pulled up one of Edward's eyelids. The pupil stared blindly, but narrowed when the doctor flicked a torch light into the pupil.

'Reactions are OK for now. Keep a close eye on him. If he starts to vomit or pass fluid from the bowel, he could go down fast. They are not usually unconscious when they are like this.'

'I see. Should I let his wife know?'

The doctor looked at him in surprise. 'Where is she?'

'London.' David said flatly.

'No, not yet. We will observe him for the time being. See what happens over the next few hours. No use in alarming her.'

'Right you are. Thanks doctor. I'll call you in a few hours to let you know how he's going.'

'Good. And don't forget to check his pupils every now and again.'

The doctor put his stethoscope away and snapped the medical bag closed. He extended a hand to Edward's forehead. 'Lucky for him it happened when it did. Can't say what he would do otherwise.'

'Good timing I suppose.' David was non-committal. He watched the doctor walk to the door and close it behind him. The doctor's concern alerted him to keep watch over Edward. David settled himself next to Edward's bed as the junior officer returned with some folded towels.

'Will he be all right Sir?'

'Not sure at this stage. Tell the Major that I won't be in for the next 24 hours. I had better stay with him until he is through the worst.'

'If you think so Sir.'

'Yes I do.' David's words were short and definite. 'Anything you need?'

'That will be all.'

The young officer backed out of the room. David picked up the towel and pressed it lightly against Edward's forehead.

'Poor man. You're in for a surprise when you come through it.'

It took 12 hours before Edward stirred. David remained by his side except for the occasional visit to the bathroom.

'You'll need something to eat Sir.'

'No doubt I will.' David was reluctant. 'No food near the patient thank you. I can last out a bit longer but a cup of tea would do very nicely.'

David was resolute. He had hardly noticed the hunger pains in his own stomach as he watched for movements in Edward.

'God man. Where are you? You can't go out stone cold for no reason.'

David felt Edward's pulse, but it was still steady. He had no way of checking the blood pressure. After two hours into the illness, Edward got the violent shivers, and did not rise to consciousness. David ordered more blankets and covered him from head to toe, wrapping him in a cocoon of warmth and security. Edward's body continued to shake then beads of sweat broke out on his forehead, under his armpits and poured onto the sheets. David stuffed towels at his sides to absorb the sweat and used smaller towels to catch the river that ran across his forehead and accumulated on the pillow. From time to time, when the shivering quietened, David pulled back an eyelid. The pupils were still, staring and not upturned. He was tempted to ask for a torch, but resisted the urge. At one stage, Edward convulsed and retracted into a foetal position.

David put the bowl next to Edward's mouth expecting the worse, but nothing came. The fever continued but there was no vomiting and mercifully, no diarrhoea. David could not imagine the difficulties in changing an unconscious man, lifting him in and out of bed, dragging sheets sodden with waste from beneath him, only to repeat the same process again and again until the voiding ceased.

David had had dysentery several times. He knew too well how futile were efforts for comfort and decency. Often, there was no time for the usual dignities of toileting and bathing. Dysentery grasped the body in a cruel torture of rapid voiding simultaneously from both ends. He was grateful that Edward had so far, been spared the indecency. Perhaps he had contracted malaria. The doctor had after all, noticed Edward's distended and touchy liver.

The hours passed in the silent communion of David's conscious concern for Edward and Edward's unconscious weariness. David moved mentally closer to his charge, wondering whether he could sense whether Edward was dreaming or simply blanked out. He could almost feel Edward rise to semi-consciousness to express feeble gratitude at his friendship before slipping away again into deeper silences, unreachable spaces that were much darker than David had imagined possible.

Edward was dangerously close to death. His mind was for much of the time, elsewhere. He had no absolutely no control over the flight of consciousness into the far reaches of unconsciousness. In the extreme distance, a silent hand, untouchable, unknowable, tended the soul. When the distance between them became extreme, David shook Edward to rouse him to semi-awareness. He wanted to touch and feel the illness as one would feel the living limbs of a child.

Edward only ever briefly glimpsed the light of David's presence. From time to time he was dimly aware of the dusky outline of the room and shadowy movements that accompanied David's ministrations before again descending into the abyss. Edward's momentary engagements with 'just-below-consciousness' were more for David's reassurance than the natural course of the illness. The hint of life was sufficient to allow David to relax and attend his routine gestures towards the unconscious man.

'Dying? No surely not. Edward, you can't die. Not here!'

David panicked and adjusted the towels and blankets, lifting Edward's hands as he rolled him onto his back. He packed another pillow under Edward's head and pulled his body higher. 'We'll get you out of this my man.'

Chapter Sixty Five

EDWARD WAS MOTIONLESS the atmosphere filled with a strangeness as if his mind was separate from his body, watching the illness from a distance. His mind was still as the fever took hold of his body and brought with it rivers of cleansing sweat, expunging disease from his organs. Edward was safe in hands that held the strings of his life. That was it, he had handed over control of his life and with it he handed over the fight of life over death.

David watched in amazement. He withdrew from Edward's body and for the first time noticed the calm repose, the unmoving faith in the man as if it matter not whether he lived or died. That was it. It did not matter! Life was of no more significance than death. Life and death were equally balanced on the scales of eternity. David looked at his hands as they shook with the realisation that his own moment could come at any time. At ease with the philosophies of India, he had yet to cognise the transience of existence. Rooted in Englishness, David remained firmly in the belief that one-day he would return to England after a 'lifetime,' a 'career' on the Subcontinent.

Now he had Meera to think about. Meera was the jewel of his eye, the beauty who tore his heart away from the dryness of work and stayed social life into a romance far more beautiful than he had ever imagined. David resisted at first, then allowed himself to be carried on the waves of her coquettishness, the sweetness of her manners, her coyly dropped eyes, the fall of her unbraided hair that swept behind her in a fully blossomed train. David observed Meera's careful footsteps, always inoffensive, sure, yet playful like a child's. He wanted to understand her immense inner poise but never imagined that he would fall in love. Inevitably, he did, absorbed in the resonance of her wiser and more refined soul, his senses dulled to the separation and differences of nation and culture.

Edward moved his leg. Lost in his private world, David did not register the change, until Edward rolled to one side.

'Edward. Edward!' David sprung from his chair. 'Edward, it's David. Are you awake?'

Edward's head rolled forwards onto the pillow as he slumped back into unconsciousness. David hastily shifted the pillow to give Edward air and, for a moment, felt the soft flicker of eyelashes catching the back of his hand. Edward half-opened his eyes, groggy, but out of the deep sleep that had possessed him for so long.

'Edward. You're all right. Thank god for that.' David shook him lightly, desperate for the long-awaited response.

Edward nodded slightly, his head heavy, neck and shoulders aching with the last of the fever. The pain felt like a dead weight against his limbs. 'What happened?' His mind was sluggish, painful. He could not recall. There was no memory. 'David. Is that you?'

At last, words.

'Yes. You're back at the compound with me. How are you feeling?'

'Feeling? I'm so tired. I feel as tired as if I have been travelling for ages. How long have I been here David?'

'Over 12 hours.'

'Is that all? It seems like forever. I can't believe it. I feel as if I've been so far away. Why am I in bed?'

'You fainted. In the car. We were quite worried about you. The doctor came.'

'Oh? I don't remember.'

'You were unconscious.' 'How did that happen?'

'I don't know Edward. When I picked you up from the airfield. You were feeling a bit 'queasy' as you put it, then on the way back you lost it old man.'

'I remember the airfield. There was a riot wasn't there?'

'Yes. You're lucky to be out alive. Are you sure nothing else happened out there?'

'No. I don't think so, at least, not that I can remember.' Edward struggled to get a grip on events.

'Don't think about it for now. Would you like some water? You lost a fair bit with the fever.'

'Thanks. I'm thirsty all right. Do you think it was the water David?' Edward tried to remember.

'The doctor doesn't think so. Too soon.'

'There was something about that man, something about his manner, his eyes. I felt locked into him as if I had no control over whether or not I took that glass of water. Strange David. I tell you, very strange.'

'I see. A few of them out here have occult powers. Perhaps he thought you were ripe for a curse.' David muttered angrily.

'A curse? Strange you said that. Yes, it felt ominous. The water I mean. As soon as I took it, I felt this rush of danger, like a warning. Still, I'm here now with you.'

'Yes, and now back to consciousness Edward. Where have you been all these hours?' David felt tears at the corners of his eyes. He was tired yet more relieved that it was over.

'Been? Nowhere that I know of. Can't remember a thing.' Edward sipped the water, carefully.

David sook his head qiuetly. He did not want to share his fears with Edward, not yet at least.

Edward looked into David's eyes, a memory emerging of the bond between them whilst he lay on the bed. 'Ah yes, now I remember David, you were here all the time.'

'Yes I was. How did you know?'

'How did I know? I don't know how. All I remember is that you were here all the time. Thank you. I'm sorry for being so much trouble.' The colour was returning to Edward's cheeks.

'Don't think of it. Now, can you handle tea?'

'Tea? That would be superb.' Edward responded.

'Tea for two coming up.' David smiled and called for his officer.

It was three days before Edward recovered his full strength. David attended him like a nurse, making sure he ate properly, watching that he drank copious amounts of fluids and assuring him that it was 'really no trouble.'

After two days, Meera arrived at the door with fresh towels and sandalwood soap.

'These are for your friend David. I'm sure he'll find the soap refreshing.' David demurred and accepted the humble gift.

'Thank her for me David, for her care.' Edward was grateful.

'She thinks you need extra. She would nurse her yourself if she could. But Meera is somewhat shy.' David placed the soap on the dresser. 'She's very affectionate with me but a little reserved with other men. Once she gets to know you and if, she likes you, she'll move mountains to make you happy.'

'Oh? Sounds as though I'm reaping your luck David.'

'Indeed you are my friend, indeed you are.' David laughed.

'I *am* lucky David. Imagine, if it weren't for you, goodness knows where I'd be by now.'

'Could be very serious indeed. I mean, losing your way as you did.' David appeared distracted as he adjusted Edward's pillows.

'Losing consciousness you mean.' Edward was comfortable with the thought.

'I haven't seen it happen like that before Edward. You know, I haven't seen anyone else come into this country and change within themselves so much in under a fortnight. What happened to you out there?'

'Out where?'

'Well, you have been around a bit; Amritsar, Lahore, Srinagar, Karachi. You are not the same person Edward. There's something missing and there's something new, but I just can't put my finger on it.'

'I wasn't aware.' Edward was mildly curious. He pulled himself into the sitting position. 'I feel so much better now David. You're an excellent nurse.' Edward smiled broadly.

'Thank you. But you haven't answered my question.'

'David, there are some things that I don't fully understand myself, but what I do know is that 'out there' as you put it, I discovered I love my wife more than I ever realised.'

'Is that what happened?'

'In Karachi David, I met a most remarkable people. I have never met anyone like them before, never.' Edward paused to recollect. 'Well, this young teacher Rajika whoever she is, reminded me about myself and how to love myself. Then an old man said something like *"Call her."* Can you imagine that! I hadn't even met any of them before and they sensed so much about me.'

"Quite an experience.' David noted softly. I have to admit I am out of my depth Edward.'

'When I was there at the ashram, there was a sense of so much love and acceptance, as if it hadn't mattered what an selfish idiot I had been. I also suddenly realised what Ruth meant to me, I mean how much she means to me. Especially after the baby. I guess I have been acting like a child myself. Imagine, poor Ruth, pregnant to someone else then losing the baby. Oh my God, I've been so blind.' Edward wanted to weep.

David walked to the door. 'I'll just be a moment Edward.'

Edward looked towards the window. The afternoon light dappled in slow rays towards the bed, the light catching the folds in the sheets. He crumpled the top edge of the sheet, watching the light straighten and push into empty space and onto his wrist. The light caught his skin and softened into a broad bangle, moving and dancing as Edward rotated his wrist from right to left and left to right. The time! How long had he been here? Ruth! She must have received his telegram by now. David mentioned a telegram when he arrived in Delhi.

Edward sunk into the pillows and breathed deeply. The air was slightly scented with rose. Meera certainly had an enchanting influence on David. The stoic English seemed to became either more entrenched or ridiculously exaggerated in the east, otherwise completely subsumed by the beauty and subtle nuances of the Subcontinent. Edward relaxed, allowing himself to luxuriate in the cleanliness of David's cottage, the peaceful here-and-there touches of Meera, and the unexpected and highly welcome nursing care. This was not what he had expected from India. Even better, he felt more at peace now than he did, even in his own bed at home in England. He stretched his legs, pleased to discover that the aching was relieved and that the pain in his belly was now a dull resemblance of its former intensity. There was nothing much to do or think about, except to wait until he was strong enough to travel. David insisted that there was no point in visiting Gandhi whilst he was as sick as he was. It seemed less and less likely that he and Gandhi would meet. Ruth was more pressing on his mind than further adventures into the mysteries of the subcontinent, even if that meant meeting the Mahatma.

'Edward, here it is. I've been keeping the telegram until you were well enough to read it for yourself.' David said carefully as he walked back into the room.

'Oh. I was just thinking about Ruth David. Thanks.'

David handed him the telegram and sat on the chair at the base of Edward's bed. David watched Edward; his expression neutral yet supportive, not wanting.

Edward to know that he knew the contents of the cable.

'Edward, Chris was concerned that I was here when you opened it.' David broke the silence.

Edward dropped his head and began to cry softly into his hands.

David sat motionless; his face unflinching as Edward averted his eyes. 'It's alright old chap. You're with another man.'

'Thanks.' Edward let his tears flow watching them fall onto the sheet where the light continued to dapple and play at its edges. For a moment, Edward felt the presence of David's brotherly compassion suffusing the room.

'Edward, can you manage a reply. Your wife must need you.' David attempted.

'Yes, you are right. I should not think of myself. She must be feeling desperate.

There is only so much a doctor can do. Dr. Anderson can't replace either her father or Thomas.'

'No-one can replace her husband Edward.'

'She seems to think that's all over.' Edward choked back the grief.

'It could be just a call for help you know. She has been through rather a lot.'

'You know?'

'Chris told me the broad details, nothing much. He was concerned about you.'

'Good old Chris. That's what he's all about David. The most patient, kind and loving employer anyone could wish for.'

'You *are* lucky then.'

'David, since I've been in this country, I've come to understand a lot of things, but nothing has meant as much to me as my family and friends. It's something I'll never forget. And Chris is one of the best, believe me.'

'I do.'

'I am forgetting myself. You've known him a lot longer than I.'

David smiled and suggested more tea.

'That would be sensible David. I'd better make arrangements for London.'

'Gandhi?' David opened the door of opportunity for Edward. 'It's your choice. He's close by and you are in India after all.'

Edward paused, his mind deliberate, detached. 'What would you do David?'

'I'm not you. I'm not your wife and I'm sure it's what is most important to you Edward.'

'I suppose it is a bit unfair to ask someone else to answer for me. I thought as a man, you might understand, you know, the dilemma between professional life and marriage. Of course, you have not had to confront it yet.' Edward suddenly felt old.

David stretched his arms above his head, as if looking for answers. 'Edward, when I came to India I thought that reputation and career was everything. I found new things in doing the job well, in being important, in taking part in the making of history. It meant so much to me. After a while, I realised that all that was superficial, that men were ambitious and self-serving, that principles were easily sacrificed for personal honour and that people without power, wealth or position didn't matter. They didn't matter to those who made the decisions. Poor people are inconvenient to those with power.' David looked unhappy in the memory. 'Then I met

Gandhi. Gandhi was different. He has none of the airs about him that the British have. He has no signs of personal gratification for the work he is doing. Gandhi simply has a deep, deep concern for the untouchables, and his heart is wrenched each time he hears the news of communal violence. 'David stroked his chin. 'Gandhi has complete and untiring commitment to free his beloved India through an almost savage self-searching, as if he needed to remove every stain on his character before he made his next move. That is why Gandhi is different Edward. He is the politician that everyone would want to be; yet, he is not a politician. He is a leader, a man of greatness, of awesome personal power. Gandhi is a man of god however you perceive your god. Essentially, he is simply a humble petitioner for the liberation of the human soul, no matter the colour of the skin, country or religion. That's what struck me about the man. He cares deeply, not about profession, career or politics. None of that counts in front of Gandhi. The Mahatma exudes an enormous sense of peace, and a hint of a plan far greater than even the Independence of India. That's what I like about him, his intrigue. There's no one in this country like Gandhi Edward. The Jinnah's and Nehru's have their own power and personality, but they're not Gandhi, none of them are. Do you see my point?' David looked directly at Edward.

'I think so David. I think I understand what it means to see one's facades dissolve in the face of something far more enduring and powerful.'

'You know, the Lahore Resolution deeply hurt Gandhi. It tore at his very soul that people would see Hinduism and Islam as antagonistic to one another. Gandhi sees communalism as the denial of god. Have you seen the *"Harijan?"* '

'Gandhi's newspaper?'

'Yes. This is the latest edition.' David picked up the newspaper from the dresser and threw it lightly onto the bed.

'Thanks.' Edward tried to prop himself up on the pillows, but the effort was too taxing.

'Here.' David caught him under the elbow and placed a free hand around Edward's back and under his other armpit. 'Heave ho.' David hoisted him to the sitting position and adjusted the pillows to support his visibly thinned frame.

'Thanks. Quite an effort.' Edward wheezed slightly as he spoke.

'Is that usual old man?'

'What, the chest?'

'Mmm. Sounds ominous. Not asthmatic are you? Never had TB?'

'I don't think so. Perhaps it's the dust. Not used to it out here.'

'Maybe that's all it is. But be sure to have a complete check up when you get home though won't you.'

'That I will. Now where's that paper?'

'Gandhi has quite a good turn of phrase if I may say so. It's hardly the journalistic style that you are used to. More of a platform for his "*Satyagraha*."'

'Well, perhaps Churchill can learn something from him. Hitler might need more than just arms to contain his ambitions.'

'I am afraid the Jewish community are not pleased with Gandhi. They asked him what a *Satyagrahi* Jew would do in the face of Hitler.'

'Really? What did Gandhi say?'

'Gandhi said that if he were a Jew in Germany, he would stand as tall as any of the gentiles and challenge the Germans to shoot him or cast him into the dungeon. He would never submit or let his self-respect be crushed. For Gandhi, the joy of suffering for dignity far outweighs the hostilities of any of Britain, America, France or Germany. Even if Hitler retaliated with a massacre, that would become a day of thanksgiving and joy to Jehovah for granting them their deliverance.'

'How did that go down?' Edward was mystified.

'Not well. Greenberg thinks that Gandhi is unfair to make the comparison.'

David paused, staring at a distant point through the window. 'But Gandhi is nevertheless convinced. He's challenging the Jews to find someone with courage and vision, to lead them into non-violent action, so that the German-Jews score a lasting victory over the German gentiles through changing a degrading manhunt, into an a statement of human dignity.'

'Much like the Salt March David.' Edward stated flatly.

'And with whom do your sympathies lie Edward?' David smiled.

'The Indians of course. Gandhi's actions made us look like cowards.'

'Indeed we were. In the name of a measly tax and authority we committed an atrocity.'

'How many died?'

'Oh, it wasn't the deaths Edward. Several hundred were wounded, mostly through blows to the head with those lathis. It was the manner in which they continued to strike them when they were totally and utterly defenceless. That was the death knell for British-Indian relations. Same thing in Bombay, only there were thousands of them there, over fifteen thousand.'

'And they were also attacked for what was it, *"civil disobedience?"*'

'Race, religion, money, territory. What does it matter? One human being wanting to exert control over another.' David sounded bitter.

'And we're a party to it by virtue of our nationality.'

'We are.'

Edward picked up the *"Harijan."*

'I can't read this David. It's in Hindi.' 'I know. But I thought you might like it anyway. Keep it.'

'Thank you.'

'Meera can read some of it for you later.'

'I'd appreciate that.'

Edward placed the paper on the bedcover.

'Gandhi would have us submit to Hitler and Mussolini, to simply let them walk in and take Britain and we ourselves walk out.'

'To where?'

'Who knows. But he thinks non-violent retaliation will save our souls whereas retaliation through arms and violence will lose us both our soul and our dignity.'

'Perhaps he is right David.'

David looked at Edward and smiled. 'So you agree with the Mahatma.'

'I agree that the bloody war is destructive and will achieve nothing.' Edward said resolutely.

'Including Independence?'

'What do you think David?' Edward's tone was neutral.

'I think that if Congress were more active in the war, then they would be les inclined to take advantage of Britain's weak position.'

'Then Britain would reciprocate with Independence?'

'Perhaps.' David was non-committal. 'A coalition could be more workable than the Constituent Assembly that Congress demands and at least that way, Jinnah would be appeased.'

'You're saying of course, that the Hindus are too insistent on their own claims and are ignoring the practical realities of the situation.'

'Yes Edward, I am. If the Hindus were more Gandhian in their attitudes towards Jinnah and Britain, the situation might have resolved more quickly.'

'But would Jinnah accede?'

'Jinnah is no fool. He is as astute as Gandhi is. But Gandhi won't back down on his principles to take advantage of Britain, even if it does mean Independence.'

'What?'

'Gandhi wants true Independence, *"Swaraj,"* not the opportunistic Independence that arises *"out of Britain's ruin"* as he puts it.'

'Very noble.'

'Noble? No I think not. Gandhi's veracity is based on his unswerving commitment to his God.' David looked at Edward with total sincerity.

'You know David; I think that you are right. One has to be true to one's inner convictions and follow the way of the heart.'

'You'd like to meet Gandhi then?'

'I think I already have.' Edward folded the *"Harijan."* 'I'll look forward to Meera reading some of this to me.'

'He wrote of course, about the murder of General O'Dwyer as *"an insane act"* that caused him deep pain.

'Really? He didn't think that it would further the cause of *"Satyagrahi?"'*

'On the contrary. He immediately thought it would damage the cause of Independence.'

'You could hardly blame am Singh or anyone else connected to the Amritsar Massacre though David.'

'It is very difficult of course to separate out political injustice, oppression, human trauma and horror.'

'Especially if you were involved in the horror as was Ravinder.'

'Ravinder?'

'Robin didn't mention him to you? At the well at Jallianwalbagh?'

'Of course. He did say that he chatted to a fellow from time to time. The young man who survived the shooting.'

'Hmm. Not your Udham Singh, not by any means.' Edward mused.

'A much more personal connection with that fateful day Edward. Then, his reconciliation with his past is an ongoing private journey.'

'A journey that you think that the Mahatma would approve of David?'

'Gandhi is a man of peace Ed. When he heard about the murder of O'Dwyer and injuring of Secretary of India Lord Zetland, Gandhi said this his own heart was wounded.'

'He cares about the English?' Edward could hardly suppress his surprise.

'He would care about *you* Edward.' David gave him a broad smiled and slapped him lightly on the back. 'Why not meet him?'

'And what would Gandhi say? Is that what you're mean?'

'What I mean is if you think you understand the power of the man, and you don't need to meet him for *"The Reporter"* or for personal reasons, then return to your wife and think nothing more about it. Then you have an opportunity right now that many would give their right arm for, then I would encourage you to meet Gandhi before you leave.'

'I understand a lot more than I ever thought was possible David. But I would still like to meet Gandhi.' Edward vacillated. 'Quite an opportunity as you said.'

'It is.' David paused, his mood sober and searching.

'I want to meet him David. I want to meet Gandhi but I also know that I love Ruth and I don't want to lose her.'

'Of course.' David said nothing further. He walked quietly to the head of Edward's bed and placed a hand on his shoulder. For a moment, the two men exchanged silent thoughts before David walked to the door. He felt that in Edward, he had met someone and something he liked immensely, something he would hope to find in himself one day.

Chapter Sixty Six

DAVID SET ABOUT organising the train travel for them both from Delhi to Nagpur - one of the oldest and in David's opinion, most beautiful of the railway stations that were a continuing legacy of the British Raj in India.

'Ed, without the British railways in India, Gandhi would have far less access to his people in India and far less influence.'

'That is a paradox. How does that sit with his 'Independence' ethics?' Edward smiled for the first time in it seemed, days.

'Intriguing isn't it. The postal and rail system is so much of a part of the fight for freedom in India. You couldn't imagine this country now without the rail services especially.'

'Who started the Free India movement anyway?'

'A British Civil Servant Allan Hume virtually started the whole process with Indian National Union, then Congress. It was virtually a forum for dialogue between intellectuals from both countries and the idea quickly took off as it happens.'

'Dialogue!' Edward raised his eyebrows. 'Diplomacy also uses the hard worn path of dialogue.'

'Indeed Edward. The Muslims felt left out thought, as Congress was Hindu dominated and some of the people very anti-British so that was never going to help the cause. So the formed the All India Muslim League, with the assistance of the Raj of course.'

'So you are not totally anti-Raj.' Edward laughed.

'Not at all old chap. Not at all.' David said quietly. 'We have our place and role and especially so, in these new chapters of India's destiny, to make the transition smooth if you know what I mean.'

'And Gandhi? Not anti-British either?'

'Gandhi is your ultimate diplomat with extraordinary powers of persuasion. Take his ability to subdue communal hatred and killing. It doesn't matter whether it is a Muslim or Hindu man, Gandhi is *'Bapuji'* to both.'

'And a father figure to you also David?' Edward said kindly.

'In this land, with its many gurus and vast population, it pays to have good friends.'

'I see.' Edward smiled broadly. 'Gandhi was the main agent of the Free India movement in the last twenty to thirty years I take it?'

'Well yes in a sense. But it is also a matter of good timing. Annie Besant actually, the Irish freedom fighter, was the person who formed the "*All India Home Rule League*" and she literally galvanised interest right across India as well as bringing together Muslims and Hindus under one banner. Remarkable really. The movement really took off then the British put her under house arrest in India in 1917.'

'Seems to be a habit. Gandhi seems to have spent a fair bit of time as a political prisoner of the Raj.'

'Yes he was, but back to the timing thing. Gandhi returned to India just as the Home Rule idea was taking off. He soon became the president of the All India Home Rule League and quickly merged the organisation with Congress, and the rest, is well, clearly history with his impact across the Subcontinent.'

'A smart move by any account.'

'Gandhi is streetwise if you could use such a term in India, the place of over 900,000 villages!'

'Our train to Nagpur will take us through some I expect David.'

'You will love the journey. We have our friends in the centre of India and Nagpur itself has quite an impressive history.' David said.

'What an amazing role David. To be a part of the Independence movement, to be Gandhi's friend..'

'If an Englishman were ever to use the term"*guru*" then of course, Gandhi would be mine.' David sounded as excited as a schoolboy. 'We can stay at his ashram at Sevagram if you wish Edward. He has a guest cottage where we would be very comfortable.'

'I would be delighted David. What an honour.' Edward was clearly moved by the offer of hospitality.

'Well then. Let's finish our packing. We catch the Grand Trunk Express just after 6.30 p.m. tonight Edward.'

'Overnight?'

'Overnight sleeper First Class - courtesy of the Raj of course!' David smiled broadley. 'When in Rome….'

'Enjoy the ride.'

'We will be in Nagpur for lunch then we can meet Gandhi once we are in Sevagram.'

'Excellent David, I am excited.'

'As excited as I am Ed.' David beamed.

Chapter Sixty Seven

Nagpur, Central India

NAGPUR STATION WAS as David promised, delightful. The first class sleeper was as comfortable as Edward had hoped. He awoke feeling rested, his mind clear and confident that he had made the right decision to travel to meet Gandhi. In any case, Chris would want him to meet the Saint and listen to his perspective on the murder of General O'Dwyer and the mood in India at present. Edward did not have any illusions that Gandhi would give anything away from a political perspective, but he was intrigued how a skinny old man dressed in virtually, a 'loin cloth' as Churchill described him, could hold such sway over the millions of souls that were India.

David's friends in the British Civil Service waited patiently at Nagpur Station to whisk them away for a private luncheon. It was clear from the moment that they stepped into the car and their luggage was firmly clamped into the boot, that there was a tacit understanding, that Edward would have limited time with Gandhiji, that he could ask a few questions, but there was nothing to be said or done that would rock the British-India boat. This was wartime.

'Ed, we will enjoy ourselves nevertheless. See this as an insider's view, from the British perspective of course. All very delicate at the moment. We need to step carefully and not offend anyone.'

'Of course. I will follow your lead David.' Edward was used to having his own head, but understood that he was David's guest in India and now, Britain's guest in India visiting Gandhi on their terms.

Luncheon was, less boring than he imagined.

'David. How lovely to see you old chap.' Sir Henry Twynam stretched out his hand.

'Sir Henry. This is Edward Thompson from *"The Reporter"* in London. He has been here on business covering the Amritsar story.'

'Very sad business. Very sad. Still, we shan't dwell on that now shall we.

Edward, I take it you are here to meet Gandhi.'

'Sir Henry. Good to meet you.' Edward extended his hand to the Governor. 'I am honoured to meet you also.'

'No need to flatter me. Of course you are welcome here. A bit tricky having the Saint right here under our feet.' Sir Henry's eyes twinkled.

'He is quite the character from what David has told me. Very persuasive.'

'Aah. So you have heard about some of his antics, pushing us towards relinquishing the colonies.' Sir Henry sighed. 'Then, it is probably time we left as I am sure David has already told you.'

'Actually, David hasn't given away too much if that is what you mean.' Edward stepped in briskly to defend his friend.

'David is very discreet, yes.' Sir Henry concurred. 'Luncheon is served. Let's not keep them waiting for us. Hope you don't mind David. Thought we'd make an occasion of it. Can't let Edward leave India without the right impression of us all here.' Sir Henry smiled conspiratorially.

'I am sure that Edward will have all the right impressions Sir Henry. Apart from the final leg of his journey to the Ashram.'

Sir Henry laughed loudly. 'Can't do much about that I'm afraid. The old chap insisted on living in the middle of nowhere making it virtually impossible for us to talk to him.'

'Edward, we take the car to Wardhu but the last leg, of the journey into Sevagram is by the *"Oxford,"* a little homemade to say the least.'

'Oxford?'

'We had to cut the back, off a Ford motor car and attach it to a couple of bullocks to make it easier to cross the muddy and malaria ridden fields to Gandhi's place.' Sir Henry looked amused and distressed at the same time.

It was Edward's turn to laugh, surprising himself that the last of the tensions of his trip appeared to suddenly dissolve in the unexpectedly, welcome company of the true British Raj.

'And, we made him accept a telephone line. Imagine the Viceroy trying to talk to him about matters between Britain and India and having to catch an ox cart each time he wanted to talk to him.'

Edward found the image intensely amusing and had to work hard to stop himself from laughing again. 'You mean, he runs his Independence campaign from out here?'

David stepped in quickly to save Sir Henry from the embarrassment.

'Sevagram is the non-government capital of India Ed. This is from where Gandhi launched his *Satyagraha* campaign. So you will be in the centre of the action here, not that Gandhi does a lot apart from his prayers, and letters.'

'And sits at that damned spinning wheel of his.' Sir Henry was clearly not amused, especially since the demise of the Lancashire cotton mills.

Chapter Sixty Eight

Sevagram, Wardhu, India

DAVID AND EDWARD unpacked their belongings in the guest cottage at Mohandas Gandhi's Ashram in the small town of Sevegram, fifty miles from the administrative heart of Central India, Nagpur. The cottage was sparsely furnished yet comfortable, the most notable feature the absolute silence, as if the world had suddenly come to a complete standstill and time was suspended in an unexpected sanctuary of total calm. Edward looked around the neat room, the simplicity, the cleanliness, the lack of unnecessary clutter; the honesty of the space refreshing and humbling.

'Let's rest Ed. We have plenty of time until Evening Prayers with Gandhiji.'

'He won't mind if we join him?'

'He would be delighted. Are you religious old man?'

'Me?' Edward stopped for a moment. 'I am used to listening to my brother-in- law's discourses if that's what you mean.'

David nodded and sat on one of the beds. 'You won't mind if I do, have a nap for a couple of hours.' He smiled openly like a child who had just won a treasure hunt.

Rested and refreshed by a simple wash with water drawn from the Ashram well, David and Edward walked around the grounds of Sevegram.

'You know David, I am sure that Gandhi has absolutely the right idea here.'

'What do you mean Ed, taking down the British Empire from an isolated village in the middle of India.'

Edward laughed. 'I meant, living simply. Look at us out here. We could have anything we wanted. The Raj I mean. Yet somehow it is far more peaceful here than anywhere I have ever been.'

'That's exactly Gandhi's point. It is the villagers that he wants to look after. He is fighting for their freedom, their self-determination and it doesn't take an army to deliver that to them. It just takes a spinning wheel, a pen and paper and evening prayers.'

'Evening prayers?'

'You are coming? 7 pm. You will enjoy it.'

'I don't really understand all these Hindu gods David. A bit complex for me.'

'Don't worry old chap. He usually reads some Christian verses as well.'

'Oh.'

'It will open your mind a bit, listening to a couple of Suras from the Quran, verses from the Bible and of course, readings from the Hindu texts.'

'I might remember some of the stuff Thomas used to teach me.'

'Then you have had your preparation. You should feel quite at home.' David grinned and took his elbow, guiding him towards the evening prayer ground.

Gandhi sat motionless on his mat looking straight ahead as if the world were unfolding before his eyes. David sat quietly, cross legged on the ground amongst the half dozen people attending the prayer meeting that night. Despite his best efforts, Edward could not sit cross legged. Someone quickly brought him a small stool to take the strain off his back and legs, unable - as much as he tried - as he was to flex into the sitting position on the ground. The pain eased and for a moment, Edward was able to focus his mind on the people around him and then, on Gandhi, now picking up a piece of paper and reading it quietly to himself. He then lifted his eyes to the gathering and from memory sang the hymn.

> "Lead, kindly Light, amid the encircling doom,
> Lead Thou me on,
> The night is dark and I am far from home,

Lead Thou me on;
Keep Thou my feet, I do not ask to see,
The distant scene, - one step enough for me."

They woke to a clear morning, the temperatures already rising to what promised to be a hot day. David slept like a baby but Edward, simultaneously excited about meeting Gandhi and worried about leaving Ruth for so long, tossed and turned until finally, he crept out of the bedroom and slept on a grass mat on the verandah. The cooler night air eased the pains in his limbs that were a warning of early arthritis, and settled his mind into a dreamless few hours before dawn.

'Ah, there you are Edward. I was wondering where you could have wandered off to in the middle of the night.'

'I couldn't sleep. Perhaps it was the heat David.'

'Gandhi likes to sleep outside. So I see you have already found something in common with the old man.'

'Right. Then we meet him this morning David?'

'Yes of course. What did you think of the prayer meeting last night?'

'Actually David, I was stunned. I had no idea that Gandhi would sing a Christian hymn.'

'His favourite of course. He would have the whole of India sing the hymn, if but they would.'

'I thought he was devoutly Hindu.'

'The title *"Saint"* tells it all don't you think?'

'You mean souls who understand all.'

'Or remain above all it all and return to the basic premise of human rights, human dignity for all, no matter your station in life, your caste, your creed.' David said humbly. 'There is something I am not quite yet above though, and that is breakfast!' David announced.

Chapter Sixty Nine

GANDHI WAITED QUIETLY for David and Edward to enter his 'meeting' room, which doubled as his private sitting room, at times bedroom and place where he would pull out his spinning wheel every afternoon and produce the khadi cotton that he hoped one day, all Indian villagers would spin to liberate themselves from poverty and oppression.

'David, my friend. Welcome.'

'Ghandhiji.' David folded his hands together in a namaste to his venerated friend and hero.

'Sit, sit. And your friend also. Sit comfortably. Here, there is another little stool for your friend. I note that his legs are still stiff.' Gandhi smiled at Edward.

'Sir,' Edward was lost for words.

'Nothing so formal. Sit. Edward Thompson isn't it? David has told me something about you.'

'Yes, Edward.' award stated simply.

'Very sad, my sincere condolences to you all in England for losing General O'Dwyer and for the injuries to his friends.'

'Thank you but…'

'You are here of course, reporting on the murder?'

'Yes I am. Amritsar was…'

'More than you expected?' Gandhi looked directly at Edward.

'It certainly wasn't what I expected and I wasn't ready for the feeling that I was right there, when it happened I mean.'

'You saw it?'

'Saw it and heard it more likely. I couldn't imagine what it must have been like, except for the flashes as if someone played the events out aloud in my mind.'

'A vision. Then you are blessed to have such clear sight.' Gandhi said simply.

'I wish it were so. Sometimes I feel so confused.' Edward confessed.

'We all do at times young man. That is why we must meditate and pray for insight and clear sight, a gift that you already seem to have. David tells me that your wife has been unwell?'

'She lost her baby, our baby.' Edward added.

'I am so sorry my friend.' Gandhi reached forwards and patted Edward's hand.

Edward looked up into the old man's eyes. The deep brown pools seemed to have no beginning and no end, taking him away from his personal pain and into a place where he felt relieved of his burdens, light, free, happy.

'No doubt our British friends are interested that an old man such as I, could worry about the murder of the people responsible for so much unhappiness on our Indian soil. Then we are all human aren't we Edward and one murder does not absolve the crimes of so many more. Murder is a mortal sin. We are here claiming back our destiny through non-violence and so of course, I abhor any violence in the name of the freedom and Independence of India. We will achieve our ends by peaceful means.' Gandhi stood up and excused himself leaving David to wind up their business in Sevagram.

'Come, we must pack our things Edward. Our train leaves for Delhi at 12.30 p.m.'

Chapter Seventy

England

RUTH, RUTH? IT'S Edward. Can you hear me? Ruth I'm home.'
'Edward.' Ruth, caught between her newfound freedom and the sudden relief that Edward was home, choked on her reply.
 'Edward are you all right?'
 'I'm still at the Base Ruth. I'll be there in about an hour. See you then.' Edward replaced the receiver on its hook. He felt contented and thankful that there was none of the coldness and distance he had felt from Ruth through her cable. The airbase was as efficient as he had left it over three weeks ago. There was a sense however, of the shortness of time, a need to move faster without losing the customary calm of the well-oiled British military machine.
 'Petes!' Edward was surprised to see him. Petes touched his peaked cap and smiled.
 'You're home. Enjoy your trip?'
 'You could say that.'
 'You'll be returning to India?'
 'Not straight away Petes. I'm happy to have my feet back on British soil for now, and in any case there are a few more urgent items on the agenda at the moment. The War in Europe!'
 'Glad to hear it.' Petes collected Edward's baggage and signalled for a car.
 'You people certainly do a lot without much asking.'
 'Part of the service. The Old Man would hardly want us to leave stranded Englishmen wandering through the Kashmir.'
 'You heard about Srinagar?'
 'Quite a story you've got there.'

'I imagine so. But it was mostly for the holiday Petes.'
'What did you think of Karachi?'
'The Major was very hospitable.'
'He is. You left quite an impression on him I understand.'
'Oh?' Edward said lightly. 'Nothing passed these lips except for, the alluring sights of Solomon's Throne and Clifton Beach.'
'You missed the Taj.'
'Next time.'
The men shook hands.
Edward got into the car. 'Petes - Baghdad?'
'After the war. See you then.'

The Riley was roomy and warm. The driver adjusted his seat slightly forwards, briefly studied his passenger in the rear view mirror then quickly began to fill Edward in on the war news. As the car pulled out from the base, Edward glanced sideways just in time to catch Petes pulling a small notebook from his breast pocket.

'Curious. Petes certainly did not waste time pencilling in the details.' Edward half muttered.

The Riley swung abruptly to the left and Petes disappeared from view as the driver engaged second gear. The engine purred, and the driver, clearly enjoying its easy power and handling, grinned at Edward through the mirror.

London was a crowded and misty reminder of all that Edward had left behind. The cluster of newsagents and cafes surrounded him in welcome warmth, but the shops had lost their usual edge, the somewhat depressive edge of routine life. Edward felt buoyant and free. Ruth suddenly flashed into his mind. Her innocent face, the gold-brown hair swept aside with a pale hand and her soft red lipstick reminded him of her, when they first met. He opened his briefcase and unwrapped the silk scarf, folding it into the marble casket. She would like it. On top of the scarf, Edward placed a tiny gold brooch, delicate, filigree and shaped perfectly into a peacock. He closed the casket and returned it to his briefcase. It would be better to wait until they were inside before he gave Ruth the present. He wanted to make sure that they were relaxed, drinking coffee together so that he could gather the frail threads of their relationship and mend them into a tender bridge of new friendship.

The Riley pulled close to the kerb, engine idling as Edward slammed the door and reached into the boot for his luggage. He gave the driver the thumbs up and walked to the front door. Edward looked up to see the window to Ruth's bedroom. The curtain fluttered aimlessly in the morning eddies of rising warmth. She opened the door and looked at her husband with steady and open eyes. Edward bent to put his luggage down and clasped both of her hands in his.

'Hello Ruth. I'm back.'

'Edward.' Ruth dropped her head and looked at their entwined hands.

'Let's go inside. I have something for you.'

'Yes. There's some fresh coffee brewing.' With a brave and womanly smile, Ruth lifted her eyes.

'Ruth. You surprise me. You look somehow, more mature.'

'Thank you Edward.' Ruth nodded gracefully and unclasped her hands. 'Your bags.'

'I'll manage them. You go inside.'

Edward was taken aback by Ruth's demeanour, her quietness. He had watched her many transformations. Before him now was woman he had never met. Their silence was initially awkward, but neither Ruth nor Edward felt the need to find words. Ruth soundlessly poured the coffee and waited for Edward to sit down before she did.

'Ruth… I… '

'It's all right Edward. I know.'

'How?'

'I am a woman after all. Is she beautiful?'

'She was, though little more tangible than a fleeting thought. I'm sorry, I didn't realise… '

'You didn't realise that it could happen to anyone.'

'Ruth, I've brought you a gift.'

Edward placed the package in front of his wife.

Ruth searched his eyes for a long moment and got up to refresh the coffee. 'Edward, I can't. I'm different somehow. I don't want another baby.'

'I don't mean that… 'Edward stammered.

'I'm free Edward. I don't need you to look after me anymore.'

Ruth turned to face him. Edward could not find the words. He looked sadly at Ruth, her unfamiliar beauty and unearthly glow.

'Ruth, open it.'

Ruth looked at the package sitting on the table. She walked slowly to her chair, eyes fixed on Edward, then began to unwrap it. A soft flicker of pleasure toyed at her mouth and eyes.

'Edward it's beautiful.'

'I thought you would like it. I chose the scarf myself, but I got some help to find the right brooch.' Edward tried to hide his relief.

She picked up the delicate peacock and placed it in her palm. A sudden flash of fear crossed her eyes. It was impossible to escape his searching gaze. He raised his eyebrows.

'Edward…' Ruth paused, helpless before her admission.

'What's wrong?' Edward leant forward to catch the thoughts ready to flow through her eyes. Ruth could not speak for a moment, but with Edward holding her in his concerned gaze, it was impossible to hide the truth.

'Edward it's the pearls, and the brooch.'

'You haven't sold them Ruth.' Edward teased. They were hardly important.

'I threw them away.' Ruth's voice wavered slightly.

'You threw them away?' Edward looked at her in disbelief. 'Edward, I couldn't wear them anymore, not after… '

Edward stood up and walked around to his wife. He placed his arms around her and pulled her close to his chest.

'Ruth, I'm so, so sorry.'

Ruth allowed a few tears to drop; feeling more surprised than sad. 'Edward, I'm so glad you're home.' Ruth finally allowed herself to feel his warmth and comfort.

Edward held his wife close, stroking and caressing her hair.

'So am, I Ruth, so am I.'

Chapter Seventy One

THE NIGHT PASSED in the relative seclusion of their home. Edward and Ruth explored their new friendship, holding one another but not daring to speak or return to the familiarity of their former selves. The atmosphere was silent, almost sacred, but without desire. Since his meeting with Rajika, Edward could not find it in himself to be the man he once was. His wife, delicate, barely recovered from the trauma of miscarriage was still lost in the uncertainty of their relationship. Ruth lay close to him, unconcerned about his caring detachment. She appreciated the chance to be held, luxuriating in the safe warmth of Edward's arms. They lay together, still and subdued as they discovered in one another, a selfless and tender intimacy. Edward briefly wondered about Ruth's diamonds, his mind flitting to the brooch on green silk in Karachi.

'Uncanny.' Edward thought quietly. His felt rather than saw, another man taking his place, taking Ruth far away from her pain, far away from the cheap, charity balls and false jewellery and into the shelter of loving arms.

Chapter Seventy Two

'MANI, MANI, COME here child.' Ami's exasperation was visible in her voice. 'Mani, I don't have time to waste with your nonsense. Come when I call you child. There. That's better. Now, your hair. It is getting too long. Look, it is nearly at your waist! Goodness child, the gods have been kind to you.' Ami pulled and tugged at her daughter's hair with her brush, the perfect strands sparkling with a golden sheen on sheer black. The morning sunlight streamed through her fingers, caressing her the child's scalp her hair cascading in a delightful flow of light and dark, sun and heritage; a perfect river of unbraided youth.

'Mani, what am I going to do with you? You are too bright to become a wife for some ungrateful man. And you are naughty! Taking jewels from the gutter and hiding them from your own mother.' Ami yanked at a knot.

Mani yelled. 'Ouch. Mama. Don't tug so.'

'What else have you taken without telling your Mama? Tell me child? Do you hide things other so that I won't find them?' Ami put the brush aside and took the weight of her daughter's hair in her right hand and divided it into three to begin the long braid. The plait started high on Mani's neck, folding into a thick twine under Ami's expert fingers. Ami quickly became absorbed in the slippery silkiness of her daughter's hair, intent on making each twist as even as the one before and checking the alignment of the braid against the child's spine. The weight of the braid was heavy on her arms and she wanted to rest the plait on the back of the chair, but to do so would disturb the perfect placement and spoil the effect. She grasped the bottom of the plait, pulling it deftly into a single, tight strand for the ribbon. Ami worked a ribbon around the base of the plait three or four times, her fingers moving with a speed that

Mani herself could never manage. Then she doubled under the base of the plait securing it with a ribbon, winding it around and around until the plait felt snug and secure.

'There child. Now you look as lovely as the Sisters of Mercy in Karachi.' A few tears gathered defiantly in the corners of Ami's eyes. She missed her home badly, the sound of the street vendors and the cluster of women at the market. She wondered if her husband Hanif thought before he sent them away, so far from the comfort and warmth of their relatives, the chatter of children, the ever-present sounds of the Mosque and in the distance, the bells of the Christian Church where the Sisters of Mercy gathered around their Mother Mary.

Yes, she could hear those bells here, but the sound was not the same. Here, the bells competed with the sound of bombs falling like rain on the solemn head of London, its skyline and roofs now shattered in submission to war. This European war was not for her or the child. Hanif was right about that.

The large and small markets of Karachi were filled with colour and the resonance of timeworn tradition. London was dull and depressing. There was no spontaneous combustion of passions at the height of business, nor the rapid exchange of goods and money. London was the place where deals were hidden, secretive, laced with quiet, copious greed in the hands of the few. There was nothing open or abundant about these people, no one as alive as Hanif and his markets friends.

In England, Ami felt unsure and afraid. The climate was dim, business people were sour and one could not easily judge whom to trust. Yes, the grand buildings of London overawed her with their wealth. But how could they compare with the ageless architecture of her India, the grand arches of the Moghul emperors, the delicate flutes of the carved marble and stone Hindu temples or the golden dome of the great Sikh temple? Here, the people in the streets never looked happy. They could not enjoy the colours or fabrics of India; her silks, Khadi and carpets or be swept away by the impulse of a passing moment; a chance for a bargain in any one of the thousands of village markets. London did not have the same markets with their flurries of women escaping the tentacles of trade as street vendors plied their wares.

London did not understand the intricacies of bargaining and the thrill of winning an anna or rupee over the marketwallas. London was staid and steady, incapable of sweeping Ami, laden with goods, from the market, into the rivers of culture that wound past her home. London was boring, lonely and frightening. The old ladies here were as grey as their skies, their hair knotted in impossible buns, and bodies wrapped in mournful and woollen coats. In London, the angry roads scoffed at shoes, threatening to topple the women from their precarious heels. Her own sandals were well-worn, soft and stable beneath her determined feet. Ami was footsure even though far from the uncomplicated sands of Clifton Beach.

'Mama, you don't need to do it anymore. It feels quite tight. I don't think it can fall out.' Mani felt the top of her braid, her little fingers exploring the neat and inseparable twists of hair.'

'Don't touch child. You will loosen the braid.' Ami scolded.

'Thank you Mama.' Mani hopped to her feet and turned to face her mother. She swung he braid from side to side, giggling like the child she was,

'Imp!' It was Ami's turn to smile. 'Go inside. We have work to do.'

'But Mama, you promised.'

'I promised nothing child.'

'Mama you promised that we could go to the grocer's this morning.' Mani's voice quavered.

'I know child. I know. Perhaps little later would be better. It's too early now. Ami suppressed her cough, surprised that she was frequently sick, more so than she had ever been in her life.

'Mama, we can buy you something beautiful if we sell the jewels.'

'We will do nothing of the kind Mani.' Ami was adamant.

'But Mama, you need so many things.'

'Mani, that is the end of it. Your father will send some money when he is able to. Until then, we just have to do the best that we can.'

'Yes Mama. I only thought…'

'Don't think Mani. I did not ask you to think for me.' 'I know Mama.'

Mani picked up the chair sitting stubbornly in the wan patch of sunlight. Their yard was small, but sufficient for her to reproduce at least part of her normal domestic ritual. She enjoyed plaiting the child's hair and God knows how little sunshine the child would get in this land. At least she, Mani's mother, could drag the chair into the light, long enough to brush and braid the hair even if the neighbours were not ready for such an open display.

'Like apes they are. All the time picking at the hair as if they have fleas.'

Ami was aware of the antagonism. It was not easy to be a woman in a strange man's land. At least at home, she knew the rules and the women found one another and looked to each other for support and company.

Here, there was nothing like that. Some of the women were frightened and because of their fear, cruel with their gossip. Ami ignored it. She would content herself with the child and in keeping their home. From time to time, she would allow herself to dream about when Hanif would leave his dedication to Allah and call them home. Once they had settled, her uncle busied himself once more in his own affairs. Yes he brought them money every month, but it was company that Ami craved.

Ami was rarely wrong. She 'knew' that the jewels had to be returned. If she kept them, they would almost certainly bring death upon her and the child. She must be find the owner! Later, when the child was warm, they would go to the shop and place a notice in the window. She make sure that the owner would instantly understand that the lost jewels were found. Ami did not even think of a reward. She only wanted to rid herself of her child's unfortunate treasure and hear no more about it.

Chapter Seventy Three

CHRIS ANTICIPATED EDWARD'S return with the happiness of a schoolboy. He tidied the office, putting papers and pens in places and dusting shelves that had remained unnoticed for six or more months. He wanted Edward to feel valued and that he was to Chris and *"The Reporter,"* essential. Most of all however, he understood the boundaries of Edward's professional ego had been diminished and blurred and that he would need reassurance. Chris planned to remind Edward of the warmth of their close newspaper family, to downplay 'office roles' and 'personalities.' He was conscious that his role as 'editor' was simply a role. First and foremost, he was Edward's friend and that is what mattered.

Today was going to be a gathering of friends, people who came together according to the nature of the world, to earn their living, to use their talents and hopefully be an asset for England during the war.

As editor, Chris had the final say as to the nature and quality of the material, its subtle inflections and impact on readers as a sober, mature and honest reflection of the world around them. He fully realised the tremendous impact of any media, the newspapers and the radio. People were ready to believe what they read and heard, and Chris accepted full responsibility for what *"The Reporter"* put out onto the streets of London. His dry humour frequently dominated the Editorial page; London needed to laugh at herself along with putting down Jerry in this war, that would be won on the psychological as well as physical battlefield.

'Have you ordered the buns?' Chris asked Jenny.

'I have Chris. Breakfast as usual.' Jenny piled the buns on his table.

'We will do it a little better than usual Jenny. The prodigal son returns!' Chris smiled wickedly at his new 'reporter.'

'Let's do that Chris.' Jenny too, was ready to celebrate.

Chris looked around the office. He was pleased with the result, at how the staff entered the spirit of *"Welcome Home Foreign Correspondent."*

'You have all done me proud,' Chris announced. 'Imagine, one day it could be any one of you coming back from an overseas *"assignment!"*

'Can't imagine it Chris. But you don't know, do you.' Jenny announced.

'You never know. *"The Reporter"* might become more adventurous. Any one fancy a trip to the western front?'

'You might lose half your staff that way Chris.' The oldest in the group, Robert remarked.

'Just joking. That's why I sent Edward to India Robert. The world's vision is on the war, but whole different drama is taking place in India. I wonder whether Gandhi is ready to hold the reins of India.

'Edward will fill us in on that no doubt.'

'He will, but it may take time for him to recover his health and be back on form.' Chris said more seriously. 'David cabled me from Delhi. Edward was virtually unconscious for the better part of twelve hours and out of action for another few days.'

'Can't be cheap sending him all the way around the world for a short story.' Robert remarked drily.

'We have friends in the business.'

'Friends in the War Office?'

'You might say that. What could they do without the enthusiastic support of the London press.'

'The question is, what would they do Chris if you weren't hanging around them like a?..' Robert let the sentence hang.

'Like a…? '

'Like someone who knows more than he should.'

Chris laughed uproariously, his head thrown back and stomach shaking at the joke. 'That's what this game is all about. If you don't look over their shoulder from time to time, they get away with far too much.'

'You mean Colonel Dyer?'

'Precisely.'

'Well I'm not sure that everyone would agree with you Chris.' Robert was attuned to the general English reaction to General Dwyer's death.

'There are truckloads of Indians in England who would.'

The conversation hung on the timely warning. Edward's visit appeared more as experiment in British truthfulness than an, aimless meander into the middle of pre- Independent India.

Edward climbed the stairs to the office. He was glad to be back, happy that Ruth was comfortable to have him home, neither repelling him nor clinging to him as she had done in the past. He wondered how Chris would receive him, the prodigal journalist, empty-handed apart from a few snippets from Amritsar. He would write about Gandhi, and how the Saint sympathised with General O'Dwyer.

The office door swung open to a warm and unexpected welcome. Chris stood boyishly next to the table covered with plates of food, coffee cups and fresh flowers. Edward looked at Chris, fighting desperately to contain the emotion choking in his chest.

'Good to see you old man. Welcome back.' Chris walked towards Edward and put his arms around him, holding him until he felt Edward regain his composure. Then with a hearty slap on the back, he pulled Edward into the gathering. Edward slipped quickly into the joviality, smiling, greeting his colleagues, and accepted from Jenny, the life giving liquid for journalists - hot coffee. Chris moved easily in and out of the room, attending minor matters of the day whilst keeping the celebration alive. He gauged the visible changes in Edward, how he seemed more emotional, more sensitive, more open. He would accommodate the changed Edward in context of the daily work of *"The Reporter."*

Chris had also faced his own painful moment of truth, of being aborted from the temporary womb of 'career' to confront the harsh realities of transient and changing roles, as if his lines were cast for someone else's drama. He was at the time, heart-broken to realise that *"The Reporter"* was a futile gesture of validation for an otherwise mortal and insignificant life.

Edward had also experienced the death of his ego, only his journey was amplified in the vast arena of the subcontinent, complete with its spiritual giants, numberless millions of rural Indians living in virtual poverty and a tiny Saint spinning India's future. It was a humbling, sobering and at times, excruciating experience to lose oneself totally, and then find oneself, totally dependent on other people to reconstruct that same self. The entire process of loss of self and recovering self, could take place as quickly as a vision, or be drawn out in tortuous days, the mind stretched like catgut in a tapestry of pain, suffering and anonymity. India affected the most seasoned traveller at a deep and soul changing level.

Edward nodded, grateful for Chris's wisdom, his gentle and well-chosen actions to reorient him back to the clockwork efficiencies of English life. The breakfast party concluded with the simple ease of telephones, cables and the soft clatter of cups and plates collected into the office sink.

Edward stepped into his boss's office. 'Thanks Chris. That was very good of you old chap.'

'Don't mention it Edward. Good to have you back. How is Ruth?' Chris was genuinely concerned.

'She is better than I had hoped.'

'Thank goodness Ed.' Chris's smile and relief was genuine.

'I appreciate what you did for her Chris. Seriously.'

'Think nothing go it old man.'

Edward nodded gratefully.

'David was quite worried about you too. You have no idea what caused the illness?'

'None. One minute I stepped off the plane and then within half an hour, it was as if an iron hand had a grip on my innards. I have never felt pain like that before Chris, never. I'm not as strong as I thought I was. I imagine that's why I passed out.'

'Take it easy for a while yes? Just familiarise yourself with the usual routine, war news, updates from the Old Man, you know the score.'

'I do have plenty of notes from The Subcontinent.'

'Whatever you write will do nicely Edward. Just do what you can today. I don't want you relapsing into unconsciousness.' Chris joked carefully.

'I will. Perhaps it is partly the strain of Ruth's illness and losing Tom. That's in the past now. I'm sure I'll be feeling on top of it all again by tomorrow.'

Edward already was tired and happy to sit at his desk.

Chris withdrew to his own desk and began to patiently and methodically sort the morning's correspondence.

Chapter Seventy Four

Karachi, India

SESHETA EMERGED FROM behind the shop curtain. She had become increasingly interested in her studies and now, was able to memorise and repeat several verses of Kabir. She often pleaded with her uncle to recite the Suras. There was something unreachable in the verse, something masculine that she could not touch, not in the same way that she could touch and embrace the gentle lyrics of Rumi and Kabir. As she remembered and recited Kabir with his soft verses, she felt that she were a part of the same lover's embrace with the Eternal Beloved. Sesheta allowed her thoughts to wander over each passage, exploring truth, reality and the existential; the boundaries expanding and merging into the unknown. Her heart breathed with new life; fluttering like a bird freed from the human cage of gender, religion, culture. Long after the poetry had faded from her lips, it continued to chant in her mind. Now she could read Hesse.

'Sesheta. Sesheta.'

'Papa? '

'Sesheta. What is this book on your bed?

Sesheta hesitated, frozen by her father's rage, his fury unmasked.

'Answer me Sesheta. Where did you get this? And who, who is this,' he shrugged his shoulders in disbelief, 'this Edward Thompson!?'

'Papa, it was a gift.' Sesheta tried.

'A gift. What sort of a gift is this rubbish girl!' Her father's eyes blazed, his mouth curled into a dangerous snarl. 'Is this your Uncle's doing? Is this what he does when I give you to his care? Tell me girl? Where did you get this book?' He stepped close to her, one fist clenched, the other shaking the book in her face.' Fahisha!' He swung an angry back-hander across her face.

Sesheta reeled to the floor stunned more by his words than the blow that caught her cheek. Her father moved closer and dragged her to her feet again.

'Answer me girl! Who is this Mr. Thompson? What are you doing reading this trash? Is this what you do when you pretend to study? Meet foreign men! Have you no respect for your father's honour?

'Papa… '

'Don't answer me!'

Sesheta fell to her knees, confused and unable to comprehend his anger. The book was to help her with language, not with men.

'Father, it's in English.'

'I know it is in English. Who said for you to learn English!' Her father paused, uncertain of the significance.' You should be with your mother, working, not showing yourself in the market.

'But..'

'Go to your room before I thrash the life from you girl.' Sesheta was too afraid to move.

'Get up!' Her father lost his patience and pulled his daughter by her hair. Sesheta screamed. 'Papa, Papa, no!'

'Do as I say Sesheta. Go to your room.' His anger darkened to black rage. Sesheta wanted to face him, to order him out of the shop as Hanif would order any man who threatened her. Her eyes, flashing with the fire of rebellion, caught his.

Dada saw the power, the sudden strength in his daughter and raised his fist, smashing her forehead with the full force of his wrath. The single blow forged a fatal signature into the idol that was his daughter.

Sesheta fell beneath his force. Her head struck the counter and the blood spurted from her temple, staining and soaking the piles of grains delicately arranged on trays of brass and steel.

Dada did not see her fall. Blinded by hate, he gripped the book with shaking hands ripping and tearing the pages in his impotence, before scattering the, fleeting testaments of death, onto the shop floor.

Sesheta's body lay prone and lifeless in her own blood for two hours. Then Hanif found her. He returned from his evening prayers to close the daily accounts in th shop. As he opened the door to the shop, he immediately knew that something was wrong, terribly wrong. At first, he thought that a wild goat or a wandering cow had strewn havoc into the grains and piles of nuts. Then he saw the book, the pages of *"Siddhartha"* lying scattered, littering the floor. The rounded character of the language caught his eye. Sesheta would hardly let the treasured book out of her sight! Now the pages, cast like throwaway catechisms, littered the soiled and bloodstained floor. Hanif's eye caught the cover consecrated with the blood of his niece and the flecks of blood on brass trays; darker stains, polluting and poisoning the grain. His heart pounded in horror.

'Sesheta. No!' Hanif screamed.

He found her, wasted like a sacrificial goat on the altar of impotent belief. 'No! Not this way.' Hanif cradled his niece in his arms, pulling the strands and thickened clumps from her face; the eyes dull, disbelieving, staring soullessly into his. He bent over his niece, tears blinding his eyes. The blood matted her hair and the wound that gaped obscenely.

Sesheta, his lovely niece, was totally lifeless; dead. Hanif wanted to wrench his eyes away, to escape her pain, but he was transfixed, trapped by her death, feeling Sesheta's fear of her father's hatred and rage.

Hanif closed the shop with a broken and heavy heart. He had not wanted to leave his business in this way. The soundless call of the Mosque resonated in his mind, its soft tone lifting his spirits in a joy that he had once tasted as a boy. It was the same joy of unshod feet, running free across sands of Clifton Beach as if there were no boundaries and no limits. Now, all that was shattered. The walls of the shop, were nothing more than a crumbling reminder of all that he once held dear and precious. Sesheta, Sesheta; so rare, like a well- tuned sitar, the strings willing and ready before the master's bow, was no more.

Chapter Seventy Five

THE IMAM INSISTED that they put Sesheta to rest according to their custom. Her father refused at first, still angry at the girl's learning, her literacy in life that defied his unspoken command. Ultimately, Dada had no choice. His hand at her death would instantly be known if he did not display the normal play of grief. Hanif questioned his brother, the bruising on Sesheta's forehead, the scattered pages in his shop. The child was defenceless, harmless. There was no other answer in his mind, but Papa protested any knowledge of her death.

'Hanif, you accuse your own brother! Would a father kill his own flesh and blood?' Dada defied.

So, Dada remained safe from the echoes of his mortal and hideous sin.

Hanif blamed himself. Sleepless nights and hour upon hour of prayer an numbed silences later, Hanif finally accepted Sesheta's death. There would be no justice. Of that he was sure. He blamed himself. Yes, in good faith he had encouraged her to read and study. There were few like Sesheta who understood the lilting lines that revealed the mysteries of the one he knew; Allah, the same One Sesheta longed to meet in life as she had now had, no doubt met in death. Hanif knew that Sesheta would only wilt in marriage, lost like a lotus in a desert storm. Perhaps this was Allah's way.

At least Sesheta had only lost her life and not her soul, that would be inevitably squandered and gambled in the hands of a careless and prideful man. They could destroy her body through death, but her spirit remained untouched, like a virgin goddesses, a Sufi Priestess, free upon the forgotten plains of time. Hanif mourned Sesheta like a daughter. Yet she was more sacred than any mortal child, her soul steeped in a spirituality and sweetness that few other Muslim girls would ever discover, hidden as they were cloistered worlds. Yes, Sesheta was gone, but the memories of her spirit burned in Hanif's chest almost as brightly as his longing for his Allah, his deep desire for his own ascension into grace.

Chapter Seventy Six

England
'MANI. COME CHILD. It is time.' Yes Mama.'
Ami collected her scant valuables into a cotton bag and gathered her child close to her. 'Now say nothing Mani. Understood?'
'Yes Mama. I promise.'
'Good. Then we must go.'
The mother and child, secure in one another's company, stood alone in the street, the door to their tiny sanctuary closed tight. Ami was pleased that the house offered at least shelter and warmth. In this unwelcoming land, at least they had somewhere safe and private. Outside the confines of their home, Ami was acutely conscious of her dress, the obvious and hidden barriers of culture and language that made her more alone than she had ever felt in her life. She spent as little time as necessary outside their home, unable to confront the faces that grimaced with the fear of difference, unsure of the meaning of Italy coming to England. The women often turned from them, muttering into themselves as if she Ami were to blame for the weather, the price of milk or the planes that loomed across the city at impossible and frightening hours. Ami stepped hastily onto the road, one hand clutching the child and in the other, the bag hiding the notice, carefully written in a coarse and uneasy hand.

Together, the mother and her imp for a child, stepped into the tiny shop. It was like stepping back into Karachi. Shop was cluttered, untidy and she could smell the stale smells of cooking from behind the curtain that hid the grocer's own kitchen. He suddenly slipped from behind the curtain into the shop. The grocer was unkempt, small, ugly and with cunning eyes and a drooping lower lip that constantly dribbled. He smiled crookedly at Mani and immediately offered her boiled sweets from a large glass jar with a battered metal lid.

Ami looked sternly at her child. There was nothing she could do! The grocer was far too clever and had already tempted the child before she, her mother could speak. Ami had very little choice but to give in to both; the cat and the mouse. Ultimately, it was the mother's purse that was of more interest to the grocer than his corruption of the child.

Finally Ami soke.' Leave the child alone. She has enough to eat from her mother's kitchen.' Ami admonished.

The grocer smiled unpleasantly.

'Ah, for you my good lady, some rice perhaps? Flour? You must need eggs for the child, she is still growing.'

'I am not your "good lady." Nor does she need eggs. We make our own chappatis and pooris and don't need your eggs.' Ami said in broken English.

'Perhaps fresh bread?'

Ami softened with the memory of Hanif's shop, the scent of freshly baked breads, the inviting array of pooris, the grains and lentils carefully arranged on sparkling metal platters patterned with the blue and gold of peacocks.

'A loaf then. I have only this much until next week.' Ami freely displayed the emptiness of her purse.

'So I see you are a good mother. Keeping a little somewhere safe perhaps? Under the bed is it or behind the stove?' The grocer knew the secret ways of women all too well and when they promised payment next week or the week after that, he could cleverly extract from them, the location of their private store.

'There is nothing. But, please place this notice on your door.'

'Ahh. Let us see.' The grocer paused for effect. '"Found. Precious belongings from a lady's bag. Enquire with grocer." It does not say much my dear woman.' He hung the sentence expectantly.

'It is as I want it to be and if you'll be good enough to keep the name, of any lady who asks.'

'From a lady's bag... that could be anything; her compact, her watch.' The grocer was deliberately evasive, enticing an answer.

'Mister, it is...'

'They will understand what it means if they have something to claim.' Ami cut her daughter off, aware that the grocer had fooled the child into speaking. 'Now, the bread and I won't keep you any longer from your honest work.' Ami was emphatic.

The grocer filled the bag and added a boiled sweet for Mani. 'Just one. Let the child enjoy herself.'

Ami, keen to leave accepted the sweet without a word. She dragged Mani to the door and onto the street. 'Child. I told you to promise.'

'I am sorry Mama. He was guessing so I thought... '

'One day child, you will learn. Never let a man know any of your secrets. Never!'

'Yes Mama.'

Ami hurried faster than her dignity and caution normally allowed. She wanted to be as far away as her feet would take her from the grocer with his seeping eyes that glinted with his lust for money and drooping mouth shadowed in ugly unkemptness. The grocer also smelt. As he breathed in and out his thoughts, it was not with the sweet smell of rose and jasmine that followed Hanif. This man smelt dank with sweat and deceit. Ami had no choice. There was nowhere else to post the notice.

Alone, solitary in his business, the grocer pretended innocence, forgetting the rules of English culture

Chapter Seventy Seven

'MADAM, PLEASE COME to my shop.'
'Your shop? Who is this calling?'
   'Sayed the grocer?'
   'What do you want?'
   'Madam, please come as soon as you can.'
   'Sayed? Of course. I remember. You sold me the beans.
   'What is it?'
   'Madam, please come then I will explain.'
   'OK Sayed. I am not sure what it is you want but I'll be there in fifteen minutes.'

   Ruth replaced the receiver on the hook. How odd! She rarely shopped at the grocer's yet he seemed to know her well. She gathered her purse and powdered her nose before drawing her dark grey coat around her limbs against the London fog. She was happy to walk and feel the sharp tap of her heels on the road.

   Ruth opened the shop door and entered the dark den filled with smells of smallgoods and cooking from behind the curtain. Sayed stood behind his counter, measuring and weighing barley onto a pair of scales. The grain threatened to spill as he carefully placed counter weights until satisfied with the measurement.

   'Four pounds exactly. Ahh. Mrs. Thompson.' He drooled, inclining his head slightly to invite her closer.

   'Yes Sayed. And how do you know my name?'

   'Your husband of course. He comes for the morning paper and ahh….. Turkish coffee; *very* strong.' Sayed underlined the very.

   'So that was it. He did mention your coffee. He seems to like it.'

Sayed gave her a sideways grin, measuring the thinness of the pale woman against the prospect of reward.

'Madam, have you lost something precious.' Sayed rolled the 'r' across his tongue.

'What do you mean Sayed. I am not sure that I know what you're talking about.'

'Madam, you are the queen of the night. No one else wears the same, beautiful trinkets that you *"The Charitable Queen of The Night"* do. Sayed lifted his eyebrows revealing the secrets he did not hold. 'Perhaps, perhaps....you have lost some valuables?' Sayed lifted his right hand, dancing his fingers into the stale air as if the invisible jewels hung from an imaginary mannequin.

Mouth slightly agape, Ruth observed the craft of the man. How could he know anything about her? *"Surely, no Edward, you wouldn't..."*

Ruth's thoughts ran like quicksilver.

'Madam, perhaps you have forgotten… maybe something slipped from your neck one evening after…' Sayed let the question linger.

'Sayed, if you have something to tell me, perhaps you ought to be more open about it.'

'There is a reward…' his tongue quickly explored the margins of his lips. Ruth noticed for the first time, the roughness of his beard, his unkempt appearance, the paunch of his unseemly belly.

'First tell me what you've found, then we'll see if it belongs to me.'

'Then your jewels aren't so important to you that you would not think of a tiny reward for a kind grocer who takes his own time to…'

'All right. If there is anything that belongs to me, of course there will be a reward Sayed. Now, what have you found.'

'Madam, first you must come here this evening, at about seven o'clock. Then there will be someone for you to meet. Perhaps also, some way of thanking a hard working grocer for his troubles.' Sayed's mouth curled, but his eyes glinted like hardened steel.

Ruth drew in her breath, exasperated by the manner of the man, aware that he was perhaps the key to her discarded jewels. 'Seven o'clock then Sayed. And my husband will accompany me.'

'As you wish Madam. Now, some more beans?'

'No thank you, at least not now.' Ruth caught the sharpness in her tone before she caused offence.

Sayed inflected his head slightly to indicate victory and moved with exaggerated politeness to open the door.

'Madam.' Sayed held the door open just enough to let her pass, his fingers resting lightly on the door handle. Ruth smelt the excitement in his breath, fresh sweat pricking under his arms, and the tang of curry and garlic seeping from his pores. She stepped hurriedly onto the street, the door closing swiftly behind her.

Ruth felt dazed and disoriented by the encounter. She wanted to walk home quickly, angrily; but her steps faltered before she found the footpath. For a moment she was torn as to whether to return to the shop, to yell abuse at the little man, or to remain rooted in rage where she was. She was soundly trapped between the grocer's taunts and her own curiosity over the 'jewels.' For a few minutes her breath caught in her throat then, she eased into a steady walk. 'Fool Ruth' she told herself. Sayed used her husband to manipulate her for his own private game. There was little point in getting angry. The jewels were gone although strangely, not far as if they were meant to return to her, tarnished only by the grocer's greed it seemed. She felt as cheap as a lady tramp, reduced to trash by the glinting and beady eyes of Sayed.

Ruth opened the front door and strode straight to the kitchen angrily lighting the gas for tea. The routine and rhythmic actions of preparing the tea calmed her and allowed her to gain perspective. She was pleased that the jewels had surface - if indeed they had - yet felt detached from the discovery as if they had lost all importance to her. 'In any case,' she reasoned 'Sayed has blemished any hope of happiness in their return. *"The Charitable Queen of the Night"* indeed! What would he know about charity balls and how indeed did he know about her life in such intimate detail. Perhaps he had overheard some gossip in his shop, the wives....'

Edward would want her to claim the jewels but how could she wear them now? Ruth stilled the stream of invective towards the grocer that threatened to course through her mind. The little man was interesting in his muddiness; there was something authentic in his cunning behaviour, more real and tangible than the ephemeral flattery and platitudes of the charity set. He was repugnant to her, tangible and transparent in his ugliness. At least in Sayed there was no mistaking his greed. He was measurable and predictable, unlike the men who hid their lust and private wars behind the screen of civility and the fragile mask of charity.

Tonight, she would ask the grocer for new delights; sweet meats laced and perhaps some Turkish Delight for Edward as a treat.

Chapter Seventy Eight

RUTH ARRANGED HERSELF comfortably on the sofa, book in one hand and a rose-patterned china teacup in the other. Home was warm, cosy and comfortable. Edward could no longer bring himself to be solicitous or protective and Ruth was happy with the change. It was a rare luxury as amidst the fears of war, to curl into the sofa, knees covered with her grandmother's crocheted rug and eyes heavy with contentment.

The telephone jolted Ruth awake. She was surprised that the book was open in her lap, the cup and saucer on the table, a still life sculpture of liquid sweetness.

'Edward?' Ruth sprang to her feet to answer the hall telephone.

'Yes. It's me. How was your day Ruth?' 'I fell asleep reading on the sofa.'

'Wonderful. The rest will do you the world of good.'

'Hmm. Are you hungry?'

'No, Not yet. Would you like to go out for dinner?' 'I can't, I mean we can't Edward.'

'Oh? Why not?'

'The grocer called, the one where you buy papers and coffee. I think he has found the brooch and necklace.'

'Really?' Edward was surprised. 'Where?'

'I have no idea. That's just it Ed. He phoned here and said to come to the shop at seven o'clock. He was talking about a reward.'

'I see. Then we'd better go and see him.'

'I thought we might have shepherd's pie for dinner.'

'Sounds good to me Ruth. I am not so keen on mince any more. Can you use beans instead of mince?

'Are you still feeing sick Edward?'

'No, but I have lost my appetite for meat. It must have been Delhi.'

'Perhaps you'd better see the doctor.'

'I feel alright, but nothing too strong for the stomach Ruth. See you at six.'

'See you at six.' Ruth put the telephone down. She opened the cupboard. No beans? And Sayed had asked her - curious!

'Edward, go home early this evening. There's nothing much to do until the reports come in tomorrow. First day back and all that.' Chris instructed.

'Thanks Chris. Ruth has something planned, I'd appreciate it.'

'Don't mention it. Edward, it is good to have you back on board. I mean it.' Chris smiled humbly. 'You'll need to read this before the reports come in.'

Edward took the file pushed it into his briefcase. 'I'll have the story on Amritsar ready by tomorrow lunchtime.'

'Good. Don't forget to include the bit on sedition. Gandhi must have known there would be repercussions.'

'The point is, even if he did, would he have taken a different course?'

'You've been closer to the man than any of us Edward. I trust your judgement.'

'According to David, Gandhi is somewhat of a Saint so it's hard to imagine he would willingly put so many people in danger through a little, shall we say, *"old man's rebellion."'*

'The tyrant beneath the homespun dhoti!' Chris retorted. 'Now, enjoy your evening. Is Ruth cooking something special for you?'

'Shepherd's pie, without the mince.'

Chris roared with laughter. Don't tell me Edward, even without meeting the Mahatma, he has influenced you!'

'I hadn't thought of it like that. I thought it was just a sensitive tummy.' Edward said whimsically.

'I doubt it. Hard to imagine you would change your favourite dish for something as minor as a tummy upset.'

Edward had no reply. He smiled at Chris and pulled his coat and gloves on. 'See you tomorrow then.'

Chris was already buried in his papers, cables and reports.

Chapter Seventy Nine

AMI PAUSED OVER her cooking. The faint smell of tomato was both tempting and pleasing. She tasted the vegetables and added another pinch of salt. The sauce needed more time. Carefully she added more of the diced tomatoes assembled at one side of the pan. Their food was simple and nourishing. Ami could only afford the basics and her usual fare of homemade sweetmeats were now a luxury. The burden of lingering poverty rested uneasily on her shoulders. Now, she was annoyed that the grocer had offered his rude temptations to her daughter.

'Stupid man. What does he want from us?' Ami banged the roller onto its board. At least he had posted her notice at his shop so there was nothing further she could do until someone came forward and claimed the jewels. More than once she had considered wrapping the brooch and necklace in newspaper and throwing them into the dustbin. At least that way they would be off her mind, but the image of a woman, wondering and pining after something that was precious to her, deflated the impulse. Although her life was simple, she had in any case, an innate love for beauty and fine jewels. She could not deny the joy of another woman in wearing what she Ami herself longed for.

Ami gazed absently into the vegetable subji, softly simmering on the stove. It was just about right, not over cooked and the mixture not too oily. She lifted the pot onto the table and turned down the stove. The food was hot and the subji with its small collection of home-made pooris would soon fill the corners of her child's willing stomach. Ami was proud of her humble and honest kitchen. She spent a few solitary moments thanking Allah for providing for them before preparing the table and hurriedly heating milk for the child. Mani was still undersized for her age and not that strong. Ami worried about her, but knew that no amount of food would change nature of the child.

'Mani. Mani. Come.' Ami called through the doorway.

The smells from her mother's kitchen, lifted Mani from her studies. She happily pushed aside the books and stretched her arms. She enjoyed the pictures, but she struggled with strange words of English, finding the language boring and confusing, not like their native tongue Urdu, which was easy to read and sounded like a song.

'Mama, why can't I dance and sing?' Mani announced in a miniature tantrum.

'Mani, this is England. You learn what the teachers tell you to learn and that is the finish of it.' Ami responded, as exasperated as her child by he futility of her education. As soon as she was of age, she would ask the local women if they would employ the child. Even a little cleaning would be sufficient. Mani was young, but anything it seemed, was better than learning from the unfamiliar and foreign books.

'Mani, Come now!' Ami commanded.

Mani pushed her chair away from her battered desk, scraping the chair legs on the floor. She wished she could sit and watch her mother work. She would help with the dishes, and then her mother would forget the homework.

'Sit little imp. Drink your milk.' Ami heaped spoonfuls of the vegetable subji onto two plates. She expertly replaced the pots on the stove in a single movement and sat opposite her child. Ami wanted to talk to the child but the words stuck in her throat. So she ate silently, watching Mani play with her subji.

'Your food will get cold Mani. Eat it. Don't play with it.' Ami relaxed, in fond chastisement of her daughter.

'Sorry Mama.' Mani pushed the piles of food together and tried to look interested. Her mind wondered to the grocer and his sweets.

'Later Mani, I will make you something sweet.' Ami guessed.

A light knock interrupted her train of thoughts. Ami pushed herself to her feet. 'You finish your food Mani' she instructed.

She opened the door to the urgent face of a boy, perhaps eleven or twelve years only in age.

'Yes?'

'Missus, you must come this evening to my uncle's shop. Seven o'clock.'

'Seven? Who told you to come here.' Ami tried to be stern, but the frightened young face softened her. For a second, she was tempted to invite the boy to join them at her meal, but her memory of the grocer warned her that she should not become too familiar.

'Uncle Sayed said that you would know and that you should come at seven.' The boy's eyes, innocent and lonely, begged for the warmth of the familiar. Again, Ami struggled with her instinct to bring the boy to their table.

'One minute child. Mani. Bring the tin.'

Mani obeyed and brought her mother the slightly battered vessel, salvaged from their home. Ami, a sentinel of maternal warmth and familiarity, opened the tin and placed a biscuit into the boy's hand then gave one to her daughter before closing the tin and shooing Mani back to the table. 'These are homemade. The best. Tell the grocer I'll be there at seven.'

Ami gently shut the door and returned to the table. She said nothing.

Chapter Eighty

RUTH AND EDWARD ate slowly, luxuriating in one another's quiet company. Ruth, amused by the 'bean' shepherd's pie, ate with good humour and wondered whether the seasoning was to her husband's taste.

'Wonderful Ruth.' Edward complimented her. 'How did you get the right consistency?'

'A little cornflour and water. Acts like glue.'

'It tastes much better than mince.'

Ruth laughed.' Just as well for you. How was your first day?' 'Chris turned on a do for me. He's incredibly generous.' Edward looked up from his plate.

'So you're not tempted to leave us all for the Far East?'

'Ruth, you know I couldn't do that.' Edward said.

'I know. Just teasing Ed. All those exotic foods, colourful clothes, jewels…' her voice trailed away.

'Something up?'

'Ed, I don't know about the jewels. I don't know whether I want them any more. It's past. I don't belong in that group any longer.'

Edward looked at his wife with clear eyes, burying the old pattern of "I told you so." 'If that's what you think best Ruth.'

'It's not that it's better or best. I just don't belong there anymore.'

'Ruth, you don't need to explain. It's good. Have you thought about what you want to do with your jewels then?'

'I honestly don't know.' The decision troubled Ruth.' Any ideas?'

'Not a one. You could always keep them for a rainy day.' Edward suggested. 'I don't think so. Edward, maybe the jewels haven't been found. The grocer, you don't think…'

'What else would he want Ruth. *"Found, a lady's precious handkerchiefs."* Edward's eyes gleamed mischievously.

'Sayed? I can't imagine he would have such an interest. Then, he's not the sought of man I feel comfortable with.

'Oh. You women are always so sensitive.'

'You wouldn't know Edward. You're not one.' Ruth said, the mock exasperation lifting her voice.

Edward studiously observed his napkin.

Ruth rose from the table and collected their plates. She returned with a baking dish still steaming from the oven. 'Sweet cardamom and coconut tapioca, laced with rosewater and topped with lightly roasted almonds.'

'That sounds exotic Ruth. I'm not at all sure where you find all the ingredients!'

'Tomorrow I'll make sure you have some halva. Sayed must have some semolina tucked away in his vast empire.'

'My word Ruth. You are breaking out.'

Ruth smiled daringly. 'Wouldn't want to miss out on all the fun.'

'Then perhaps you'll come with me to India sometime. I'm sure David would love to meet you. And Robin and Marion will love you, you'll get on like a house on fire.'

'I'll think about it Edward. Seriously.' Ruth spooned the sweet onto Edward's plate and then a smaller serve onto her own.

'Don't you think we'd better go Ruth. It's nearly seven.' Edward placed the last spoonful into his mouth. He rose to gather their plates and napkins.

'Leave it Ed. There's no rush.'

Edward looked at his wife. He had not expected the change; she was definitely more relaxed and contented.

'OK then. But I should be serving you Ruth, not the other way around.'

'Is that how the men in India treat their wives?'

'Hardly. I did learn a few tips from David and Robin. They didn't go along with the Raj bit and seemed almost embarrassed to have servants.'

'Surely Edward!' Ruth admonished.

'There seems to be a very fine line between servitude and marriage don't you think Ruth?' Edward said half-seriously. 'And I'd hate to think that I'd fallen by the wayside and that I use my wife as a slave rather than a person.'

'Edward! That's a bit extreme.' Ruth was amazed.

'Not at all. Can't have you under my thumb now.' Edward gave her a quick peck on the cheek.

'I'll get my coat.' Ruth left the dishes on the table and went upstairs for her purse.

Ruth draped a scarf around her head letting it fall softly over her shoulders.

Edward caught the delicate line of her profile, framed by the folds of her scarf. For a moment, he felt Sesheta's presence in his wife, her pure beauty and peace trapping him the aching memory of their meeting.

Ruth pulled on her gloves and coat. 'Ready?'

Edward gasped slightly as if in pain and for a second, turned his eyes from Ruth in case she saw his feelings.

'Are you feeling up to it Edward?'

'Of course. Edward managed a brave smile.'

Chapter Eighty One

SAYED COVERED THE shop window with black paper then a corded blind. It was sufficient to keep out the light. He would rather a curtain, but there was nothing he could do for now. Sayed was quick to realise that even a fleeting façade of middle class British life, was important to his custom. He kept a watchful eye on the window, from time to time, pulling the corner of the blind open to the street. Then the boy arrived, eating the last of his biscuit.

'Oh, so you have found another grocer? From where did the biscuit come if not your uncle's shop?' Sayed scolded.

'Mrs. Ami. She gave them to me.'

'And the message? Did you give her the message young scamp?'

'Yes uncle. She has the message.' The boy closed his mouth as if he was afraid he would lose the last of his biscuit.

Sayed turned into his shop, his mind tantalised by the prospect of…..fortune? What good fortune had visited him? There would be a small reward for his troubles and the child, would probably ask her mother for sweets. Sayed shut the door and collected his grocer's broom, sweeping away the day's litter of brown lentils, spilt beans, rice and the remnants of flour. Amongst the little piles were hours of dust, gathered like detritus of the past, waiting to be discarded as surely as the wasted spoil. He was pleased. The day's trading was modest, though sufficient. He would wait until after nine to complete his books and make notes in the margins about the rising cost of produce, the waste of semolina and the need for more coffee. Mr. Thompson he was sure, would buy more coffee if the price was right, adjusted down a little, he would order for both home and the office. For now, Sayed would prepare the finest brew to greet Mr. Thompson his wife. As for the mother, she would not take coffee; tea, sweetened with crystals of sugar would please her mature and wholesome mouth.

Ami arrived first, the child clutching her side, slightly fearful of her mother's stern warning. 'Say not a thing child. No speaking unless I speak to you. Understood?'

Mani nodded mutely, unsure whether she was in trouble because of the jewels, or the sweets.

'Ah, my dear. You came in time. Good. Please,' Sayed opened his door his arms waving them inside in an exaggerated welcome.' Please, sit over here with the child.'

Ami felt deep discomfort creep around the borders of her scarf and settle in ominous thrills over her shoulders. She snatched Mani to her breast and sat the child on her lap not wanting the grocer to catch her eyes, and trick her into temptation. Then Mani would be lost to her, caught by generations of masculine greed and lust, concealed carefully beneath a grocer's sickly-sweet smile.

Sayed's eyes narrowed. The woman was not generous with her child. 'Come my dear, a little sweet for the child.'

'Please Mama.' Mani, her hopes already caught in sticky strands of temptation, gave her mother little choice.

'Just one Sayed.' Her look was fierce, not of the lioness but the tigress ready to kill and defend.

Sayed purred over his minor victory. 'Which one?' Temptation oozed toward his prey.

'Just one!' Ami felt panic rising in her chest.

The door half opened as Edward pushed into the dimly lit drama.

'Ah, Mr. Thompson and Mrs. Thompson. Do come in. We were expecting you, weren't we Ami?'

Ami choked with rage as she squeezed Mani closer to her body.

'Mama!' The child's head banged against her mother's breast.

'Ah, she needs a little something I see.' Sayed moved with the smoothness of a cougar towards the sweets.

Edward watched him catch the jar into his left hand the right hand un-twirling the lid and in the same movement, extract two or three boiled sweets before re-twirling the lid and positioning the jar exactly from where it came. Then in a blur that left no space between him and the mother, his hand extended the sweets into the child's open and innocent palm.

'Say thank you Mani.' Ami was instantly ambushed Ami into politeness.

'Thank you Mister.'

'That's all right my sweet.' Sayed caressed the girl's cheek with possessive fingers.

'Mrs. Thompson, you must be cold.' Sayed moved with cold calculation to catch the back of a chair and swing it towards her. 'I have prepared coffee, just the way your husband likes it. Please,' he motioned generously at the chair, 'come, it is better to sit.' The grocer ushered his guests into the confines of his shop and shut the door. He rubbed his hands in satisfaction. 'Ah, this is pleasant now. So warm inside and such a.....cold evening. Mr. Thompson...?'

'Yes Sayed, it is cool outside. Ruth? Can I take your coat?' Edward placed a hand on her shoulder.

'Allow me.' Sayed bent towards her, pulling the coat from her shoulders and carrying it like a trophy to a loose hook, nailed ostentatiously behind the counter.

'Mr. Thompson?'

'It's all right Sayed. I'm not over warm and this coat is light.'

Sayed feigned disappointment then half-ran to the table. He uncovered a tray laden with cups, coffee, cream, sugar and sweets.

'Sayed, that's very kind of you.' Edward complimented him, aware that the image did not suit the man.

The women exchanged glances, their silent rage forging resistance to Sayed. Ruth observed Ami's hunched posture; her powerless protection over the child now absorbed in her second sweet. Ami looked alone, very alone and lost in the poverty of motherhood created by Sayed's adeptness and singular power with the sweets. The child sucked the sweet, unaware of her mother's defeat, the defeat of her womanhood and of her motherhood. Ruth fought the desire to embrace Ami, to pull the woman out of the web. Ami looked at her and smiled. She noticed the other woman had understood. She briefly admired the English woman's silk scarf, still draped loosely and softly just as her own half-purdah fell and dropped onto her shoulders. Ami's eyes hung with pain, grateful that another woman knew. The women looked quickly away, aware that the men should not see that they had registered in one another's disconsolate eyes.

Sayed passed a cup to Ruth. She was untouchable, distant and he could not identify how she so easily evaded his grasp, aloofly accepting the coffee with the formality of culture and class.

'Thank you Sayed. That will be fine.' Ruth firmly declined the sugar.

'Thank you Sayed.' Edward's hand was rough, warm and friendly.

'Now, what can you tell us good man?'

Edward's genuine attempt at friendship took Sayed off guard. He looked to Ami and the child, but Ami was staring at a far world on the wall, transported by Ruth's unexpected warmth and grace.

'Come Sayed. You must want us here for something. Is it about Ruth's jewellery?' Edward came straight to the point.

Ruth looked to Ami, but the woman sat unconcerned, her shoulders suddenly relaxed and dignified. The women sat soundlessly waiting for Sayed to speak.

'Mr. Thompson......'

'Call me Edward Sayed. We're all friends here.'

'Mr. Thompson, Edward...' Sayed paused to make the point, his accent thickening, 'You must be aware that someone, sometime would shall we say, return the jewellery. Isn't that right Sister?' Sayed looked condescendingly towards Ami, still wrapped in her scarf as if a nun's veil.

Ami said nothing.

'Ami!' His voice was a sword cutting through the ambience.

Ami looked carefully at Sayed, her repose unbroken by his sharpness, her eyes placid and unmoved.

'Perhaps I can help.' Ruth cut in. 'Ami, I hope you don't mind if I call you Ami?' Ruth paused. 'Have you found the jewels?'

Ami nodded, unwilling, unable to speak, lost for any and all words of English.

'I told you so!' Sayed said triumphantly the beads of perspiration breaking onto his brow.

'So you told Sayed Ami?' Edward tried to relieve the grocer of his obvious embarrassment. The coffee gritted into his throat, causing him to cough.

Sayed leant forwards to take the cup, brushing against Ruth's shoulder and dislodging her scarf.

Ruth smiled widely at Ami who returned it with an equally amused smile. The women adjusted their headdresses.

Sayed noticed Ruth's movements and blushed with surprise. He turned to Ami but she too pulled her scarf closer to her cheeks, her eyes bright and mouth curved into feminine victory. The little grocer wanted to scream, to bang his fist onto the table and tear Ami's hair. Edward looked at Ruth, sobered by the rush of unspoken aggression from Sayed.

Ruth dropped her head slightly; her eyes and mouth unsmilingly locked into fierce loyalty to Ami.

The men were momentarily bewildered, unable to speak yet aware that they were not part of this new play. Edward caught Sayed at the elbow giving Ruth an out to talk privately with Ami. He drew Sayed into the coffee, asking for more, 'only a little less cream, ah sugar, and not too hot. Wonderful, such flavour…where do you get this coffee Sayed? Can I buy some from you?'

Sayed's grocer's sense of a sudden sale consumed him just slightly more than the flattery of unexpected friendship. 'That I cannot tell you. It's my offshore secret. You understand.' Sayed recovered with astounding speed slipping quickly into business drone, humming and seducing the buyer with tempting tones of colour, taste, *"so cheap, so scarce, for you I'll keep some especially"* - supremely content in his world of petty deals.

Edward massaged his ego with well-timed praises, 'oohs' and 'ahhs' as Sayed showed him the range of coffees, sweets… *"please, you must try these."*

Edward patted his arm, assuring him that they would come each week to see what new stock, what new delicacies, despite the war, that he could provide. He absorbed himself in the produce, catching the aromas of this or that variety, weighing, wondering, and deciding *"yes this one."* He would take a few ounces at first. If Chris liked the flavour, then he would buy more. And for home, something softer…subtler for his breakfast palate… a thick, roughly roasted brew for the evening when he liked to put his feet on the coffee table, newspaper and pipe in hand and turn on the radio.

The opportunity, the fuss, the attention overwhelmed Sayed, although the pennies spent at first would be few. He breathed out happily; thankful that the man's presence saved him from the surprising smile, the unruffled poise of Ami whom he had so carefully contrived to control.

Ami accepted Ruth to her ample bosom and in between, Mani protested that she could not breathe. The two women relaxed their mutual embrace and Ruth pulled a spare stool close to the mother. She adjusted her headscarf now slightly off centre and smoothed the fold to cover her eyebrows. Ami looked down as Ruth concealed her Englishness with familiar gestures of modesty and then timidly, met her eyes.

Ruth herself carefully shy smiled softly and the two women engaged themselves as if nothing but the child sat between them.

'It was the child. She found them.'

'Oh?' Ruth stroked Mani's glossy hair and tucked a finger under her chin. 'And what did you find Mani? Ami, she looks as perfect as a pearl.'

'What did you find Mani? Tell Mrs. Thompson.' Ami's words were at last friendly and at ease.

'Please, call me Ruth. Or Aunty Ruth will be fine Mani.'

'Yes Aunty.' The child was instantly responsive and comfortable with her adoption. 'Are they yours?'

'Are what mine Mani?' Ruth could hardly hide her genuine pleasure at the child's response.

'The pearls, Mrs… '

'Aunty Ruth.'

'The Pearls Aunty. And the brooch.'

'Oh. Well it must be them then. Where did you find them child?' Ruth spoke like a mother.

Mani looked down. 'I was playing outside before school and then when I walked along the street I saw them, shiny and sparkly in the sun.

'So you went to see what was there.' Ami was keen to hand over the responsibility of the jewels to their rightful owner.

'Yes Mama.' Mani turned to her mother in angelic obedience.

'And…' Ami prompted.

'And so I found them Aunty.' Mani turned to Ruth, whispering with the same sweetness and respect with which she had just addressed her mother.

'Oh. May I see them?' Ruth affected her curiosity without betraying the wrenching in her gut.

'Mama?' Mani had come to the end of her carefully spoken script. 'They are here Mrs. Thompson.'

'Ruth.'

'Ruth.' Ami smiled, again warming to their womanly communion. 'Here.' She unwrapped the black cloth tucked into her shawl. Then she reverently placed jewels in Ruth's hands.'

'Yes. These are mine. Thank you Mani.' Ruth turned to the child and patted her cheek. Ruth watched as the jewels in her hands blurred out of her view. The brooch melted like butter before her eyes, the sparkle of the diamonds merged into a golden pool that spread across her palm and dripped in molten light through her fingers. The pearls once creamy-white reflected the rainbow as if they were balls from a Christmas tree strung into a necklace of colour. Her hand vibrated with an ethereal heat and the jewels weighed heavily, forcing her wrist into her lap. The light spilled from her hand in waterfalls, surrounding her body in an aura of gold. Ruth let the jewels go. She raised her head her quiet eyes finding the mournfully lonely eyes of Ami.

'They are for you Ami. Please take them.' Ruth could not move her hand. 'Ami, they are for you.' She repeated.

'I can't Ruth, they don't belong to us.'

'Mama…'Mani tugged her mother's scarf.

Ami remained frozen, unable to comprehend the gift, what it could mean for them.

'The jewels are not mine Ami. They don't belong to me any more.' Ruth's voice was stone cold. Her hand moved as if powered by a distant force and lifted them into the air, slowly, slowly across the bridge of love and friendship between her and the mother from Karachi. She held them out for Ami to accept.

Ami's breath caught in her throat, unable to move in or out, unable to direct her life force to retreat or to accept. Then her own hand moved imperceptibly, slowly in a gesture of feminine intimacy towards Ruth. Ruth turned her hand over and pressed the pearls and brooch gently into Ami's open palm. Their hands met, the jewels melting between them.

Ami pulled back, aware that she now held the precious stones and pearls in her strong and steady hand. Her eyes searched Ruth's face, sensing the thinness of the woman, the loss, and the death in her eyes and her loneliness.

'Oh Ruth. Thank you.'

Ruth felt the rush of maternal love from Ami and desperately wanted her embrace. Ami felt her own tears of loneliness flow as she stroked Ruth's face, the pearls swinging from her free hand like the rounded beads of a priest.

'Child!' Sayed reprimanded his nephew who was now busily exploring an open jar of sweets. The boy needed no further warning and let the jar go. The lid, loosened by inquisitive delight, clattering to the floor.

Edward smiled at the child, catching his shirt. 'Here young man. These are on me.' Edward gave Sayed a shilling and held the jar to the boy.

Sayed stared at the shilling in his palm then at the boy, unable to prevent him from reaching into the jar, his eyes curious with wonder.

The child lifted his face to Edward. 'Thanks mister.'

'That's all right son. You can call me Edward if you like.'

'No, he must be polite. Mr. Edward will do fine.'

'OK, Mr. Edward.' Edward agreed.

The boy could not repeat the *"thank you,"* his mouth already jammed with sweets. Edward grinned and topped the jar as he handed it back to Sayed.

Sayed, suddenly thought of the women. He turned towards Ami impatient and annoyed that he had forgotten her. The two women were sitting hands clasped together talking as if they had known one another forever, the child bobbing around them tugging at Ami's dress and stopping to catch Ruth's occasional caresses.

Edward followed Sayed's gaze. 'Well Sayed, it looks as though that's sorted out. Now, let us see about a reward for you.'

Sayed was nonplussed. He had completely lost control over the women and could not make a fuss in case Edward changed his mind about the reward.

Edward reached into his coat pocket and pulled out a book, beautifully bound in handcrafted leather. Like musical notes from an ancient score, the gold script swept across the cover.

Sayed stopped and looked at Edward, his mouth falling into gaping wonder.

'Mr... Edward. Where did you get this...this..'

'A kind grocer like your good self gave it to me as a gesture of our friendship.' Edward bowed slightly.

'It is beautiful, beautiful.' Sayed whispered. He looked at Edward then thrust his hand into Edward's, his eyes touched with emotion. 'Thank you. Thank you.'

'You are very welcome Sayed.' Edward smiled, fighting to steady himself after the vigorous handshake.

'And such perfect binding.' Sayed slapped the cover with one hand.' This is the best, the best. How did you know....'

Edward stepped towards Ruth before Sayed took his hand again. 'We had better go Ruth.'

Edward assumed command and patted Sayed on the back. 'One day you'll have to teach me all about the book Sayed. Meanwhile, you can supply Ruth with more spices and beans. We are going vegetarian Like Gandhi!' Edward laughed lightly then made to collect Ruth's coat.

'Yes, yes Mr. Thompson.' Sayed's eyes were still fervent and excited. 'And Mrs. Thompson?'

'Ruth. Call me Ruth Sayed.'

'Yes, I will tell you how to use spices and beans. There are *so* many ways.'

'I'm not sure that I have the same talent for taste as as my husband does Sayed, but no doubt I can learn something about the spices of the Orient.'

'I can teach you to make vegetable subji Aunty.' Mani piped.

'No, not you my child. You are far too young.' Sayed attempted to silence her.

'I'll tell you what. You can bring your mother Mani and together, you can teach me how to cook and speak a little of your language.' Ruth concluded.

'Can we Mama, can we please?' Ami hesitated.

'At least come to our house Ami. I can teach the child English.' Ruth offered. 'And I'm sure the company would do us both good.' She said practically.

'Of course Ami. That's a wonderful idea.' Edward confirmed. 'And Sayed, once you have read the book from cover to cover you teach me about your history and the journeys of your people along the Silk Road.'

Sayed grinned, patting the cover of the book as if it were a long-lost friend then disappeared into the shop and returned with a short length of midnight-blue velvet. 'I will keep it safe beneath the counter for quiet times.' Sayed informed Edward upholding the dignity of his profession.

'I'm sure that you're quite busy Sayed, but there's always a quiet moment in anyone's work.' Edward replied tactfully. He caught Ruth's arm and walked her to the door. 'Thank you for your hospitality Sayed. Goodbye Ami and little imp.' Edward tweaked Mani's chin. 'Save some of those sweets young man.' Edward did not forget the boy. 'One day youngster, you'll make an excellent shopkeeper like your uncle.' Edward opened the door for Ruth and followed her into the night breeze. 'A bit cool tonight. Are you warm enough Ruth?'

'Perfectly Edward. Edward, she looked so sad and alone.'

'Who, Ami? I thought you were the one who looked a bit sad and alone Ruth.'

'Oh Edward, she needs them more than I do.'

Edward pulled Ruth into step with him. 'Are you sure that's what you wanted?' Edward said quietly.

'What can I do with them now Edward. They're gone, they're in the past.

Chapter Eighty Two

EDWARD AWOKE FEELING nauseated and weak. It was now several months into the war. Churchill, now England's wartime Prime Minister, faced the irritating enigma of Gandhi, the ridiculously simple and frail revolutionary with indisputable charisma and power. The intellectual giant of war strategy and the little old man were at philosophical loggerheads. Gandhi was clearly as intent on dismembering India from the empire as Churchill was on preserving Britain's honour and tradition. Gandhi's gall inevitably, deeply infuriated the war chief. There was little dissuading however, the immovable Mahatma. His ferocious hold on *Satyagraha* disallowed in Churchill, any possibility of fully harnessing the forces of India for Britain's war effort. Hitler had entered Norway, Denmark, Holland and Belgium and had his sights firmly set on France. Britain was vulnerable and Gandhi was aware, fully aware of India's critical role for Britain. He decided to play fair. It was not the time to exert civil disobedience at Britain's expense. Gandhi continued to advocate non-violence.

> *"I do not want Britain to be defeated, nor do I want her to be victorious in a trial of brute strength… I hope you do not want me to enter into such an undignified competition with the Nazis. I want you to fight Nazism without arms or, if I am to retain the military terminology, with non-violent arms. I would like you to lay down the arms as being useless for saving you or humanity. You will invite Herr Hitler and Signor Mussolini to take what they want of the countries you call your possession. Let them take possession of your beautiful island with your many beautiful buildings. You will give all these, but neither your souls nor your minds… you will allow yourself, man, woman and child, to be slaughtered, but you will refuse to owe allegiance to them."*

His support in principle of Britain's predicament was gracious, but Gandhi would not sacrifice his ultimate goal of the unity of India, the preservation of the moral, spiritual and cultural integrity of the nation he adored, through opportunism. Congress veered dangerously from the moral path of total non- violence dictated by Gandhi and offered conditional co-operation to Britain. The resolution stated that if India were granted complete Independence and a central government, Congress would throw its full weight *"in efforts for the effective organisation of the defence of the country."*

Gandhi was almost singularly opposed to the offer, save for the support of one Ghaffar Khan. Ultimately, the Viceroy rejected the offer of Congress, tinged by the hope for political gain, India's complete Independence and the establishment of a provincial government in Delhi. Instead, he put forward his own version of *"Independence"* and insisted that constitutional matters for India could not be decided at the very moment when the Commonwealth was engaged in a struggle for existence.

The Viceroy invited a select handful of Indians to join his Executive Council and set up a War Advisory Council. Linlithgow's tone and unspoken intentions to limit freedom of speech and various liberties were not well received. India felt betrayed. Angered, Congress turned once again to the old man for support, declaring him their leader.

Gandhi responded diplomatically. He did not want England to be defeated or humiliated. Instead, Gandhi announced that he was committed to the greater cause of the human family.

> *"I can keep India intact and its freedom intact only if I have goodwill towards the whole of the human family and not merely the human family which inhabits this little spot of the earth called India."* Gandhi proclaimed with complete sincerity.

Gandhi wanted nothing of the fratacide in Europe and wanted that neither he nor Congress participate in the war. Again, he offered limited support to Britain, conditional on *"the reasonable request of Congress for full liberty to preach that we cannot aid imperialism."*

The Viceroy said no, and Gandhi, equally stubborn in his conviction and determination, launched his own unique form of defiance, non co-operation through civil disobedience. Congress rallied with a campaign of anti-war speeches. Bhave was imprisoned. Then Nehru, following in the chivalrous manner of Gandhi, informed the police of his intention to follow suit. Ten days later, he too was arrested and imprisoned for four years, without having made a single speech. Patel followed by Naidu and Azad followed the same path. The leaders, the backbone of Congress, were imprisoned and Gandhi's *"The Harijan"* was temporarily closed.

Chapter Eighty Three

EDWARD COULD NOT believe the pain in his gut. *"The Reporter"* was busier than usual with reports flowing into the office in a tide of misfortune, warning of worse to come. Chris and Edward managed the deluge, grappling with signs of worsening conditions in Europe and the tightening grip of the Nazis. David, more carefully, continued to supply Chris with updates on the situation in India. Edward was glad that he left India when he had. It was enough to deal with events from a distance. Today would be no exception. Chris had to sift and sort the cables, the typed transcripts of radio reports, letters and postcards, into logical and accurate impressions to form the news. Chris was keen to keep the tone of reports low, not to cause alarmist or negative feelings in the public.

Edward was however, more pragmatic. He knew that by giving the real impression the seriousness of the European tensions would enhance Britain's unity and efforts. However, today was not going to be easy. He grimaced at the thought. It seemed hardly likely that he would make it to the bathroom let alone the office. The pain stabbed at his belly, a sharp reminder of his short illness in Delhi with the overwhelming loss of consciousness. Edward struggled against the impulse to faint whilst Ruth busied herself in the bathroom. The radio hummed over the sound of his breathing, now in gasps as he fought the pain.

> *"We are in the preliminary stage of one of the greatest battles in history.... That we are in action at many points—in Norway and in Holland—that we have to be prepared in the Mediterranean. That the air battle is continuous, and that many preparations have to be made here at home. I would say to the House as I said to those who have joined this government, I have nothing to offer*

but blood, toil, tears and sweat. We have before us an ordeal of the most grievous kind. We have before us many, many long months of struggle and of suffering. You ask what is our aim? I can answer in one word, Victory! Victory at all costs. Victory in spite of all terror. Victory, however long and hard the road may be, for without victory there is no survival."

It was Churchill. Edward felt a thrill of anticipation pass through his body, as if the giant had spoken to him personally. *"For without victory there is no survival."* His mind grasped and tried to hang onto the words, fighting the waves of dizziness that began to wash over him.

Ruth returned to the bedroom, mildly surprised that Edward had barely stirred.

'Edward. You'll be late.'

Edward opened his eyes. 'Ruth, I feel awful.'

'What's wrong?' Ruth drew in her breath in a short gasp.

'It's that pain, the pain I had in Delhi.'

Ruth felt Edward's forehead and lifted a limp hand to search for the pulse. 'You had better stay in bed. I'll call Dr. Anderson straight away.'

Edward groaned and closed his eyes. The pain gripped him in a powerful spasm of helpless finality. It was definitely worse now than when he was in Delhi. He had been careful with his diet, reducing fats and cutting out meat altogether until he had eliminated all disturbances to his system. The pain was very real, and now nausea carrying him into new dimensions of fear and depression. There would be no containing this relapse.

Ruth hurried downstairs to ring Dr. Anderson.

'Yes Ruth. He's that bad? OK. I'm on my way. Keep him cool and try to turn him on his side if he looks as though he is going to lose consciousness.' Ruth replaced the receiver and raced back upstairs. Edward was half hanging out of the bed, sweat rolling across his forehead.

'Edward.' Ruth yelled. 'Edward, what are you doing?' She tried to lift him, but he was too heavy managing only to pull his legs further onto the bed. The slight scent of vomit warned her to find a bowl. Edward clearly had tried the bathroom, but could not make it. He was groaning softly and retching now in gentle and rhythmic heaves. Ruth returned within seconds, placing the bowl under his chin and turned his head to the side. She hung onto the bowl, not wanting to look, but determined not to flinch at the sounds and smell. After being sick, Edward regained some strength, enough of life to push himself to the side of the bed.

'Thanks.'

'Don't talk. Dr. Anderson's on the way.'

Edward slumped back onto the bed, his arms outstretched. He felt like death and knew that today was going to be long and painful. His abdomen felt as though it was etched with acid then clamped into a vice. His throat and nose burnt from the remnants of vomitus and his breath was shallow and laboured.

Chapter Eighty Four

AUBREY ANDERSON ALLOWED himself a few minutes to dress and adjust his bag. There would be no sense in arriving out of sorts. The minutes and seconds often counted, but his professional edge relied upon his composure, his ability to think, precisely and clearly. He walked quickly to the front door, collected his hat and coat and locked the door behind him. The black Daimler shone dully, rarely used now except for emergencies. His income was modest, but he had the fortune of inherited wealth and enjoyed a few select luxuries in life. His car was one of them. The engine sparked into the fog and he counted the seconds until it was warm and responsive to his touch. The first moment was tense, waiting for the familiar purr of the engine before he would release the handbrake and engage first gear. Then he manoeuvred carefully off the kerb, worried about the condition of the road and unexpected obstacles. London was under siege.

It was ten minutes before Dr. Anderson arrived at Clarkenwell Green. Ruth was waiting downstairs, the front door open before he had stepped out of the car.

'He is a bit better. He was sick and that seems to have relieved the pain.

'Right. Can you bring me some towels Ruth? I want to examine him here before moving him.'

'You don't think… '

'I don't know, but I am not taking any chances. Oh, and I'll need a bowl of warm soapy water and a hand towel.'

'I'll bring them straight up. You know where the bedroom is.'

'Thanks Ruth.'

Dr. Anderson acted with economy and concentration. His thoughts were few, running over possible diagnoses, noting tests that would bring him closer to a course of treatment. It was true that he could have been more thorough when Edward returned from India, but the symptoms subsided and there seemed to be no immediate cause for worry. When he reached the bedroom, Edward was dozing, the nausea and vomiting leaving him weak and tremulous. Dr. Anderson moved with consummate ease to the bed and felt his pulse. Edward relaxed, semi-aware that he no longer had to hold on. The pain was coming in waves accompanied by a deeper pain gripping his lower abdomen.

'You haven't had any diarrhoea Edward?' 'Not yet. But I can feel the cramping.'

'We had better get you to the bathroom. Then I'll give you an injection.'

Dr. Anderson was not a young man, but he still had the strength of a bull. He put an arm behind Edward's back and heaved him into the sitting position. Edward leaned forward slightly fighting the dizziness.

'OK? Do you think you can manage it?'

'I'll try. Can you steady me as I walk? I'm feeling a bit off centre.'

'Swing your legs over the side of the bed Edward, then put your arm over my shoulders. There's a good man. Heave.' Dr. Anderson pulled Edward to his feet. Edward battled the looming blackness. It seemed for a minute to Dr. Anderson, that he would be unable to support Edward's weight. He pressed his calves against the bed to regain his balance then shuffled Edward to the bathroom.

Ruth returned with the soapy water, her arms draped with towels. 'Do you want some help?'

'No Ruth. Wait there please.' Dr. Anderson kicked open the bathroom door and half-dragged Edward through it. He kicked the door shut and positioned Edward closer to the toilet bowl. I will hold you until you are ready. Edward struggled to loosen his pyjama cord. Dr. Anderson felt him slipping. He pulled the trousers loose, setting Edward firmly on the bowl and pushed his head between his knees.

'Don't move Edward. I'll be right back. Ruth, give me the bowl. Make it quick.' Dr. Anderson half opened the door, his hand outstretched as he gave the command. Ruth handed him the bowl and retreated to the bed. She could hear Edward heaving and hoped Dr. Anderson had made it in time.

Edward's discomfort was over in less than a few seconds. A violent voiding from both ends left him gasping, the pain wrenching his belly and darkness threatening to descend like a vulturous cloud over his consciousness.

Dr. Anderson waited until his dizziness passed then pulled Edward to his feet. The smell of diarrhoea overwhelmed him for a brief moment, the taste of vomitus rose in his own gullet. He repressed the urge within, and, with his free hand, tore a towel from its rail and shoved it into the basin. Aubrey Anderson let the hot water soak into the towel before squeezing out the excess and quickly cleaning Edward, removing all traces of his waste. Then he dropped the towel on the floor. His arm ached as he strove to hold Edward upright and pull his up his pyjamas with the other. 'Hold them up for now man.' Edward caught the front of his trousers and Dr. Anderson opened the door with his foot. 'Come on then. Back to bed.'

Edward clung to his pyjama trousers as if this was the last vestige of hope in the world. The bed swum in front of his eyes and he could feel Dr. Anderson almost push him onto it and draw the sheets around him.

'Pass me my bag please Ruth.' Dr. Anderson was official and detached from her.

Ruth obeyed and placed the bag on Edward's bed.

He opened it and pulled out a glass syringe and two vials. Dr. Anderson rolled Edward onto his side and jabbed the needle into his buttock. Edward flinched involuntarily, the loose muscles automatically contracting. Another jab and Dr. Anderson rolled him onto his back and pulled the covers to his chin.

'That will stop the vomiting and diarrhoea Ruth. I want you to make sure he drinks at least half a cup of water each hour until lunchtime, then if he can manage it, increase the quantity. Let him sleep, but keep an eye on his breathing and pulse. There's a good girl.' Dr. Anderson patted her hand. 'I'll look in on him again this evening.'

Ruth nodded mutely.

'Don't worry Ruth. He's not a hospital case. Not yet. Ring me straight away if he slips. Will you be OK? I can send a nurse if you would rather.' He raised his eyebrows in expectation.

'I'll be fine Dr. Anderson. Thank you.' Ruth was genuinely relieved.

'That's perfectly all right Ruth. Now, if you will excuse me, I must go to the surgery. I'll let myself out. Don't hesitate to call me if you need to.' Dr. Anderson made a brisk yet calm exit.

Ruth slumped onto the dressing table chair. Edward was already falling asleep. He looked totally at peace, the pain and nausea eased by the injections. It would be safe to leave him at present and she badly wanted a cup of tea.

Ruth walked down the stairs and headed straight for the hall telephone. 'Chris? It's Ruth. Edward is sick again.'

'Oh. What's wrong?'

'I'm not sure. But it looks like a relapse of whatever it was he had in India. Dr. Anderson has already given him a couple of shots to stop the nausea.' Ruth paused. 'I think he'll sleep for a while.'

'Did he say how bad?'

'No. He wasn't as sick as this in Delhi was he?'

'I can't say Ruth. He was out to it for over 12 hours.'

'Oh.'

'Don't worry Ruth. You know Edward. He'll bounce back and be on his feet in no time. Let him sleep it off today. Call me this evening and let me know how he is going.' Chris made his voice sound cheerful and unconcerned. Underneath he was deeply worried.

'Thanks again Chris.' Ruth put the telephone down.

Chris Cooke placed the telephone on its cradle and returned to his breakfast, sober and thoughtful. David's cables from Delhi were graphic and telling of how close Edward drifted towards the border of life and death. It could be simply a relapse. But Chris felt it in his gut that this was something more sinister, as if, death had found a foothold. The early morning bustle of London usually uplifted and intrigued Chris. But not this morning. Even during the war, the busy movements of buses and cars, the endless foot traffic and the tolling of city clocks meant that all was well. At least in London, there was a sense of urgency, a sense of the immediacy of the war and the pressing need for the shops to remain open, for commerce to continue to stimulate the will and spirit of the nation. Chris Cooke felt his own part, his own pivotal role in the in-depth, weekly analysis of the war, carefully constructed to be both accurate and encouraging. He knew that through *"The Reporter"* he could lift the mood of wartime Britain. His opinion was respected as a neutral and detached slant on the war. And Edward was his right arm, diligent and rigorous in his study of cables, photos and 'word-of-mouth' messages that ultimately formed the backbone of the war reports Without him, Chris would be at a loss, not just as editor of *"The Reporter,"* but also as his close friend and mentor. Chris trained the entire staff of journalists and above all others, Edward was more than just his first rate reporter, who continued to provide clear and insightful reports. Other matters could slide for the week, but not the war reports. The stories had to be written and photographs collated, sorted and matched to the stories.

Chris wondered for a moment whether he had made a mistake sending Edward to India. He could not bear the thought of losing the man. Edward was his friend and almost, soul mate if there were such a thing! Edward had matured and changed more than a normal man would in decades and it was not only Ruth who reaped the benefits of his change. At least the marriage was intact, at least they had one another and continued live as man and wife. Ruth continued to prove herself to be a real brick, lively, strong, now rarely showing the signs of losing either Thomas or the baby. Chris was content. The outcome of India was nevertheless good, despite the fact that Edward's health had suffered, now it seemed, irreparably. He walked into his office, his mood slightly jaded by news of Edward's illness nevertheless, mildly jubilant at the prospect of the next challenging edition of the paper. Littered amongst the telegrams, the half-typed reports and scribbled notes was a cable from David.

> "Mother and baby boy doing fine. Tarika at ten weeks is as strong as a Bengali tiger. How is Edward? Regards, as ever, David."

Chris folded the telegram into his pocket. He would drop in to see Ruth and Edward on the way home. Tarika the tiger! Trust David. He would need all the diversion he could find if Gandhi were stirring the British administrative pot.

Chapter Eighty Five

RUTH BREATHED DEEPLY into her coffee. At least Edward was peaceful. The months since his return had been blissfully uneventful filled with the small pleasures of domesticity. Ruth could not return to her round of social engagements and the constant shoulder rubbing that demanded of her in order to influence a few pounds for this or that cause. The war played a significant part in diminishing the social glitter she had become accustomed to. The more pressing demands of the war were for her, to reorient family and social priorities towards the needs of the nation. She was content to dress down to more sensible and sober greys and browns and to attend her business on flat and tempered heels. Her weekly routine also accommodated language classes for Mani and Ami.

Ami was at first shy, perhaps uncertain outside her own home, but Mani bubbled incessantly, curious and openly accepting of Ruth and Edward. Ruth looked forward to their coming; preparing scones, muffins and from time to time, ordering special halvas from Sayed the grocer.

The two women grew closer, bonded through the war-fated transformations in their relationships with their men. For the child, newness was no stranger. Innocent of the war, innocent of the estrangements of men from women and women from men, Mani amused the women with her chatter and predictable absorption in the delights Ruth happily produced from their meagre rations of butter, sugar and flour. Mani was happy and fascinated by her Aunty Ruth and in Mani, Ruth also, found new happiness and laughed easily in the company of the child and her mother. Mani was delightful, sweet and endearing and her mother gradually softened at Ruth's easy acceptance of them, less defensive, less hidden behind the shawl of shame that continued to frame her soul. Ruth never questioned Ami about her past, her dress or even, in her quietest thoughts, intimated that Ami should relax her guard and shun her scarf.

And so Ami relaxed, her cultural vows unchallenged in the warm company of the Englishwoman. The classes always finished before Edward returned from work and Ami was glad.

Ruth stirred more sugar into her cup wanting the sweetness to continue into the morning, warming her nostrils and easing the tightness in her chest. Inevitably, she would rise and climb the stairs to visit Edward in his confinement. It was the first time she had nursed him and she felt slightly nervous, hoping that the illness would subside, tamed by Dr. Anderson's drugs. The morning light sifted through the lace curtains softening the still life of bowls and cups on her kitchen table, now fluid as the light washed one form into another. The sun drew Ruth's attention to the window framing the reality that existed beyond their home. Set in quiet repose Ruth sensed other women sitting in their kitchens, counting the hours, waiting for the morning mail, wondering, hoping that the news would not come. The war had plummeted wives, families and communities into untimely and relentless grief. Ruth hoped it would never happen to her. Edward was safe in Britain, for now, untainted by war other than the unremitting reports and cables from abroad.

The light whistle of the postman alerted Ruth to the time. Edward would need more fluids, a quick check of his pulse and temperature and the telling glance of torchlight against pupils to prompt the ready response of life, of continuing consciousness. As she opened the front door into the passing stream of morning news and mail, Ruth wished that Dr. Anderson had not left her with his responsibility. It was too soon, Edward was too sick for her to be able to judge dispassionately whether his condition had worsened or mercifully, had receded to remission. She opened the mailbox and pulled out a thick package wrapped in brown paper and addressed to *"Mr. Edward Thompson."* It was postmarked Karachi.

'Karachi! Perhaps it was the report David had promised him, a new angle on Muslim-Hindu unity.'

Ruth turned the package over. There was no sender's name. A single piece of coarse string gathered the paper into its four corners, a flimsy attempt at security and privacy. It could wait. Edward would be unable to deal with work anytime soon.

Ruth walked back inside, quietly closing the door. She looked quickly along the length of the stairs, uplifting her face to the bedroom door. Edward would need fresh water. She turned to the kitchen her steps interrupted by the sound of a door closing.' That's odd!' She remarked to herself. 'Edward could hardly move.'

Ruth climbed the stairs in a few seconds and opened the door. Edward was out of the bed. The bathroom door pushed closed. Ruth heard the sudden flush of the toilet. At least he was feeling better.

She sat on the bed, package still in hand. 'Edward! Are you feeling better? Ruth solicited.

Edward dragged himself slowly back to the bed. Ruth dropped the parcel on the bed and stood to help him back.

'Here. Easy does it.'

'Thanks.' Edward was breathless and pale.

'You don't look so strong Edward. I was just about to get you some water when I heard the door. I didn't think you'd be able to walk to the bathroom.' Ruth smiled wanly at his attempt at Independence.

'Thanks Ruth. I thought I'd try, but I'm clearly not as strong as I had hoped.' Edward wheezed out the words.

'Don't try. Just rest.' Ruth eased him back onto the pillows and drew the covers over his body. 'You don't look at all well Edward, but at least you are awake. Chris was worried about you but said to take it easy. There's no rush back to work.' She comforted.

'You told him?' Edward was alarmed.

'Of course. He said he'd ring tonight to see how you were.'

'Oh.'

'Is it all right Edward, I mean…' Ruth started.

'Of course. It's just, I didn't want to worry him or let him feel that I'd let him down.'

'I know. You couldn't let Chris down though you know that. He's far too understanding.' Ruth soothed him.

'You're right. You seem to know him better than I do Ruth.'

Ruth smiled. 'This came for you.' Involuntarily, she handed him the brown- papered package. 'It's from India. I was going to wait until you were better. Looks like work.' Ruth smiled, relieved that Edward was conscious and obviously stronger.

Edward accepted the package, his eyes fixed in gentle contemplation and appreciation of his wife. 'Can you open it Ruth. My hands aren't so steady.'

'Of course. Here.' Ruth took the package and turned it over to untie the string. She felt the tension in Edward's hand as he released it into hers. She looked briefly at his face, noting the paleness darkening under his eyes. Dr. Anderson had warned him that his liver might produce changes in his skin colour, but this looked more like deep tiredness than disease. She opened the parcel and caught together the loose pages before they scattered onto the bedclothes and handed the bundle to Edward.

Edward fingered the pages and let two or three drop onto his lap. He held the broken book in hands, paralysed by disbelief. The life drained from his cheeks, accentuating the deep and dark valleys underscoring his eyes. Edward's change in mood charged the atmosphere. Try as he may, he could not hide the sudden realisation, the instant plunge into the yawning cavern, the magnetic vortex that pulled him, despite his struggle to resist, the inevitable descent into the same dark hollow that had absorbed Sesheta's life. *"Midnight Pearl"* came to him, her blood spattered onto the pages in his hands and the knowledge of her death flooding his body with waves of grief. Edward wanted to scream and wail, but in front of the softly enquiring eyes of his wife could say and do nothing. Tears flooded into his eyes and his mouth opened in horror as the truth sent shocking arrows into his heart.

'Ruth…' Edward collapsed into the pillows as he tried to shut out the horrible news.

'Edward, what's happened.' Ruth now noticed the blood spattered onto the loose pages of the book lying across Edward's chest. 'Edward.' Ruth tried to reach him, sensing his pain, not wanting to see into the world that he had not shown her.

Edward's body heaved in silent agony, he looked at Ruth, pleading an apology, forgiveness and for help. His mouth opened as if to offer an explanation that was beyond comprehension, then, silence. 'Edward!' Ruth screamed. 'Edward.' Her mouth went dry and chin trembled in shock. She shook Edward's arm and tried to find his eyes with hers. Something, someone had penetrated his heart, his soul, and his life. Ruth pulled back in sheer horror.

'No, it couldn't be true, he couldn't be…' She ran from the room, shocked, almost falling down the stairs. Then her cries came from deep within, cries of rage and disbelief. 'No Edward, not now!' Ruth yelled into the hollow hallway. In her fear she dislodged the telephone from its cradle, and grabbed wildly at the hand piece until she had it securely in her grasp. Her fingers, trembling with sick fear dialled slowly, deliberately. She was not going to make any mistake, not now. The numbers rolled one by one as she kept her finger in the dial. Then the bell, its perfect ringing; one second, two seconds. 'Dr. Anderson? It's Ruth…' she whispered.

'I'm on my way Ruth.' Dr. Anderson put down the telephone.

What had gone wrong? What could have happened! Ruth was competent and he was sure that Edward was safe. 'My God, how could you have misjudged man!' Dr. Anderson was instantly angry with himself. Edward was stable when he left, weak, but with no signs of deteriorating. Edward's unexpected deterioration challenged his professional edge. Predictably though, now his detached discernment kicked in sufficiently to allow him a few seconds of total clarity, uninterrupted thoughts, the room to judge, weigh and decide.' Perhaps he had slipped and fallen, tried to walk to the bathroom, fainted onto the floor.' Dr. Anderson bargained with himself. He hardly noticed his ritual of collecting bag, coat, keys, walking to the car door, unlocking the door, closing the door, turning the key in the ignition. It was only when he was aware that he had placed too heavy a foot on the accelerator than he normally allowed that he was already moving, driving towards Ruth and Edward. He needed the speed to erase the unwanted questions threatening to consume his thoughts. At least the speed would push his mind to concentrate, to watch the road and not think about the worst.

Chapter Eighty Six

DR. ANDERSON WAS trained in mind, body and will, to perform his duty, above and beyond all other influences. He arrived at the Thompson's house nevertheless, in an almost, semi-daze. He pulled the car off the road and switched off the ignition. Ruth had left the front door unlatched. She sat slumped on the hall chair, her eyes glazed over with pain and limbs numb with disbelief. This time, Dr. Anderson was immensely grateful for his training, his capacity to sum up the situation in less than a second, to switch off his thoughts and direct his attention to the immediacy of the situation. Quickly he shot a compassionate glance at Ruth and took the stairs two at a time up to the bedroom. He allowed himself, seconds only to perform the almost automatic routine of establishing life support; the airway, the breathing, pulse…..'

None of it was necessary. Edward lay like a statue, his limbs collapsed in line with the torso, the head slightly tilted to the left and the dry line of tears lining his cheeks. Aubrey followed the line of tears to the unfettered pages, scattered across Edward's chest and on the bedclothes, their unspoken innocence somehow linked to his death. He stood still, his medical sensibilities frozen into hopelessness and impotence. He was unsure whether to mobilise himself into routine actions; measured, aimed at deliberating over the death, checking, noting and certifying, or whether to retreat downstairs, abandon Edward and the postmortem medical necessities, or secure the floundering sanity of Ruth. Aubrey Anderson's feet would not move; the dilemma casting him deeper into immobility. Finally, the sound of the front door shutting prompted him to decision.

'Hello Ruth. It's Ami.'

'Ami. The Indian woman and her child. Oh God. Not now!' Dr. Anderson swore quietly. He turned his back on Edward, instinct propelling him towards Ruth.

Ami instantly caught onto Ruth's pain; her pleading eyes, wounded, like a child. 'Ruth, what is it?' Ami knelt before her friend, grasping both of Ruth's hands in hers.

'Ami.' The words choked in Ruth's throat. The older woman flung her arms around Ruth, absorbing her brokenness into her bosom, rocking her, stroking her hair, letting her break the numbness in wailing, shrieking tears.

Ruth hardly felt her sobs. Her body racked by grief found comfort in Ami's gentle arms, moulded by innumerable trials and tolerances. Ruth relaxed. The older woman had clearly known death, pain, and grief. Her burden eased, Ruth released herself from the crucifix of loneliness and death into the breast of her friend.

Dr. Anderson witnessed the scene from the top of the stairs. He saw the two women bound by a bond he had not seen in years. The older woman, with her quiet restraint, embodied sensitivity, respect, humility, and the younger, acted out the play he had seen so often; sudden loss, the unexpected departure, the disbelief, the shocking denial of all that was familiar, safe. So many times, he had seen the cycles of life and seasons of pain wash as predictably as the flow of moon tides through families, and now, through the woman he loved as a daughter. As if by instinct, he felt Ruth's mind buckling under the sheer weight of her grief, her will to live teeter dangerously close to the point of submission. Her sobbing was from a distant place as it often was, separate from the world she knew. Ruth's wails emanated from the limitless pool of human grief and emotion; storms unleashing unbearable tempests, marking the passage of time, the otherwise unwritten rites of the soul on its journey from the known to the unknown.

Ruth was unaware of the flood of tears raging through her as she clung to Ami like a child at a familiar breast. The older woman remained steadfast and patient holding Ruth in her grief. Then it was over. The sobbing subsided and Ami drew her friend closer, breathing her own life into Ruth's frail chest. Ruth stilled in enormous relief, the fear of loss and grief now gone.

Chapter Eighty Seven

EDWARD WAS SNATCHED away from their lives without warning. The book of his life snapped closed and lay still, the covers perfectly aligned within a masterful final act of his destiny. There were no loose leaves to gather and reorder into the dignity of his character, the perfect reason of his life.

Ruth registered the presence of the child tugging at her mother's side, her sympathetic eyes pressing her own with their tiny tears of selfless remorse. Then Dr. Anderson caught her in his arms, hiding her exposed wounds in his healing embrace. Ami moved into the kitchen. The sounds of crockery and the gas singing under the kettle for now, silencing her pain and providing urgent comfort to her still, grief stricken mind. Dr. Anderson seated Ruth on the sofa and gently took her hands, offering his compassion and sympathy through the kind lines etched into his features, innumerable pages from countless lives. Ruth's hand shook slightly, then let go as she found the strength to face death one more time. The maturity of the doctor facing her with the timeless theme of life and death, allowed her time to gather the courage to face another loss. First it was Thomas, then her child, now Edward, and ultimately her own death that would inevitably visit her one day. He felt the current of recognition surge through Ruth's slender fingers entwined in his own immaculate hand; strong and unwavering, instruments of life and death. He willed his accumulated wisdom and strength from a lifetime of dedicated care, to steady Ruth's hand until she felt the joy, the wonderful celebration of Edward's liberation and the extraordinary beauty of grace. He sensed in her a witnessing of the sacred and the unfathomable. Edward was gone, but in his death, Ruth had found life, truth, and immutable strength. Ruth turned and looked at her father-mentor, her eyes shining in a moment of unexpected victory; now filled with the intoxication of realising a truth far deeper than the medical profession either acknowledged or allowed for.

'Ruth, I have to certify your husband deceased.' Dr. Anderson became official to create a separation. 'If you'll allow me, I'll examine Edward then write the certificate. Will you be all right for a few minutes?' Ruth nodded her head. She felt older, matured beyond her years and grateful for the clink of cups.

Ami settled the tea tray between them, the wafers delicately arranged and arrowing towards the centre, a silver spoon carefully placed at the side of each cup. Mani followed her mother into the room, bearing the teapot in both hands. Ami took it from her and put it on the tray.

'Ami. Could you stay tonight?' Ruth could not bear the thought of being alone in the house. She caught the child's eager eyes entering the sanctum of their discourse. 'Stay tonight Ami please; both you and Mani. I would appreciate the company.' Ami looked frankly at Dr. Anderson as he packed his notebook into the bag. His eyes were soft and respectful like the humble vision of the St Assisi.

'Yes Ruth. That will be a good idea.'

Ami rose to the occasion. She nodded quietly and placed a firm hand on Ruth's arm.

'Thank you dear Ami.' Ruth resigned herself to the inevitable.

I need to make arrangements with the hospital Ruth.' Dr. Anderson stood quietly in the living room.

'Hospital?'

'I am not sure how he died Ruth. I will need to arrange for a post mortem.'

'Oh.' Ruth dropped her head.

'I am sorry Ruth. There's no way around it.'

'I understand.' Ruth sounded like an obedient child.

'I'll call you at six.' Dr. Anderson collected his coat and walked to the front door. 'Call me if you have to Ruth. I mean it.' As he passed the hall mirror, he caught the reflection of two women, their heads close together and a child sitting between them on the sofa, watching wafers on a tray.

The front door clicked shut, the two women and the child alone in the silence, Mani skipping uncertainly between the kitchen and living room.

'Ruth. Drink this.' Ami poured the tea. They drank silently, Mani bobbing around the sofa, nibbling her biscuit and quietly observing her Aunty Ruth.

'Come Mani.' Ruth called. She pulled the child to her chest and hugged her, deeply, as if afraid that she too would disappear into the darkness.

Chapter Eighty Eight

CHRIS WHISTLED AS he drove out of the city toward Edward and Ruth's home. The day had been good. Chris felt considerably cheered by the news of Tiger Tarika.

A Hindu wedding and now the baby boy! For David, it was exciting and Chris shared in his excitement. At last, a new life in the midst of the sea of death and destruction. David would want to invite him to Delhi as soon as the war was over. Chris felt that the child was a good omen, a good omen for India and a good omen for England. He parked close to the house, but not immediately outside, maintaining his personal code of respect for other's space and privacy. He closed the car door carefully and quietly and trod along the path to the front door.

Ruth sat downstairs idly fingering her cardigan. She did not want to go upstairs, not yet. Ami and the child had left to go to the grocer's for more supplies. Then, when they were all home in her house, they would attend to Edward's body. She would then she would ring Chris and tell him the news.

Chris banged on the front door with the perfectly shaped, brass knocker. He was looking forward to seeing Edward, to tell him news of David and Meera's boy child and to share a few jokes from the office. He knocked again and allowed the fragrance of the fresh bread tucked lightly under his arm to rise into his nostrils. Ruth would appreciate the gesture. He waited patiently for her to open the door aware that he was early. Ruth rose to the door, expecting Ami on her return from the grocer. Dear Ami, so shy and polite, would always belong to India!

'Chris! Thank goodness you're here.'
'Hello Ruth. I brought you some bread. How's the man?'

'Chris…' Ruth stumbled over her thoughts. She sat awkwardly beside him. 'He's…' the words would not come out.

'What's wrong Ruth?' Chris fought the impulse to catch her shoulders and shake her. 'Ruth, come on. Out with it.'

'I…it's…Edward' she stammered.

'What's wrong? Is he in hospital?' Chris felt the fear rise in his throat.

Ruth shook her head, looking down to hide her anguish. 'He's dead Chris.'

Chris took her hand and pulled her around to face him.

Ruth found it hard to meet his eyes.

Chris saw the pain in her eyes, and that it was for him.

'I'm sorry Chris.' Ruth dropped her head.

Dazed, Chris let her hand go. 'Ruth, he can't be.'

Ruth nodded and looked up at Chris, the corners of her mouth softened with apology.

'No! Ruth, what happened?' Chris whispered.

'I don't know Chris. One minute he asked me to open a package for him, then… '

Chris looked at her with quiet disbelief. 'What do you mean Ruth, he… He can't just stop breathing!'

'Chris, it happened in less than a minute. I opened the package, gave him the book…'

'What book Ruth?'

'I don't know! It was torn and I ran from the room before I could look at it properly. When I gave it to Edward, he just froze, then he looked as though he was in incredible pain. He could hardly speak. Then nothing. Nothing!' Ruth felt the tears rising. 'I tried to shake him, just as Dr. Anderson told me to but he didn't move Chris. He didn't move.' Ruth started to cry the tears of remembered shock breaking through his disbelief.

'No, Ruth no!'

'Chris, I am sorry. Ami and I were about to fix the room. I wanted you to see Edward here, not, not… '

'Thanks Ruth. I'd appreciate that.'

Ami stepped into the front room of her friend Ruth's home. She was timid, shy, respectful and aware that this was a moment when grief was about to spill into the room.

'Ami. Come in. Ami, I want you to meet Chris, Edward's boss.'

'Hello Ami.' Chris held out his hand, but he quickly withdrew it again, aware that it was shaking uncontrollably.

Ami looked to Ruth for support. 'It's OK Ami.'

'Sorry.' Chris dropped his hand and sat down.

Ruth patted Chris's forearm. 'Chris, when you're ready, would you like to see Edward.'

Chris stiffened slightly. 'OK. Are you coming too?'

'I haven't been in the room since he died Chris. I would like it if you were there too.' Chris nodded.

'OK. Let's go up then.'

'Ami?' Ruth wanted to console Ami that she was part of the family.

'I'm not sure I can Ruth.'

'Of course you can. Please.' Ruth put her hand in Ami's and gently encouraged her to join them.

Chris allowed the women to climb the stairs in front of him. Ruth was slow to ascend, keeping Ami at her side, measuring her thoughts, gauging her reaction in advance. Chris followed them into the room and walked to the side of the bed.

Edward lay totally still, as if an unseen hand had halted him in mid-life and taken the breath from his body. The book lay beside his right arm where Dr. Anderson had placed it. The face was pale, lifeless.

Chris looked at Ruth and picked the book up, closing it and placing it on the bedside table. It could wait. The two women were at the head of the bed, Ruth stroking Edward's forehead and Ami placing her hand on his breast. Ami found Edward's hand by the side of the body, and attempted to rest it respectfully over the heart. It was heavy, resisting.

'It's OK Ami. I think we might just cover him. What do you think?'

'Good idea Ruth.' Chris pulled the cover to Edward's chin.

'Ruth, where does he keep his comb?'

'In the bathroom cabinet Chris. There's a washer near the sink as well.'

Chris disappeared into the bathroom, aware of the slightly acrid smell of vomitus and diarrhoea. He opened the cabinet, took out Edward's sponge bag, and wet the washer with warm water. He returned to the bedroom, mindful of the peaceful glow on Ruth's cheeks the gentleness of her features and slight tilt of her head. As she inclined her face to kiss her husband goodbye.

Ami waited, watching for the right moment to enter Ruth's thoughts and place a comforting arm over her shoulders. Ruth remained totally composed as she gave Edward a soft, parting kiss, lingering for a moment before closing his eyelids in a final farewell.

Chris waited until Ruth withdrew into Ami's arms.

'Yes, go ahead please Chris. He'll look better.'

Chris pulled out the comb and carefully arranged the hair in Edward's normal style. He took the washer and wiped the face clean, wiping away the trace of torment. The grooming complete, he returned the sponge bag to the bathroom and washed his hands.

For a few moments, they stood quietly by the bed, Ruth holding Edward's hand.

Then it was over. Ruth let go of Edward's hand and looked to Chris for her next cue, vulnerable, her heart exposed.

'Come on Ruth.' Chris took both her hands.

'Thanks Chris. Thanks for coming when you did.'

Chris had no reply.

Ami witnessed Ruth farewell her husband. She too had lost her own husband to another world, but their farewell was painful, humiliating, and unbearable to remember. Not only had she lost her husband, she had lost her family, her country her culture. Ami's tears choked in her throat and her knees threatened to fold beneath her as her own loss acutely surfaced. Chris sensed the pain in the woman and stopped in mid-stride. Ruth felt him turn slightly towards Ami - then together they moved towards her, Ruth placing an arm around Ami's waist and Chris holding her under the elbow. They left the bedroom and the shared intimacy of Edward's death closing the door to emptiness and loneliness.

Dr. Anderson arrived as he promised in the early evening, and with him, came the priest. The priest performed the last rites, chanting in mellow tones and swinging a small lamp attached to a bell to-and-fro, as one would spread cleansing incense throughout a temple. It was silent and holy and Ruth found it easy to release Edward to the care of the hospital.

Ami insisted she clean the room and scrubbed the bathroom in a manner that Ruth herself could not do. She stripped the sheets and blankets for laundering. They would soon hang on ridiculous lines, as if the last visible shreds of his life needed public airing like flags displaying past or future glories. Ruth let Ami continue into the evening whilst she cooked and prepared supper for all three. Then Ami showered, changing her clothes and packing them for boiling and airing along with the sheets and blankets, symbolic, respectful and thankful. The bedroom was ready, cleansed of death, the memories of Edward, ready for the light, and air of tomorrow to circulate in eddies of new beginnings.

Ruth was grateful to be relieved of the task, relieved of changing the bed and washing away the traces of Edward.

The women slept in the same room. Ruth piled a few cushions on the floor for herself and put Ami and Mani in the bed. The atmosphere was comforting and sweet. Ruth felt like a child in the company of Ami and her dreams were filled with alluring sights and sounds, the colours of saffron, gold and peacock blue and the distant hum of a flute. In and out of her mind, drifted images of a woman with child, happy, laughing, surrounded by family and friends. From time to time, the woman saw Ruth, and from across the seas, eyes filled with compassion and love. Then the woman was gone and in her place, a single child appeared, happy and sparkling, a tiny girl sleeping in a woven basket, lined with gold and sheets of spun silk. Ruth enjoyed the perfect bliss of the woman and innocent joy of the child and her heart filled with peace.

Ami hugged her daughter close, whispering quiet words into her ears, lullabies of assurance. Ruth was their friend, her house, their second home. It was good to sleep here. The women slept in the cocoon of one another's company and their dreams. Ami wanted to hold Ruth, but Ruth insisted that she was all right as she pulled the blankets closely around herself. Then Ami also fell asleep, wondering about Hanif, the shop, his Mosque and the god who protected the English and, for whom she found little evidence. Ami thought of her husband and their home that no longer existed and she was glad of the presence of Ruth.

It was morning. The sky was slightly overcast, dim but not threatening. Ruth wanted to sleep longer, to rest near the warmth of her friend but Mani needed attention, a visit to the bathroom then to drink warm milk to soften the dullness of the day. The child raced upstairs to the bathroom and came back with the book and its discarded wrapping.

'Mama, what's this?'

Ami was not amused with the child. She had respectfully left the book on the bedside table for Ruth to dispose or keep it, as she thought fit.

'Child! Who told you to touch things that do not belong to you.'

'Ami, it's all right. Mani, bring it here to me.' As Ruth spoke, Mani had already placed the book and wrapping into the lap of her mother. Ami lifted it smiling at Ruth, conscious of the innocence of the child. As she adjusted the wrapper, her breath exploded as a tiny necklace dropped into her lap.

'Ami, what is it?'

'Look Aunty Ruth. It's pretty!' The child piped with enthusiasm.

Ruth stood up as the wrapper dropped from Ami's hands onto the floor. Ami cradled the necklace, her body rocking back and forwards as if she had been struck a mortal blow.

'Ami! What is it?' Ruth could not contain the fear in her voice. 'Allah forgive him.' Ami wailed.

'Who Ami?' Ruth picked the wrapper up from the floor then opened the cover of the book. She gasped in horror; Edward's name and address written on the inside cover in his own hand. Then for the first time, she saw the blood. Finally, Ruth saw what shocked her husband into frozen terror and death, the loosely held pages spattered with the drops of life, someone's life!'

'Ami what does this mean? How did this happen?' Ruth stared at her in disbelief. Ami clutched the necklace, racked with the terror of the truth lying in her lap.

It was an hour before Ami relinquished her wild-eyed terror and faced Ruth. The intuition that gnawed at her heart told her that something was desperately wrong. Now she knew that the omens of death had come to Ruth's home and she had nothing but her faith to comfort her.

'Mama, Mama what is it?' Mani implored.'

'Child. There are things it is better you do not know.' Ami closed the subject.

'But…..'

'Child. Mr. Thompson is at peace and that is all that we know. He is gone and Aunty Ruth must be very sad.' Ami's words were disconsolate, empty.

Ruth held Ami's arm and asked Mani to bring the biscuits, desperately hoping that it was not true. She wanted to know, she wanted to know about the passage of death that visited them. The wrapper, the book, were indisputable evidence that there was someone else's blood staining Edward's life, his character, his soul. Ruth placed the book and wrapper on the telephone table. They would decide later what to do. The book belonged to the past, it was unthinkable, but certain that Edward died from the shock of its revelations.

The child returned, wary and insecure with the biscuits on a plate. Mani was numb with the exhaustion of being away from her familiar home and drained of childlike curiosity by her mother's display of emotion. She urgently wanted her mother's warm and loving arms.

Ruth caught the child into her lap, stroked, and kissed her face. 'Thank you Mani. You've been a great help to both of us.'

Ami recovered, grateful for Ruth's ease with her daughter and wiped her tears in long downward strokes. Then she tucked her handkerchief into the loose folds of her bosom and pulled her scarf straight. Ami looked to Ruth, the wisdom of love and death passed between them like an ancient tide. There was something in war that women would never understand, but also never forget. She desperately wanted to forget death and she knew that Ruth also wanted to forget. War only ever brought death and gouged valleys of pain into their hearts and souls.

The morning passed quietly with Ruth idly putting things away in the kitchen and Ami resting on the bed, holding and cuddling the child, in order to ease the memories of India. Karachi, how far away was Karachi! Ami had never realised how much she had longed for good company; a woman's company that would not gossip or betray her to her own kind. And to her surprise, she found in Ruth what she doubted she would ever find amongst her own. Yes, her friends and family were loving, close, and protective; but Ruth, Ruth was different. In Ruth, Ami sensed a deep respect that allowed her to find, for the first time, her identity, her sense of herself, her own being. Ami rejoiced in the discovery, becoming more attentive to her daily life and the little actions that created the warmth of the kitchen, the cleanliness of the bathroom and the functionality of the bedroom. She basked in the freedom to think of her own domestic life as important, liberating her from the depressing bondages of her birth. In her liberation, was the liberation of her girl child.

Mani was eager and happy to explore her new environment and delighted in the unusual ways of her Aunty Ruth. London could never be the same as their home. Yet, the weekly visits to Aunty always brought surprises, scones and jam, teddy bears and lessons in English and piano. Aunty Ruth always gave her a big hug when she arrived and patted her head when she left. She was glad that her mother and Aunty chatted and she explored the piano with her tiny fingers. Today, the child was at loss. Today was different with mother and Aunty crying and holding each other. Mani did not understand their sadness. She looked with open and unabashed eyes at their frequent embraces and accepted them. After all, Aunty was her mother's only friend, someone she liked and trusted. Mani stirred next to her mother. She felt warm snuggled into her soft body. Then she was fidgety, excited and pulled at her mother's clothes, waiting for the chance to run downstairs.

Ami stirred, refreshed by sleep but still drained by the emotions of the morning. The shock registered deeply within her heart but she had already distanced herself far from India, from her husband and his preparations for his war. Nothing, nothing could rebuild the bridge. The wrapper with the familiar writing, Hanif's writing, scrawling out the name of Ruth's husband, the necklace…..it was an omen, a death knell on Sesheta's life. Ami sat up dislodging the loosely arranged blankets that draped English warmth across her body. It was time to wash. She spent a few minutes in the bathroom daring to look frankly at her lightly lined faced, to straighten her hair and set her scarf. Then she went downstairs calling quietly to Ruth from the top of the stairs.

Ruth emerged from the kitchen. 'Ami, you must be feeling better.' Ruth was relieved.

Ami said nothing. She walked to Ruth; her arms open without any trace of confusion or question. They embraced, mature and resolved, a communion moulded by circumstance, death, separation, and courage.

Chapter Eighty Nine

London 7 September 1940

CHRIS FELT HE had been at war for years. Hitler refused to take his eye off the ultimate prize; Britain. For months, he had targeted the RAF, sending the Luftwaffe into the skies between the continent and the tiny island that was the heart of the allied forces. Believing he had won the battle of the skies, Hitler, turned his attention to the English coastline to try and systematically destroy British industrial and military assets.

Chris closed the file spilling over with clippings from the last month's major newspapers detailing the war effort. It was going to be a long struggle, that much he knew. Already, the days were shortening, the autumn skies softer and the light fading casting a sombre hue across the city. It was nevertheless, the end of a long day. He stretched in his chair and moved to the window in his office. The city appeared to have disappeared, the usual thrum of citizens strangely muted. He pulled his coat off the rack and walked slowly towards the door.

Then it came. The whistling sound, eerie, as though there was nothing else in the silence apart from the imminent thud as the first bomb hit the city.

It was London's turn to feel the full impact of the war, the bombs dropping day after day on the docks in a "Blitzkreig" that appeared to have no end. The relentless bombing campaign of London had taken a heavy toll on life and property. The citizens of the Empire - now struggling for its very existence - continued to huddle every night in the deep shelters and the underground network of railways, far below the thud of metal falling from the sky. The physical city was broken, yet the morale of the city remained resilient.

Chris knew that it was his duty to wake every morning and organise his thoughts carefully, to write uplifting stories in the middle of the greatest battle Britain had ever faced. This was *his* war service; to use his skills and his newspaper to lift the city's morale, to tell her people, that Britain could and would win the war. Their lads in the skies would bring down the German planes, one by one until there were no bombers left to raid London.

It was all Chris could do to lift his own spirits yet he knew it was his task to stoke the fires of hope, resilience and a determination to to fight, survive and thrive - a power that not even Hitler could crush.

The pattern of bombing continued night after long night for seventy one nights until there could be no more hope left that the madness of war would ever end. But end it did the night skies were finally silent and the citizens of London at last, slept in their own beds at night.

Churchill too mourned the city he loved, a city that was the envy of Europe in a nation that was part of an Empire that spanned the oceans and spilled onto the major of continents across the world. At the same time, he shared his incredulity that Britain, London continued to live, to function, its people rising again and again to defy destruction, death, annihilation.

"London is like some huge prehistoric animal, capable of enduring terrible injuries, mangled and bleeding from many wounds, and yet preserving its life and movement."

Chapter Ninety

CHRIS OPENED THE telegram lying on top of the folders and files in his in tray.

> "November 1 1940.
> David, Congress leaders imprisoned over anti-war speeches. Civil disobedience sweeping India. How can Gandhi persuade the Indian soul to act peacefully for Independence? Chris."

"Act peacefully for Independence?" Would there be any end to the madness? How many lives would be lost for freedom?

It felt to Chris that the whole world was on fire.

Chapter Ninety One

India

ON DECEMBER 7TH 1941, the Japanese bombed Pearl Harbour and effected a swift advance through Malaya and Burma, leaving trails of young Japanese dead through combat, and longer trails of Burmese fleeing into India.

Congress saw the opportunity and tried again to barter for India's Independence. However, Gandhi resisted, insisting that opportunism was incompatible with non-violence. Then he withdrew his leadership of Congress in protest whilst across the oceans and continents, Roosevelt and Churchill forged the Atlantic Charter.

India was delighted. A new window to freedom was open. Churchill, his bile still stale from the memory of the Mahatma, refused its application to India, Burma and 'other parts' of the British Empire.

Roosevelt could not agree with his wartime counterpart and encouraged Churchill to make India a reasonable offer. But Churchill continued to be stubbornly unwilling. Roosevelt stepped around the obstacle, around Churchill, and sent his envoy Johnson to India. Under the pressure of Japan at the eastern edge of India, Churchill had no choice but to reconsider constitutional solutions for India.

Chapter Ninety Two

England, March 1942

"CHRIS, JAPAN HAS taken Rangoon. Britain stands between India and her safety."

David sent the cryptic cable then languished in the afternoon heat, amused by Roosevelt's footwork. As the cables and reports passed his desk, he chuckled at the prospect of the towering giant Churchill toppling before Gandhi's spinning wheel, the old man buoyed by his ally, appearing before India at the final hour. David noted the correspondence in the register, fastidiously sorting the urgent and non-urgent messages before forwarding them to the Viceroy. Linlithgow was, in his opinion, too remote from the feelings of India, too aloof to allow sympathy to temper his cold logic. 'To yours and India's detriment old chap' David muttered as he gathered the pile for the Viceroy. He never enjoyed their encounters, but exercised sufficient wisdom to engage with the man in a manner that was without sycophancy or insubordination lest the Viceroy gauge David's true feelings about the British Raj in India. David was aware that his sympathies for Gandhi and Independence had been 'officially noted.' Now that he and Meera were married and with their infant Tarika, his impartiality was more so viewed as 'compromised.' Nevertheless, the Viceroy could not dispense him to Britain. David's service was exemplary and in him, the Viceroy had an administrative link to his predecessor.

David idled with thoughts of Roosevelt's challenge to Churchill's domain. The literal answer came with surprising speed. Churchill despatched Cripps to India with a limited proposal for dominion status. David watched, as the fortunes of India washed across his desk in a flow of cables and letters.

Predictably, Gandhi was offended and insulted by the lesser offer and suggested to Cripps that he take the first plane home. India was in no mood for Britain's insults and as the disposition of Delhi darkened, Congress demanded cabinet status and the appointment of an Indian Defence Minister. Cripps refused and returned to London with constitutional Independence for India no closer.

For the first time, much to Jinnah's delight, Britain publicly acknowledged the likelihood of a separate 'Pakistan'. The battle lines were drawn.

Gandhi wrote in *"The Harijan"*;

"I waited and waited, until the country should develop the non-violent strength necessary to throw off the foreign yoke. But my attitude has undergone a change....I have decided that even at certain risks which are obviously involved, I must ask the people to resist the slavery."

Gandhi wanted no part of Britain's war with Japan and demanded Britain's immediate withdrawal from India, bluntly asserting that it would be better for Britain to leave India to God at best, otherwise (and preferable to British rule) anarchy! Congress similarly insisted on the immediate end to foreign rule in order to allow a free India to defend herself against the European war. Churchill's Cripps had done nothing for India except to escalate anti-British sentiments and inevitably, rebellion.

Eagle-sharp, Jinnah wasted no time in aligning himself with Britain.

The pace quickened and by August 8, the Working Committee passed the *"Quit India"* resolution.

The British administration ordered Ghandi's arrest and instantaneously, a series of mass demonstrations erupted throughout India. The era of *"non-violence"* was over. As the fires of anarchy swept across India, indignant at Britain's indecent and unwelcome hold, Churchill dug in his heels and refused to liquidate Britain's grasp.

David swept aside the litter of papers and annals on his desk. British administration was becoming more tedious by the hour, the blatant need for a timely and neat exit more apparent than any other time in her history of occupation. The atmosphere in Delhi was stifling. India needed a quick release from the stranglehold of the Viceroy, now convinced that the issues were personal between himself, and the Mahatma, and not those of national and historic consequence. The Viceroy in cold anger, suggested that Gandhi should starve himself to death rather than have him released from prison for his fast. David was horrified having already detached himself from the atrocities inflicted by his English colleagues.

'Meeraben, if I could leave the Civil Service, then I would do it now.' David lamented over dinner.

'No David. Not now. It is better to wait until these untidy affairs have been completed and then retreat with grace. Otherwise they will see you as a supporter of Congress and send you home to gaol.'

David glumly agreed. He was unhappy with the business of the past few months and imagined that there would be further disquiet in Delhi. There was little Gandhi could do to stir sentiments now that he was interned. He could not rouse the masses in his usual style.

Chapter Ninety Three

England

AMI AWOKE TO a grey day in London. Nothing seemed to change in Europe and the fortunes of war continued to send Londoners scurrying like rabbits into their holes at the sounds of sirens and searchlights blazing the sky. On more than one occasion she hid, the child beneath the bed rather run to the community air shelter. Ami would rather die in her own home than be suffocated like an animal in a cold, desolate and premature grave. War-torn London seemed little safer than Karachi, but at least here was a sense of belonging, that they were fighting a common war, not brother killing brother, neighbour betraying and slaughtering neighbour amidst the fires of communal violence. In London, a common fate bound them, and along with the imminence of death, they shared feelings of hope and trust.

The war flung the mother and child into a new community. London was more than home now; it was the place that surrounded them in grey mists, in moments of both, depression and unexpected friendships. London had given them Ruth. Otherwise, the city was yet another man's world, this time of smoky buildings and low flying planes skidding over the tops of houses. It was all that they had. If Hanif could ever know how close death had come, how they ran more than once from the rain of dust, debris and the threat of their own roof falling in a heap of useless rubble around them, he would regret his noble decision to send them into safety! Yet, amid the destruction of Europe, Ami found Ruth and through Ruth, the opening of her own womanhood in a way that she had never known.

Ruth did not wear the elegant fashions of the Continent, but she did have a sweetness of tongue, gentleness of nature and beauty of temperament that Ami wanted for herself and her child. She was warm, loving, and safe. In Ruth's home, Ami knew she could always find the friend she loved more than any of her own neighbours and relatives. The men's world of meaningless wars and artificial lines in the sand could never destroy the bond between her and Ruth. It was a sacrilege to imagine that ambition and greed for land and wars could ever regulate the love of friendship, the bond between she and Ruth. She wondered whether the men of her Karachi really believed in their make-believe war. Ami could not imagine that the men seriously believed in themselves, their hatreds or their wars.

'What do their beliefs and wars have to do with collecting jars of water, feeding the children and finding warm clothes to keep them covered and protected from wandering eyes?'

Ami shook her head as if her thoughts were flecks of dust. She sighed, wondering why she allowed herself to think of Hanif and his brothers and cousins, of their useless plans to join the British war. She looked around their tiny kitchen. It was warm and predictable, the pots and plates carefully and deliberately positioned by her economical yet artistic hand. Soon Mani would want her breakfast; warm milk, perhaps a little fresh and hot halva as a treat Although she was still Indian at heart, Ruth had cultivated in her and Mani, English tastes. The child was happy. Ami was more than content to let Ruth mother Mani. Silently she watched the Englishwoman and her child warm to one another, and neither noticed her quietly thanking Allah for bringing them together. Ruth was at first hesitant, her maternal instincts eventually pulling her to the child. Mani opened in her, the maternal love that she longed to feel Ruth patted the child's head. Mani continued to stumble over new piano tunes and English words. Ami too learned to relax and released the child to stay at her Aunty's more than once. Mani would clap her tiny hand when it was time to stay again. Ruth and Ami would laugh at the child's delight.

'You know Ami I don't think that I could ever have had a child as beautiful as Mani.'

'Nonsense Ruth, that's not true and you know it!' Ami was alarmed that Ruth could think so little of herself and wondered whether within Ruth there was still the grief of her losing her baby.

'No I mean it Ami, sincerely. I'm proud to be Mani's Aunty.'

Ami hesitated at the door. It did not seem right to leave her friend alone and without the warmth of a family.

'Ruth, I wonder if I could stay tonight as well. It's getting late and I don't like the thought of walking outside when it's so cold.

'Of course you can Ami. I'm glad you mentioned it. Come; let's make that cup of tea. Mani, find the biscuits, the ones we were saving.' Ruth's smile widened in open appreciation of Ami and the child. The tea was pleasantly sweet as Ruth sucked on her biscuit, curious at the thought of India. She would let Ami know of her plans this evening.

'Ami.'

'Yes Ruth.' Ami smiled warmly at her friend. 'I'm thinking of going to India.'

'India!'

Ruth paused. She was unsure how to proceed and looked towards Mani as if to find inspiration. Mani played with her food making patterns on the plate, then rearranging them into new configurations of childlike intrigue.

'Chris promised to take me to Delhi. What do you think?'

'I, I don't know what to say Ruth. I think it's wonderful of course, but why India? Why not holiday somewhere safe?' The immediacy of India, of her past, took Ami was taken by surprise.

'Chris has friends in Delhi. David was the last person to see my husband before he became critically ill in India. I need to know Ami, you understand.'

Ami was silent. She too had lost her husband, but didn't even know which questions to ask to find her way through the morass of grief, humiliation and abandonment. She could not even imagine a reason with which to challenge Hanif. The past was incomprehensible to her. All that she knew was that now she was safe with her daughter and their friend. She did not want to open the door to India yet; it would only bring pain.

'I am sorry to bring it up Ami. I know how painful it is for you to think about home. But I have no choice. I have to let Chris know of my decision. Apparently it's still too dangerous, but we plan to go early in the New Year.'

Ami was frightened as if it were she who had to return to the scenes of death, loss, of uncertain futures and the grinding reality of deep rifts in her own and other's families. Her shattered world was for so long contained in the pleasant warmth of Ruth's home, and now Ruth herself planned to enter that world lost to her. Ami fingered the long scarf draping across her shoulders. Why not? If she could not taste the familiar sounds of her India, then why not encourage Ruth to enjoy the forgotten delights?

Ruth waited for Ami to come to terms with the idea. She needed an opening to invite Ami, to take them both with her. But Ami's expression told her that it was too early, that she would find too much sadness in returning to India when she was just making this land, England her home.

'Ami, will you come here while I am away? The blinds need to be opened and I would feel better if I knew that you were here sometimes.'

'I would love to Ruth.'

Ruth took her friend's hands. 'I wish you could both come Ami.' Ruth implored.

'It is better that I stay here Ruth. The child feels safe here. I would not want her to see so much killing. Already, there has been too much death.'

'Of course.' Ruth looked into the eyes swollen with unshed tears and thought of the sleepless nights Ami must have spent, locked in the memories and stories of her past.

Ami looked at her child. The child had a natural love for life that no man could create. Men may try to build nations and draft laws, but they could never make anything as beautiful as this one. And here, the child was safe, far from the grasp of the men in her home. Nevertheless, as long as men continued to wage war the children would never sing. No man understood at least that much.

It was the same in India. Edward had told them both about Nehru with his starched collars and Jinnah with flowing pronouncements of separatist ideals and Gandhi, Gandhi hardly clothed, preaching as he did to women. At least Gandhi had considered abstinence, but remained in Ami's eyes, unclothed and indecent before all women. Even though he lived amongst the poorest of the poor, his lack of modesty in dress, meant that, all women were also stripped by exposure to his beliefs. In Gandhi's world, the child would simply be stripped bare and made vulnerable; her innocence gambled at the hands of careless men boasting high ideals and ridiculous laws. What difference did it make? In her eyes, Ami trusted no man; not even the Mahatma with his cloth spun on his wheel of belief. Of what benefit was Gandhi's private war if it stole from women and their children, modesty, their safety and if it robbed the English of their livelihoods?

Ami wondered about the women in London. Were they not well clothed? Even the poorest were covered. Ruth always dressed sensibly, her shoes flat and her cardigans knitted in a calm array of contentment and Ruth flaunted, neither her body or talents from beneath her English wool. Ami was sad. Now, the violent storms of war tainted and tore the at the veils of women in Europe and India. Who had allowed men to trespass into the sanctuaries of women; their homes, their churches and temples? Only in their hushed whisperings, would women find a way to comfort themselves, something that men could never do.

Through her eyes, so often, the men of the Cloth who transcribed, translated and taught, were little more than common thieves, stealing and young girls and women to satisfy themselves. Men could claim and possess the bodies of women or children, but they could never, confine or contain their souls! No matter the faiths men professed, women were their common commerce.

'Go Ruth. You must go.' Let Ruth witness for herself, the mindlessness, the childishness of men consumed and overawed by their own learnedness, their business and quick money floating from hand to hand. Let Ruth see what she had seen, the futility of men's wars, men who hated women and amongst them, some who denounced the womb as *"the gateway to hell."* Men could never enter a true womb without women. Instead, they built artificial wombs; temples, Mosques and Churches, lifeless forms fired from empty ambitions. Men birthed in their artificial wombs of religion, distemper, dissatisfaction and death.

Women were blessed with the power to create, to bear life in their wombs, a power that no man could ever have. In Ami's experience, women were the pathway to life, to a heaven on this earth. She was immune to the bribes of men, their mirages made from broken poems and illusory veils; promises winnowing on winds of pretence. They could never steal a woman's soul. She knew it in her heart. Ruth also knew the same truth, the same secret that all women shared without ever having to speak of it or turn it into texts that men chanted in their Mosques, Temples and Churches.

Ruth caught Ami's elated mood, her eyes blazing and shining with fierce victory.

'Ami, they can't do anything to you here. There is no one to stop you from doing what you must. Besides, they wouldn't dare now.'

Ami smiled at Ruth, her breasts heaving with passion.

'I know Ruth. Hanif is weak. He doesn't even know himself so how can he possibly know me?' Ami sounded strangely sad and bitter.

'They don't understand Ami. No man does. Not even Edward could ever understand the pain of childbirth or the pain of losing a home.'

Ami looked softly at the child. 'Ruth, one day our men will come running back, wondering why they have destroyed the crops, why they have burnt and ruined the markets and raped the women and children. Then they will be filled with remorse, but it will be too late. It will be too late for anyone to protect them from themselves.' Ami wiped a weary hand across her forehead. 'If only they had listened in the first place to their mothers and sisters and wives. Then none of the deaths would have happened. I would still be in my own home Ruth.' Ami pleaded against the insanity of the war.

'What you say is true Ami. If the men had more respect for their mothers and the homes that nurtured them, there would be no war. They could never rape and they would have no reason to kill.'

'I don't understand it Ruth. To destroy one's country! To destroy one's own land or the land of any other man! Is that not to rape one's own mother?'

'Yes Ami.' Ruth said quietly. 'To wage war is to destroy the very mother's womb that bore them life, that held and nurtured them! I think that for men, pride and honour is greater than life. Yet in war, they lose all honour in a single moment. If only they knew it.' Ruth also could not conceive of the senselessness, the futility of war.' They have no respect, so how can they have love, and without love, there is no home for them, not anywhere on this earth.' Ruth brought her hands together. 'Most men are orphans cast upon one of the many battlefields on this earth; India, Europe, England. What does it matter? There is only one field of war anyway, and that is the field within their own hearts. It is one earth, one home and one hearth upon which they sacrifice themselves.' Ruth surprised herself with her unexpected passion.

'It is through self-hatred and not honour that they kill Ruth. Men kill to salvage their lost honour, the honour of themselves they carelessly throw away in a moment of passion. They slit one another's throats not because their wives or daughters have lost their honour, but because they themselves have squandered their own honour by giving in to their own weaknesses. That is what they are most afraid of. Then, when they cannot confront themselves and their own weaknesses, they hide from themselves, in their Temples and their Mosques and Churches.'

Ruth listened to Ami, wondering what secrets, what memories and pain she was hiding.

'Ami, if a mother loved her son enough, do you think it would stop the fighting and killing?'

'Mothers love their sons too much Ruth. That's the problem. If mothers loved other's sons as much as their own, then all the fighting would stop. It is the pride and jealousy of mothers that prompt their sons to fight for false honour. It is the attachment of mothers to their sons that creates wars in the first place. So the mother is responsible. It is then that the young women suffer. Men rape girls for the honour of mother and country. Then they call it 'war!' So many rapes Ruth. So many innocent young ones lost!' Ami wrung her hands. 'A virgin is hated for stealing a son. His mother hates her if she does and a father defiles her if she does not consent to uphold his honour through marriage. If she relents before her time, she is abandoned, humiliated and outcast to the world of ridicule and contempt. She cannot win Ruth. So it is the mother who starts all wars and condones all rapes.' Ami looked at the playful form of her daughter. 'The mother alone is responsible. She alone can quell the fire of passion that burns away the hearts and souls of men.'

Ruth nodded quietly.

Chapter Ninety Four

India

TWO YEARS PASSED and Congress remained immobilised, its key members imprisoned. Meanwhile, Jinnah waged a private war with India, carefully reconstructing the Muslim League and preparing for Partition. Then, sixty thousand Indian troops surrendered to the Japanese as POWS under the command of Bose. When the time was ripe, Bose equipped with his long-awaited army, stormed Manipur and Imphal. By 1944, his troops were imprisoned, this time in Rangoon. The forces against violence took an unprecedented turn as Gandhi continued his quiet routine of letter writing, reading, spinning and prayers from prison. As the Mahatma's health failed, India called for his release from prison. The Viceroy finally relented. Gandhi, at last, was free.

'Well, at least there is a little morality left in our lot after all.' David slammed the paper onto his desk and walked into the hot compound.

Only weeks away from the monsoon, the air festered with the omens of change. David strode to his cottage, wanting the privacy and coolness of his own company.

Meera, now heavily in child again, waited.

'David, you must not concern yourself too much in these affairs.'

'Then why am I here in India. in Delhi Meera?' David sat at the table. 'Of course. I nearly forgot, I came to India for you Meera.' He joked. 'How is the mother-to-be?'

'The pains started this morning David. I think it is a girl.' Meera sat quickly, the colour draining from her face.

'You can tell that it's a girl from the pains?' David was incredulous.

David, I have a bag packed ready. But you know that I would prefer the birth at home.'

'I know that. But I'm not taking any risks.' David was unsettled.

'Let's start here and if I can't manage or the midwife thinks that there are problems, then we'll go to the hospital.' Meera gasped to ease the pain in her belly. She smiled, contented and glad that the child was ready.

'Of course. Let's have lunch then you must rest.'

'I can't eat David, not now.' Meera looked into his eyes, her own dark eyes smiling and sparkling with the prospect of the birth.

David grinned boyishly. 'This is far better than worrying about the dying Raj. I'll telephone the office and let them know I won't be back today.'

'Thank you David.' Meera pulled herself off the chair. 'David, I am going in now. Come when you're finished lunch.' Meera walked to the bedroom, leaning briefly against the doorway before positioning herself on the bed. The pains were more intense and frequent and she knew that this birth would be different, not easy as Tarika's, but the child would still be born at home.

Chapter Ninety Five

Midnight, 14 August 1947, Delhi, India
BARELY TEN MINUTES before midnight, Pandit Jawahal Nehru stepped up to the dais draped with the Indian Flag. Before him were the many men and the handful of women who were the Constituent Assembly of India; people who had an investment in the past, some cynical in the present and the timing of this great day, this great moment; many hopeful that they too would have a part in the future that was India.

There was one man more than anyone else that Jawahal wanted to be before him in this hour. He looked at the faces in front of him. Gandhi, Bapuji was not here with him. For a moment, his heart missed a beat. The man who was as a father to him, the mentor who had guided him towards this moment in his life, the very same moment that was now India's destiny, was far away in Calcutta.

With a heavy heart torn by news of the day's events, the violence in Lahore, the killings and bloodshed, Nehru raised his head and commanded attention from the noisy gathering. He could not waver in heart or mind; not now in this moment, not for any single moment in the future. The man destined to lead India to her future decided that he must bring an end to the pain within his own heart and the hearts of his brothers and sisters across the entire subcontinent that was soon to become both India and Pakistan.

The first Prime Minister of India knew he must rise to the occasion and with him, India and all Indians would rise to become a new nation, a nation where the shocking memories of communal violence would fade, hearts could heal and some of the tears at least, be wiped away for ever. He hoped that at the midnight hour, as India separated from the soul of Pakistan, she too would rise to become a nation of peace. Pakistan,

"*The Land of the Pure!*" How could either of the twin nations birthed by the conch at midnight 14 August 1947 claim any moral purity? Perhaps Bapuji was right after all. The first Prime Minister of India should be a Muslim!

The subtle scent of the red rose in the buttonhole of his silk jacket, calmed his mind. Nehru placed his notes on the dais. He looked around him. He looked into the eyes of the people he knew had faith in the future, the people he knew had faith in him, the new father of India. The words that India and the world needed to hear, spontaneously flowed from his mouth.

> "Long years ago we made a tryst with destiny, and now the time comes when we shall redeem our pledge, not wholly or in full measure, but very substantially. At the stroke of the midnight hour, when the world sleeps, India will awake to life and freedom. A moment comes, which comes but rarely in history, when we step out from the old to the new, when an age ends, and when the soul of a nation, long suppressed, finds utterance. It is fitting that at this solemn moment we take the pledge of dedication to the service of India and her people and to the still larger cause of humanity with some pride. "

David looked across the gathering and glanced at Nehru. The man he had come to know so well was absorbed in the moment as if it was written deeply into his soul, as if it were a part of him. For months, he had witnessed the meetings between Mountbatten and Nehru, the chemistry between the two people that would ultimately change the course of history, change *his* history and the lives of all the people that mattered most to him in the world.

> "To the people of India, whose representatives we are, we make an appeal to join us with faith and confidence in this great adventure. This is no time for petty and destructive criticism, no time for ill will or blaming others. We have to build the noble mansion of free India where all her children may dwell. The appointed day has come - the day appointed by destiny - and India stands forth

again, after long slumber and struggle, awake, vital, free and independent. We are citizens of a great country, on the verge of bold advance, and we have to live up to that high standard. All of us, to whatever religion we may belong, are equally the children of India with equal rights, privileges and obligations. We cannot encourage communalism or narrow-mindedness, for no nation can be great whose people are narrow in thought or in action."

David wanted to weep, but he was transfixed, as if time stalled in the seconds before midnight.

"To the nations and peoples of the world we send greetings and pledge ourselves to cooperate with them in furthering peace, freedom and democracy. And to India, our much- loved motherland, the ancient, the eternal and the ever-new, we pay our reverent homage and we bind ourselves afresh to her service. Jai Hind."

Chapter Ninety Six

New Delhi India 12.20 am 15 August 1947
LORD LOUIS MOUNTBATTEN accepted the Prime Minister of India Jawahal Nehru and the President of the Constituent Assembly Rajendra Prasad in his private study. David stood quietly amongst the press as they witnessed the formal notification by Nehru that they had taken over power and that the leaders requested Mountbatten be the first Governor General of India.

Then Nehru presented to Mountbatten a carefully addressed envelope.

'May I submit to you the portfolios of the new Cabinet.' Nehru said solemnly.

David watched as Lord Mountbatten placed the envelope on the side table, to be opened later in the privacy of the office.

The two men chatted briefly and smiled. The deed was finally done.

Lord Mountbatten look at David and nodded. David smiled, but he felt like weeping. The burden of Independence was finally off their shoulders, they the British were no longer in the Empire, they were guests in another country, of the new leaders who were now India.

'We must retire now David. It is a long night and I feel, a long day awaits us.' The brilliant smile flashed across the Last Viceroy's face and David smiled back. Ever gracious in victory or defeat, Mountbatten continued to inspire in him a loyalty that surpassed any feeling for Britain he had ever found within himself.

Chapter Ninety Seven

INDIA RADIO BLASTED into the airwaves at 5.30 a.m. It was August 15, 1947.

'India is a free country.'

David stirred from his short sleep after the long night spent with Lord Mountbatten that marked the birth of the new nation, India. He felt, elated, deeply relieved and immensely satisfied that India at last belonged to India.

It was a great pity in his opinion, that Gandhi was not present in Delhi for the announcement. His passion to curb communalism had detained him in Naokhali. Of all people, Gandhi should be first to hear that Independence for India had finally come. David mused at momentous presence of the moral giant. Ever-vigilant, Gandhi remained at a distance from the hubbub of politics. However, his impact found its mark in Nehru, the ably crafted vessel for his illusory *"Ramraj."* Perhaps the Allah of Jinnah would also now ordain him with *"Bahist!"* Then there would be no need for separate arrangements for the newly birthed nations. In any case, who knew whether Rama, Allah or God would bring any relief to the mindless and childish altercations of India? David certainly didn't. He resisted the impulse to relapse into sleep. Was land at the core of religion, or was it the other way around?

David turned the volume knob higher until the lilting sounds of the broadcaster filled the room. Nehru's speech pounded into the first morning of India's new destiny. The radio announcer was contained but David could detect the emotion, the surge of feeling tinged with elated pride, and *"aaah, at last"* national identity. With that, came the promise of freedom, liberation from what he, David represented, and before him, the Moghuls and before them, the feudal lords of India. He, David, the

Raj, represented the oppressor; except, David was now a part of India. He had sworn allegiance to India by virtue of his Hindu marriage to Meera and then the children, their second hours away from birth.

Angeline suddenly came into the world; beautiful, unblemished, and perfect. Nothing would change the fact. The child came into the world that morning. In a rush of labour, that gave Meera little warning, her waters burst. It was time. But the baby did not present as she should. Meera stirred aware that she was now in labour and that this pain was different, not like the intense pain of childbirth, but the pain of her womb tearing and dying. The breathless labour, the tearing of her mother's womb and leaking of fluids into the peritoneum shadowed the child's birth.

Meera fainted in mid-labour, overcome with pain and exhaustion. After a short hour of agonising contractions, Meera's will, could no longer overcome the the power of birth at any cost; at her the mother's cost. As the child was born, the life drained from Meera, her legs shaking uncontrollably with humiliation at defeat in her hour of victory. The midwife had urgently called for the doctor in the final hour, but it was too late. Nothing could save Meera.

Meera had returned to consciousness briefly, repressing her rage and the urge to scream at David to take the doctor away, that the midwife was sufficient. David was obstinate, insistent that the doctor knew best and could deliver the child with the minimum of pain. He had medicines and injections to dull both the pain and divinely ecstatic moment of delivering her child into the world.

Eventually the drugs knew better than her own instincts, at first dulling her pain, then her strength to fight. Meera relented; her spirit crushed, her cries dying with the ebbing pain.

Silence. Deadly, horrible silence. Her cries stopped, her energy and will was totally spent. The doctor was forced to operate. He lifted the child out of Meera's belly before it completely stilled; a blood-stained and lifeless tomb. The newborn cried, bleating above the wails of Meera's mother and sisters as they watched her suffer, struggle and finally succumb.

'How could it happen, how could it be possible for her to die!' David momentarily gave way. It was unthinkable. Why had he not taken her to the hospital?

David had never imagined how blissful his life with Meera and their little boy Tarika could be. The boy, peaceful, smiling, with an innate wisdom invested in his huge and depthless eyes, had blessed their lives. Now the girl-child Angeline was born, motherless like the new India and Pakistan, her soul torn from a ruptured and damaged womb, her life emerging directly from death.

He could hardly comprehend the depths of his loneliness without Meera. Not only had he cast off his own culture and rejected the trappings of an office, the status and privilege, but he lost the woman he loved, the mother of his children and the angel who had bonded him to the culture to which he was now wedded. Without Meera, their cottage was instantly sad, its walls dismal and kitchen empty of the love and warmth to which he had grown so accustomed.

'Sahib, Sahib.' It was the houseboy.

David propped himself on one elbow and looked wearily into the dimness of the dawn.

'Sahib, chai. Very hot!'

'Thank you, Thank you.' David was grateful, grateful for the remnants of the Raj that allowed him to enjoy without conscience the luxuries of having tea brought to his bedroom. The chai smelt sweet. David relished the precious moments left this morning to absorb the realities of "*Ramraj.*"

The children were still sleeping, Tarika easily roused by the excitement of the new day and Angeline, slow, ever sleepy, content to observe each moment as if it were an external event filled with intrigue and curiosity. She would never stir to action but simply watch, unruffled by Tarika's impatience and impetuosity.

Tarika, rising to battle before he was two years old, jumped out of his cot, toy sword in hand as if to slay his imaginary dragons. Meera had tut tutted over his nature, a little warrior filled with fire and bravado. But there was the other side to the boy also, his insatiable need for books, not to read but to leaf the pages one by one as if in each were treasures known only to his tiny mind. Tarika was intrigued by the sounds and soon, the sight of poetry; Sanskrit, Persian, Arabic. So Meera plied him at first with picture books and comics, and soon, placed copies of the Gita, Quran and Bible in front of his thirsty eyes. It was Tagore that enraptured him and again and again, he would ask her to read it to him as if the verse were the very soul of life.

David wondered about the boy Tarika. If anyone, he was the living testimony, the proof positive of reincarnation. How else could the child be so drawn to books and learning when neither he nor Meera were especially fascinated, although happy to collect and keep the texts? In their child, there was a maturity of understanding. He possessed a wisdom that far surpassed his tender years of life. From where he came, David dared not think.

Now there was Angeline to think about and care for. Born in death, this child was as innocent as a tiny Saint. For answers to the questions that had no answer, David turned to India. In this vast and great nation, there was a heart of tranquillity that could quieten the questions and calm the soul. The great wheels of time and fortune steadily turned, axled together by the cultural traditions and religions that were India. David was now a part of that tradition, deeply involved as a member of the British Raj, in the making of its history.

He allowed himself time to soak in the news and digest the significance of nationhood for himself and his motherless children. It was inevitable that the children would have to know why their mother abandoned them when they needed her most. It was still too raw for him to think. His grief would wait, in any case now overwhelmed by the greater truths that were the new India, the new Pakistan. He knew this much, that the children were his; they were his life as much as new India was a part of all of their lives. He could return to England and take up residence in the well-heeled comfort of post-war Britain, or he could ensconce the children in a life in India and in so doing, keep alive the memory of their mother.

David chose the latter. The children belonged to him, but they also belonged to the new India and India, to them.

It would take time before the final arrangements were made for his transfer to the new Indian Civil Service under the Governor General Mountbatten, or at least, the fledgling British Consulate. Either way the children would have a father and a father who would work and serve to ensure the stability of the new nation that one- day, they would inherit. Even whilst the political, cultural and spiritual milieu of India was volatile, the children would survive and thrive, they would learn about her past and future just as they would learn about the past of their mother, the wife that David had now lost.

The tea sweetened more than David's tongue. He was endlessly fascinated how food could flavour ideals and comfort the insatiable inner palate as much as it nourished the physical being. David was glad that he elected to stay in India. Although the future was distinctly uncertain and unsavoury, the hearth and heart of India continued to provide spiritual homage and culinary delight to the now, more than 380 million souls and bodies of India. The hubbub of life on the ancient continent would always revolve around the humble stove and central cooking pot. Today, breakfast would be served at the usual time of eight o'clock. David wanted nothing more than fruits. Undoubtedly there would also be the usual assortment of steaming griddlecakes, tea, semolina and perhaps even, a hot dahl. He always found it hard to convince his wife that he needed less but could not find the heart to refuse her. Since her death, little had changed in his household other than the welcome presence of the children's' nurse and the more frequent visits of the children's aunties and uncles.

The houseboy interrupted his deliberations. 'Sahib. A cable for you Sahib.'

'Oh?' David was surprised. Yesterday's afternoon mail was delivered on time. This one must be important.

> *"David old chap, any news on Independence? Did you join Mountbatten at the transfer of power or were you relegated to message boy?"*

It was Chris in his usual semi-bantering style, open, cheerful yet deliberately probing for news.

> "Appreciate whatever you can give me. Am thinking of a short trip Delhi - with Ruth. She wants meet you - something to do with Edward's death. Holiday would probably do us both good. Is India quiet or are you expecting more riots?
> Ever yours, Chris."

India quiet?! With communal violence sweeping the streets and blood flowing in Delhi as men raped women and gangs of lathi wielding youths destroyed temples and Mosques alike, India could hardly be called quiet! The reverberations of the slaughter in Calcutta, Dacca, Noakhali, Tipperah and Bihar echoed throughout India for an entire year leading to Independence. Gandhi, ever vigilant in his pledge for truth and non-violence, walked like the Christ from village to village, barefoot and scantily clad, beseeching his people to lay down their weapons of violence and hatred.

David soberly observed the unfolding drama from Delhi. As they celebrated Tarika's sixth birthday, Nehru formed an interim government and Jinnah repudiated the claim to sovereignty, with the declaration of *"Direct Action Day."*

Then from Bengal, the killings began. Delhi was inundated by a tide of refugees from the Punjab and North West Frontier Province.

As August 15 approached, the tensions broke and the exodus of over 15 million souls from the Punjab began. With the flow of human pilgrims, came the unprecedented and horrific levels of violence and rape.

The slaughter of a million Hindus and a million Muslims was more than *Bapuji*, the father of the nation could bear. Gandhi finally reversed the wave of death from his prayer meetings in the colony of sweepers.

When Independence finally arrived at the midnight hour, the old man refused to celebrate. Gandhi absorbed himself in fasting and spinning and refused the BBC a *"Message for the World."* The Mahatma was solely intent on quelling the Calcutta riots that followed the separation of Hindu from Muslim. And the fate of the Punjabi Sikhs with nowhere to go, deeply troubled the soul of the Saint.

David shook his head more in exasperation than disbelief. No Englishwoman was safe in India.

"*Chris old boy, you need to have your head read!*"

David thought about his reply. The obvious mischief and mirth in Chris's cable, broke his incredulity. Indeed, one should not become morose over the riots and killings. At least he and the children were safe.

'What a blessing you were Meera.' Here, at least they were safe from the marauders and murderers of post-Partition India. Chris and Ruth would have to wait. There was no chance that Ruth's civility could survive the current climate of the subcontinent where entire communities were nothing more than moving chunks of humanity. Entire states and cities were reduced to a patchwork of refugees. David wondered whether Ruth would be ready to witness the game of living chess with thousands upon thousands of household pawns lost to the urgent moves of Jinnah and Congress. Only Gandhi could embrace and subdue the tiger of Bengal and David knew that he lived precariously close to the tiger's paw.

Perhaps Ruth blamed him for Edward's death. It was true, Edward might never have ventured into the Kashmir, or Karachi for that matter, if it were not for his, David's encouragement. One could in any case, become sick anywhere in India.

'But that's ridiculous.' David rebuked himself. 'That's bloody stupid. You know that you could not have done a damn thing about it.'

David was as shocked as anyone was by Edward's death. However, he never imagined he would face a post-mortem of the man's life by meeting his late wife Ruth! As if he didn't have enough think about.

The prospect of English company, the company of a real woman, was however, refreshing. Apart from the vibrant presence of the lovely Lady Mountbatten, the English women in Delhi were, on the whole, stuffy and boring. Meera and Lady Edwina clicked like old friends in an unlikely acquaintance of Indian and English wives of civil servants.

David smiled to himself. He had privately enjoyed the catty stares after his announcement of his engagement to Meera. He could laugh about it now and wondered whether it was he or the Indians who were meting out bittersweet revenge on English civilisation. It did not matter.

He was sufficiently independent of the British 'club' that he was no longer affected by their opinions.

Thank goodness for the precious time he had had with Meera, the pure lotus of contentment that shone amid, the muckiness of British-Indian sentiments.

'Ruth!' David exclaimed aloud. He had often wondered about the woman. How much the death of her husband must have shocked and saddened her. Perhaps she was curious, curious about the maturity and wisdom India emerged in her husband, a wisdom that was untouchable, untouchable even to his wife.

The cascade of violence was a depressing blanket over the elation of India's freedom; a hole in the aura of new beginnings and it appeared for now at least, that only England would come out of the situation, of long-awaited Independence, relatively unscathed. Why should the Muslims and Hindus continue to carve one another into carcasses through their desperation for homeland and religious identity? What was the point of deepening their despair at Partition, when both had worn the yoke of oppression? Britain had ruled them all and now, freed from her oppression, they turned on themselves in an orgy of unprecedented hate and violence.

David slapped the cable onto the bedside table, aware of a mild curiosity, a strange and welcome happiness. Chris was bringing Edward's wife to India, to Delhi, and that thought, lifted the mood of the morning to something close to joy.

There was little time for pondering this morning. This morning they would be busy with the celebrations; Mountbatten's speech, the parade before tens of thousands of Indian people, the hoisting of the flag and finally later that night, the celebratory gathering of princes and British officials.

David had spent frantic days working long hours under difficult conditions. The office felt as though it was awash with crisis after crisis as the Maharajas of each state met with Lord Mountbatten, some changing their mind as to whether they wanted to be a part of Pakistan or India, or they simply did not know. The day of transfer was upon them and

David, like Mountbatten, held grave doubts as to whether the Boundary Commissions had made the right call on the line in the sand between the two nations about to be birthed in the office where he stood. He knew that ultimately, the border between India and Pakistan was an arbitrary line, a line that could and would be disputed, a line that could and would divide communities in the Punjab, whether or not they were ready for the vivisection. The Sikh princes were about to lose everything; land, titles, position, possessions; there was no guarantee under either India or Pakistan that they would prosper. For centuries they had endured the rule of both adopting as they had, the sword to protect their identity, their religion, their homeland. Now, they had endured an open caesarean section, right through the centre of their homeland to deliver the two new nations; the twins, India and Pakistan. Unlike the birth of a child, the birthing of the essentially Hindu and ultimately Muslim offspring of the once great and united India, would be painful; non-identical twins who would lose their single *"Mother Bharat"* as they came into the world.

For a moment David felt the emotion grasp his chest as he remembered his wife Meera, her pain, the losing of the love of his life as she brought forth to him the children who were now the most precious things in the world to him. The pain was too much to bear. How much pain would Bharat suffer and would the two children be unscathed as was his beautiful child?

Quickly, he brushed away the thoughts. There was no time to turn back. The tide of events now completely overwhelmed them all, Jinnah, Nehru,

Mountbatten....Gandhi. They teetered together at the precipice, save for the tradition and order instilled by Mountbatten. That they all knew that the transfer of power would incorporate the usual 'order of the day' at the Government Houses in Karachi and in Delhi.

David cleared his desk and pushed himself up from his chair. It was almost time. He would eat alone and settle in the children before joining Mountbatten for the ceremonies of the day. For a moment, he thought of Edward, joining him in India, talking as if in a dream about his *"Midnight Pearl,"* the unknown temptress that soon manifested as the beautiful Sesheta; innocent, intellectual, inquisitive. If only Pakistan were her, *"Midnight Pearl,"* endlessly beguiling, openly enquiring, self-willed and ready to embrace a world larger than herself in her love of life and learning. If only she Sesheta and he Edward had survived their love affair, their soul connection, their embrace of the heart; pure, uncomplicated, instant. If only Pakistan and India would fall in love with one another, embrace ideas and cross the cultural divide in a dance of eternal discovery.

David doubted it. There was no romance in his opinion in Partition. By its nature, it was a process of separation, male egos tearing at one another, sacrificing hundreds, thousands, millions.

Chapter Ninety Eight

THE GIDDY NIGHT and now day of events came into sharp focus in the extraordinary light of the new day as David sat in the front seat of the car following the State Coach that carried Mountbatten. Literally hundreds of thousands of people lined the streets and climbed atop the roofs to witness the parade, the last passing of the British Raj. There was no chance at all of solemnity. Mountbatten and Nehru road together in the carriage, Nehru later seated like a little boy on top of the carriage for fear that he would be consumed by the crowds. The bodyguards and their crowd-patient horses, struggled to push away the pulsing mass of people thronging towards the carriage. Suddenly the chaos appeared to be ominous and quickly Mountbatten and Nehru decided to immediately hoist the flag of India.

David, worried by the throng, kept a close eye on the two men as the flag unfurled towards the sky and in the same moment, a brilliant rainbow with its multicoloured shafts of saffron, white and green light erupted over the gathering. The crowds burst into wild rejoicing and India was finally birthed in the bright light of the new day.

'David, join us won't you.' Mountbatten signalled to the waiter to bring over the drinks tray laden with crystal glasses. 'To us. To you David, my loyal friend.'

'Governor General.' David eyes twinkled as he cast his eyes around the room.

'Yes indeed, a gathering of Princes, Maharajas and of the best civil servants a man could ever wish to have with him.' Mountbatten turned once again to David. 'Are you planning to stay David?'

'I have children here Louis.' David said quietly.

'You must stay then. India is your home now. You won't be alone. There will be a British diplomatic and civil service to participate in the transition of the new nations.'

David nodded.

'Look, the Sikh Princes seek our company.' Lord Mountbatten bowed slightly then greeted the new rulers as old friends.

Chapter Ninety Nine

Karachi, Pakistan 15 August, 1947

KARACHI AWOKE TO the unfamiliar glint of victory. Previously, Viceroy Lord Mountbatten addressed the *"Constituent Assembly of Pakistan"* and now, the Assembly fated by the masterful strokes of Jinnah, waited to taste the essentially Islamic stirrings of a new nation. The metallic hub of the marketplace was both victorious and ominous. Nothing was surer for Hindu and Sikh, the Punjab was no longer their homeland.

The Imam sighed, wistfully aware of the enormous responsibility now weighing on his shoulders, not that it had been any easier prior to Partition. So many unnecessary deaths. As spiritual counsel to the developing soul of Pakistan, *"The Land of The Pure,"* the Imam was caught in the unenviable position between religion and politics. He didn't doubt the Quaid's motives, but he could hardly be fooled into thinking that only Allah or Rama lay between Jinnah and Nehru. Who was the true *Mahavir* of this land?

Land; land was the driving and sharp wedge between brothers. Land, territory and identity robbed them of their essential goodness. Now, there was no guarantee of workable relations between India and Pakistan, of profitable trade and stable social life. The worst was to come, of that, the Imam was sure. The rising passions of his people were not, he surmised, simply about their respective Lords but fuelled by the indignation of premature identity and misunderstood, misused power, the power that rendered individuals unconscionable and destroyed entire families.

Despite his own, professed and undeniable loyalty to Allah, the Imam had no personal argument with Gandhi's Rama, or his brother-priest's God or even any one of the many gurus that journeyed his part of the globe. In fact he delighted at the opportunity for spiritual and social discourse, to gauge another enlightened, albeit different view. He was deeply grateful to Allah for Hanif, his unassuming and devoted understudy of rare and sober nature. How lucky he was that the grocer surrendered his trade in nuts and grains for the service at the Mosque. Allah was good! The Imam felt fortunate. Hanif now belonged to the Mosque, to Karachi and her people.

Jubilation worthy of a new nation would undoubtedly fill this morning's news. Nevertheless, the Imam could not shake his deepening sense of foreboding. It was nearly a century since the War of Independence. Then, the British effectively wiped out Muslim identity in India and cast their spiritual hopes, like refuse into the pit of oblivion. At the hands of the British, Muslim culture crumpled threatening to obliterate Urdu and along with the language, any real hope of identity and self-expression. The All-Muslim League was in the Imam's opinion, a beleaguered attempt to resuscitate Muslim identity in India and safeguard perhaps, against Constitutional fraud by Congress. He was convinced that the British had different designs for the Ottoman Empire other than its revitalisation and he doubted the League's alliance with the Hindus.

Gandhi alone, was the willing glue for the disparate beliefs of his beloved nation. Free from spiritual or secular bias, the Mahatma cemented relations through his charisma, integrity and commitment to truth, But in the Imam's mind, not even Gandhi could settle the bitter dispute of the rivalling brothers Jinnah and Nehru. Certainly Lord Mountbatten had failed to dissuade Jinnah from anything other than, a united India. The *"Khalifat"* and *"Swaraj"* movements were temporarily synonymous, yet ultimately collapsing in bitter enmity and communal violence.

The Imam shuddered. He foresaw the venting of bitter rivalries and avenging of past hurts. In the vivisection of the new nation from the greater body of India, there could only be pain. Through his Islamic eyes, he discerned the war of personalities, the clashing of bulls' horns over the dusty plains of the Punjab. In his humble view,

"Independence" Midnight 14, August 1947 was dangerously similar to 16, August 16 1946 and, by association, there would be more violence and the unnecessary letting of blood, of lives and of souls.

Already the naval uprising in Karachi and berthing of American ships for the Japanese war had stained the new soul of Pakistan. Now, Britain's interference interrupted the fair and peaceful apportioning of Muslim identity, of land and of constitutional power. The Imam knew that the Partition of India and Pakistan was unavoidable, inevitable, but sadly reflected that it would neither, rectify the ageless problem of Muslim identity or stem the violence. What would Allah think? What could Allah do with his sons bent on mutual destruction? If only they had listened to Gandhi and fought their wars on mythical and not worldly battlefields!

The Imam wanted to put the recent history behind him, but it continued to loom in front of him in a series of illusory arguments that spelt more deaths. The seed of war was greed and lust for land. Of that he was sure. Why could they not at least share land and a common identity of nationhood; the Muslims, Sikhs, Hindus and Parsis of one India? Even the Christians belonged here and his brothers in their Church were friends in kind.

'Imam?'

'Hanif!' The gentle yet respectful intrusion of his clerk surprised the Imam. 'The Quaid-i-Azam will want your blessings.'

'Thank you. I'm sure he will.'

The Imam stirred from his prayerful thoughts. In Hanif, Allah softened the daily blows of news and challenges to his faith. Hanif's quiet movements around the Mosque counterpointed the rude shocks of the slaughter and the ugly appearances of human nature. The Imam looked carefully at Hanif. One day he would rise to higher office. The man had all the necessary virtues but needed experience and time-forged wisdom. He had remarkable resilience and a deep patience that would prove to be invaluable when the political sentiments and passions exploded and spilt over into spiritual life. For now at least, his clerk Hanif was reliable and predictable.

The Imam steeled himself for the day. He would meet with Jinnah, then, talk to friends in both Hindu and Sikh communities. Already there had been too many deaths as passions flared without warning. The Christians were safe, for the time being as was the fledgling community at the ashram. This war with England was not religious. It was not a war with Christianity. The tensions with Britain were simply the fallout from the commercial, military and later, the political intrusion of the British into the age-old traditions and rhythms of the subcontinent. Perhaps if the Thomas of Christ had never come to Sindh, if the trade routes were denied the Europeans, there may never have been any British, Portuguese, Dutch or French in India! Inevitably, Bombay attracted greedy foundlings to suck India dry.

Chapter One Hundred

TARA SAT BETWEEN her parents. Her uncle Hanif sat opposite sipping coconut milk and quietly turning the pages of the morning newspapers. The atmosphere was calm but Tara was not happy, her mood captured by the mourning of India and Pakistan. Her father wore a long scar down his right forearm. Tara could see the scar's coarse edges through his shirt. It was ugly, purple and slightly raised.

He tried hide it, but from time to time as he raised his arm, the scar pulled and caused him wince.

'Saadi, you might like to read this.' Hanif passed the newspaper to his brother. 'Page two.'

Saadi took the newspaper from his brother.' Hanif. You are thinking about your friends. They will have to leave Pakistan.'

'Saadibhai, Allah is good. If He wills, then we will remain in Karachi. There will be no further deaths.'

'Hanif you of all of us must know that Allah cannot intervene in the affairs of men. If Jinnah were here now, what do you think he would say? What would he say Hanif? That all were safe in Karachi? That all had his personal blessing, Christians, Hindus and Sikh. Do you think that Jinnah will welcome to Pakistan your friends when so many Muslims die in Delhi? Do you think so Hanif? No brother, you must accept it. The die is cast and there will be more bloodshed.'

Saadi's wife drew her breath in quickly. 'No, there will be no more bloodshed.'

'Mama.' Tara looked anxiously into her mother's face.

'Child. Go and bring some fruits for your uncle.' Kahina instructed her.

'Let the child be Kahina. It is better that she learns the things of her new country.'

'She is too young Saadi and her innocence should not be spoilt. Don't you agree Hanif?' Kahina sought his support.

Hanif looked at his brother and his brother's wife and shook his head. 'I do not have the answer to that Kahina. Your Saadi is right. She needs to learn. Nevertheless, nothing must spoil her innocence. In this new nation, there will be a need for learned women.' Hanif paused. 'Kahina, there is nothing as beautiful as your home and your hospitality always brings so much happiness. However, your daughter! Your daughter is a part of the future of this land, whether you like it or not. She must learn the ways of the world as well as how be a good wife and mother.' Hanif consoled her.

'You mean like our Sesheta.'

'Kahina!' Saadi rebuked her sharply.

'I'm sorry Hanif.' He turned his brother. 'Perhaps the child needs your help woman.'

'It's all right Saadibhai. I too wonder sometimes about Sesheta's death.'

'But the Imam...'

'I know.' Hanif sounded weary. 'I don't think that anyone can explain her death. I am sorry brother. Today should be a day of celebration only.'

The mother and child returned with fresh fruits for the men. Kahina carefully spooned sliced mango and dates for Hanif.

Hanif thanked her quietly, trying to hide the pain in his eyes. He ate the fruits, but felt the fire of anger and unresolved grief.

Kahina pulled Tara onto her lap and stroked her hair absently.

'Kahina. Let the child sit. She can feed herself.' Kahina sullenly obeyed.

'Hanif it is no wonder that women are unable to learn your teachings. They are too absorbed in petty affairs.'

Hanif remained detached, unwilling to enter the tensions of married life. He was glad that he had joined the Mosque and that he had sent Ami and Mani to Calcutta.

'Have you heard from your Ami?' Saadi asked as if he had heard his brother's thoughts.

'They are both doing well.' The change of topic cheered Hanif.

'They must miss their home Hanif.' Saadi persisted.

'Yes.' Hanif spoke softly.' So many have died Saadi, so many.'

'Then the Mosque has not protected you from violence after all Hanif.'

'Allah's ways are very mysterious.' Hanif was aware that his objection to violence and war left him more exposed now he had entered the Mosque. At least he had the power of his prayers, the protection of the Imam, something to steel him against the waves of death. 'There are so many who have died. So many unnecessary deaths.' Hanif finally found the words for his own defence.

'You have seen too much brother. I am sorry for my words Hanif.'

Hanif said nothing.

'You also will go Hanif?'

'I will consult the Imam. Perhaps it is better to spend the time in silence.'

'Allah will keep you occupied no doubt.' Saadi said jovially.

'Allah has His own plans.'

'Uncle?'

'Yes child.'

'Uncle, why aren't you happy about our freedom?'

'Since when did you have an opinion child.' Saadi laughed.

'Then she has already learned too much brother.' Hanif saw his own trap. 'I am happy Tara, that one day you will become a great leader for this country and for other little girls like yourself. One day, you will give proof that a good education is a far better liberation than simply dividing Hindu from Muslim and India from Pakistan.'

'Tara, you had better go your room and practise your reading' her father said. Saadi and Hanif exchanged amused laughs.

'Kahina, you must show her how to write letters to her Aunty and cousin in England.'

'Saadi!'

'What is wrong with you wife. Teach your daughter! Already she shows a keen interest in reading and if you help her, she will learn to write. Now brother,' Saadi turned to Hanif, 'for the Imam.' Saadi gave him a tin crammed with fresh dates.

'Thank you brother. The Imam will be grateful.' Hanif bowed humbly to his brother and his wife.

Saadi showed Hanif the door. The two brothers embraced briefly and Hanif lightened his step. He was glad for the visit. Saadi at least understood his pain, his lingering guilt over Sesheta and was determined to relieve him of the discomfort. It was strange how his brother became his counsel. Hanif wondered about the ways of Allah. Family life was the practical path yet also created the most pain and challenges to his faith. The dilemma had not eased despite his prayers. Still, he had occasional thoughts of returning to the family, of restoring Ami to her former status as his wife and mother of his child and he to the humble, yet well-respected role of grocer. Even then he was a loved and well-regarded community figure, the one person in the market place who was known be scrupulously honest, sincere and trustworthy. However, it was far too late go back to that world as he knew it and too late to recover his wife from her complete shame, an outcast from her own family and community. For that, Hanif could never forgive himself. Ami's sacrifice and obedience had made it possible for him to enter the Mosque; he knew that. Hanif had hardly to mutter 'yes' to the Imam and it was settled. Yet without doubt, Ami's life was shattered in an instant in order indulge him in his sentiments for his Allah. Hanif could easily appease his conscience, convincing himself that his small sacrifice of his wife and child would ultimately benefit so many more. How could he minister to the thousands whilst entangled in the petty affairs of his own life, his small business and family? Surely, Ami would understand the greater plan, his divine wisdom and guidance? Surely, the child would have a better chance, an education to pave her way in life? Hanif felt confident blessings filled their sacrifice.

Chapter One Hundred One

England

THE DIRECT DETAILS and news of Partition came to Chris's desk. Chris was horrified. It was as though no family would be spared the violence, and somehow, here in London, the war was over and they were spared the atrocities. After the Holocaust, no one wanted to hear about any more violence, about needless slaughter, about the sacrifice of innocence lives for ephemeral, transient ideals. Chris threw the sheaf of reports onto his desk in tired resignation. It had to stop. The killings must stop and he wanted that David would hear and tell him nothing more.

Chris knew that it could not be so, that it could not happen so easily that India could wrest Independence from the Empire without pain, death and sacrifice. He know that both Independence and Pakistan would be birthed in blood, just as any child entered the world. He abhorred the thought of more reports of limbless children and raped women. Both were brutally sacrificed at an imaginary altar; the hope of land, territory and nation. Nothing was achieved. The girls and women were endlessly humiliated, desecrated and defaced; broken dolls destroyed in crumbling temples of belief.

Chris knew that in Delhi, David would weep uncontrollable tears of shame for India and Britain's part in the slaughter. No woman, Muslim, Hindu, Sikh, Parsi or Christian would be protected by the promises of Independence. There would be no stopping the slaughter in the Punjab. The blood of generations poured into a single pool of sorrow.

India wept beneath the butcher's knife.

The insoluble paradoxes of death plunged Ruth and Ami into a vortex of disbelief, their faith shattered by the horrors of both wars, in Europe and on the Subcontinent. The women clung to their womanhood and to one another, hoping for a reprieve from the news, as Chris continued to inform them on a daily basis of the horrors unfolding in India.

Chris and Ruth decided to wait to travel to India. It was too soon, to close to the violence. For now, Ruth was content to wait. The journey to the Subcontinent would come later. She also knew that in India, the crucible of Edward's transformation, she would find the reason for his death.

For now, neither of the women wanted to hear about war, let alone the deaths in India. Overwhelmed by powerlessness, cheated and robbed of all they loved, they had shared in their grief. Now, they simply wanted peace. No matter the culture or country, the waves of destiny washed over them as if horror alone could cleanse the world of hate. Centuries merged into a moment. Yet within the unimaginable losses, the light of hope penetrated with bright promise of a new tomorrow. A decade, two decades, five decades? What did time matter? Ultimately it would be the power of reason, the power of love and the power of family that would rule the blood-soaked plains of India and the warlords would once again be humbled.

As the oceans of death flooded into their lives, the women were conscious of their immortal resilience. They felt their potency and victory.

Epilogue One

DAVID'S WORST FEARS were realised. India descended into her darkest night as communalism scourged her soul. Gandhi continued with his prayers and fasting, but the old giant had lost his will. David despaired. Gandhi represented to him all the hopes he held for India and within India's future, his hopes for the children. Without the old man, he would have no mentor, no spiritual light to find his way from the valleys of destruction into the golden world of God's Kingdom on earth, the "*Ramraj*" that Gandhi longed for. Now, David longed for the Kingdom of God also. The Saint understood that home and community ties were often far deeper than the ties woven by religious belief and nation. The Muslims of Delhi wanted to return from Karachi to their homes and the people of Sindh, also mourned the loss of their homeland, now the new Pakistan.

Gandhi committed to deliver to Delhi, a peaceful and reasonable resettlement.

David fretted as the Mahatma's health gradually broke down under the rigours of his *'final purification'* of the spirit. Finally, the old man had his way. The pledge for peace from all quarters in Delhi; Hindu, Muslim, Christians, Sikh and Jew, even the fundamentalists and fanaticists, promised Gandhi that Delhi would unite. So persuaded, Gandhi broke his final fast, his thoughts first and foremost for Pakistan.

It was late in January 1948 when the Mahatma walked solemnly through the crowd assembled at his prayer meeting. The atmosphere was jubilant. India's liberator and mentor was once again amongst them. Then, as Gandhi accepted a garland at his feet, reaching to bless the Hindu man before him, the assassin's bullet rudely and fatally interrupted his life. As the Mahatma uttered his final homily to *Rama*, he crumpled into the land that he so loved; the land and people that so loved him.

Gandhi, was no more, his life squandered in a flash of insanity. As *Bapuji*, *"The Father of the Nation"* died, India's soul tore and divided. The Saint departed and with him, his hopes for the unity of India's sons and daughters.

David listened to Nehru mourn his beloved mentor-father and he too mourned.

"The light has gone out of our lives and there is darkness everywhere."

David sat on the banks of the River Jumna with Lord and Lady Mountbatten in a crowd of over half a million as the Dakotas sprinkled rose petals on the funeral procession. Amongst numberless Indians, David also wept as the flames consumed Gandhi's pyre and the remains of his bones were scattered and swept towards the sea.

As David sat in his office and scribbled a cable to Chris. It was January 1950 and the British administration was little more than a skeleton of its former self. Mountbatten had left handing over to the new administration of the *Republic Of India* to Nehru.

> *"Chris old man. Come when you are ready. Bring Ruth if you like. From Delhi, we'll go to Karachi (business of course). The children are as excited about your visit as I am.*
>
> *Yours,*
> *David."*

Epilogue Two

CHRIS AND RUTH arrived in Delhi on a sunny February morning and David greeted them as if the last decade had separated him from his most precious memories, his friends, his life and London. Chris grabbed David in a bear hug and waltzed him under the wings of the Dakota.

'Ruth, meet David. David, Ruth.'

As David and Ruth searched one another's eyes, David pulled Ruth into a warm embrace.

Ruth felt the compassion for David well into her eyes. 'David.' She wiped the tears from her cheeks. 'It's so good to meet you after all these years. You are every bit as cheeky and wonderful as Chris and Edward said you were.' Ruth's cheeks flushed with happiness and David stood as if rooted to the past.

'I'm so sorry about Meera, David.' Chris began. 'Are the children…'

'Thanks Chris. The children,' he turned to Ruth, 'the children are looking forward to meeting you both.'

Tarika and Angeline scampered about them; their high spirits a refreshing reminder to Ruth of the imp Mani.

'You must both come to London, and your father.' Ruth invited noting the enchanting, midnight-blue eyes of the little boy.

'That will be wonderful Ruth. But first, dinner and then, plans for Karachi.'

The two days in Delhi, were to Ruth, the most silent and humble she had spent in all her time with Edward. David repeated, hour by hour, the details of Edward's illness and his gradual recovery under the cotton quilts in his cottage. When it was time to go, Ruth turned to David and touched his arm, unable to express her gratitude and the fact that she understood that once he had visited the subcontinent, that his life now belonged to India and not to her or England.

The three adults and two children journeyed uneventfully to Karachi. David consumed himself with paperwork for the new British Consulate. They stayed at the British Compound in Old Clifton. David bobbed up and down like an excited schoolboy, as he met in the new Pakistan, his old friends from Delhi.

That evening, David took them to a reception at the Gymkhana Club.

'What about the children David? You can't hide them away while we cocktail into the small hours of the morning?' Ruth asserted.

'Children strictly allowed.' David announced sombrely. Then he broke into the laughter he had enjoyed before Meera died.

'Ruth, you could offer to take the children back with us. I'm sure David wouldn't mind.' Chris joked.

'Not these ones - they are more precious than a thousand jewels strung on the silken skies of India.' David claimed.

The party was a stunning success in the fledgling British-Muslim-Hindu relations, celebrating the business, academic and religious leaders of Pakistan. David moved with ease in the gathering, familiar with the mix of British cuisine, Indian dress and manners. He wished that Meera were by his side, but the tugging of Tarika interrupted his thoughts.

'Papa. Papa. Can we meet them?' Tarika pestered. 'Whom child?' David smiled in amusement.

'Over there! 'Tarika pointed to the Muslim family. One of the men was dressed in a long robe as handsome and regal as any of the priests of St Paul's Cathedral. Alongside the Imam was a women, dressed in robes, her sari carefully covering her head. For a moment, as David's thoughts stopped, he felt afraid that his mind would dive and disappear forever into the pool of silence that surrounded her. David felt the rush of maternal love that Edward had so carefully related on his return to Delhi. He felt the assuring and gentle caress of thoughts, free from any intrusion that could suddenly embarrass or frighten. The eyes remained steady, gauging his soul as if a parent quietly observing a child, lost and defenceless. Then the waves of compassion struck to the core of his heart. David felt himself pulled away from Ruth and Chris and into the presence of the Hanif, the Imam and the saried woman, now silently slipping away.

Just as David reached the outstretched hand of Hanif, Tarika raced across the room, oblivious to the fine silks and jewels glittering under the light of the chandeliers.

'Hello. My name's Tarika.' He announced in English.

'Hello young man. Hanif.'

Tarika looked at Hanif, his eyes widening and mouth opening in surprise. Hanif flicked a glance at the Imam then turned his attention to Ruth, Chris and Angeline as they walked towards them.

'Ruth, Chris, this is, Hanif and The Imam.' David obliged with the introduction.

'Peace be with you all.' The Imam quietly greeted them.

'Hanif!' Ruth could hardly suppress her surprise.

'Madam. The pleasure is all mine. Hanif bowed gracefully. And this is my brother Saadi and his wife, and of course, Tara, the 'true star' of Karachi.'

Ruth gasped. 'You aren't the same Hanif….as Edward?..'

'Yes.' Hanif said lithely. 'He left such a powerful impression on my niece Sesheta.'

'Then this is your writing, on the wrapper. The book arrived in the post just before….' Ruth fumbled in her bag and pulled out the brown paper that had covered the package that arrived so fatally at their door. Hanif took the wrapper and turned it over carefully.

The Imam skilfully eased Hanif's obvious pain. 'Hanif. You have new friends from London I see.'

'My wife received Hanif's package in the post. It had Edward's name inside. It seems that there was a problem…. 'Chris started to explain.

'My niece. She loved to read. Your late husband gave her his copy of "*Siddhartha.*" We were both very touched. Thank you.' Hanif bowed to hide the sudden resurgence of his grief.

'I'm so sorry Hanif. I didn't realise.' Ruth gently touched his arm. 'Ami, Mani… they are friends of mine, of ours.' She turned to Chris for support.

'Ahh, Hanif.' The Imam once again stepped into the conversation. 'Sesheta was such an inspiration to all who knew her and her fortunes of course, brought these good souls to us.' The Imam smiled at Ruth and Chris. 'Without the change in Sesheta's fortunes, Hanif also may never have come to me in the Mosque' the Imam smiled at Hanif, 'through a most difficult time in our history. Hanif, I was hoping to suggest it to you privately of course, but now that you are in the company of these gentle British souls I am sure that they will be happy to share in the news. Perhaps you could consider the call to tend Allah's tiny flock in London.'

The searing grief lifted from Hanif's heart and eyes.

'I'd be delighted Imam.' Hanif turned and bowed stiffly to his counsel. He placed the brown, slightly crumpled wrapper under his arm and nodded to Ruth.

Ruth caught the thrill of expectation in Hanif's arm. She turned to see the Imam's eyes sparkling with contentment.

'While you are in Karachi, please be the guest of my brother and his family.' Hanif turned to Ruth.

'Thank you Hanif.' Ruth was touched by their manners and hospitality.

'Oh, I'm sorry David. I was…' Ruth remembered her host. 'No, it's perfectly all right Ruth.'

'David. My old friend.' Hanif gave David his hand and then full embrace.' And of course, your lovely children, Tarika and Angeline.' Hanif patted Angeline's head.

'Here comes the Major!' David touched the light warning with obvious humour.

'It seems as though Tarika and Tara have already met.' Chris pointed to the children.

Tarika turned and smiled briefly at the sound of his name, his midnight-blue eyes flushed with happiness. Tara stood like a tiny Saint, her hand resting softly in Tarika's.

The Major suddenly interrupted the meeting, slapping David on the back then thrusting a powerful hand into Hanif's. 'And you must be Ruth and Chris. Come Ruth. I want you to meet some very special people,' The Major invited her to join the English ladies gathered together, sharing stories of their new lives in Pakistan.

'Now if you will excuse me.' The Imam turned to leave the gathering. Chris watched the Imam walk across the polo field, as he quietly retreated, saintly in his demeanour, no doubt to the sanctity of the Mosque and the solace of his prayers for India and Pakistan.

www.ingramcontent.com/pod-product-compliance
Lightning Source LLC
Chambersburg PA
CBHW030258080526
44584CB00012B/364